Autobio

KATHLEEN RAINE

Autobiographies

Coracle

San Rafael, Ca

First published in Great Britain as
Farewell Happy Fields (1973)
The Land Unknown (1975)
The Lion's Mouth (1977)
by Hamish Hamilton Ltd
Copyright 1973, 1975, 1977.
Copyright © Kathleen Raine 1991
First American Edition published by
Coracle Press, an imprint of Sophia Perennis, 2009

For information, address:
Coracle Press, P.O. Box 151011
San Rafael, California 94915, USA

Library of Congress Cataloging-in-Publication Data

Raine, Kathleen, 1908–2003.
Autobiographies / Kathleen Raine. — Reprint ed.
p. cm.
ISBN 978-1-59731-332-2 (pbk.: alk. paper)
1. Raine, Kathleen, 1908–2003. 2. Poets, English—20th century
—Biography. I. Title.
PR6035.A37Z46 2008
821'.914—dc22
[B]   2008005735

Contents

Preface / vii

Farewell Happy Fields

The Land Unknown

The Lion's Mouth

Preface

To WRITE a new preface for an autobiographical record written half a lifetime ago raises many reflections. Why did I—why does anyone—write such a record? And, in publishing, for whom? Who will profit by reading the story of another person's sufferings and mistakes, quest, occasional insights into the meaning and beauty of the world? At eighty-three the struggles and failures and passions and blindness of a young woman finding her way through life, trying not to lose the end of a golden string but lost in the labyrinth, seen retrospectively, look very different; why I did certain things and not others seems now often inexplicable. Yet, more than once, some friend or stranger has confided to me some episode in their own lives, great or small, heroic or foolish, but always the story has ended with the question, 'But what else could I have done?' And there is no answer to that question. What we did we did—alternatives do not exist. Did they ever exist? We scan our memories and our consciences to see where the fatal mistake, the fatal choice, was made. Sometimes we think we know—but causes are complex and unfathomable, the whole of our own and the world's past bears down on every moment of every life. And yet the theologians speak of free will and something in us knows, also, that at every moment of every life there is freedom.

As to why I wrote my story the answer is, simply, in order to understand, and by understanding to endure, my life—not my life as such, but as my individual way, insight, into life itself. When the soul comes to crisis the need to understand, and to survive, is there. Never have I thought life meaningless or trivial—we are impelled to seek for meaning. Of that need the Book of Job is the supreme expression. We are all, in some measure, Job, who demands an answer from mystery itself. Certainly I could never have claimed, as did Job, to be righteous and blameless—that in itself (or so Blake thought) is a foolish claim, that all must relinquish: we cannot be other than we are, limited and imperfect. Yet how hard we try! Would I in what I imagine to be my greater wisdom live my life differently if I were to begin again? Could I have reached that supposedly greater wisdom without that enactment of catastrophic mistakes? A very humbling question. When I was young I was, appearances notwithstanding, always trying to get things right. Too hard perhaps; then years of useless remorse. Perhaps we expect too much of ourselves. But then again I think of Eliot's words 'We are only undefeated because we have gone on trying'. Or are we here in Keat's 'vale of soul-making' only to learn by our own and one another's mistakes?

As to publication—and one respected friend's only comment was 'you should not have published'—I could say, that I have never had any sense of my life's being my own property, as it were, and it being all I had to offer, I could do no less than make my contribution to the whole, for others to learn what they could, from my example good or bad. Why should I withold anything from what belongs to all? What is civilization but an unending communication and participation of shared thoughts and visions, a shared pilgrimage, or quest? What have we to offer but our lives? Every life is an unique story in the thousand nights and one night, the thousands of thousands, never two alike. We can't read them all or hear them all told, yet whatever has been surely for ever is. Often in my old age I find myself saying, 'One lifetime is not enough!' The thousand and one lifetime could never exhaust the marvels. But then, all those multitudes of lives are the same life, all the multitude of stories are our own story. I do not need to live all those multitudes of lives for all have been lived, or will be lived, obscure or illustrious, terrible or conventional, happy or in sorrow, by someone; and are we not all the numberless expressions of the one Self? We are all participants in the *Divina Commedia*, the *Comédie Humaine*. Anyone is welcome to whatever I have been and seen and known and done, who can make use of it—better use I hope than I myself—as a record of mistakes and wrong choices; or sometimes perhaps as gleams of reality penetrating the obscurity of this world.

Autobiography is not much practised or valued in this country—in France it is different, and from Rousseau and Stendhal to France's great epic, *À La Recherche du Temps Perdu* autobiography has been valued; and is not the telling of our own truth a responsibility to ourselves and to others than which there can be none greater? Autobiography, that is, as a form of literature, not those memoirs of some more or less distinguished career, outer events, anecdotes, meetings with once famous personages? There are beautiful exceptions like Edwin Muir's *The Story and the Fable*, and Yeats's *Autobiographies*, that book of the 'Acts' of the poet whose thoughts and deeds rose so high above personal trivia.

My record is of course a woman's story—Heaven knows I am no feminist, but my truth, such as it is, as I have sought to understand it, my insights and my sins are those of a woman. And if my life is a 'work', it is so not only as a piece of writing, but as a work of living. And what is civilization but the sum of these 'works' of living a participation in the creation and discovery of the depths and the heights of human experience? In my old age I ask these things as questions—I have no answers! A journalist friend recently asked me why I had not written my story as a novel—it would have had better sales! (Only in France was *Adieu Prairies Heureuses* briefly a 'best-seller'). It was the fashion a generation ago for women novelists to fictionalise their lives, and readers would speculate about which character was so-and-so. But no poet could ever have done this, for the poet truth alone counts—how easy in a novel to falsify here and there, to depart from reality, to tell a different story. Well, might not that different story have been closer to our inner truth what we meant, tried to, would have liked to live? I am not considering such novels as those of Balzac, or Faulkner, or Henry James, those gifted with the power of inexhaustible invention of characters and stories. But if the story is our own 'confession' then the only measure is the depth of understanding we have been able to attain. Never enough! Yet to certain moments of truth we feel the need to 'bear witness' in the name of that universal Being in which we participate; be these moments visions of beatitude or of hell's deepest sorrows.

Often over the years I have been asked why I don't write another volume of autobiography. Now I have done so, published under the title *India Seen Afar*; but it is another kind of book altogether. We have each our unique 'story' which we enact but once. Some live their story early in life, others late, but when our time comes, we know our moment, enact our part well or ill as it is decreed in our deepest nature—we enact what we are. Perhaps there may be second chances for some, whose part was not played out. But in their nature these stories have a beginning, a middle, and an end; we become what we are as the Greeks long ago observed, as Chaucer knew and all story-tellers since the world began. The story, in this sense, is more true to life than the 'soap-opera' in which episode is added to episode endlessly. My 'story' is told in this volume, there is no sequel.

In the intervening years I have been otherwise occupied than in the living of my own 'story'. Who in any case was 'Kathleen'? I never quite felt that I answered to that name—do we ever feel that we are really that person whose part we play? Are we not all nameless, boundless, something beyond our individual selves? That is not to say that I have ceased to participate in life—on the contrary, I have never participated more fully than since my own 'story' became but one of the thousand-and-one, a story told, a book closed. As scholar editor of a Review of the Arts, speaker at conferences, answerer of endless letters, as, occasionally, poet, I have been carried on the stream of life. As for myself, I am no longer much concerned with her, not even with the remorse she was so long to feel for her life. Moments of insight—and surely these come to us all at times—have nothing to do with the wish that has so beset Christendom ever since St. Paul, for forgiveness, personal salvation and the rest, Bunyan's Pilgrim's 'What shall I do to be saved?' Lost or saved, what does it matter, in terms of our poor, brief mortal selves, good bad or indifferent as our cases may be. These flashes of insight being an altogether other way of seeing those selves and other selves. We are, as my friend Hubert Howard used to say to me, a part of something so much greater.

Kathleen Raine. February 28th 1990

Farewell Happy Fields

(1973)

Farewell Happy Fields
Where joy for ever dwells

Paradise Lost

CHAPTER ONE

O flowers,
That never will in other Climate grow

I REMEMBER, in the beginning, a place of perfect happiness, filled with the bright sun of Easter, pure living light and warmth. My place was my state and therefore in it I knew myself where it was mine to be. That was the beginning of a dream which recurred again and again in early childhood; the dream, as I now suppose, of my birth into this world.

So it always began; but I did leave that place, caught up, as it seemed, into a gentle drift as of existence unwinding itself, flowing out of the timeless state in which I still reposed as I floated along the peaceful river past beautiful fields of flowers bathed in living light. But little by little I would find myself drawn irresistibly into the flux; and as I realized that it was no longer in my power to return or to stop, I began to be afraid. The sides of the stream grew steep and dark and dangerous, then rocky cliffs towered like great walls, and then these no longer resembled nature, but a modern city. Between towering buildings I was swept along against my will, my fear increasing as I was carried towards the machines, throbbing and grinding. Down the rapid current I was plunged into a narrow passage where the machines caught me at last among their rending wheels. At this point I always awoke, in terror.

The dream was always the same; and I knew that from bliss I would plunge into terror, from the freedom of being into the power of an irresistible mechanical destruction. I also knew that the dream was my life; the pattern it would follow of necessity; the substance, I might have thought, of all generated life. But in dreams we do not generalize, we experience.

A little hand of flame, blue-tipped, thin, labile, without substance or constant form, dancing gently on a gas-jet from the wall. In my warm cot gently laid to sleep I watched those luminous fingers dancing for me, for me. I found a song to rise and fall with the hand of the flame, glimmer and glum, glimmer and glum, glimmer and glum, and so on and on. The living flame was a being, strange and familiar, familiar and strange. My father would turn it out, send the little hand away.

Flowers. The pink aromatic clusters of the flowering currant bush hung over my pram. I looked up at those flowers with their minute perfect forms, their secret centres, with the delight of rapt knowledge. They were themselves that knowledge. Not discovery but recognition; recollection; not as memory brings the past to the present but as something for ever present coming to itself. In the manifold, the innumerable I AM, each flower was its own I am. A bush burning green and rose in the light of day. There were other flowers; chickweed's slender chalices did not then seem small or insignificant, but filled my beholding as full as a rose window in a cathedral, in all their minute perfection of beautiful form. In that garden there was a face; or rather not so much a face as a smile; a maiden's face embracing me with that smile painted ten thousand times, the smile the Virgin shines for ever into every cradle. May's long hair was golden as sunbeams seen through half-closed eye-lashes spreading the golden light into long rays. May was the little girl next door, and I loved her. The rest of her family were ugly people with loud voices. They had a little greenhouse with spiny cactuses.

I lived in a world of flowers, minute but inexhaustible; the wild fragrance of thyme on the moor outside my grand-father's stone garden wall filled me to the brim with itself; it was the moor and the light high air and the thrilling bird-voice on the moor. In the shade of the north wall there was a bed of mint and cool pansies I was allowed to pick; and these flower-faces looked at me, each and every one greeted me in a here and now that had no beginning and no end. All were mine, whatever I saw was mine in the very act of seeing. To see was to know, to enter into total relationship with, to participate in the essential being of each *I am.* Strange and mysterious some seemed; the little grey-dusted lichen-cups on my grandfather's stone wall, some with what seemed like scarlet eggs in a nest; jagged forms, without a predictable pattern, never twice the same; and yet their beauty was, again, distinctly intelligible to me, was knowledge of essential meaning which, in living form, states itself more perfectly than any words can name it. The forms of nature mean what they are, are what they mean, endlessly and for ever, and their meanings are the ever-varying expression of the one life. The language of Eden—do we share it in some measure with the animals and birds and all the conscious creatures of the earth?—may be forgotten, but it is not to be learned: it is innate knowledge, and each recognition is like a remembrance of something for ever known.

Behind my grandfather's vegetable garden was a pinewood, a dark secret world of its own. From that pine-wood came the cock pheasant I saw standing in his living glory among the rows of peas and grey-leaved young turnip. What was he? So perfectly himself he was, with his golden eyes and his gold-brown train; he was himself to the least spreckle of his feathered breast, his small proud head observing me. The fear I felt at the otherness of his life was part delight in his beauty, part awe in the presence of his touch-me-not, his 'I am that I am.' Every creature has a measure of power peculiar to itself and to its kind; I was in the presence of his bird-kind, his pheasant-kind, and the proud life that informed that feathered dress, that jewelled head and harsh beak, that deliberate gait; the absoluteness of his being there before me. I beheld and worshipped.

I remember the palpable stillness of that pine-plantation, the fir-cones lying where they fell on the carpet of needles muting sound in a place shunned by all life but that of the trees themselves, with their branches for ever dying away below to form overhead an endlessly entangled dead thicket. In my fear of its dusk was also an exultation in the experience of the wood-in-itself, as another vista of awareness into which consciousness could flow. The circumference of consciousness was the circumference of the perceptible world; the world perceived was that consciousness, that consciousness the world: there was no distinction between seer and seen, knowledge and its object. All was mine, because myself.

Perhaps those called 'nature-mystics' simply retain longer than others our normal consciousness, our birthright, lost sooner or later, or returning only rarely; or it is we who return only rarely, and lose Eden by a turning away, a refusing to look. Our separate identity grows over us like a skin, or shroud.

Places have their identity as flowers or creatures have, their soul, or *genius loci*. A place, in nature, is, after all, only a larger and more complex organism, a symbiosis of many lives. All inviolate places have this wholeness of essence; their perfection lies in their remaining intact, undisturbed by the intrusion of any life which does not itself participate in that harmonious organic unity; the shepherd and his dog, the ploughman and his plough, but not the bull-dozer or the motor-car or the actively or passively destructive presences these bring. I think of the little glen of a burn that tumbles down a series of falls into the Tyne. A path winds up beside it to the pool where the highest fall of the linn pours its fluctuating veil of water into dark turmoil. Never, in later life, do we experience that sense of perfect arrival that is, in childhood, the term of every walk; we bring the whole of ourselves to the very place, we have not already in thought moved on, or away; our thought is what we see and love and touch. We bring no ghostly memories, no pictured fantasies, with us. We are eternally there, outside time or change. That is perhaps the secret of our power of returning to certain places in memory: to places to which we never truly came, we can never return. So I call up before the mind's eye that sounding misty linn of white water falling over dripping rock, fringed with emerald liverwort and maiden-hair and yellow pimpernel. A single noble spray of the pale blue chimney bell-flower leans and nods in the commotion of the fall. Stream and rock, tree and fern, down to the most minute frond is formed each by the whole, and the whole by each. A leaf turns here to reach the light, another is pale in the shadow; the moss advances towards moisture, the twining honeysuckle ascends towards the light. Rock is shaped by water, water flows as rock bars the way or makes a passage; the dark shadow of trout, their heads upstream, fins in balance with the weight of the flow; the black slugs in their world of decay and moisture, their glossy, embossed skins as beautiful as the leathery liverwort of their habitation, the toadstool, pullulating with maggots into liquefaction, all these held within one harmony. Within that larger unity each centre of life unfolds its own unity of form in perfect and minute precision. The whole is made up not of parts but of wholes. Nature a whole made up of wholes, perfection in the most minute particle sense can pursue. The tall spray of campanula holds in balance air and water and light as these pass through it on their way; yet each bud of flower and leaf is signed with a geometric form peculiar to that species and no other, down to the smallest curve of leaf-margin and the peculiar roughness of hairs on the stem. No less formally ordered is the movement of the plant through time, its two years of life from seed to decay bringing it to perfection in the month and week appointed; for the harmony of nature is in continual motion and metamorphosis, the coming and going of forms in time. The whole of organic life—the soul of nature—is engaged in nothing else but the embodiment and unfolding of forms, in all the intricate and complex delicacy of veining, colouring, feathering, spot, stripe, notch, fleck and scale: how should the creatures not in some sense know and enjoy what they are about, what, indeed, they simply are, intricate patternings and evolving forms of mathematical art? The sense of the beautiful has deep roots, it is a knowledge that is at the same time our occupation and our delight, intuitive in earliest childhood, and rooted in our very nature, in the growth in which our bodies are engaged. 'And perhaps this faculty pronounces by comparing the object with the form which the soul herself contains and using it as a basis for judging, as a rule is used to compare straightness.'

I remember, too, a little dark paved yard behind the village post office kept by a second cousin of my father's in County Durham, where a few ferns grew, and the yellow-flowered oxalis, undisturbed in their green lives, scarcely breathed on by human presence. The little secret place had the numinous quality of a sanctuary where plant-forms had composed

4

themselves into a harmony of equilibrium, in which even the smallest moss-scale had achieved its orientation towards the great sun. As a child I learned from these minute harmonies in which every leaf and tendril is in balance with every other, and all with the light, to know when I was myself in orientation; a faculty we share with the animal and perhaps the vegetable kingdoms, but tend to lose through disuse or abuse. The gift is one whose possession is in itself a source of deep happiness, when we are in our due place, but of the unease of warning when we are not—the unease which sets animals wandering and searching for a place they feel to be right for them. So women know when they are wearing the wrong clothes not by reason but by a kind of instinctive misery. I had a scarlet coat when I was four or five years old in which I experienced all the malaise of a white blackbird, and cried and protested until my mother gave up the attempt to make me wear it.

But the surface of this endlessly unfolding veil of nature is not solid. The knowledge that existence builds its beautiful forms over who knows what abyss terrified my infant soul. Fear centred upon two dangerous thin places in the texture of the world, both on the moor above my grandfather's stone house, Hollinwood, near Kielder: a bog, and a powder magazine.

Up onto the moor my father used to carry me, so I remember, wrapped in a brown plaid shawl; secure. The way passed—or is this all a fantasy woven about some trifling patch of wet ground?—between two bottomless bog-holes, treacherously mantled over with pale green sphagnum moss. To sink there was to sink out of life; mouth and nose and ears choked with black mud, I would sink down into the bottomless place. I clung to my father as we passed between those perilous mouths. The other terror was of another kind of annihilation. Perhaps for some stone-quarry, perhaps for the outcrops of coal mined at Plashetts, there was a small stone hut, far away from every place (so it seems to memory) a house with a door but no window, where nobody lived or ever would live. There, my father told me, gunpowder was stored, for it might at any time explode and blow to pieces everything near. That is why the stone hut stood isolated and shunned. Then why was gunpowder kept at all? my infant self asked; I cannot remember my father's reasonable answer to my unreasoned protest against the very fact of destruction; for the idea of violent destruction was an outrage to some essential organic creaturely sense in me. My father, whose father was a coal-miner in County Durham, would certainly not have understood that he was, in bringing to my notice so useful and powerful a thing as gun-powder (one of the tools of the miner's craft) filling me with such a sense of outrage. The moor was beautiful, for the heather and thyme, grey lichen and green grasshoppers unfolded each to its term of perfection; the place was woven of their many lives; but the blasting and shattering of rocks and earth, the uprooting of heather and tormentil, the destroying of the nests of the stonechat and the lark was a destruction of being and meaning by the meaningless. How could an activity intrinsically destructive not be evil and its agents evil? 'For since everything formless is naturally capable of receiving shape and form, in so far as it does not participate in reason and form, it is ugly and apart from the Divine Reason; and it is in this that ugliness of every sort consists.'

Yet I gathered flowers with never a thought that I was destroying them in my desires to possess them, to hold them in my hands. I loved also butterflies; and my father must have caught them for me, shown me how to catch them under his straw hat. I must now have been four or five years in the world. I had been taught that what you must do with butterflies is to kill them, then pin them on a cork, in a box, their wings outspread. They were then called specimens; and I had seen a box covered with glass, hung on the wall, filled with dead butterflies: a *collection*. My first deep betrayal was to kill the butterflies; Red Admiral, Tortoise-shell, Peacock butterflies from the nettles. I had been told that the way to kill them is to pinch their thorax with the nails of thumb and finger. I did as I was told, unquestioningly: then I saw them with horror moving their legs slowly, but not dead; and knew what I had done.

I understand now that it is to my mother I owe the happiness of my infancy as I remember or have since imagined it. I could not have come and gone among my flowers had not her remote presence assured my freedom. She never constrained me, and to her I owed that most precious solitude in which I could lose myself. I do not remember her face or appearance then so much as certain phrases which return; of a poem by George Macdonald she used to say to me: 'Where do you come from, baby dear?/ Out of the everywhere into here.' The poetry of infancy was vivid to her. Thank God, she was a poetic mother, not a practical one. To the baby in her pram how early she communicated her own sense of the mystery and beauty of the earth. Doubtless it was from her I inherited my love of wandering the moors; for not so long before my birth she had herself been the young girl who among that same heather recited to the winds *Comus* and *Samson Agonistes,* of which she knew all, and *Paradise Lost,* of which she knew most by heart. Yet it was not the freedom of Paradise but a first foretaste of exile that first awakened the poetic instinct in me; the first intimation of a beauty inaccessible. In my infancy the pattern of my life was already indelibly drawn; there began my longing for that legendary land which some call Eden, some Erin, some Zion, some Tibet; I called it Scotland. From Scotland my people had come, my mother's people; for my father's people were never my people, in any living sense. Scotland is to this day a matriarchal country, and my mother's family naturally regarded me as my mother's daughter rather than my father's. My father, besides, had no continuity of tradition to pass on; if from my mother's side I inherited however small a portion in the memories of Scotland embodied in song, speech, and heroic story my father stood for progress, education and the future. These two influences formed me; but if I am grateful for the education to which I was subjected by my father, it is because it has given me that sad knowledge of 'good lost, and evil won', and the words in which to lament the destruction of tradition by education; for my maternal inheritance is too far away from me, too meagre for me to have preserved more than its shadow and the sense of its loss. Yet far as I have been carried from my origins, meagre as was my inheritance, the poet in me is my mother's daughter, and owes more to that lost birthright than to all the extraneous book learning I have since acquired.

The Cheviots were the hills to which (in words then familiar, for the learning by heart of the psalms was no less a part of childhood than the hills themselves) I lifted mine eyes; from them came my help. To this day a range of distant hills is to me like a promise of paradise. Beyond those hills, so they told me, lay Scotland, 'over the Border'; our own country. Displacement was already my inheritance, but by so small a distance that I could still see the country to which (so I was given to understand, not in so many words but by a thousand expressions of that profound love of a native place which among country people is as strong, perhaps stronger, than the love of persons) we belonged.

My mother's mother was a native of Edinburgh; of her people I know nothing except that an aunt who kept a dame's school had been a friend of Mr. Gladstone, who called her the most intelligent woman he had ever known. Whether that was a compliment I do not know. There was some remote kinship too with the Adam brothers, the architects of Edinburgh.

A great-grandmother, remembered by my mother, was called O'Hara, and smoked a pipe, kept secretly in a box which my mother was sometimes asked to bring her, with warnings not to look inside. My grandfather came from Forfar; from his father he had inherited his skill in fly-fishing, his knowledge of Milton's poetry, and his addiction to whisky. Was it the songs, sung not as songs learned, but as if the spontaneous utterance of some immediate feeling, or as the telling of our own story, that so early gave me the sense of identity within the tradition of Scotland? Or that

7

speech, with some qualitative implication of feeling in every noun and verb, so fitted to express the life I myself knew, of open moor and sheltered barn, of cow-byre and kitchen, sweet Maiden's Blush roses blooming in the shelter of stone walls, a poverty redeemed by a natural setting both noble and free, fine and delicate, of a consciousness, a knowledge indistinguishable and inseparable from a country of hills and mountains and streams, of bird and blossom. In my infancy the resolution to go straight back to my true native land was pure and passionate; little did I then know the great distance of that journey back. So near the Border, all that was to be loved and desired, all of which the songs told, seemed to be not quite out of reach, near enough to arouse and to betray hope continually. I see nothing arbitrary in the process by which our lives at every moment give us symbols appropriate to what we are; and to say that imagination is 'conditioned' by an accident of geography seems to me quite inadequate as an account of the journey of consciousness through the ever-changing landscape of a life. It may be the other way round, and the scene set by imagination itself.

The sense of living as an exile in a foreign land, of being of another race and kind from those among whom I have lived, has not weakened to this day, so deeply was it implanted in me, in my infancy, by my mother's kin; they themselves already exiles, though living only a few miles over the English border, but as race-proud aliens in an alien land.

Yet my infancy and childhood had 'one foot in Eden' in a sense more than symbolic: we were to the north of Hadrian's wall, in *Scotia irridenta;* beyond the reach of the imposed law of the Romans, on the side of the unconquered people. Here the legendary Picts had defended our sanctuary against servitude and civilization; and there I felt myself to belong with the untamed creatures of the wild sanctuaries of whom the songs of Scotland tell, with deer and curlew and lapwing of the moor, not to the trammelled history of civilization. Yet living as we did south of the modern frontier (an invisible one, however, less majestic and ancient than that wall I later knew well, whose hewn stones, whose fosse and vallum, sometimes lost, yet so persistently reappear, running on and on, from Corbridge and Chollerford over the Nine Nicks, bare moor and crag farther than eye can follow) we were nevertheless in some sense excluded. I did not know what those mysterious frontiers were that lay between my world and the country of the poems and the ballads. The place of poetry seemed to me, then, a place in this world, of this world, and only a few miles away.

The place I was later and for years to come to love most in the world was within sight of the Green Rigg where the Douglas had died under the same tall bracken that was higher than my head when at last I climbed its

8

slope. There was a loch, and a crag called 'the old Man of the Wannies' because its rocky fall had the profile of a man's face; and a pair of ravens (the last in England, it was said, though this may have been a poetic more than a literal truth) nested there. But before I ever saw that place, 'the wild hills o'Wannie', a line perhaps from some poem by a local bard, spoken by my Aunty Peggy Black in her sweet treble, was as the 'ξιζ 'οροζ in *The Bacchae*, a summons to that other world. It was the phrase itself which acted on me as a spell: *wild hills*; and they were there, visible far away, where my Aunty Peggy pointed. The phrase named those hills as a place not in the world so much as in the poem; promised in that very place the wildness-in-itself of all hills. I had only to reach the Wannies to be in that essential world.

So it was that at last, one day, one fair northern summer's day, we set out, my mother, my Aunty Peggy and my infant self in my little push-car. We crossed the farmyard with its scent of camomile and cow-dung, and through the one of its several gates which opened upon the high bare pasture where the peewits are always wheeling over the outcrop of rock where they nest, their high domain, set out towards the wild hills. We were already above the level of trees, and as we climbed the turf became finer and softer, with wild pink and wild thyme and rock-rose. We came to the little crag where in the warren there were always a few black rabbits among the brown—I knew the place well later. Wild it seemed, without wall or man-made road, the creatures wild in the rocks, and far and wide. Was this 'the Wild Hills o'Wannie'? No, I was told, farther on, could I not see them in the distance? And there—so memory has composed the picture, or imagination has—the sun was setting their crests on fire with gold, and we were walking along the green road of the long summer day towards those bright hills until it seemed to me I could see the purple of the heather on their slopes. We were on our way, we were going to the place itself.

Until we came to the farm of Sweethope, where my mother and aunt were merely going to take tea with the farmer's wife and daughters. Would we go on after tea to the Wild Hills o'Wannie? Oh yes, after tea; be a good girl and wait; and after tea we walked long in the garden among the phloxes and sweet peas and the late summer flowers. I must have given a good deal of trouble, for not for one moment did I relinquish my quest, or realize that this was the end and not the beginning of that for which we had come. The fair promises had all been a ruse to keep a baby happy on a walk across those long Northumbrian pastures.

After tea in my push-car I was again happy: we were setting off at last, for those beautiful hills; but the push-car was turned round towards home, myself crying and struggling. They promised that I should go there 'someday'— that beautiful horizon of time, where as upon mountains distant in space, resides that same imagined beauty. They thought I would forget, as soon as they themselves, my purpose to go to that place; but I was, on that day, not the baby in the push-car but the self I was later to become, or already was. At last poetry came to my aid, and I fell into a chant, repeating the magic phrase over and over until the words became a sort of mantra. 'I want to go to the wild hills o'Wannie.' By incantation I tried to bring near the far bright beauty of the hills. In need of magic for so specific an end I discovered the use of poetry.

I later learned that not only were there certain places which belonged to that world of which poetry tells, but also certain animals, and birds. The hawk, the heron and the raven, appearing in all the power of their magical significance, would write across the sky some word of ill-omen or of splendour. To see the heron, or the crow, was, in that remote world, an epiphany of indescribable mystery; not the mystery merely of the bird itself (though that was part of it) but of something which concerned also the seer of the bird, a confluence of our existence with the existence of the bird and of both with something else otherwise inexpressible. This was something more than a child's *participation mystique,* it was a mode of knowledge communicated to me by my elders in the tone of voice in which it would be said 'there is the heron'—or the corbie, or the hawk—it was always 'the', not 'a', for any individual bird or beast was as if endowed with the full identity of all its kind. (Such lowly creatures as rabbits were not so distinguished by the definite article, but were only named by the collective form, or the plural.) We felt, I think, that the bird itself knew that which to us it communicated. Thus the corbie was 'an evil bird', condemned by us for that dark nature of which it told, as if a conscious agent. But to put it so is to translate—and how inadequately—into the language of words what was itself a language far more powerful and no less exact; a language in which bird and beast and tree were themselves the words, full of otherwise inexpressible meaning. Poetry was not then words on the page, but birds in the air, in the dusk, against the wind in the high blue air; it was trees, it was stones and springs, an ever-changing face of things which communicated knowledge words can only remotely capture or evoke.

To that order also belonged certain people; and with these people, belonging as they did to the world imagination seeks always to enter, I felt some deep link. The old hierarchic society had subtle virtues for the imagination, most of all perhaps for those who had least to gain in material terms from the caste system. Imagination loves nobility and splendour and tragedy and beauty and kingship; loves all great things; of equality, that doctrinaire abstraction, it knows nothing. It is very likely that our neighbouring Armstrongs and Shaftoes and Douglases or even the Percys themselves no longer participated in the living tradition which for their tenants they continued to embody, bearing as they did names from those ballads which were our sole cultural heritage long after they had ceased to be theirs. Doubtless education had brought them into the twentieth century while their tenants continued to live on in legendary time; yet they continued to nourish our imagination, as those Guermantes whom Marcel was later to meet in Paris had existed for him, as a child and a young man, with another kind of reality, of which social status is itself only an image, a metaphor.

My mother's family inherited, however tenuously, the archaic attitude of the clan towards its chieftain. It is forgotten in these envious egalitarian days the extent to which the cement of such relationships was neither the compulsion of tyranny nor of economics, but imagination. It was at its roots a blood-kinship, or, what is almost as strong, a kinship through a common love of the land, of the same mountain and river, the same fields, the same prevailing wind and the sun and the stars rising and setting beyond certain abiding hills. There is a sense in which each creature possesses its world far more real than the mere token ownership conveyed by deed of property. 'That all the world is yours, your very senses and the inclination of your mind declare.' Clothed with the heavens and crowned with the stars, each creature is 'the sole heir of the whole world, and more than so, because men are in it who are every one sole heirs as well as you'. Every child knows this; and country people who, enjoying the beauty of some tree or the flowers that grow by the side of the road, are not troubled by thoughts of ownership. There is a kinship of Eden itself among all who are in Traherne's sense co-heirs of the same parcel of earth and sky. In the present world it must seem incredible that, in that old unbroken pattern, envy played no part.

There is, besides, a kind of being 'in love' with those who often bear the names, and are from legendary time associated with such enduring and continuous places. Bearing those names they embodied, in some measure, the sense of identity of the nameless people of their land, with its intangible heritage of imaginative riches. Their lives possessed a dimension which common mankind lacked, the dimension of tradition, of poetry; yet they were at the same time extensions of the lives of their nameless tenantry. No lords can so much speak of 'their' tenantry as the tenants of 'their' lords and ladies; for no economic bond has in it the immortal quality of the instinct for poetry. The names written in 'the book of the people' are not those who have done most 'good', or worked in 'the people's' cause, but those whose stories have the most poetry in them, the most of the human qualities all possess but not all can realize; the 'black' Armstrongs and Douglases, the bride-stealers and murderers and fratricides, the vanquished no less than the victors on legendary battlefields.

Song and legend were a birthright which to the poorest lent the dignity of an identity conferred by ancestral participation. What are the legendary rivers of epic and ballad to strangers? Academic scholarship does not so much inherit as usurp and obliterate the living tradition it replaces. By her speech and her music, Scotland, like Ireland, had kept, even to my childhood (though not unimpaired) her imaginative identity; and my mother's share, small as it was, in this birthright, is the only inheritance I ever had. I learned with love the words of the Scottish speech, because these were 'our' words.

My father spoke 'educated' English, learned as a foreign language at Durham University, and acquired by the help of his fine fastidious ear. But my mother's family spoke 'braid Scots' bringing out, in moods of excitement, whether of tenderness or scorn, uncouth words like treasured heir-looms; for the words of a living dialect are not abstract terms, they are an imaginative map of a country of the imagination, and of experience, feelings and perceptions inseparable from experiences in, and of, that world, caught up into regions of consciousness, with the peculiar light and climate of the place. The words are concrete as if the landscape itself had uttered them; 'In behint yon auld fail dyke' can no more be translated as 'close behind that old turf wall' than can 'corbie' as 'crow'; for the words bring with them the context of their world, are inseparable from that total experience. The words of the ballad evoke an expanse of treeless moor, and lichened stone, where the harsh dialogue of 'twa corbies' is carried on the delicate air over miles of bare hillside to the ears of those who themselves participate in that total consciousness of which landscape and language are alike regions. Nor can those regions be entered by visiting the geographical site: Tweed and Till, Sweet Afton and Flodden Field are regions which cannot, in that sense, be visited.

Now that I speak only a well-learned acquired Cambridge English I wonder if any other kind of poetry is possible than one so rooted in the unbroken continuity of language and place; a language which itself transposes into words that earlier, more richly meaningful language of bird and weather and hill, inseparable from the people who created it, and the continuity of a culture in the places named by speech. When Indians (for instance) send me poems written in what they take to be the English language, I invariably ask them why they use it; and I have never heard again from any Indian to whom I have put that question: for had they understood the answer they would not have been writing English in any case. Yet I am no better myself; an exile, even linguistically, looking back with nostalgia into a world to which in infancy I thought I belonged, but from which my people had already travelled too far for return to be possible, even for themselves, far less for me.

So it was useless for my father to oppose the doctrinaire abstractions of socialism (for he came from the world of the dispossessed who hated and envied those who inherited their place and portion in the old social order, the dispossessed already bent on its destruction) or the alien themes of 'education' to the flow of talk in the kitchen of Hollinwood; of the Duke, of the proud Duchess, of the young Earl Percy whose life was ruined through family pride, who died young, killed in a duel in France, so it was said, romantic Byronic victim of a broken heart and the legendary proud mother of the ballads who counselled her son against his true-love. There was Lord James, fair-haired as the young lords of border history, who died tragically young, and in whose sickroom his tame birds flew free; and the lady Victoria's great coils of fine-spun hair my mother had admired as she sat behind her and her sister the lady Mary in the Kielder Kirk, of the bright gold so praised in ballad and song. Of all those conspicuous in our eyes as those who once walked on the Akropolis of Mycenae, the stories were woven into that unbroken thread of the memory or imagination from which Shakespeare and Homer drew only a few strands.

Such were the first stories I ever heard; and it seemed to me then as if my very identity was bound up with those stories and with the people who enacted them; figures who belonged, like the hills and rivers, to the world of my inheritance.

Was I—have I all my life been—the too much doted on child of my poetic mother, cast by her for a part not in the peasant activities of her mother's world, but in poetry? Or did I myself intuitively know that the aunts and grand-mother who pampered and bored me, the next-door-neighbours and indeed almost all the adults of my world and most of the children, were not of my kind, not concerned with the things which concerned me? My mother's business that I must be about? Or was it my mother's sense of innate difference, was it her inhabiting of a world whose atmosphere was freer, clearer, more wonderful than theirs, which from the beginning of my life imprinted upon me the sense that I was not of their kind? That I belonged with the golden race? For the golden race is not to be identified with class (though the class system has given it some protection) but is sown broadcast over the earth, like the wheat in the parable, to starve, or wither, or bear fruit. I was born with gifts, inherited as I now realize from my mother, and by her from her father, or perhaps merely God-given; and when I am judged it will not be for my knowledge of their possession, but for the small use I have made of them. I might, I ought to have achieved more, to have left more and better poetry than I have done. How clearly childhood knew; but choked by thorns how fruitless I have been.

My Aunty Peggy Black was not my mother's sister, but her first cousin, who had come to live with my grandparents as an orphan at the age of ten or eleven. She was less 'educated' than my mother and her sisters, and I suppose of commoner clay; for it was from my handsome grandfather, who though but a village schoolmaster, knew Latin, wrote political verse-lampoons, and read aloud to his daughters (as in the evenings they sat sewing and embroidering—I have a patchwork quilt which my mother made in those far-off days when even the poor had leisure for such skills) the novels of Meredith and Thomas Hardy as these appeared in serial form, that my mother and her sisters inherited, along with their beauty, something rare, altogether out of place in the world in which they lived. My Aunty Peggy too was a village schoolmistress, and reigned in the hamlet of Bavington; but she (not being a daughter of Alexander Wilkie) had neither beauty nor dreams to unsettle her; she was therefore at one with her world, as my mother and her sisters were not; she taught the children of farmers and hinds in her single schoolroom with its big iron stove, and its high windows, and its lobby smelling of miry clogs and carbolic soap. 'You cannot make silk purses out of sows' ears' summarized the wisdom of her years of experience with the 'gowks', 'donnarts' and 'gommerels' who made, all the same, very good pig-skin leather in the long run. In a farming community, heredity ('like father, like son') had not, as in an egalitarian urban society in which all alike are stripped of individual qualities, been censored from the laws of nature.

It is to my Aunty Peggy Black that I owe the only years in which I was ever to know the sense—even though it was an illusory sense—of having a place on earth to which I truly belonged, and of being in that place; for in my parents' house this was never so, as will be told. How could it have been so, my mother herself living as she did as a stranger in a strange land?

My Aunty Peggy lived, at the time of my first memory, in a two-roomed stone cottage at the top of the outcrop of rock that was our only village street. There, I remember my mother, young and full of laughter, and myself (the infant in the push-car) lifting from the earth numbers of small brown snowdrop bulbs. Perhaps the clumps were being divided, or some being given to my mother to take away. I had not known before that under the earth there were these mysterious roots of things; not shapeless like pebbles, but formed according to a pattern, and glossy and living down under the soil.

Later Aunty Peggy moved into the manse, a stone house with a big garden sheltered by beeches, and a field where the Minister had kept his pony or grown his hay, and the burn running along the bottom of the garden, its sound of swiftly running water ever my companion at night when I too lived at the manse. In that garden snowdrops were in multitude without number. After the snow they broke the ground, clumps of short green shoots tightly clasping the green edged white flower-buds stiff upright. Then a few would break their glassy sheaths and bend their graceful necks, the petals still closed; then many, then innumerable, their flowers would open, some single, some double, nestling near the house, or scattered in the half wild undergrowth down to the 'syke loning'. I can see them now in my mind's eye; but the mind's eye is a poor thing in comparison to that marvel of reality, that immaculate freshness, and the light cold early spring scent of the green-white flowers in the air fragrant after the melting of the snow. 'Ten thousand saw I at a glance', Wordsworth said of his daffodils; surely exaggerating a little. But when I think of the snowdrops in the manse garden—in the grass, under the apple-tree, cascading down towards the bordering beech trees—I see multitude as the peculiar delight of that vision. Wordsworth's ten thousand is to be read in the same sense as the 'ten thousand creatures' of Lao-Tze. That they were countless, that there were always more, gave a kind of knowledge that nature is inexhaustible, that multitude is her secret, her deep mystery. There could be no end to snowdrops. When, much later I suppose, I heard of 'extinct' species, of the last of the Great Auks slaughtered on St. Kilda (with all the wild glory of Kingsley's Mother Carey's Chickens) I felt that deep sense of sorrow and outrage as at the blasting of the moor at Plashetts. For what is more 'against nature' than the killing of her creatures, the blasting of her fecundity, the erasing of one of the moulds of creation?

Bavington might itself have stood in legendary time; built of the stone of the hills, it had no age, but perfectly belonged to its place at the top of the outcrop of rock that paved the farmyard and the village street. Up and down that slope of rock, worn by clogs and hooves, came and went the dwellers in the row of three cottages below, the manse, the byre, and all who came on weekdays to the school, and Sundays to the kirk. Living in the manse, my Aunty Peggy enjoyed with the house some of the status it conferred. The school and the adjoining cottage were of great age; some said the cottage, with its mullioned windows, had formerly been part of a monastery. None who lived there had yet moved out of ancestral continuity, and the texture of their lives was inwoven with the land on which their fathers and mothers had been born before them: Hallington and Throckrington and Hare-Laws, Three Farms, and Clay Walls, and

Sweethope. The texture is broken now; the children no longer walk or ride on horseback over the moorland pasture to the village school (belonging, with barn and byre and kirk to that world to which each was sole heir) but are driven away in buses to the nearest town, or the farmers' sons sent to public schools, there to lose, in exchange for education, that sense of identity with a place (which I and my own school-fellows were, I suppose, among the last to know) which belongs only to people of intact inheritance.

Bavington's 'time immemorial' can, of course, be given dates. The little Presbyterian church bears the date of its building—1725; records of a congregation go back to 1662 and the times of the Covenanters. The manse was built in 1855, when the earlier manse (contemporary I suppose with the church) became 'a respectable school in which the highest branches of education' were taught. The school's founder (the Rev. Mr. Forsyth) wished 'to make the Institution of such a character as should induce the wealthy farmers and graziers of the neighbourhood to send their children to it instead of sending them to boarding-schools to finish their education'. Mr. Forsyth went personally to Scotland (for where else would a Border Minister look for a sound dominie?) to search for a teacher of 'superior qualifications'; and whether because of the excellence of the school, or because farmers had at that time little regard for book-learning, the wealthy farmers and graziers did indeed continue to send their sons and daughters to be licked into more or less silky purses by my Aunty Peggy Black, herself a native of Edinburgh.

As for the manse itself, the *Morpeth Herald* in June 1855 described it as 'neat and chaste in design, substantial in structure, and commodious in its arrangements. In honour of its completion, a social entertainment, or a "house-warming", was held. The tea-tables, sumptuously furnished by the ladies of the congregation, were laid out in the several rooms, and crowded with a large and respectable assemblage of guests, consisting of the members of the congregation and their friends from different quarters. The utmost hilarity prevailed on this occasion. The draught "which cheers but not inebriates" was copiously supplied—and its accompaniments reflected great credit on the taste and liberality of the entertainers.' (This I can well believe; the cookery book issued on the 200th anniversary, 'which took the form of a sale of work, tea and concert' and on which occasion Miss Black's name appears among the Robsons, Waltons, Slessors, Fenwicks, Patersons, Carrs, Browells, Scotts and Bells, contains recipes for those cakes I myself remember and whose like could not now be obtained at Fortnum and Mason's.) 'In the evening the party withdrew to the Church, when they were successively addressed in very interesting speeches by the Revs. A. Forsyth, the Minister of Bavington; Fergus,

Thropton; Anderson, Morpeth; Cathcart, Harbottle; Wrightson, Wark; and Lennie, Glanton.' That innocent merry-making must have left something of its sweetness in those familiar rooms that even now I so often revisit (strangely altered as they always are, but still and for ever the place of my homecoming) in nightly dreams.

The house-warming, with its six addresses, must indeed have been a grand occasion; but later members of the congregation and their friends from different quarters were always ready to attend and to enjoy, with sober hilarity, those permitted festivals, a sale of work, or a whist-drive and social. Those of us pupils at the school with the best handwriting (copperplate as it still was) would copy some dozen or more announcements of the event to be held in aid of Bavington Church on such a day; and these were nailed to certain gate-posts where they could not fail to be seen by the farmers, rich graziers, etc., and their wives; who would arrive in their traps on the day appointed to partake, in the school and the manse, of the cup that cheers, and its accompaniments of sponge-cakes, 'melting moments', singin' hinnies, gingerbread, sultana cakes, and pasties made of the fruits of every tree in the garden.

When last I saw Bavington the texture of woven and interwoven lives which had made it, in the human sense, a place, had been destroyed; the school was a youth-hostel, George Carr the school caretaker its warden; weekenders from Newcastle occupied the cottages; the retired schoolmistress who at that time occupied the manse (where the two silver Cromwellian Communion-cups and the six 'tokens' had been treasured in a cupboard with deep idolatrous reverence) was 'a Roman Catholic'. All was in confusion and decline. Yet we were the first unwitting agents of the process of change; for it was my Aunty Peggy Black herself who brought to Bavington its first motor-car, and I whose task it was to open and shut the five-barred gates across the grass roads over those high moorland pastures, and to move in order to do so (along with their clouds of flies) the five or six ruminating steers or heifers which would be lying on the sun-warmed outcrop. There were some five gates between Bavington and the main road to Newcastle; they guarded the magic, the *genius loci,* such as it was; but no gates can prevail against the encroachment of the machine age which obliterates all that has unique identity.

Yet Bavington, as I remember it, seems to have stood outside the millrace of history, abiding still within the covenant of God, 'While the earth remaineth, seed-time and harvest, cold and heat, and summer and winter, shall not cease.' Time was cyclic, not linear.

The experience of each season was, in that distant world, like a change of consciousness; and it was winter especially which then had the power to remove every farm and hamlet from common time, bringing healing isolation as its most delicate secret. The arrival of winter had a grandeur, as of the approach of that God 'who maketh the clouds his chariot: who walketh upon the wings of the wind', and whose breath comes out of the north. It was in terms of the grandeur of the God of the Psalms, of Isaiah and of Job (whose Word we gathered to hear every Sunday, read by the Minister in the little church, and whose memorizing was my Sunday task) that I saw the elements unloosed upon us, snow-clouds on the North wind that travelled unhindered over the sweep of the moors. Because of their greatness, and because they were the vehicles of God, I rejoiced in the arrival of storm, wind, snow, frost and thunder. These were attributes of the divine majesty, and the coming of a great storm the approach of the God who 'did fly upon the wings of the wind'; a dignity conferred upon our high lonely house as by the progress of the Elohim.

We knew of the approaching snow-storm not from any weather-report but from watching the 'weather-airt' of our own sky. Aunty Peggy would close the school early to let her twenty or thirty pupils get home to their remote farms in safety; she and I had only to cross from the school to the manse; we used the door through the back-kitchen, where the iron pans, soot-encrusted, in which we boiled the porridge, the potatoes and the broth, the coal-shovel, the water-dipper, the ash-riddle and the zinc pails all seemed to have grown inimical, emanating an icy coldness that clung to the skin like fire. Many years it is since I have known, as then, the ordeal of the body which winter brought, feet frozen and leaden in heavy clogs and hands stiff and red in gloves with holes in the fingers, miserably comfortless. Last thing at night when all the tasks were over, my Aunty Peggy and I would draw up our chairs to the kitchen range (where the kettle hung on its hook over the fire, and the steel dampers of the oven shone spotless at all times) to thaw out the cold of the day, the wind rattling and battering at the shutters, and the voices of the air howling as the smoke blew in gusts down the chimney. Yet these ordeals of winter seemed to raise us towards the grandeur of those elements visiting with their presences our remote hamlet.

No room was ever so cold as the blue bedroom of the manse on a January night; but the feather-bed of that icy bedroom was my refuge and my only hope of ultimate comfort from the misery of having a body in winter; when after what seemed like hours I would venture, little by little, to thaw those frozen feet against warmer parts of my small shivering body, and a glow of warmth would come at last. In the night the wind drops and I wake to the silence, a stillness as intense as the sound it replaces. The tinkle of the little burn at the foot of the garden is muted and muffled; and the light is white, reflected back from the transfigured earth to the grey sky. Immaculate snow on garden and moor, on the tops of the dykes, on the window-sills, all is drifted into lovely and simple curves, hollows and ridges the shape of wind, the shape of eddies of wind, of gusts, and long smooth sweeping waves of wind. The wind is a subtle mathematician, a Platonist impressing on the snow an image of invisible forms ruled by number and geometry. The house, sealed by drifts of snow, its doors and windows softly barred by mysterious barricades of myriads of delicate crystals, seems removed during the night into another mode of being. Our solitude seems to set upon us some seal, as chosen and set apart by the snow, the snow-clouds and the sky, in their sanctuary. All within safe from all without, nothing the heart loved could spill or flow away. The white cups and plates, with their pattern of a gold circle and a clover-leaf; the eggs in a bowl, the loaves in the bread-crock, the paraffin-drum in the back-kitchen, the lamps, the clock on the wall, the magenta bells of the Christmas-cactus, the empty rooms of the house itself, purged of all invasive and obliterating and blurring irrelevances; space and time no longer flowing away all round them, stood in their own principle, their absolute identity. All I loved in the world was in that place, encircled within that white horizon.

I wished that our sanctuary could remain for ever within its white barrier; but soon came Grannie Carr, a woollen cap on her toothless head, strong as ten old women, making her way in her clogs through the drifts to see how we fared; and presently George Carr would come and dig us out, baring a raw path to the door of the back-kitchen. But if the innermost sanctuary was now destroyed, another magic circle remained intact about our little hamlet; which had, overnight, drifted away from Northumberland, England, the world, into its own sphere of separate time and space. Our lives, so implicated one with another, came into a completeness. We travel in search of experience, yet nothing so enhances the real as remaining in one place; and when our frontiers were closed, all humanity seemed sufficiently represented by Granny Carr and George, and George's wife Annie, and Annie's baby Francis; by old Maggie who lived in the two-roomed cottage where she raised young turkeys in a barrel turned on its side, and kept a box of 'Dainty Dinahs' and bulls-eyes to sell to the children at the school; by the unshaven farmer and his slatternly wife, with their unbroken row of annual boys, ending with a baby girl, Minnie; all their heads, cropped with the sheep-shears, patched with ring-worm and their corduroy clothes smelling of milk and cow-dung. The vague figures of the butcher, the grocer, the post, the coal, Mr. Howatson the Minister, the invasive distant world, none of these could reach us. There would be no school until the thaw, no doing sums on slates with squeaky slate-pencils, no dreamy chanting of the multiplication-tables and the rivers of England; no learning by heart of *The Revenge* or *The Lay of the Last Minstrel,* or how Horatius kept the Bridge across the Tiber, no clatter of desks and clogs as a score of children sat down after reciting the Lord's Prayer (hands together, eyes closed) in broad dialect as ancient as the boundaries of their fathers' fields; no washing of hands in school washbasins or comparing of warts as we dried them all together on the rough linen roller towels before the children from distant farms gathered round the great iron stove to eat the huge pasties they brought for dinner. Until the thaw, all that hum of life and effort of learning was over.

The farmyard had become a labyrinth with passages cut between walls of snow, from house to byre, from byre to barn. I wished those walls would stand for ever, and the world they so briefly and marvellously built, so strangely unlike the familiar farmyard with its outcrop of rock streaming with mud ('clart', we called it) and fragrant with camomile. Of course it ended; and perhaps it was very brief, though now it seems without beginning and without end, that condition I have tried to describe in which each thing, as if unique and altogether itself, attained its full identity in a timeless state. You can find that experience, once winter's most delicate secret, only in pictures like those painted a thousand years ago by Chinese sages whose magic brushes were able to express at once the great emptiness, and the eternal existence of every frozen twig and dry grass-stalk.

One of the foundations of my happiness in that vanished world was the security of a life in which children as a matter of course helped in the work of the day. All my school-fellows returned home, the boys to feed the beasts, the girls to milk and bake and gather eggs or pick gooseberries; and in hay-time all helped to gather the hay into pike and stook and cock. There were not two worlds, one for children and another for adults; nor for adults two worlds, one of work and one of leisure. There still remained, in the country, the integrity of that ancient way of life in which work, and whatever pleasures we might find or invent, were woven into one texture. If at times the tasks laid upon our childhood seemed hard, we had in performing them the sense of participating in the real world, whose wholeness embraced all within the horizon our eyes saw, crag and pasture, byre and garden and kitchen. Extraneous knowledge (how Horatius kept the bridge) occupied a place in our lives relatively small and quite unimportant. The poetry of life lay at hand, as in country gardens clumps of double daffodils bordered the rows of early potatoes and winter kale. We took our pleasures as we came and went upon our tasks; we were at once occupied and free, nor could we have said where tasks ended and pleasures began. We could enjoy our Maiden's Blush roses as we picked the gooseberries; and who can say whether gathering raspberries or

seeking eggs be work or play? As for 'education', 'school' was not in those
days seen as 'work', but rather as a respite from the hard tasks of life,
which lay at home. To write a good copperplate hand was an
accomplishment rather than a necessity; and who, once school was over,
would ever again need to recite by rote the rivers of England? Yet we did
learn the structure of language, to parse and analyse sentences, to spell,
and to know what were called 'Latin roots' with a thoroughness that has
served me well in a life undreamed-of at Bavington school. The great
virtue of that outmoded education—and that surely for all of us—was the
number of poems, psalms, and passages from the Bible we learned by
heart. Memory makes our own the words of power in a manner far more
complete than the mere reading of them, or the knowledge of where we
may look them up on our shelves. My Aunty Peggy's tastes were for
rousing heroic narrative—the *Lays of Ancient Rome, The Burial of Sir
John Moore at Corunna,* or *Nobly, Nobly Cape St. Vincent/ To the north-
west died away,* or *The Revenge.* My own preferences—though I learned
all these, and with them the simple heroic values they express—were not
ballads of tragic love *(Fair Helen* or *Lord Ullin's Daughter,* and still less
The Bridge of Sighs) but the simple nostalgia of 'I remember, I remember/
The house where I was born', and Cowper's *Poplar Field,* and 'My
Heart's in the Highlands, my heart is not here'; imperceptibly leading, by
way of 'He has gone from the mountain/ He is lost to the forest', and 'The
harp that once in Tara's Halls' to the exultant war-songs of Scotland,
'Scots wha hae wi' Wallace bled' and *The Gathering Song of Donald
Dhu.* To childhood patriotism is innate, for places are more dear than
people; and there is no deeper love than that given once and for ever to the
place on earth which childhood held dear.

The poems of Burns and Thomas Moore I knew as songs not poems; as
they are meant to be known. With some surprise I find, as I write, calling
up from the long past forgotten lines, and with them the emotion they first
aroused in me, that these are the poems that still have the power to move
me to tears; while I can read dry-eyed all the canon of English Romantic,
Metaphysical and philosophic poetry I have since studied. It is these older
strata that made me whatever I am.

Among my daily tasks at the manse was the carrying of the water. The
soft-water barrel stood behind the back kitchen, on the sunless end of the
house, where the beautiful green liverwort, whose strange and mysterious
indusia filled me with a kind of learned botanical awe, advanced over the
naked rock. As I lowered the dipper into the water the larvae of mos-
quitoes which, undisturbed, hung as if suspended from the surface, would
dive wriggling into the gloomy wooden depths. A few of these creatures,
or their sloughed integuments, whose exquisite fragile delicacy of form

fascinated as it repelled, found their way into my dipper with the inexorability of the laws of probability (so many to the cubic foot—I could not cheat chance) sooner or later to be poured out of the bedroom jug, their reappearance a kind of malevolent pursuit, like Pandora's troubles. There even one of them produced a scunner which marred the luxury of feeling the softness of that water (mellowed with brown fragrant Pears' soap) as I washed my hands and face in the bedroom wash-basin.

Our drinking-water I had to bring from the well in the farmyard; a task which burdened me to the extreme limit of my strength but whose imaginative delight was of a quality to which I find it difficult to give a name, for it seemed to touch springs of thought at that time unknown to me; and not altogether (like my daily delight in nature) something child-hood may share with the animal creation. I took with me the tin dipper, and two buckets, held apart by a square wooden frame which prevented them from jolting and spilling against my thin young legs in their black woollen stockings. Empty they were no burden, but full, the handles of the pails cut into my hands and their weight dragged at my shoulders, so that I had to set them down more than once between the well and the water-crocks in the manse larder, under the cold stone slabs on which stood the pats of butter and the bowls of milk set for the cream to rise (to be skimmed delicately with a spoon into a glass cream-jug for tea). To drink that well-water, cold and clear, was a kind of austere luxury, almost a rite; my Aunty Peggy never failed to praise, as she drank it, the water from that well as the best she had ever known; as people praise wine. Years later, in the Highlands, I again met country people who spoke of the water of their wells and springs in that ancient way as in the Book of Kings ('Give me to drink of the water of the well of Bethlehem . . .'), or in Greek mythology.

The well must I think have been very old; the roughly-hewn well-head which covered the spring might have dated from the forgotten monastery; and simple as it was it spoke a language entirely strange to me at that time, not of nature, but of a different kind of meaning, which I recognized because this primitive shrine (for the well had, for me, a kind of numinosity) was raised upon a marvel of nature itself whose magic it served to enhance. I shared, as I drew my water, the wonder of those who had built the well-head, recognizing in it the expression of a mind for which, as for my own, a spring was something pure, mysterious, more than natural. The spring was not deep, and I could plunge my arm to the depth of the sand-grains which danced on the bottom perpetually, as the cold clear water welled up. This perpetual welling up of the water was to me a marvel, that emergence from the rocky darkness where water has a secret life of its own, profound, flowing in underground streams and hollows under the hills which none can know or enter. It was as if at this spot a mystery were perpetually enacted. If I found in the stone basin leaves or water-shrimps I removed them as from a sacred source.

The sense of sacred places, natural shrines, was strong in me (the Covenanters notwithstanding); one such I had made for myself on a rock upon a certain crag, where I used to sit, remote as a hare on its form, looking out over the moors to the edge of the sky in a kind of religious ecstasy. I felt I ought to take there that simple symbol of the divine, my Bible, but, finding that the book did not fit the genius of the place at all, I took it home again, replacing it with treasures of my own, banded snail-shells and the like. That was my first, but by no means my last, unsuccessful attempt to attune the reality of my experience with accepted modes of religious expression. Child of nature that I was, I perhaps grew up too long without access to civilization. But I would have well understood those Buddhist stories which tell that the most sacred scriptures are the unwritten pages, an old pine-tree gnarled by wind and weather or a skein of geese flying across the sky.

Yet once it had left the well-head the little trickling stream which overflowed continually did not seem to me in any way sacred or mysterious. In it paddled the farm-yard ducks and geese, and a few yards below the well it gathered into a small muddy pond where the beasts drank. From the pond the water ran on, through the bull-field and under the high stone wall of the manse garden, swiftly running between abundant banks of saxifrage, under the luxuriant blackcurrant bushes which love cool moisture, through the manse hay-field and across the 'syke loning' to which it gave its name. Two fields away its waters were still pure enough for watercress to thrive in abundance, whose dark fresh leaves I often gathered for our tea, to eat with our homemade bread, and salt; and there were wild flowers, water-avons, brooklime speedwell, marsh-marigold and many more I then knew, before the Bavington burn joined the Wansbeck, somewhere beyond our world.

The water was my morning task; and after school I fetched the evening milk, from Clay Walls, two fields away from the manse, the enamel milk-can swinging and jolting on its wire handle, the milk splashing into the inverted cup which formed its lid. Sometimes when Grannie Carr's cow was in milk I was allowed to milk her, squeezing the white jet from the rough udders of life; something I did not (strangely enough, perhaps) find magical, as the well was magical, perhaps because the cow's udders were so like my own body, only coarser, and not very clean.

Sometimes Grannie Carr would take me into her parlour, there to show me her treasures—a set of biscuit-coloured Wedgwood dessert plates, and fern-leaves shaped into jugs and other forms; these I knew to be of incalculable value, something altogether of another world than ours; for Grannie Carr was an illegitimate daughter of the gentry, and the Wedgwood came from that mother, who, even after she had been married off to a groom, kept certain standards which Grannie Carr inherited and prided herself upon: always polishing the soles as well as the uppers of shoes was one grain of gentility which had survived all these intangibles which cannot survive in an illiterate world. The Wedgwood plates I thought beautiful because they were like real ferns and leaves; but also because of their almost legendary origin, and the value set upon them as treasures once of ladies of the Hall.

In the manse kitchen I would find, on my return, the day's work over, my Aunty Peggy (whom I identified in my own mind with Ellen's upright but severe aunt in *The Wide Wide World* and Marilla of *Rebecca of Sunnybrook Farm,* my favourite books at the time, both held in high regard in the Presbyterian world, and permitted reading even on Sundays, along with missionary books now entirely forgotten). The iron kettle would be singing as it hung from its hook over the kitchen fire, the clock ticking on the wall, a white cloth spread on the table for our tea, a loaf from our weekly batch, butter from one or other of the neighbouring farms marked in the pretty lozenge-shaped pattern traditional in the neighbourhood, our own raspberry jam, in a ruby glass jam-dish; my glass of milk set aside from the morning on the cold slab of the larder, its cream a band at the top, narrower or wider as the cow was newly calved or going dry. After tea, on the big rag hearthrug by the kitchen range, glossy with black lead, its steel dampers spotless and shining, Aunty Peggy would sit in the rocking-chair, taking from under its cushion (the place where newspapers and catalogues of all kinds were kept) the *Northern Presbyter* or the *Newcastle Daily Journal;* and I in the windsor chair, my feet on the steel fender, its lustre soft with much polishing, embroidering some afternoon-tea apron (those eighteenth-century garments were still worn on Sundays by the ladies of Bavington), handkerchief-sachet, or table-centre; french knots, feather-stitch, cross-stitch, faggoting, chain-stitch, satin-stitch, button-hole stitch, hem-stitch, whipping and smocking; I name them all, so far have those once familiar occupations of childhood's evenings—those satin-stitch violets and wild-roses, once in my eyes so beautiful, or that cross-stitched cats' tea-party I once embroidered on a tray cloth for my mother's birthday—receded into a past as remote as that of the Mithraic carvings and hypocausts of Housteads a few miles away. No more than the stonecutters on the Roman wall did I know as I embroidered, in cursive chain-stitched 'B.S.' (Bavington School) on the roller-towels for the school lobby, or laboriously copied 'A whist-drive and social will be held...' in copperplate script with those heavy downstrokes and fine up-strokes which I never mastered, that I was anonymously signing the imprint of a period.

These were the evening tasks, the evening pleasures, accepted as both task and pleasure; and because so accepted, the tasks and the days ('six days shalt thou labour and do all that thou hast to do') built round my childhood then a shelter of reality I have never since known: all was as it must be, could not be otherwise than be, secure and familiar.

But at bed-time the immeasurable forces of the dark were waiting beyond the kitchen door to seize upon me, to dissolve me into nothing, snatch me away from the small charmed circle of safety cast by the light. To leave the lamplit kitchen, to carry my enamel candle-stick with its precarious flame up the stairs to my cold bedroom with its blue wallpaper overgrown with patches of damp, each with a life of its own, in daylight like a plant of moss or lichen, but at night like some conscious presence, was to venture unprotected into the region of unknown powers. Safe I was if I looked at the candle-flame; but on the wide landing where along the book-shelves a fox's mask looked down and many closed doors led into rooms full of darkness, what lurked in the shadow that moved with me and behind me? Children sense how precariously the phenomenal world is held together, how thin the texture of its appearances, how easily torn to let in nothingness.

I was advised to say the Lord's Prayer when I was afraid; but the presence of God everywhere seemed then not the least terrifying aspect of the Great Mystery; and in terror I implored the Holy Ghost not to appear to me, in tongues of flame and with a sound like a rushing wind. Yet living as I did in the manse, with the stone kirk in our own garden and field, I had the sense of personal involvement with the things of God, feeding my imagination with those two books most accessible in all Bibles to the very young, Genesis and Revelation. On Sundays a fire was lit in the parlour where the piano stood, and the fragile porcelain vases with dried grasses, and I would read, too fearful to look up from the page, of the Apocalypse. During the first World War, Armageddon and the unsealing of the Seven Seals of the Book of Judgement seemed, to country people for whom the Bible was the true Word of God with the same literalness as the news in the *Newcastle Daily Journal,* the simple history of the near future. The advent of those crowned grasshoppers with the hair of women and the teeth of lions, the stars falling from Heaven and the moon turning to blood were events daily to be expected, though none knew when. Perhaps after all they were more right than subtler symbolists; I did not doubt that I should be among those present at the End of the World. Frightening as they might be, and strange beyond the power of invention, my imagination recognized in those dread visions an aspect of its own world.

The harsh Calvinism of the Presbyterian Kirk (my mother had suffered from Sabbaths behind drawn blinds, allowed to read only, besides the Bible, Fox's terrible *Book of Protestant Martyrs)* I never experienced; my terrors of the darkness had certainly nothing to do with the God of Calvin and Knox (such was then my innocence that it never occurred to me that I might be one of the wicked for whom Hell burned) but were archaic and instinctive; whatever it was I feared was not Hell, or punishment. That fierce morality was not the only aspect of the Old Testament which spoke to the Scottish temperament, after all: there was also the nature-poetry of Job and the Psalms, all of storm and wind and mountains and the deep, peculiarly suited to the landscape of Scotland, and to the way such children as myself responded to an untamed land. As for the Sabbath, my own memories have fashioned that day in an atmosphere of staid yet delicate sweetness.

On Sundays the heavy door of the little eighteenth-century stone church, locked at all other times, was opened for the one service— morning or afternoon on alternate Sundays—for which the Minister bicycled from Stamfordham to our outlying congregation. Farmers and their tall Northumbrian wives came in traps, and the church stable was opened for their horses. The Minister and one or two of the farmers and their wives would stay to a sweet solemn Sunday dinner with us, in the dining-room never used but for guests; for since we lived in the manse, some of its dignities and its duties devolved upon us. The pasties, apple, rhubarb, gooseberry or raspberry (successors of those which so sump- tuously furnished the house-warming) were made by myself, under my aunt's stern step-by-step supervision; they were always undersweetened— it was wartime, and this may have been a reason, but not the only reason: undersweetening, like the convention which permitted the sucking of acid-drops but no other sweet during the long sermon, had a moral, or perhaps it would be truer to say, an aesthetic value, impossible to define but impossible not to sense; austerity, plainness, is always most admirable when it is a matter of style rather than of principle, and our under- sweetened pasties partook in that subtle beauty of living signified by the grey Quaker gown, the Rule of St. Benedict or the Pythagorean abstinence from beans; abstinence from alcohol was a matter of moral principle, and therefore without that finesse which belongs only to manners, not to morals.

The front porch of the manse was opened on that day alone, a door of sacred dignity; no part of our lives on the six days of doing all that we had to do. There hung the Minister's black cassock; the Cromwellian Communion-cups and the tall slender church vases of green glass rimmed with gold were locked away in a cupboard of varnished pine. To find flowers for the church vases was my Sunday morning task; and in my pale blue wool-backed satin dress, embroidered with violets, my hair brushed loose, and scissors in my hand, I walked the garden-paths to cut suitable flowers; godly flowers.

To know godly from ungodly flowers is a part of my Presbyterian education that has remained with me; an instinctive sense of their intrinsic natures and symbolic, 'signatures'. Tall white pheasant's-eye narcissi; daffodils white or pale (but not the double yellow sort that grew in great clumps along the border of the vegetable-garden), white phlox (though with some reservations on account of its strong scent, distracting from devotion), and a certain white mallow were permitted. Madonna lilies, by their very name, were suspect, as idolatrous; the rose, the flower of love, was not encouraged; and once I was seriously scolded for bringing crimson peonies (too riotously loose-petalled, and to the rose as profane is to sacred love) while to put tiger-lilies in the church vases I did not need Blake's Tyger to remind me was unthinkable. Not only was a combination (a 'clash' not a harmony) of black and orange manifestly ungodly, but the form of the flowers, with the tense recurve of the petals, the long filaments, too delicately extended, and hung with their heavily loaded anthers, spoke of nature's unconsecrated mysteries. There was something in so intricately perfect a form, besides, to arouse the intelligence, and by so doing to ruffle the surface of the glassy sea of calm devotion. Poppies verged on wickedness even as a garden flower. A pale yellow species of asphodel, long ago planted in the manse garden by a minister who had some knowledge of rare flowers, I myself spared; for I had a secret understanding with the asphodel, as a plant sacred to the Greek gods; its alien evanescent form, like its alien evanescent name, made it a flower apart, like the white Grass of Parnassus that grew high on our northern moors in certain wet places, but which participated in the nature of all that the name Parnassus signified. All wild flowers were, of course, altogether ungodly; to be 'wild' was, by definition, to be outside the Lord's Sabbath.

Yet I loved those Sundays, days kept as holy, wherein laborious people did no manner of work, and exchanged their week-day character and dress for something unaccustomed, dignified and refined by a grave sweet light shed about them by the archaic Word of God from the Holy Book. By those words, and those stories, so alien yet so familiar, we were all drawn away from ourselves into other selves with modes of thought and feeling unfamiliar and unpractised. Those unpractised other selves of simple people were like their polished parlours, with piano or the more holy harmonium none had skill to play, the family Bible, photographs of their ceremonially robed bridal selves, and of their dead, including the newly dead young soldiers killed in the war, enlarged from some stiff snapshot, as strangely unlike their homely selves as the sons of the wife of Usher's Well whose hats were of the birk; theirs the trench-caps of the British Army. These rooms were kept with reverence like a shrine, opened only upon the Sabbath Day, or for christenings, marriages, and funerals; those so deeply spiritual, and also so deeply carnal moments when life seemed raised into a higher and more solemn mode, struggling out of itself towards something which could be sensed but not described. In those ceremonial rooms exotic flowers bloomed with marvellous abundance: Christmas-cactus, maiden-hair and pheasant ferns, pendant white campanula, pelargoniums, treasured for their beauty as works of art in higher social spheres, but even more for their rarity, or because grown from a cutting from the greenhouse of some Trevelyan or Shafto; plants of unknown name, valued for their strangeness as if perhaps there were no other on earth, like that Chinese orange tree which grows only in the Emperor's garden, or the small bindweed on Eriskay, planted by Prince Charles Edward Stuart which they tell you there is none like elsewhere in the world; so great in all humankind is the desire to possess one treasure beyond all price and peerless. These scarcely literate country people did not live always and only in the profane; they felt, however remotely, the upward pull of simple and time-honoured observances through which they felt themselves securely bound within an order of values dimly and remotely glimpsed; as it were at the foot of Jacob's Ladder leading into that heaven whose glory, on holy days, unveiled itself a little. And it is perhaps those at the foot of the ladder who best can see its height.

In the evening when Aunty Peggy and I were left again in sole possession of the manse and the kirk, I was allowed to play on the church harmonium tunes from the hymn-book with its India-paper leaves, thin and holy, with their oval breves and semibreves. The engraved script of music seemed to me extremely beautiful, like an unknown sacred language, Sanskrit or Tibetan, a high language known to the angels themselves who to the sound of harps and trumpets sing hymns continually; a language I could divine but not decipher, full of intelligible meaning as yet unknown to me, speaking of a world remote from Bavington. The harmonium's strange voices, vox Humana, vox Angelica and Diapason (a name, to me, conferred on the thing named the nature implicit in the name), its windy petals, its groans, the stiff rattle of the damp keys, and my own child's voice singing holy words, exalted me into a Sunday rapture. 'They shall rise on wings, as eagles,' the Minister had read from the Holy Book, 'they shall run and not weary, they shall walk and not faint.' The eagle-wings were for youth, he had told us, as we sat, stiff and still in the varnished pews; the running for grown men, the walking for the old. Mr. Howatson was old; but I was young, never would I run or walk, but would rise always on wings, always and only soar.

And all the time it was growing darker and darker until the shadow invaded the holy sanctuary itself. Over the varnished pitch-pine of the pulpit a brass lamp twinkled faintly from the failing light outside. The red carpet led between empty pews (were they empty?) to the dark porch; and there, I knew, lurked evil-ones mustered against the holy as negative electricity is attracted towards positive. The more angels were gathered in the dim sanctuary of the church, the more demons thronged against them in the outer darkness, always in equal strength; for the outer darkness is their kingdom, boundless, immeasurable; and the angels (of course) could not leave the church, where they belonged. My heart thudding and my tongue cleaving to the roof of my mouth with terror so that I could not utter a prayer, I made my way between those empty pews, plunged into the gathering night, and along the church wall where lady's-mantle grew rank among coarse grass. Never have I known panic fear like that which possessed me as I fled along the side of the kirk, across the field into the manse garden and up the path past the yew-trees that led to the door of the back-kitchen, behind the little wall overhung with ivy-leaved toad flax; lifting the latch I plunged into the darkness among the drums of paraffin, storm lanterns, buckets, the wooden washing-tub, the hip-bath, the wave of terror mounting behind me as the sneck of the kitchen door delayed my rush for safety. There the wave that had swept me in its course would break and those powers of immeasurable evil ebb into the ocean of outer darkness, as I reached the safety of the lamplight, my Aunty Peggy's human presence, and the table laid ready for the breakfast of a morning not holy: the sabbath, with its heights and depths of the numinous, was over.

I had at Bavington my first bosom friend, Sally Walton, one of the daughters of the farm of Throckrington. She was a year older than I and she seemed to me, with her dark brown hair, her rosy cheeks and her vivid red lips, altogether beautiful. Her voice was a rich contralto, with a kind of break in it, indescribable as voices are. She was strong and gay and she knew everything about animals and birds, about hay, and all the world of barn and byre to whose fringes I so precariously clung. Sally and her two younger sisters sometimes came to school on horseback, sometimes on foot, and in the evenings I would go with Sally half way home, or all the way. Through the farmyard; along a length of stone dyke; then through a gate onto a wilder pasture, with a ferny crag; to the Onsteads farm, and past a plantation of wind-scaped beeches. From there we could see Throckrington Church, and were on the land of Sally's own farm. There was a pool where a grebe nested, and once Sally showed me the nest and its clutch of wild eggs. On the way we asked one another riddles as old as the hills (where did we learn them? Why can I no longer remember them?) and told stories about 'an Englishman, an Irishman, and a Scotsman' which seemed to us inexhaustibly funny. There was no irony, no cynicism in our laughter; it was as classical as the jokes in Aristophanes and much less sophisticated. At Throckrington we would catch wild litters of kittens in the hay-loft where the swallows built in the high rafters, or seek eggs, or I would watch Sally while she milked with her skilful fingers. For her day's work began when she returned home. Her father was said to be immensely rich; but in those days farmers' sons and daughters worked on the farm, becoming farmers and farmers' wives in their turn, their knowledge passed on from father to son and mother to daughter—the best recipes for jam and cakes and the skills of baking all the loaves and pasties and rabbit pies that sustained their labour.

Why did I love Sally? Why she rather than her sister Molly, nearer my own age? Why did I despise Mrs. Carr's freckled granddaughter Hetty Thorburn, who lived much nearer to me than Sally? Who knows the answer to a question no child ever asks, love being so simple, so spontaneous when one is a child. Sally was my 'best friend' beyond all doubt or question. It was not that we had 'tastes in common'—though we had a world in common. Such relationships are a blessed gift of nature while we are still within our own nature.

It was many years later that I met Sally again; she had a handsome son of twenty-one, and a daughter called Kathleen. So it would seem that that thin-legged far away Kathie had remained a part of her life, even as Sally of mine; though now we must meet as strangers. Could we ever have believed it? In the grown-up world others might grow estranged, might go away to far-off places and never return; but we never would, for Bavington was the place of our happiness, and never would we go into the far world among strangers. Sally, married to a farmer, moved only a few miles; her sister Bella, married, lives now at Clay Walls; while I—can never return.

And yet it was not on the merry walk to Throckrington with Sally and Molly and Bella, but on the walk back alone that I was most companioned, was nearest to the being of beings I loved: nature itself. I was an 'only child' and my solitude never seemed strange to me, or lacking anything heart could desire. Stories about the Englishman the Irishman and the Scotsman were one thing; but that was all a world of play and make-believe. Alone, the wind blew through my hair and through my heart, and every stone, every stonechat, every flower of eyebright or thyme, the polypody fern, the clouds far out over the moors, were as if part of myself. To be with other people, even with my best friend, was to be diminished to the stature of a little girl with mouse-coloured plaits and a velvet bandeau. Alone, I was all the earth, as far as the horizon and to the depths of the sky. Lacking nothing, desiring nothing but to be for ever in that place of all the earth that was mine, I knew—I think I am not inventing this in retrospect—perfect happiness. I knew that I was where I alone desired to be. It was by no will of mine that time moved on, and tore me from my early and humble roots.

Yet if I must tell all, I must tell of an episode which I can never forget, in which I was, God knows, the victim not the guilty, though it was I who killed. My dear grey tabby-cat, Graysie, a gift from Sally from the Throckrington barns, tolerated but not welcomed in the manse by Aunty Peggy, was the being I most loved at that time; for what child can ever love a human being with that osmosis of understanding with which we are at one with the animals? Animals never speak, and therefore never accuse, never blame us, always accept us just as we are. Graysie was my cat utterly; and when, though supposed a Tom, she proved a she, I remember how her striped body grew pear-shaped, and how I could feel the kick of the kittens inside her when I stroked her lazy pregnant side. And there one morning, in the box I had prepared for them, were the kittens, a warm snuggling pile. I was prepared to love them too, all of them. But my Aunty Peggy not so: it was my cat, it was my responsibility that these unwanted kittens had been born; and it was I who must drown them.

Country people are cruel and realistic; my Aunty Peggy saw nothing more in this command than in an order to fill the water-crocks or to fetch the milk. So I must fill the zinc bucket, and I must drop in the kittens. They were asleep, they were quiet as I dropped them in; so quiet that I hoped death would not waken them. But they came alive, they struggled for life, I heard their tiny claws scratching the zinc. I trembled, my knees grew weak, I fled. Yet it was I who was made to dig their grave, to empty the contents of the bucket into the hole, to fill the hole in. That was the price of having a cat, and it was I who must take the consequences; I must 'learn my lesson', Aunty Peggy said. And all this I did. So young, blood was already on my hands.

My friend Sally perhaps would have thought little of drowning a litter of kittens; I do not know. Farms are places where birth and death are everyday events and no guilt attaches to murder. But it was not so with me.

It was winter, and I had caught a feverish chill through staying out in the icy wind for many hours, high up on the moor away from the houses, because Grannie Carr's pig was to be killed that day; my friend, to whom

I had given bunches of elderberries and cabbage-leaves, visiting him in his stye, sometimes letting him loose in his field and there playing with him. So on that day I ran away far enough, as I hoped, not to hear his shriek. I was not sure whether or not I heard it, after all; in imagination I did, and yet still listened; the wind itself seemed to carry his death on it. All was long over when at last I returned; I had walked on the thin ice of a cattle's drinking-trough, and going in up to the knees my clogs and stockings were soaked with cold water. Knowing that I would be scolded for getting my feet wet, I lingered in the steel-like wind hoping it would dry me. My teeth were chattering with cold when at last I was undressed by the kitchen fire and my feet restored to life in a footbath of mustard-and-water. There were no hot-water bottles in those days; or if there were, not in the manse; and in the always-damp feather-bed I first shivered and then burned. Next day I had a fever, and a fire was lit in my blue bedroom; and lying in bed I watched the flames and glowing palaces; a fire in a bedroom was a luxury which made illness a pleasure. But I remember watching as I lay the shifting and writhing patterns of ribbons and roses, and the patches of damp on the blue wallpaper, and the waxing and waning of the substantiality of the room, upon whose reality I could keep no hold. Neither the Fifth Commandment in its gilt frame, with painted angels blowing their trumpets among calligraphic scrolls of red and blue and green; nor the wool sampler, *I am the True Vine,* cling to them as I might as icons of the holy and secure, could hold my world together.

I do not remember the way of transition from that feverish room into the freedom of the clear dark sky in which I found myself travelling accompanied by a dark winged companion, a sort of bird-angel or *alter ego* whose features I could not see and did not try to see. We were rising swiftly and beautifully through the night, and I knew the destination, towards which I travelled as a place I had always known. There was a sense of perfect familiarity, as of something formerly known and now remembered. We were travelling, as I thought, to some star; but I cannot be certain for we never reached that place, and the pull of the earth began to draw me back; alone now. Presently I saw the bedroom, as another kind of space, another world coming into place. I remember how small the window with its sixteen panes looked, as I came back into my body to find my mother putting water into my mouth from a teaspoon.

Yet I came back willingly enough; indeed, as it seemed to me, of my own accord; for I was happy on earth, then, and loved no place on earth as I loved the manse, and its garden, and its moors and the horizon bounded by the three humps of Simonside. I came back as gladly as that other Cathie whom Emily Brontë. describes weeping, in a dream, until the angels should carry her back to earth and put her down at Wuthering

Heights. Like a wild animal I loved my wild lair; and to return from my night-journey of the soul to the manse, the moors, the crags, the burn running at the foot of the garden under the black-currant bushes and the mounds of saxifrage, to the raspberry canes under the high stone wall overgrown with its mosses of many beautiful forms, the liverwort on the outcrop of rock by the outhouses, the scent of the cream-flowered daphne on the thaw-fragrant winter air, seemed not a grief but a delight. Even so, I knew on my return that there had been a closing, a limiting, a diminution as the world slipped into place. That leaving of the body was for a state not tenuous and fragmentary or dreamlike, but more clear, more real than normal consciousness in this present world. As into this world we wake from sleep, so into that we wake from waking.

Of my excursion out of the body I did not at the time, or for half a life-time after, think as perhaps a foresight of the road all travel at death; and I continued to regard death with the same grief and horror that drove me away onto the icy moor when the pig was slaughtered. The violent parting of soul from body, commonplace as it is to every country child, the instinctive energy of life refuses to accept. How much does the pity and terror of tragedy itself rest upon this bodily *timor mortis?* Traditional wisdom, whether of Vedanta or the Buddhist scriptures, of the vision of Dante or Blake, precludes tragedy; for the possibility of the hells (whether of finite or of infinite duration) is not the same thing as Aristotle's 'pity and terror', which is of this world, and at its centre such a death as we share with the animals we slaughter.

Over the high moss-grown stone wall of the manse garden, behind the raspberry canes where on hot summer days I basked and read the novels of Sir Walter Scott on the wooden bench of a little holly-arbour, was the bull-field. There the bull lived his solitary life, marked out from the herd by the brass ring in his nose, and the heavy wrinkled folds of his head and neck. We children used often to play a dangerous game of 'last across' the bull-field, climbing the five-barred gate from the farmyard when he was quietly grazing at the far end of his field; or we would provoke him with sticks, poked with safety over the wall, to make him advance with lowered head, that ominous slowness gathering to a rush that filled us with delight and terror. His high-pitched bellow was well known to me, for from my bedroom window I could see into his field when the other children had gone home to their distant farms—in a special sense he was my neighbour.

Anyone who has lived on, or by, a farm, knows in what respect a bull is held. There is no other creature on an English farm who has the power of death in his horns. For this reason, and also no doubt because of his sexual potency, equated with 'sin', he was the evil-one of our world. Yet by us children the bull's *mana,* his magical animal power, was recognized;

he was a power among us; no human being in our world had such greatness as his. Theriomorphic gods are older than human, and children, like archaic man, recognize with immediacy the quality of animal-souls. He was, besides, not *a* bull, but *the* bull. Like the priest of the sacred wood, there is never more than one.

One day—I think in March, but this is no more than an impression of a clear cold sparse day of early spring—the news passed round among us that the bull had gored the farmer; not fatally, as it happened, for his eldest son, a boy of thirteen, and still one of the back row of pupils in my Aunt's school-room, had arrived on the scene in time to save his father's life. But the butcher had been sent for, and the bull was to die.

So it was that I was one of the row of children who stood in the farmyard, where on an outcrop of rock the camomile was trodden by the clogs and hooves of all the village; the same farmyard where daily I filled our two buckets from the well. The farmyard was our Akropolis; and there we gathered to witness an event that held us not in partial, but in total, all-excluding participation. Never in amphitheatre nor temple of the gods nor circle of stone menhirs did the fate of consecrated victim more totally absorb the minds and souls of the spectators; what the theatre only represents, the bull-fight simulates, this was.

I recall the hush as the butcher drove his low dray into the farmyard; it stood there, empty, while the butcher walked over to the byre; empty; but we know what it was—a hearse for the dead. And the great one who was to be dead still lived, not knowing he was to die. The human world had passed judgement on the animal; the evil beast must yet again be slaughtered. Behind the immediate crime—the attack upon man—lay who knows what remote echo of archaic man's profound self-condemn-ation of his own animal nature, still not extinct in men so primitive as to be scarcely themselves securely rooted in the human principle to which on the Sabbath Day they aspired. Unreflectingly these hamlet-dwellers passed on the beast the age-old human verdict, laid down for the animal in the antiquity of pre-history; yet for them there was drama in his death as though the struggle between man and animal remained still undecided, still to be waged. There was in this death the suspense of a struggle undecided: why else did we gather and stand so attentively on our lime-stone akropolis?

But to me the pity was greater than the terror: I was on his side. Everyone knew, as I did, that Farmer Bell was but a poor specimen of mankind; his stone dykes were falling unmended, his children were dirty and covered with ring-worm, his wife a slattern and he himself was good for nothing but breeding his kind; yet now all but I sided with him against the innocence of nature. Such was human solidarity; but I was on the side of nature against man; I felt the wrong man was committing against the wildness of the beast, who, having no conscience had not sinned. Surely, surely he must not die! Justice would intervene, what justice I did not know, but I believed the world to be just.

There was the long waiting; the butcher, alone, crossing the yard, gun in hand; a muffled bellow; and as in a Greek tragedy the king is slain behind the heavy doors of his palace, so we waited for the shot, and knew that the great one of our small world, the creature of power, had once again been slaughtered; the strong by the weak, the great by the small. Presently, as from those palace doors, the great body was dragged out of the byre and onto the dray, limp and powerless. I saw his pepper-and-salt purplish-brown hide with a sense of infinite compassion: I *was* him. My body suffered in itself the death of the beast, my skin mourning for his skin, my veins for his veins, my five senses for his; and when from his anus slipped a mass of faeces, I was ashamed for the abasement of his death.

In another death my participation was of a darker kind. I had a boy-cousin, a year younger than myself, with whom I had often played as a child; he must, when his sudden death put an end to his childhood, and, as it seems, to my own, have been eleven years old, I twelve. It was Easter, and I, with my parents, was at the manse; not any more living there, but already moving away into an exile from which I was never to return. I was a visitor to what had once seemed my own place. We had scarcely, as it seems, arrived, when a telegram came to say that my cousin was dead. My father, I remember, knelt down and prayed on the stone flags of the manse kitchen floor, my Aunty Peggy weeping loudly, and I myself strangely embarrassed by my father's act, which seemed so out of keeping with the familiar manse kitchen; and by my Aunty Peggy's loud weeping, strangely out of character. Then we all left for the Midland town where his parents then lived, to attend the funeral. I think I was more sorry to leave Bavington than that Jimmy was dead.

He had been, on Easter day, to the Presbyterian church; and on the way home (his parents had stayed on for the Communion service) had said to another boy with whom he was walking, 'It is so dark and cold on this side of the road, let us cross into the sun.' Then he had collapsed and had never recovered consciousness, dying two days later of cerebral meningitis. I did not see him dead; dared not, would not go to look at him; but his death invaded and possessed me.

The horror that took possession of me was, literally, a darkening of the light. The light was filled with blackness, the light itself was emptied of light; not figuratively, but in a way those only who have known the like will understand, the phenomenal world ceased to be accessible to me. For me the bright Easter sun was dark, shedding blackness. I could see objects about me, and people, but I could not reach them; they and I were in the same physical space, but between them and me there was a great gulf fixed. Was I possessed by my cousin's young and too suddenly banished spirit, whose last conscious act was to seek the light? Was what I then suffered not my own, but an invasion of what he was suffering in the darkness of his sudden death, unable either to reach the people or the things of this world, or to make his way elsewhere? Are our spirits in truth so separate that such influx and possession by the thoughts of others may not occur? It was as if I as well as he had died from the living world and that bright Easter sunlight.

No one had any idea of what I was suffering, for who has words to describe those states that absolutely remove the normal aspect of the visible and tangible world from the reach of consciousness? I was in terror, even in broad daylight, of being alone, lest the gulfs of darkness should swallow me.

My mother must have stayed to comfort her sister; for I remember going on, with my father, to stay with his two second cousins, Marie and Sally, at the little village post office in County Durham, and the blackness went with me. I remember looking at brilliant golden dandelions in the sun, and their being entirely filled with blackness, emptied of all substantial reality. I clung to my father's hand as if only physical contact with his calm life, as he walked with God, could hold me to this world.

What I suffered was not grief; not mourning. I was sorry for my cousin's death but not as they grieve who lose one deeply loved. It was not even 'fear of death', but rather an invasion of consciousness by death, if so I may call the total removal of all contact with what we are accustomed to experience as a world. There are states of insanity in which the loss of reality is continuous; but to call such a condition insane is to evade the most obvious conclusion to be drawn from the experience as such: that the sensible world coheres not by physical but by mental agency. At best it coheres precariously; there is nothing inherently safe or solid about the sensible world, even though normally, at least by daylight, and in adult life, we accept it for real without giving the matter a thought. It is a marvel of adaptation that we do so.

Bavington seems, in retrospect, to have ended with that Easter. Perhaps it was in truth many years before I returned; or perhaps memory has now amended the pattern of the outer to fit the inner reality, which engulfed my own childhood in that annihilating darkness.

My father's people I scarcely knew; and the only house on his side of the family in which I remember having stayed was the little village post office at Newfield kept by Marie and Sally Pearson, his cousins; the house where the ferns and oxalis had made for themselves a sanctuary in the enclosed back yard. But I must have visited other houses; for from them I retain an impression (remote perhaps because I have put away from me such memories) of the crude raw stench of the poverty of the working-class. I remember the dirty miners' children who came into that little post office, very often sent by their mothers to ask for goods on credit; I can remember hearing Aunt Marie sending away a little girl, telling her, as it now seems to me, that her mother could have no more until she paid. The episode shocked me, though from what point of view I don't know; I think just the uncovering of unhappiness and anger and the sense of lives irremediably wrong. I remember that some of those children took me one day into a stifling kitchen, where a slatternly woman was frying onions. The strong smell overcame me and I held my nose. The woman laughed at me for this, and I was overcome with shame at having seemed impolite; I denied that it was the smell of her kitchen I minded.

Another impression is of a narrow and squalid brick yard in a pit-row, perhaps the house of one of my father's brothers. On the ground was the dirtiest crawling baby I had ever seen, her bottom and legs ingrained with dirt as she dragged herself about on the ground. The smell of the human animal nauseated me. And yet I have another memory, of walking hand in hand with a gentle bearded old man, my father's father. I was gathering sea-pinks on a shore, and he holding them for me; so the place must have been Newbiggin in Northumberland, where one of my mother's sisters had the infants' school.

It was natural that, coming from such a world, my father should look forward to a better future, and not back into a legendary past; yet his people too had lived their banishment within sight of the countryside from which their fathers had been driven by poverty from the fields to the pits. For my father lost Eden was not over the Border, but, no less inaccessible, in the pre-industrial England of Gainsborough and Surtees and Constable and Bewick that still survived between the pit-villages. These were the painters (as Cowper and Wordsworth the poets) my father most loved. I have seen him stand, lost in memory, contemplating some country lane or painted plough like the one he had learned to guide seventy-five years before. To him Constable's plough was a transcript of that real plough he had himself known the feel of in his hands, and the horses and the fields and the lanes and the cloudy skies not a world of imagination but reality itself, recaptured in a pictured world. For as a schoolboy he had played truant to drive the horses on a neighbouring farm, and at the end of his childhood wept when he was forced against his will, being a clever and docile boy, to become a pupil-teacher. At eighty-five his bitterest regret was that he had not been allowed to become a labourer in the fields of that lost paradise of the English countryside. His first love was a daughter of Sir William Eden's gamekeeper; and with the loss of that early love he lost, too, all hope of any return to a way of life and a world as a tiller of the fields from which his forefathers had been driven.

My father's lost Eden was the English countryside and English nature-poetry and landscape-painting spoke to him and for him; but from his boyhood his only cultural heritage was the Methodist Christianity his father had inherited from his grandfather who had walked, so my father would often tell us, twenty miles to hear John Wesley preach, and twenty miles back, to go down the pit on a Monday morning, strengthened in that darkness by his faith in another world than that cave where prisoners are chained. My old gentle grandfather was a class-leader among the Wesleyans, a man of blameless goodness; he had himself gone down the pit when he was eight years old, often not seeing the light of day from one Sunday to the next; yet I think he lived his life, enduring many sorrows (the loss of his wife when my father was himself eight years old and of a daughter who had barely reached eighteen when my father was at college) in the deep and abiding joy of an unshakeable faith; his favourite book, after the Bible, was Thomas à Kempis's *Imitation of Christ*. He also knew many healing herbs; centaury, agrimony, and other wild plants, hung in bunches to dry in his kitchen. With these he cured the simple ailments of his family in days when poor men could not afford to call a doctor unless in extreme need.

Yet quite unknown to himself my father was heir to a religion far different and of greater antiquity, from ancestors forgotten. But it was as a children's game, long emptied of *mana*, that he inherited the mystery of that old battle between the champions of light and darkness whose issue, however many times it be fought, remains always undecided. As a little boy in County Durham he had been initiated, unawares, into a tradition older than Christianity, surviving in the 'guiser's play', handed down by the older to the younger boys in secrecy and by word of mouth. In the week before Christmas—the winter solstice—the little boys, with faces blackened with soot and wearing their fathers' jackets turned inside-out by way of actors' costume, would go from house to house, knocking at the doors. First would enter 'King George',

> 'Here comes in King George,
> King George is my name,
> With sword and pistol by my side
> I hope to win the game.'

—then his enemy 'The Turkish Knight',

> 'The game sir? The game sir?
> That lies in my power!
> I'll cut you into mincemeat
> In less than half an hour.'

—and the King with the earth-name, the Green Knight and the black-faced enemy, would then fight until the enemy lay slain on the rag hearthrug before the kitchen fire. Then the victor himself, inexplicably and illogically changing his mood, would call for 'the Doctor' (my father usually played 'the Doctor') to come and revive the slain. 'Is there a doctor?' he says; and from the darkness outside a chorus of little boys answers,

> 'No doctor!'
> 'A pound for a doctor!'
> 'No doctor!'
> 'Five pounds for a doctor!'

Still no doctor; and the bidding would go on with mounting tension until a price was named that, after whispering and a pause outside, brought in the travelled and cloaked figure of 'Doctor Brown' ('Here come I, Old Doctor Brown, the best old doctor in the town') wearing an old top hat and carrying his famous bottle of the elixir of life. The doctor is asked to tell how he came by his knowledge; and his answer goes back to the late middle-ages when Paracelsus and his like travelled

> 'Italy, Picardy, France and Spain
> Round the world and back again.'

The Turkish knight, magically revived, would spring to his feet, and the champions, reconciled, would make a promise (not to be broken until the next solstice) 'we'll never fight no more'. The guisers still outside in the cold would then come thronging in for their share of the oranges or ginger-cordial now distributed to all. That was the Christmas play; no one thought of asking why there was no Christianity in it.

Driven underground, did an old paganism unrefined by song and poetry linger on in the imagination of the tillers of the soil of Durham and Yorkshire, unsubdued by that newer religion whose excessive insistence upon the virtues of meekness and love was perhaps the measure of the brutality of that which it was invoked to subdue? Typical of many similar stories (murder and the gallows in nearly all) was one my father told of a farmer who in his loft kept an ox-hide with horns and tail complete. On a fine evening he would sometimes put on this theriomorphic disguise, lurk behind hedges and frighten his neighbours in whose souls, as in his own, albeit unknown to themselves, the horned god still reigned. In this story there is no mention of a coven; though it now seems to me more than likely that the farmer of the story was the 'devil' of a coven. In any case, the half-animal figure of the Devil still had power over the imagination of many a respectable church-goer for whom his hoofs and horns were an article of Christian faith.

A young hired man had recently come to the farm, and had been sent to the village forge with the coulter of a plough to be sharpened for the spring ploughing. The farmer felt the urge, so my father's story went, to put on his ox-guise and to enjoy, together with the sense of power to be had from frightening his neighbours, who knows what exaltation in his temporary identification with the archaic animal mood he donned with the skin of the beast with whom his life was so closely bound up in the fields he shared with his cattle. Hiding behind a hedge he appeared suddenly with a bellow that had made others take to their heels; but the lad, coulter in hand, stood his ground and faced this apparition of the evil-one. The boy, between terror and religious fervour, attacked with the coulter, and killed the devil; but it was the farmer whose blood soaked the fields fertilized in a forgotten past, it may be, with many blood-sacrifices made to the same god who had returned unrecognized to possess the human victims of that crudely enacted tragedy.

In a story so expressive of the mode of consciousness in that dim half-awareness of ignorance and animality, I seemed to catch a glimpse, beyond the fervour of my father's religion of love and goodness, of a dark ancestral contrary, brutal and heavy; a chthonic barbarity in every way alien to my mother's world. The modes of feeling expressed by the songs of Scotland are delicate in their subtleties of tenderness, pride, scorn, nostalgia or mourning or merriment; and the 'other' world of Scotland is peopled with green-clad fairies of more than human beauty, or the bird-souls of the dead, or the terrible grandeur of the banshee not with the half-animal devil and churchyard ghosts; an elegant world.

The drama of my father's people was all a confrontation of good and evil in their crudest terms; men and womem were either good and religious chapel-goers, or violent, drunken and brutal; or so it always seemed from the stories he told, many of which were of those spectacular 'conversions' so dear to the Methodists. My father never tired of describing these, and the revival meetings at which such conversions often took place. There he had himself seen and heard, as a boy, converted men 'speaking with tongues', or walking, in ecstatic trance, along the inch-wide tops of the chapel pews. To him such things seemed marvels of God. The crucial question was, in that world,'salvation', and salvation meant some dramatic 'change of heart', a change of consciousness closely allied to mass emotion. But I found the 'salvation' of my father's world as remote as the state of the reprobate; his terms were, and have remained, alien to me.

These issues, among my mother's people, who were at once more naïve and more refined than those ardent aspirants towards salvation, simply never arose. Perhaps Calvin's doctrine of predestination precludes for those who hold it the Wesleys' wrestlings with the Traveller Unknown or John Bunyan's heart-searchings; the question of salvation or damnation rests with the Lord, and therefore there is, within that rigid doctrine, some room for freedom from the burden of personal guilt. I always had the impression, with members of my mother's family, that their religion was extraneous to themselves whereas the songs and history and fairy-lore of Scotland expressed their true natures and real beliefs. To escape into that world of poetry whose people have no morality but only life and its many moods must have seemed for them—and was for me—like an escape into reality from the acting of a tedious part; when moral censure was passed—as it often was—it might be vehement but it was never, I felt, sincere. To my father it was the other way: songs and stories and poetry he felt to be lacking in seriousness unless they had a moral; but what is the moral of the stories of Wallace or the Four Marys? The tears they brought were for beauty and valour, not of repentance and 'conviction of sin'. My mother's family put on their religion on Sunday with their Sunday clothes (which mattered to them no less, indeed perhaps much more, than religion) and during the rest of the week gave a degree of attention to this world which to my father seemed profane. My grandmother, grim slave of housework as she was (on her washing-days she generated an atmosphere of bitter and self-righteous resentment), had a certain fine fastidiousness; she would drink her tea only from the thinnest of china cups and these of gleaming cleanness; and she stirred her cream into Melrose's tea with a silver teaspoon.

My grandfather's three passions were likewise incomprehensible to my father, for none had any moral purpose; his fuchsias and gloxinias, the nemophila and the pansies, the sweet-peas and the gladioli he grew with a finesse which in my father's eye mere flowers could never deserve. When he was dying it was to look at his flowers that he came downstairs for a last time. My grandfather's second skill was dry-fly fishing; many a salmon he drew from the Tyne, and he himself made those delicate feather flies bound in the barbed hooks of which he always carried a few in his tweed cap. I loved to sit near him on the bank of the Tyne while he drew in on his line trout whose fragrance, in his fishing-creel so elegantly constructed of fine wicker, was like violets.

41

On account of his third passion—whisky—he was placed, by my father, unquestionably (though with regret, on my mother's account) among the wicked. This judgement was self-evident, and was that of his wife and daughters also. To 'drink' was sinful, sin was to 'drink'; so it was in that time, and place, and class. Such too was the teaching of the Kirk, whose moral condemnation was reserved for acts easy to discern in others, easy to avoid by the righteous. The subtleties of Dante's morality were as undreamed-of as those of the psychology of the unconscious, which has since made such havoc of these simple moral judgements. It is true that my grandfather's addiction to whisky had brought him down in the world; the hamlet of Kielder, remote from any source of supply, was the bottom of the descent. But why my brilliant and handsome grandfather had taken to drink, none asked. What my own generation would regard as effect was then regarded as cause.

Even my mother, whose real self was light-hearted, amoral and gentle had a second personality, the censorious Calvinist group-mind of the family collective, the terrible possessing devil of John Knox's Scotland. Censoriousness would come upon her, not, so far as I remember, in relation to people so much as in her relation to the inanimate world. If a weed grew in a flower-bed or a bush overhung the lawn, moral censure was invoked as if the weed were wicked and the bush deliberately doing wrong. Even chairs that stood in her way, or cups that got themselves broken, were blamed as agents—'that chair!'—whose perverse wills opposed and thwarted her. This sinister animism was, to be sure, the dark side of my mother's sense of the poetry of things; and she may after all have been right. Yet it was the inanimate world she turned her Calvinistic censoriousness upon. She had a particular voice, on such occasions, unlike her own, as if she were then possessed by a spirit of righteous indignation. When one or other of my 'aunties' came to stay, or when we were staying with my grandparents, this collectivity would reabsorb my pretty mother into itself. I would lie in bed hearing the family voices rising and falling in censorious cadences something like the crooning voices of eider-duck, but loaded with an emotion of deep moral indignation. I used to think this censure was directed against me; for all the doctrine of the reprobate was expressed in those voices whose words I could not distinguish but whose rise and fall carried condemnation until my heart beat with dread. In adolescence 'the unforgivable sin' became a terror; for none could tell me what that sin was. Might I not commit it unawares? Had I not indeed already committed it? For the sense of guilt that had been implanted in me from earliest childhood by those accusing voices, before I knew what sin was. I feared with vital dread that to commit the unforgivable sin might be my fate.

For my mother the unforgivable sin was 'drink'; or rather it was so for her second self that belonged to her family collective. And I remember an episode very clearly in which I was the observer—from another state of being, like that calm virgin in Picasso's Tauromachia—of adult morality in action.

I must have been five or six at the time; which must have been during my father's summer holiday, which we spent always with my maternal grandparents. I was walking with my grandfather through fields to a neighbouring farm; he walking slowly, quietly puffing at his pipe; while I ran to and fro after white caps in the grass which I hoped would be mushrooms but which were very often only puff-balls. The late afternoon sun was golden on the dry sweet pasture with its eyebright and tormentil and wind-rustling harebells and quaking-grass. We were both happy to be free and away from the constrictions of the house, for my grandmother had had one of her washing days. We called at the farm; and I can clearly see, to this day, the farmer offering my grandfather a dram of whisky. In my mind's eye I can still see him standing by the sideboard draining the small glass of golden liquid. Then we set off on our way home in the late summer gloaming and the shadows lengthening on the turf of that sweet pasture.

I remember nothing more until the outbreak of hatred that was suddenly shaking the house; and I was somehow in the centre of it: how could he have done such a thing and the innocent bit bairn with him? My poor grandfather at bay was allowed no word in his own defence by my grandmother, my aunts, my father, and even—to me unaccountably—by my own mother. It seemed that some great wrong had been committed, of which I was the innocent victim; but why, after that happy walk through the fields, I should have become the pretext of this ugly, devastating outburst of righteousness I could not understand. Indeed I did try to defend my grandfather; for I felt that I somehow shared his guilt, that I was the cause of this attack upon him. If he had done wrong so had I, for we had shared that walk which now appeared to have been such a dreadful thing. But I was snatched away to bed by my mother—excessively and demonstratively tender towards me—as the storm raged on. Children absorb such violent emotions by a kind of osmosis; and the sense remained with me that I was implicated in some terrible and mysterious sin. All the grown-ups had become ugly and dreadful, and now I could hear my grandfather turning on my mother, and knew not where my loyalties might lie.

My mother's one moral imperative—'never touch drink'—I could never hear without thinking of my grandfather set upon by the furies of his household; and it is abstainers rather than drunkards from whom I shrink to this day.

My father I think counted, also, my grandfather's striking good looks against him; or saw them perhaps rather as an extenuating circumstance, like a physical or mental defect; for physical beauty, whether in man or woman, constituted if not a sin, at least a predisposition to sin, a temptation greater than is laid upon commoner and humbler clay. My mother and all her sisters were in their youth beautiful, with a kind of radiance that still shines from old photographs of them; a radiance later life extinguished in them all, though all kept their fine features, their curly abundant hair, and their slender lissom figures.

My mother's evasion, after her marriage, of the religion of John Wesley was not different from her earlier evasion of John Knox; a withdrawal of attention, a failure of interest availed her more than argument and useless opposition. She had, besides, a habit of fainting in church; I never knew her to faint elsewhere, certainly not at the theatre, on the longest walk, or in the hottest greenhouse in Kew. My father I think never knew whether my mother had been 'saved' or not; for she always agreed with everything he said. But at over eighty it was the Upanishads and the works of Æ and G. R. S. Mead and even Israel Regardie that my mother would take down from my shelves, or travels in Tibet, or works on spiritualism; never have I seen her read any work of Christian devotion. The supernatural world was for her, as were her vivid nightly dreams, rather an escape from the moral world than, as for my father, a region of it. She confessed to me (she was in her mid-eighties then) that she was not 'religious' and had always found the emotionalism of Methodism vulgar; 'but I am very interested in the cosmos'. Some time before this she had had a slight stroke and thought she was dying. What was it like? I asked her; and my mother's eyes flashed like those of a hawk whose hood is lifted and she said 'I was very interested'.

And later still—in her nineties now, and after my father's death—my mother saw me with a little Victorian copy of Bunyan's *Pilgrim's Progress* given me by a friend to pass on to my grandchildren. 'I have never read it', she said; and I— missing her point—offered it to her. No, she said, 'I have avoided reading it all my life. But I know pretty well what is in it.' (This I can well believe, for to my father it was a sacred book.)'I think it is a book that has outlived its usefulness,' was my mother's last word. And then I read it myself. She was more right than I—remembering how as a child I had loved those chained lions, and the shepherds on the Delectable Mountains with their glass through which Pilgrim saw the Holy City; how I had feared the thundering mountain, and Apollyon, and that trap-door into Hell through which the groans of burning sinners could be heard— could have believed.

For did not the Bedford Tinker's Vanity Fair hold all the glory of the

Renaissance, stifled by the 'curse of Cromwell'; the theatre Shakespeare had created to civilize a nation; Inigo Jones, and all the grace of seventeenth-century music? Ignorance then as now seeks in bewildered envy to destroy what it cannot possess; what it cannot even perceive—for if it could see the beauty it would no longer be ignorance, and no longer would wish to violate and destroy. Yet those sour world-hating Puritans my father reverenced as saints of his religion; those smashers of all the riches of English Gothic sculpture, of the images of the Virgin, Refuge of Sinners. To the Puritan to give refuge to sinners is indeed the unforgivable sin of condoning sin. For what is worse in Bunyan than his ignorant rejection of all culture as worldly wickedness is the continual censure, the self-approving condemnation of humanity as such. Those who had a 'conviction of sin' can only condemn their fellow-men and women; seeing no beauty in the joyousness of Sir Toby Belch and his night revels, in the innocence of the happy; sick of self-love indeed, they only wish to see the poor sinner brought, all his happiness turned to tears and bitterness, to the stool of repentance. Of this taint of righteous ness my father was not free; my mother, thank God, was; she never thought herself good or made any effort to be so. She had the gift of forgetting all the sin in the world in the joy of watching some falling leaf or opening flower.

My father, on the contrary, was without curiosity because for him all was settled long ago, when on the verge of manhood he himself underwent conversion to what he himself called—and indeed it was—'a living faith', a life-long orientation which needed no confirmation from books, from which indeed too much reading would have been only a distraction. Civilization with all its arts and expressions remained for him (as for those 'early Christians' the Roman slaves who were his models) beside the point. For my mother truth was imagination, was beauty, was nature. Yet a fineness of moral sense lent to my father's conduct a beauty of its own which to some might seem of a higher kind than that beauty 'blithesome and cumberless' worn by my grandfather's daughters as unthinkingly as birds wear their plumage.

Of, and into, this disparity I was born; my inheritance an irreconcilable conflict of values to which my parents dared never confess, or did not, perhaps, consciously recognize.

CHAPTER TWO

Is this the Region, this the Soil, the Clime,
Said then the lost Arch Angel, this the seat
That we must change for Heav'n . . .

I AM writing, on this day in early November, in the gardens of Ninfa. I
hear the sound of bird-song, and of gardeners at work with sickle and
spade, and of the sweet bell of the church of Norma on the hill above. All
this landscape has been inhabited by man, loved and tended by man, re-
created by man, since the Cyclops lived behind the still solid walls of their
village that crowned the crest before the Volscians gave their name to
these hills terraced with olives; each tree, as in Greece, with its embankment of stones to keep the soil from washing away. A landscape made by
man; in this garden bright with sinuous rills trout, of a species said to have
been brought by Hannibal, swim in the clear waters, sacred to the nymphs
when Pliny wrote of them. A pope was crowned in the church whose ruins
now are entwined with rose and jasmin, and the slender leaves of grey
mimosa move gently in the protection of its walls. In the Lombard tower
is set a plate brought from Persia in the ninth century; others have fallen
away leaving round discs in the tufa walls. In the apse of another church
(it shelters a rock-garden now) the rain has not washed away nor the sun
faded the contours of two madonnas, one of the eighth, the other of the
eleventh century. The indelible line of intellectual beauty is still visible
upon the crumbling plaster, as they recede in time while remaining still in
place. On yet another wall, among persimmon trees, a fragment of a
Nativity with Ox and Ass dates from the century after St. Francis.
Jackdaws live in the tower of the old castle, pink in the evening light like a
back-cloth for one of Shakespeare's Italian plays. I think of Milton's
Paradise; of Shelley writing his *Prometheus Unbound* in the baths of
Caracalla; of a letter Edwin Muir wrote me (he too visited this garden,
hospitable to poets) in which he spoke of the images everywhere of the
Christian mysteries, of the Angel who greets the Virgin in the shrines men
and women pass as they come and go in the streets of their ancient cities.
Under my window-ledge the waters race; and here grows every tree that is
pleasant to the sight, and good for food; orange, lemon, mandarin,
avocado; magnolias, roses, cypress; fish-tanks of stone; parsley and violet.
All is beautiful as that first garden tended by man; and beyond the avenue
of walnut with trailing vines between, peach orchards, and beyond the
orchards the fertile landscape of the Pontine marshes—drained by a

former Duke of Sermoneta, uncle of my hostess. Even this newest change made by man upon the old landscape of Italy has beautified the scene. Between the rose-grown ruins of Ninfa, little changed since Edward Lear made drawings of this tower, and Circe's isle set in the glitter of the sea, there lie new fields and new villages, harmoniously green and fertile under the hillside where little flocks of sheep are still penned in the Cave of Polyphemus. A gardener is passing, carrying on his head a basket of little black grapes, the last of the season, to the house, formerly the hall of the mediaeval town of Ninfa. In that hall now the newest books in many languages lie on the table of the last Duchess, patron of literature from the world of Henry James, editor, before the last war, of *Commerce,* and after, of *Botteghe Oscure,* in whose pages the poets of England, France and America were published. On the piano on which Liszt performed, a sister-in-law of my host played, on the day after my arrival, Chopin's third Ballade; my hostess paints and plants this garden, which her mother and her grandmother created. All here reflects a beauty conceived by the human imagination; and the servants in the house, the shepherds on the hill both young and old, the old women and the boys and girls in the steep streets of Sermoneta on its citadel, they too are graced with the dignity of Catholic Italy. Perhaps a generation from now this labour of ages will have gone; perhaps even sooner; for the tide of destruction is advancing, here as elsewhere. There are rumours of the waters of the nymphs being diverted for industrial development; and the civilization that here has been slowly matured and long guarded against barbarian invasion will be swept away.

With what reluctance I bring myself to look away from all this beauty (and for all it may be doomed, it is here and now still as I write), into those times and places of my own past of which I must now tell. Walking in this garden I have thought of the strangeness of the journey that has brought me by wanderings so devious, to the very heart of Italian civilization; the highest ever attained by western mankind. Soon I must leave again, travelling into the always inconceivable future; but once to have seen is to know for ever that such things are possible.

I have written of my years in Northumberland as if they had preceded in time all that belonged to other phases of my life; but that is not so. Northumberland was anterior only in a symbolic sense: not only because from beyond the Border came my ancestors, but also because there I found, in the few short years I lived at the manse with my Aunty Peggy Black, my own image of a Paradise already lost long before my birth. For I was not even born in Northumberland but in an East London suburb.

Yet all through my childhood, and for long after, it was Northumberland which seemed my home, enduring and real; and my father's house unreal, impermanent, a place not lived-in except for the time being. In part I may have reflected my mother's unspoken thoughts; but I believe it is also true that imagination accepts only what corresponds to its own nature, its innate sense of harmony, to soul's or, perhaps, body's recognition of its proper habitat. In Northumberland I knew myself in my own place; and I never 'adjusted' myself to any other or forgot what I had so briefly but clearly seen and understood and experienced. I do not believe, as Wordsworth perhaps did, that the state of Paradise is childhood itself; some children have perhaps never known Paradise, or only as a longing; and some, like Blake, who claimed to be 'an inhabitant of that happy country' have found again what Wordsworth lost. Paradise is a state of being in which outer and inner reality are at one, the world in harmony with imagination. All poetry tells of that vision, all poets remember, or seek to remember and recreate what all know at heart to be not a mere fleeting illusion, but the norm we never cease to seek and to create (however often it may be destroyed) because in that state alone lies felicity. To be exiled from Eden is our greatest sorrow, and some forget, or try to forget, because to remember is too painful, to re-create too difficult. Those who choose the vision of perfection choose to experience the pain of deprivation as the lesser evil; or perhaps there is no choice. 'You are one of those who are not allowed to forget', Cecil Collins once said to me. And ultimately the many are sustained by those images of a lost perfection held before them by the rememberers. Such, as I understand it, is the whole and sole purpose of the arts and the justification of those who refuse to accept as our norm those unrealities the world calls real.

From Bavington to Ilford.

I was born at 6 Gordon Road, Ilford on the fourteenth of June, 1908; in the house where the little hand of flame danced on the gas-jet, and the world ended in a cascade of Virginia creeper beyond the hollyhocks at the bottom of our garden. On that first day—so they used to tell me—my father put into my hand a rose from my mother's Maiden's Blush rose-bush, and my tiny fingers clasped the stem of my first flower. The poignant sweetness of the scent of that old-fashioned Alba rose has become for me the first fragrant sweetness of my mother; as a memory irrecapturable, a sweetness known before memory began.

I do not remember the house; only the garden; nor, as separate beings, my father and mother. I remember my father's bowler hat, because when at tea-time he came home from school he would give it to me, and allow me to find in the hat-band the bunch of snowdrops or violets he had hidden there; for my mother as I now suppose, but then I thought all the flowers in the world were mine.

Farewell Happy Fields

The first event I remember is an incident which obtrudes itself, clear as a photograph, and out of context like a piece of wreckage in the clear stream of life in which my three-year-old self still floated; an event in time. I am dressed in white with a blue silk sash and hair-ribbons, carrying a little straw basket of freesias and asparagus fern. Other children, similarly attired and with little baskets of flowers, are waiting, as I am, to go onto a platform and say a poem. My mother has rehearsed me and I know my poem perfectly. She asks me to say it once more before I go on stage; and I do so. Now I must go onto the platform, and I am asked to say my poem again. This seems absurd, and I merely say 'I've said it'. There is laughter, and I am put to shame. The whole situation—the poem, the basket, the platform—is false and bewildering and I want to escape. No doubt this platform was in the hall of the Wesleyan chapel of which my father was an active member. The freesias fail to console me as I turn to their beauty as to the only beings of my own kind in this place of wooden chairs and adults.

I was three years old when we moved to West View. I remember being taken by my mother one day to look at a house. It was empty and dirty and cold and a woman caretaker showed us empty dirty rooms. Later I was told we were going to live there and dismay chilled me, as if I were going to live in an unknown house of the dead with that terrible caretaker. I remember then a day—another fragment of the ruins of time—when from the window of May's house next door I watched in woe the incessant heavy rain as strange men carried our furniture into a big removal van. Abandoned and forlorn I saw my world dismantled and gone.

Then I remember a door opening—the dining-room door of West View—and I saw my mother laughing and welcoming me. I 'saw' my mother that day for the first time, laughing and happy as she held out her arms to her little girl. The room she was in was fresh and clean, and there was a Christmas-tree, fragrant, and hung with glittering beautiful marvels, coloured glass balls and tinsel, and a soap teddy-bear and a little doll made of sugar, and twisted candles, red and blue and orange; inexhaustible, countless treasures of beauty hung on that lovely tree. Incredible transformation! The two pictures would not mix, the two houses were not the same house, but different houses; and in some inexplicable sense our new house was the same place as our old house, as if with the familiar pieces of furniture we had brought the place itself with us.

West View was still in Paradise; for with the spring the fields beyond our garden blossomed, and I, Persephone in Ida gathering flowers, astray for hours of golden eternity in the meadows and along the hawthorn hedge white with may and festooned with wild roses, first the pink, then the fragrant white Burnet rose. The various scents to my young senses were more than delight, they were indescribable harmonies of knowledge and meaning. I was, unawares, learning the scales of memory; but then memory was no longer than the length of a meadow as I ran to renew and refresh my senses with the scent of buttercups or my mother's Maiden's Blush rose, brought with her from her first garden; and there, no doubt, from Northumberland.

Memory has composed those days of my childhood into one continuous day of late spring and early summer; in whose morning white stitchwort, white Jack-by-the-hedge with its fresh mustard scent, and white cow-parsley rose along the hedgerows, and the tight-folded small leaves of the elm trees began to open. As the sun rose higher, buttercups in their several kinds opened burnished chalices, and the sparser pale lilac cuckoo-flower. In the hawthorn hedge by the stile the first miniature green rosebuds open immacuate shell-pink petals about a golden crown, and the innumerable blossoms of the may, each petal a perfect hemisphere splashed with the coral of the young unopened anthers. Later came white marguerites—'gowans' to my mother, but not in those fields—and the ruddy sorrel changed the colour of the meadow of rising grass with its shimmering sprays, soon to fall in afternoon hay; and in the heat of the afternoon the scent of lime-blossom from the single tree that stood in the hay-meadow, where, lying in my bed in the summer evenings, I could still commune with its lovely shape. I knew where the sweet patch of summer-scented bedstraw was; and the germander speed-well, brilliant blue in the morning sun. There was no flower in these meadows whose place I did not know; from the pink bindweed on the dry gravelly hillocks of the paddock shared by a donkey and a tradesman's pony, to the single clump of king-cups in the little swampy ditch beyond the hawthorn hedge. I knew where the lark's nest was in the meadow grass, and saw in that small sanctuary first the eggs, then those naked wedge-shaped heads, all gaping beak and blind eyes. The lark that poured its song from the blue sky all those summer days was our own lark, lark of the meadow where I gathered buttercups.

My mother did not send me to school until I was six years old; and if I have been a poet I owe it to my mother's protection of my sanctuary of solitude in those years of early childhood when three small fields between the advancing fringe of London's East-End suburbs, and the wooden fence of Dr. Barnardo's Homes was space enough for earthly Paradise.

I remember the day of the outbreak of war. We (for my father, my mother and I were still, when I was just six years old, 'we', an indivisible unity) were on holiday at Broadstairs. The pre-war sun shone, and there were donkey-rides on the sand. We were staying in a boarding-house; and I remember the Italian waiter, whom I loved with my whole heart, and a French family with a charming adolescent son whom I admired from the obscurity of my smallness. The sun shone on August 4th, 1914 on golden sand and the happy bathing-machine that took my mother and me out into the tepid sea water among the beautiful coral-red floating seaweed. I remember my father putting the penny into my hand to give to the paper-boy in exchange for the evening newspaper which told the news. The war had something to do with France, and the elegant French boy who would have to go back at once and who might soon have to be a soldier. I remember my mother exclaiming on 'all the men who will be killed'. To me the only sadness the war brought was parting from the Italian waiter who must have possessed the gift of so many Italians of being kind to little children.

Later, 'the war' meant tea-parties, with badminton on our garden lawn, for the 'old boys' of my father's school who came, young and gay, in khaki uniforms. It meant pretty cards from 'the trenches' embroidered with the flags of France and Belgium, and edged with French lace. It meant hanks of rough khaki knitting-wool which my mother knitted into socks and mufflers; and I too was given a pair of heavy knitting needles and set about knitting a muffler; still unfinished years after in the bottom drawer of my mother's wardrobe.

But all that was outside me; my own and only participation in 'the war' was to make little crosses by binding two sticks together with pieces of grass, and tying to them the grey feather seeds of the wild Traveller's Joy; 'for the Belgians', I said. My tribute to the dead was made without sorrow, but in a kind of ritual solemnity, impersonal as a religious rite.

On the last of childhood's timeless days I was gathering buttercups in the meadow behind the house when I heard a sound new to me, of a steady relentless humming in the air ; and I looked up and saw aeroplanes approaching, with a terrible slowness; like four-winged mechanical gnats. The intensity of that sudden terror has left an imprint on my mind, like a photograph, of that moment, and the very place in the sky where I saw the enemy planes. I fled to my mother; and, as so often later, we sheltered in the cellar. I remember sometimes sleeping there, among the sacks of potatoes grown by my father on his 'allotment' just beside the house.

There were other portents in the sky in those days; I saw, from the front window of West View, the Billericay Zeppelin pass, a great pencil-like shape, and then a jet of flame, then a blaze that lit up the windows of West View. 'Are there men in it?' I asked; and when I was told 'Yes' I cried. My father told us afterwards that a dead German officer had been found by a farmer in a field, lying near his path. The man had beautiful teeth, and the farmer stamped on his face, breaking them. The Potter's Bar Zeppelin I also saw, burning in the sky, a crumpled ball of dull red fire, far away; for a long time a piece of twisted aluminium on our mantelpiece remained as a souvenir.

Which of those two Zeppelins, I now wonder, was the one Marcel saw as it passed over Paris only a few hours before I saw it burst into flames? I had been, then, only a few hours and a few miles from Marcel Proust (so I realized when long after I read his record of Paris in the war) and not only from Paris as such, but from the immortal Paris of *Le Temps Retrouvé*. Very few of the things I saw in Ilford had ever belonged, or would ever belong, to what imagination retrieves from time lost; that Zeppelin was the only object besides the sun and the moon that ever crossed the horizon of West View that has its place in the annals of European literature. Yet France in those days was ever in mind; for it was to France my father's sixth-form schoolboys departed, many never to return. And the French master at the school had been a regular visitor up to that summer of 1914. I remember, not his appearance, but a quality of his presence, quick and warm and gay and intelligent, with a charming voice. He used to call me 'la petite aubépine', making me repeat the phrase until I knew my French name. Had he read those first volumes of Proust? Diffusion of culture is a strange thing; by hidden channels did my hawthorn hedge receive an added fragrance from Marcel's? My love of France, at all events, had from the beginning the scent of hawthorn.

As I think back into those years before 1914 it seems that there was something Paradisal even in Ilford itself on whose extreme outskirts we lived. In Valentine's Park, with its artificial lakes and little grotto and wishing-well, blackbirds did 'so rinse and wring the ear' in rhododendron-dells that the park seemed still the sanctuary it had once been, when its cedars were planted and its grotto by the water. In the quiet side-turnings from Cranbrook Road (called 'Redcliff Gardens' or some other 'Gardens') the only sounds were the unhurried rattle of the milkman measuring his pints, or the horse-drawn baker's van (few cars and no radio sets in those days) and the tinkling of piano-practice. To play the piano was in those days regarded as a minimal accomplishment even amongst the unmusical; but Ilford had its Metroplitan Academy of Music where the standard available to the musical children of the suburb was of the highest. The names of more than one now famous concert performer I first heard as playing in some children's concert at 'The Academy'.

West View was not in reality (as to me it seemed) a part of the country beyond our garden-fence, but the advancing fringe of the tide which was already submerging the older, perhaps more cultured, certainly more leisured older strata of city merchants who built the ampler houses already, within my memory, being converted into schools and nursing homes; 'The Academy' was one such Victorian mansion in decline. There were 'educated people' just above our social horizon, some of whom my mother visited. My mother came to life, became more herself, in the company of the 'educated' (to use her own word, for in reality it was culture, not education, to which she responded) whereas my father seemed positively to seek out his social inferiors. This did not argue social ambition on her part, or humility on his: rather the reverse, for she loved to learn, he to do good to others.

There was an upright German lady who played her upright piano in a disciplined manner, whom my mother called 'the Bishopess' because she was the widow of a Moravian bishop. There was Dr. Carroll, with his immaculate white silk cravat drawn through a gold ring; there was Kendrick Pyne, a once famous cathedral organist, now retired and living with his married daughter, whose beautiful Victorian diction, whose well-turned anecdotes, had a charm of artistry peculiar to a culture now almost extinct. There were our next-door neighbours, the Websters, who had named their house (wedged between West View and number three Hamilton Gardens) 'Interim', because they were living in that small but hideous villa only between a Stock Exchange disaster and an anticipated recovery. Mr. Webster was an elegant, optimistic man, who had converted his interim garden patch into an enchanted spot with a miniature landscape of rockery and pool, gemmed with rare flowers tended with skills (some—burying, for example, a plant pot near the roots of a rare plant, to allow the water to go deeper—I remember to this day) which raised garden- ing to a fine art. There were besides, in that same garden, three terriers (Bobs, Jean and Lady), two cats (Satan and Tony) and a curlew with a clipped wing; which did nevertheless escape. In the front window a grey parrot in a big round cage; and a strange flask of 'bee wine' in which translucent living globules rose and sank in a truly marvellous manner. There were several handsome grown-up sons and daughters, and Gwen, a few years older than I, with whom I played. Mrs. Webster had white frizzed hair fitting her head like a cap, or the powdered hair of the eighteenth century; she wore an enamelled gold watch pinned to the fastidiously clean elaborate lace-trimmed corsage of her blouse. I could not have said wherein it was that the Webster's way of life was not as ours; I only knew that life 'next door' was as rich and full of marvels as the Arabian Nights. It was 'fun'; quite useless things were done for their own sake. That pre-war sense of play never visited my parents' house; no conversational grey parrot delighted us by occasionally laying a round white useless egg; none of the gay bursts of song and litter of bric-a-brac of the money-spinning Websters. My parents took money very seriously and literally (my father from the working-class, my mother from par-simonious Scotland) and there was an intangible atmosphere of moral disapproval of those gay Websters who did not take money seriously. Unfortunately for the moral my father might have liked to draw, that happy circus did in due course return to the world from which it had so cheerfully descended. Interim was occupied by an elementary school-master with false teeth and a small boy with a squint and spectacles. Respectability's heavy shadow fell as frivolity departed.

Even my infants' school was Paradisal. 'Miss Hutchinson's school' in The Drive was just a large house with a garden at the back where we used to feed the tortoise with leaves from the Lombardy poplar; from which it delighted us by taking clear-cut wedge-shaped bites. We made delightful little boxes out of coloured paper, embroidering them in patterns laid out for us in dots whose traces we had but to follow to create things of beauty such as we could never have imagined ourselves capable of. I could of course read before I went to school; and the weekly award of 'the button' went either to me or to a boy called Alan Prior whose handsome person I much admired. There were two beautiful ash-fair boys, twins—a magical relationship—called Brian and Willow Mackay. For some forgotten reason—perhaps because he was not good at his lessons, being delicate, or with the amoral cruelty of the healthy for the ailing—we teased poor Willow; and when, after a period of absence from school we were told that Willow was dead, there was already guilt mingled with my evanescent childish sorrow.

My second school—the Highlands Elementary School—was not in Paradise; a red-brick prison in an asphalt play-ground, where in encaustic-tiled classrooms sixty little girls sat at desks before a blackboard. What we learned from the blackboard I do not remember; but I do remember an episode—another piece of human wreckage polluting the stream of life—which shook me deeply. A pretty, precocious dark girl (she afterwards became a professional dance hostess) had been naughty in some way of which I have no memory. Much tried as she must have been in her daily struggle to control a class of sixty, our Miss Smith's usually mild temper broke, and she called dark Gwenyth to stand out in front of the class and hold out her hands for the cane. Caning was rare, at least among seven-year-olds; and the sentence struck at my life in an indescribable way. I shook and trembled uncontrollably as I sat with lowered eyes so as not to see the awful punishment carried out. Gwenyth had spirit and showed less dread than I. When the class was dismissed Miss Smith kept me back; she spoke to me as an equal, asking me if I thought she had done wrong. That a grown-up ever could do wrong had not occurred to me; and so I said, 'Oh no'; but that it had seemed such a very terrible thing to happen. My reaction was not moral, had nothing to do with justice or injustice; it was the sense of the deep dreadfulness of punishment, as if the person punished could never be the same again, would bear the scar for ever. I do not any longer know just what it was I did feel then; for nearly sixty years in this world have dulled my realization, which was then so absolute, that some violations are irreparable. Perhaps all punishment, then, had for me the awfulness of the divine punishment for sin, eternal condemnation, a judgement passed on the soul of the sinner against which there is no appeal. For I did not for a moment doubt that Gwenyth had done something very wrong, or that her punishment was just. I do not remember a time when I did not know that we must walk a knife-edge between right and wrong, and that one sin was enough to blemish the original perfection, the sinlessness of childhood. For such was the Puritan morality which hoped for each child a sinless life; seeing sin not as the human condition into which all are born, all alike sinners who need forgiveness continually; but as a series of specific acts which we must on no account commit. Girls with illegitimate babies, drunkards and the like, were as a matter of course thrown out of non-conformist chapels (and according to Thomas Hardy also from the Church of England) in those days, and morality was a continual effort to preserve virtue and to avoid, not so much sin, as 'sins'. As a child I was resolved never to sin. The contempt of these moral athletes for Catholics who would 'confess to a priest' and then light-heartedly sin the very next day was boundless; but, however sincere, the effort not to 'sin' concealed a blindness to the human situation and the real nature of good and evil. I did make friends— fascinated and venturing out of my depth—with Gwenyth after that episode; but always with the fearful knowledge that my friend was not one of the good, but one of the bad; like Hans Andersen's robber-girl.

I remember yet another, more poignant occasion; a very abject, probably poor and rather dirty unattractive little girl sobbing and tear-stained, with no handkerchief to wipe away the repulsive grime melted in tears and making her face ugly, sobbing out 'It's my *birthday*'. I felt this to the heart; for a birthday was a day inviolable, a day which belonged to each child as their very identity. If even an ugly dirty little girl could be caned on her birthday, where was justice, where was sanctuary? Some sanctities go deeper than questions of right and wrong; and there was not a seven-year-old among us who did not feel, as I did, that a great wrong had been done against childhood's birthright.

From Bavington I have few memories of books or fantasies, for I had no need of these where the world was itself the region of imagination in which I moved. But in Ilford the two worlds must early have diverged; for whereas all I remember from Northumberland is of the sensible world, nearly all from Ilford which I have not either forgotten or rejected is of dreams and fantasies, and of certain stories which had over me the magical power of dreams.

A fantasy which companioned me for a long time must come from before the years when I lived with Aunty Peggy Black at the manse. Going to bed by day, in summer, I passed the hours before sleep in the other world. Not in dream but in waking fantasy I would take off, from the bed where I lay, to the summits of some beautiful heavy elms I could see from my window which grew a field away, by a little stream, or ditch rather, which gathered in a pool where by day I watched sticklebacks, water-boatmen, water-snails, planaria, and occasionally beautiful newts, and all manner of strange lives. From the pool the water flowed away under a brick culvert into darkness and mystery; and down into that mystery, each evening, I passed, travelling with the speed of thought to 'the bottom of the sea'.

There my companion awaited me: an octopus. How came I by that fantasy? I know only that it was so, and that among the mysteries under the sea we travelled together in perfect identity of thought. I did not need Plato to tell me that the 'real' world is a pale reflection of the divine originals stored in those inaccessible treasuries.

A lifetime later I read in Jung's *Aion* of the era of the Fish, and of a round fish, known to the alchemists, dwelling at the bottom of the sea, whose powers are marvellous and whose strength can stop ships in their course. The round magic-working fish seemed to me as I read a symbol so uncouth and improbable that I was about to dismiss the account as having, for me, no imaginable meaning, when there came flooding back (as if I had eaten a crumb of magic *madeleine* dipped in lime-flower tisane) the memory of my long-forgotten octopus; a world. What the octopus meant, or was, or the round fish of the Alchemists, I do not know; but clearly others who have been where I was, have there found the same mental beings.

That night I dreamed of the octopus; no longer as a living *alter ego,* but as a lifeless diagram, a mathematical demonstration; but one last communication of wisdom my octopus gave me before vanishing for ever. The eight arms formed themselves, as I looked, with a kaleidoscopic shift, into the shape of a Maltese cross. What did the octopus mean by that shape-shifting, that transmutation of the wild hidden life of the abyss into the world-ruling emblem which so ambiguously combines the peace of Christ with the sign of the Enemy warrior, the Iron Cross of the First World War which was the background of my childhood? So astonished was I that I sent an account of my dream and the earlier fantasy to a Jungian psychiatrist whom I had lately met, saying that this confirmation of his symbol might please Dr. Jung; who himself wrote in reply that my fantasy was a sign of 'the chosen one'—such was his phrase. He spoke of 'a pair of friends like Mithras and Helios or Kastor and Pollux or Chadir and Elijah etc.' and 'the hero who recognizes the Dragon to be himself'.

Those born, as I am, under the sign of Gemini, have often, I believe, a very strong sense of their other self, the immortal daimon who accompanies every mortal. It is said of the Dioscuri that one is mortal, the other immortal; and in that sign the poet and his guide walk hand in hand, we here, they there,· in uninterrupted communion. Dante was of that sign, and Yeats (my birthday is between theirs, on June 14th). My sense of an accompanying daimon (though not in octopus-form) has been with me all the years of my poetry; but who in so strange a shape would have recognized a companion akin to Dante's Virgil or Yeats's Instructors?

As a child I had known that I was a 'chosen one'; I never doubted it. Perhaps all souls are chosen-ones, though not all awakened to self-knowledge. Certainly there was nothing competitive in my sense of vocation; for vocation differs from ambition in that it concerns no one but ourselves; it is secret; its obligations, being self-imposed, are inescapable. I had no wish to excel, or to surpass or to be admired; my task concerned no one but myself; the children with whom I played knew nothing of my inner life, in which they played no part. I felt neither superior, inferior, nor anything at all in relation to them; children do not make comparisons, things are as they are.

My land-under-wave is confused in my memory with the story of *The Little Mermaid;* perhaps my fantasy took its form from that story; or it may have been the other way, and my deep sense of identity with Hans Andersen's mermaid may have come from the archetypal character of that land-under-wave,

> The Mind, that Ocean where each kind
> Does straight its own resemblance find;
> Yet it creates, transcending these,
> Far other Worlds and other Seas.

But I would have no marble statue of a prince in my garden of coral and sea-flowers! No, indeed—for who would exchange the ecstasy of freedom, of plunging beneath the waves, of drifting on the surface of beautiful seas, a world of life inexhaustible, for so finite a passion as love? Not I! With troubled sorrow I read of her visit to the witch-woman, who demanded the tongue with which she sang so sweetly as the price of the mixed potion which should change her fish's tail into a pair of feet to walk the earth, every step a pain as if she walked on knives; of the dumbness of the soul that cannot speak its knowledge to earthly ears; and the ending I then thought sad beyond endurance. For the Mermaid, who failed to win the love of her prince, must be transmuted yet again, this time into a spirit of the air, with a far hope of winning immortality. As a child I could scarcely bear to read that ending; but now, near the end of the unfolding pattern, I am grateful for the story, which tells, in symbols so charming, the deep truth of the soul's pilgrimage. Perhaps we each instinctively recognize, among the countless possibilities of fancy, the pattern of our own life.

Another story of land-under-wave that then enthralled me was Kingsley's *Water-Babies;* and above all the journey to the North, under the wall of ice, to that pool where in a great calm the creatures are created, gull and tern and gannet and fulmar and shearwater, for ever and ever uprising on wings of immortal life in its myriad forms. Yet another was La Motte Fouque's *Undine,* whose lover came to her as the rain beat and the torrent cut off the fisherman's cottage from the world with streaming sounding cataracts. That story too had an ending too dreadful to be borne; even on the great navigable river of her descent from Paradise the fairy bride could still dip her arm into the water and bring up pearls and jewels for her knight; but in the world of men and women to which at last they came, he forgot her; no longer 'saw', her; no longer remembered; until, led away unwillingly by her own people, back into the world of spirits, bitterly weeping, she was compelled to leave her knight, married, like the Mermaid's sleeping prince, to a mortal wife; and he sealed his fountain with a stone, lest through it she might rise again. But at the end the fountain, as it must be, was unsealed; and from it the Undine rose, weeping, slowly, reluctantly, she went to Hildebrand, he too weeping now with the clouded joy of love remembered too late. Folding him in her cold reluctant arms, she was the unwilling messenger of death. But why, I felt then, did he forget her, his true love, how could he turn from the greater love to the less, from the supernatural to the natural bride? And how could the Mermaid's prince be so blind as not to understand that it was she, not the commonplace earth-born princess, who had carried him in her arms to the shores of his kingdom? Why? And to this day I have not understood why the mortal sleep must fall upon us, when once we have glimpsed immortal beauty.

West View was the last—or first—of a row of three brick houses in the style of 1908. There were two patterns in Ilford, double-fronted and single-fronted; our house was double-fronted, the dining-room window on one side of the front door, the drawing-room on the other. Over each of these rooms was a bedroom, and over each bedroom a 'Tudor' gable. Long ago these houses were swallowed up in the no-man's land which advanced into Essex, between the two wars, to meet the needs of a population multiplying with a like rapidity. But as I first remember it our house stood at the very extreme boundary, and I, a country child, could still find in the buttercup meadows and the pasture field beyond our wooden creosoted garden fence the world I recognized, nature immaculate. The house really, then, had a West View; from the front windows we could watch the sun slowly setting over misty fields bordered with pollarded elms; 'Essex Maidens' they were called, for their slender beauty, crowned with a delicate chevelure of leaves. Our own elms, one standing in our garden, and its companions across the country road (the end of an avenue which continued towards the village of Barkingside) were not pollarded, but such hedgerow elms as Milton might have loved. Only on summer Saturdays were we reminded of the nearness of London, but in a manner that would have delighted Blake himself. In the morning, the heavy clatter of horses' hooves would approach, and the sound of brisk singing; charabancs higher than any farm-cart but in the same idiom as Constable's drays and hay-wains, full of children and their elders from the East End, were on their way to some Sunday School treat in Epping forest. There were, as a rule, several of these top-heavy joyous waggons. One would approach with its happy clatter and jingle and singing, and before its crescendo had died away into a diminuendo, the next would come, pass, and go; and the next; four or five charabancs. In the evening they would return, at a slower pace, all hung with green bracken, branches of forest trees, and big bunches of flowers from Essex cottage gardens; cabbage roses and madonna lilies and pinks hanging like votive garlands all round the sides. The singing now was sleepy, sentimental and harmonious; the major key of morning hope modified into an evening *raga* as the children and their elders, drowsy with sunshine, fulfilment and the long drive home, returned, sated with country pleasures. But after the war the great 'development' of Essex began. Our country road was tarred now, and the charabancs disappeared along with the high farm-carts with their woodwork painted in red and blue and yellow visible under the mud of turnips and potatoes, the milk-cart and the baker's cart with their little ponies. There began to be cars, though at first not many.

Then a 'bus service was opened. An open-topped omnibus (so it was still called) turned round under the last elm of the avenue, a few yards from our door. The top seats were often wet and you pulled a canvas cover over your knees to keep the rain off. The branches swished over you as the 'bus made its way townwards; some of the overhanging boughs of the trees along the route were lopped off on this account. I remember the mutilated tree at the 'bus-stop, with its great scar where the branch had been sawn away, and my father's explanation, in terms of safety and utility, of the mutilation of the tree's life and beauty. My father's answers never quite fitted my questions; the good was, for us, situated differently, his in social improvement, mine in the beautiful and the integrity of nature. Elms, so he told me, are 'dangerous'; sometimes their branches fall; what if this were to happen when someone was standing underneath? I did not put into words my real thought on the matter; but not only did this seem to me extremely improbable, but by far the lesser evil, man being more common and less noble than great elms. I knew such thoughts to be, by Christian standards, wicked, but remained rebellious; for there was the scar: the tree it was that died.

But our own lovely elm was safe meanwhile, and those opposite, their lace-like dusky leaves heaped in cumulus-forms. At their foot the hedge-row plants flourished, white stitch-wort, white Jack-by-the-hedge, white foam of cow-parsley. Even so near London people still walked along country roads enjoying green hedges and birds and flowers, We are only within the world of nature (created with and for man, whether by miracle or by natural adaptation) when we are on foot; cars do not take us 'into' the country but out of it; out of nature altogether, for to see flying fields and hedges is not to be in them. My own lifetime has seen the destruction of a companionship of ages.

Higher up the road, towards the village, a manor-house stood in its deserted garden; of the period of Queen Anne, as it now seems to me. I remember thinking the mellow brick house with its broad windows very beautiful, standing in its pleasant grounds where cedars of Lebanon laid their flat branches low over the sweep of the lawn. Into that magic ground, that forsaken garden, I, with other children, timidly trespassed; climbed on those low branches and marvelled at the great cedar-cones. I sensed a *genius loci* strange indeed to me, the *genius* of the gentry; of the eighteenth century behind the nineteenth, like a vista. Nature here was refined, enhanced; here bluebells grew larger and finer than those in the woods; flowering shrubs whose names I did not know; a great hedge of sweet-briar. I had never before seen a place made beautiful by man, whom I knew better as a destroyer of beauty. The barriers between social classes were then indeed *barricades mystérieuses;* I knew that I had trespassed, had crossed an invisible barrier when I breathed the scent of cedar on that deserted lawn. I did not know it as a barrier of class or caste, but I sensed a richer and more beautiful, a less abject world, and felt drawn towards it by a kind of nostalgia for something that ought to be. I was not the only trespasser, but only a drop in a rising tide; for the deserted manor was to be pulled down; a building estate was to take its place; development, it was called: an experience, at all events, to be undergone, though a moment only in the endless metamorphosis of the world.

Our elms, too, were to go; the road had already been widened and their roots undermined. But before the fellers began their work there came a storm in the night with wind, rain, thunder, and lightning. In the morning four elms had fallen, their roots standing up in the air, their delicate leafy heads laid low. I remember how empty that piece of sky looked, a blank light that hurt the eyes. Where something had been there was a nothing haunted by their absence.

At first I half hoped that if I went to sleep and woke again, the trees would be back in their accustomed places. Spring, besides, set about its gentle task of healing the earth's wounds. The cleavers and Jack-by-the-hedge formed themselves to the new pattern, growing lush and tall by the fallen trunks. But then came men with saws and lopped off the great branches until only the trunks remained; then these, too, were gone, and the remaining elms (their torn shapes never mended to their broken sky) put, as it were, out of their misery and felled too. Then there was a time of bricks and gravel, hammering and scraping, until a row of mean shops stood in the way of our West View. At the corner, where the brick wall of the old manor demesne still hid its doomed garden, stood a sweetshop-tobacconist; then a United Dairy, kept by a greasy pig-like woman in a dirty uniform; then an ironmonger's and domestic stores kept by a strangely repulsive man, with a silent wife who sometimes hovered behind the dark counter. Her profile was fine and delicate and her abundant coils of pre-Raphaelite auburn hair gave her the dignity of beauty. She committed suicide within a year or two. To me her choice of death seemed wise and noble; to live in a mean flat above that shop with its smell of chemical products tied to so vile a man, was reason enough to drive her to the one way of escape open to such prisoners. Next, I think, came a grocer's, then a wool and needlework shop that sold odds and ends of baby clothes, stockings and the like. The unreal and the mean had moved like a nightmare into a place that had seemed as enduring as seed time and harvest, summer and winter, day and night.

To say I grieved is needless; but besides grief there had already begun to grow in me indignation and disgust and outrage and misanthropy; bitterly, but not with childhood's innocent grief, I lamented the usurpation of the beautiful world by the mean, the meaningless and the vulgar. The mean, meaningless and vulgar being was man. That transformation which I was to watch, day by day, week by week, month by month in that doomed Essex countryside has left its desolation upon me. Never have I become reconciled; the nameless nomads who swarmed into the new building estates which seemed to have arisen overnight, and as if in a nightmare, seemed to me then—and to this day it requires an effort of will to rectify the judgement—something quite other than the humanity of which I read in those books which (so the end-pages of a famous edition constantly reminded readers of my generation) are 'the life-blood of a master spirit'. Where did they come from? Who were they? Their speech was scarcely articulate, like the voices of the ghosts in Hades; they were too frightened, those timid swarms, to raise their voices. Their only refinement was a paralysis of fear; their lives were apologetic, as though they themselves doubted their right to exist. They seemed to have come from nowhere; not from any place that could be called a place; not from the Essex villages, where pinks and cabbages grew in untidy fertility. Having no past they seemed to have, even for themselves, no identity, nor could they impart any reality to the new dream into which the wind of time had blown them.

Not real people at all, I felt; not like Grannie Carr, who in her dark stone cottage set her good loaves to rise on the polished steel kitchen fender; and who in the corner cupboard kept her Wedgwood dishes, an heirloom like the d'Urberville's worn silver spoon, a link with the ways of life and values of an eighteenth-century English civilization not yet extinct in her cottage. Not like the farmers' daughters, who were my merry play-fellows, climbing among the hay in the barn to see the swallows' nests; not even like the village outcast, Bella, at The Mires cottage, with her father-less children; who at times would repent and come to church, and sit behind those sweet, narrow Presbyterian farmers' wives with their tall Northumbrian figures upright in the varnished pews. They were not real like my father's poorer people; Aunt Marie and Aunt Sally with their village post office and the little dark shop smelling of yeast where the miners' wives and dirty children came, often without money to pay; and for the love of God Aunt Marie would often give them what they could not buy. Yet even those people had an identity, a past, a place however humble. My father's father, whose life was the religion taught to his grandfather by John Wesley, was proud of his tradition; proud of Durham cathedral, the cathedral of those earlier Raines who had been country people living in Teesdale.

Did those people only seem thus unreal because they had moved into a place which had no roots in the past, no function in relation to the earth upon which it had risen? Or was that formless proliferation of low-class suburbia perhaps the expression rather than the cause of that loss of identity, of orientation either social or spiritual? The Essex Maidens, the white foam of cow-parsley, the muddy lanes bordering misty ploughed fields, farms with walnut trees, chestnut avenues, all that old slowly traced, slowly matured human pattern of life lived from generation to generation was gone in less time than the sowing, reaping and harvesting of a field of corn. The new pattern no longer bore any relationship to shelter of hill or fall of stream; fertile and barren were alike to speculative builders. Then an arterial road advanced from London, severing like a cut artery the beginning of a lane, bordered with bramble and hawthorn, bleeding away now into the cement and gravel of the ribbon-building which sprawled endlessly in roads leading nowhere. As cancer cells proliferate without the informing pattern of the life of a human body, so this new way of life proliferated, cell by cell, rapidly killing the life of villages and old farms and parishes and manor houses. I knew that something was taking place all round me which I wanted to stop, for all seemed wrong about it, as if it were some vast mistake, beyond control. Who was making this mistake I did not know; but reading its lineaments I knew its meaning. What it told in its form, or lack of form, was something immeasurably evil, if evil be not too grandiose a word for the apathetic negation of the past of the earth and all the memories of man. It was as if the earth were being killed; and humanity becoming something quite other than that for which man was created, upon that earth now stricken. Or rather, not becoming anything, only unbecoming, ceasing to be something and becoming an unreality so immense that my young soul's 'No, No' was as powerless against it as the lark's song or the petals of a wild rose opening in a doomed hedgerow. My father saw in it human progress; in the L.C.C. houses, housing for 'the people'; easy for the theorizers to dismiss the here and now, but those who prove life on their pulses are usually less fortunate. I saw with incredulous sorrow a desolation deliberately created. My mother refused to see it at all; that was how the poet in her kept faith with what should have been.

That I belonged to the same species as those who came to live in the little mean houses and shops springing up all round us, I no more realized than Mowgli in his jungle knew himself to be a man. I realize now how little I knew of the lives of these suburb-dwellers, with whom we never mixed. Behind their garden fences and little front gates which bore each its declaration of the privacy of what lay beyond on a little enamel plate with the words 'No hawkers, no circulars', the women hovered, keeping their lives hidden. The men, dressed in dark suits and bowler hats, left each morning for their mysterious 'offices' in 'the City' (reached in the packed coaches of steam trains to Liverpool Street) and returned each evening to enter their small foothold of safety, or whatever else was theirs behind the ring-pass-not of those garden fences protected by their enamel talismans, 'No hawkers, no circulars'. These indeed bore the only clue to their desires: to find sanctuary, somewhere, from the pursuit of a bewildering impersonal and hostile world. Behind their privet hedges they tended their little bright-green lawns,carefully uprooting dandelion or daisy; no weed grew among the straight rows of bright-coloured flowers, lobelia and geraniums and marguerites and, in the midst of the garden, a 'standard' bush of the Daily Mail or some other rose of the same vivid leathery kind. That was before their dreams, growing less timid, relaxed into crazy-paving, aubretia and Darwin tulips. Those stiff little plots seem, in retrospect, idyllic in comparison with the machines which have drawn them away from even that diminished Eden. The car, symbol of total displacement, and the television set, symbol of the universal invasion of the sanctuary, have banished the Daily Mail rose, the suburban Tree of Life.

Perhaps in my sense of exile, of belonging elsewhere—of belonging, above all, not *there*—I was after all not so much exceptional as typical of that place. Those tenuous and inarticulate lives must have come from somewhere, must have brought some sense of memory of an identity and a past.

In that world dreams unattainable were nourished upon the easily attainable; the powders and creams that will make the woman beautiful; the insurance policy which will give the wage-slave, in his old age (but they do not say old age; they say, 'retirement') the freedom denied him by the very nature of his life. They hoped, yet did not hope, expected, but did not expect, the realization of dreams. What they would never relinquish was the dream itself; without those dreams they would indeed be lost.

Here was neither the realism nor the poetry of the feudal world; for these dispossessed people had no conception of the ways of life of other sections of society. They did not indeed belong to an integrated society at all which could be said to have other sections. There was no flow either out of, nor into, their lives, of anything greater, or other, than themselves; only the mirage of affluence created for them by the popular press and those advertisements which for them took on the dimensions and even the function of a mythology. People of higher classes they envisaged not in terms of what these thought, or did, or were, for of those realities they knew nothing, but solely in terms of what they owned; owned in terms readily translated into currency.

Different indeed from the people I had known, who participated in the whole hierarchy of which they formed a part. This is perhaps the worst deprivation of the society called 'classless'; all is alike and all is lowered to the level of the masses who comprise it. Rich and poor, great and small no longer know one another, no longer enrich one another's lives.

But Ilford harboured more passionate dreams; there was Mrs. Thompson and her adolescent sailor lover, both hanged for his stabbing of her husband within yards of his own privet hedge; so ended a love far beyond their means, beyond the narrow scope and meagre possibility of lower middle-class suburban life; a love, one might say, above their station; for in these two the flame of life burned too brightly for Ilford, whose apathetic and timid average created a context in which their tragedy became all too explicable. Many must have dreamed what they enacted. Murder was a crime altogether apart, unimaginable; murderers were no longer like other human beings, but quite cast out and cast away. But no one seemed to understand what I remember chiefly feeling at the time of the Ilford murder, how appalling a thing it is for a man to have rights of possession over the body of a woman, young, in love; the anguish of that desecration I felt (as once the death of a farm beast) in every fibre of my own young body; I too might (so I then thought) have been driven to murder to rid myself of a possession so outrageous, against nature. Even now I find it difficult to imagine or believe that there may be women who do not mind so very much being bound in a loveless marriage; a majority, perhaps, who would find the violence of my own (and Edith Thompson's) revulsion equally inconceivable; that anyone could care so much. Blake (but I did not know about Blake in those days) would have understood how, for such enslaved Daughters of Albion, an intolerable marriage becomes a prison from which the only release is some passionate dream or fantasy, whose enactment—for such fantasies are never meant to be enacted—brings tragedy; suicide, murder, hanging. Had I not been a poet, one of these might have been my fate also; the wife of the ironmonger found with her beautiful head of pre-Raphaelite hair in a cheap gas-stove, *c'est moi;* Edith Thompson, *c'est moi:* that privet hedge in Kensington Gardens grew within a stone's throw of the Cranbrook Park Wesleyan Methodist Church, and the Highlands Elementary School playground, shades of my own prison house.

My father looked for no earthly happiness; he, and his father, and his father's father, had known that man in this world is 'a stranger and a sojourner'; all he asked was to perform the task of his life—and for him life was precisely that, a task to be performed—sure of the reward of the faithful servant in another world. 'Well done, thou good and faithful servant!'; these were the words he most wished to hear. Of his safe homecoming to Heaven he had no doubt; he lived at peace with God. Therefore, for the brief time to be spent in this world, Ilford was as good a place as another to serve his Master in. 'Whatsoever thy hand findeth to do, do it with all thy might' was a text he loved to repeat. Ambition had no place in his life; was, indeed, unimaginable to him, for he did not regard his life as his own; only as his Master's. He could never, I think, envisage any other way of conceiving a life given by God. If he had a fault it was in a sort of stubborn pride he took in his refusal to be ambitious, in his too resolute adherence to the humblest tasks. Humility can be a form of evasion; and perhaps an excessive respect for humility made him unaware of other virtues. He was proud to tell how his father had always refused promotion, though a poor miner, even to the rank of foreman; for as a Christian he had felt it wrong to hold office over his fellows. These virtues suited not only my father's religion, but also his temperament, for he was not, like my mother, or like me, driven by a desire for perfection, for the beautiful, for boundless joy and wild freedom. He liked to recount his triumphs as a student, when he came first in every examination he ever took, from the time he was a pupil-teacher in his village school, to his degrees at Durham University; but at that time coming first in examinations was a task assigned, and therefore and only therefore to be done with all his might. I could never please him; for if I ever came top in examinations (I seldom did, but I tried) it was not as a duty to be performed but because I was carried away by the beauty of geometry, poetry, or plant-forms. Whatever I have achieved—little enough—only, I think, made my father ashamed of me; for earthly glory, even the smallest trace of it, is a departure from the egalitarianism of 'primitive Christianity' as he conceived it. To him the paradox never presented itself by which, in the very act of embodying some vision of the beautiful, glory and earthly splendour are inevitably created. Yet he loved cathedrals and above all Durham Cathedral: his own. Perhaps he was not wrong in caring only for such art as expressed a vision beyond all human greatness, an art expressing the glory not of man but of his maker; Plato, after all held much the same view of art. Where he was perhaps wrong was in sup-posing 'the good', in a moral sense, to be possible in the absence of such expressions, which are the flowering of its own vitality, and the language in which alone immaterial values are communicable.

My mother never cared for what she called 'the daily round, the com-mon task'; that was her way of putting 'Whatsoever thy hand findeth to do . . .'. As a little girl on the moors her favourite books had been the *Scottish Chiefs* and *The Arabian Nights Entertainments;* a child's version, no doubt, but nothing can expurgate from those stories the thirst for luxury and the beauties and marvels of the world. Perhaps in Milton too she responded to the nostalgia for the earthly paradise Comus offered and Eve lost. But when I knew her, her unsatisfied longing for life's joys and marvels had retreated into the vivid dreams in which she lived night after night; dreams and her flower-garden. She loved poetry because it alone answered to her insatiable longing for beauty and wonder. My father, on the contrary, loved poetry chiefly for its 'message' (for him its 'message' was not its beauty) and, as he often assured my mother, with perhaps a shade too much complacency, he 'never dreamed'. Of Shelley's adolescent and vague political idealism my father approved, and on that account forgave him his entranced lovers sailing in their magic boats. But he loved also the *Ode to the West Wind,* whose 'message' for him, was the harnessing of that 'impetuous one' in the cause of 'the people'; for him the new birth to be quickened was socialism; Christianity in practice, as he saw it.

My father despised Ilford's lowest of the lower middleclass suburb-dwellers precisely because these were not, in his sense, 'the people'. They were not low enough; they were, in his eyes, little better than those abstractions 'the capitalists' for they too worked in order to 'make money', and to buy all manner of 'things' ('things are in the saddle, and ride the world' was another favourite quotation). He truly believed that if 'the people' ruled, universal brotherhood would prevail; he thought 'the people' free from all those vices they had lacked the means to satisfy; mistaking the enforced poverty of the lowest social class for the freely chosen 'holy poverty' of the saints. So he taught English literature and Latin to the sons of Ilford city clerks and commercial travellers, using both as vehicles for his 'message' in the spirit of a missionary among the heathen. He despised these suburban-dwellers because they did not live by any values above those of self-interest; and he missed, in that unoriented world, a certain reality which he had known among his own people; a truth of feeling and a fervour of religion found only, perhaps, where sudden death is, as in the coal-mines, a daily possibility. It is one of the paradoxes no social reformer has resolved, that to make living conditions materially easier does not improve the quality of the people themselves; in some respects the opposite. So my father refused tenaciously—perhaps too tenaciously—to 'rise' in society, or, rather, to admit that he had done so. What he refused to see was that when, in his new M.Litt. gown and furred hood, he had walked across the close of Durham University, he had already left that world; a process which, once begun, cannot be reversed, or arrested, perhaps, for many generations; until the new growth has reached its term. I must have been three years old when I saw my father, looking, as I now realize, both young and happy in his academic dress, crossing that ancient close. Durham with its cathedral and its university was not yet, in those days, 'red brick', but the city of the old Bishops Palatine, the city of the sons of County Durham, even the poorest of them, the miners. My grandfather was there; the city of Bede and Cuthbert was his city and the city of his forefathers. Even miners, then, remembered the valleys whence their fathers had come. It was my grandfather (and who had a better right than he?) who held me up in his arms to touch the sanctuary knocker with its lion's head, with the strange hollow eye-sockets and solar mane; he it was who told me, then or later, that anyone, no matter what crime he had committed, had but to reach that door and lay his hand upon that knocker; to be safe from the pursuit of his enemies; for the Cathedral was a sanctuary; in it all could find refuge. To the door of Christian refuge my grandfather's arms lifted me.

My mother, I think, felt herself to be living in that make-shift suburb only provisionally—only 'for now'. Even in Northumberland she had lived, a race-proud Scot, as a stranger, refusing to identify herself in any way with the English; and as the daughter of a Scotch mother I too refused to be 'English'. On my mother, besides, words acted like a spell of enchantment, and the name 'West View' made her continue to believe even when the United Dairy and the domestic stores closed our earthly view, that our mis-shapen windows looked out towards the sunset and the golden country beyond the sunset. She retreated into her dreams and into her flowers. There was a China rose that covered the back of the house (of yellow brick and of a not displeasing simplicity) with its long, strong-thorned branches and clusters of exquisite shell-petalled double roses. I have never seen its kind anywhere since, and think of it as perhaps grown from a cutting taken in some garden before suburbia usurped the land; perhaps from the deserted manor-house of Gearies. Nothing of the new desolation which had usurped the view and the fields to which she had first come to live was, for my mother, ever really there. Those mean new houses spreading over mile after mile of earth laid waste had indeed an air of the impermanent, the provisional, the make-shift; or of that kind of unreality we meet in dreams, in which a place we know is unlike itself. From dreams we wake and the illusion passes; but as day succeeded day this outrage of an earlier memory, a former aspect of things, this deface-ment did not fade. So, imperceptibly, my mother's life, itself diverged from reality; like a road that forks, at first, only a little, but at last leads us far out of our way.

Since my mother did not, ever, really live in that place, or in those days which succeeded one another without awakening to remove the desolation from before her eyes, she began to neglect her appearance. At eighteen—I have a photograph taken of her then—she was poignantly beautiful, tall, with the proud sweet charm of her race. At twenty-eight she was still so; but tamed. Little by little she ceased to care; her dresses—it was a long time before she stopped dressing as if for her native moors—would 'do for now'; and so with her cups and dishes and her furniture. Even the meals she set before us were provisional; they too, were good enough for the time being; but the loaf on the table at Bavington and the eggs, and the milk new from the cow had been the thing itself, in a here and now which never or seldom, any more, seemed to reach us in that non-time and non-place. For what now, and here, my mother was waiting she could not have said; indeed she may not have known that she was waiting, only that these days were to be lived through; not lived in. Gradually she lost some of the freshness of her Scottish speech, for lack of those with whom to speak her own language. Yet I believe her lost paradise was an earthly one; she was never content to be, like my father, 'a stranger and a sojourner' in this world. She had, as I had (and I owed mine to her, to my being her child) known the wild joy of freedom. She subscribed, of course, to my father's religious principles; and yet to her life they never seemed appropriate, as they were to his. Even among the thorns and thistles remembered the past; Adam looked towards the future: but I too was a daughter of Eve.

Every morning, after breakfast—and in recent years I have found myself falling into the same habit—my mother would walk round her garden, teapot in hand, from flower to flower, seeing what buds had opened each day, or bulbs appeared above the soil. The tea-leaves would be given to a fern before she returned to her household tasks, which she disliked; she never ceased to protest against the necessity of having to do them; she developed a resentful perfectionism, but without ever, in a long lifetime, becoming tamed to a way of life from which she never thought of attempting to escape, because no other came within her range of possibility. That round of her garden was a brief return to Paradise; she had come to terms with exile in her own way, refusing to see what lay beyond her flowers. My ever-living protest continually broke across her own way of being reconciled to her life. Refusing to see what her West View had become, she could not bear me to remind her of the surrounding desolation; she must build her refuge or have none; but I, being young, meant to escape. I knew that I was not where I belonged or with my own people; and each day I refused the proffered pomegranate. I had not needed to realize that what I felt still to be my place was no longer mine; for Bavington was still there, my Aunty Peggy lived on at the manse. But in the years that followed in the struggle to keep faith with my earliest vision of the beauty and the truth of nature, I became involved in a cruel and continuous battle against my new environment and, finally, with my parents, who attempted to hold me to the world which they had made theirs, or which had, in the end, made them captive.

My father used with me only one argument of persuasion to accept Ilford: religion. Christian charity demands that we love our neighbours (neighbours! my heart said, these are not *my* neighbours). Yet his own love for mankind was remote and idealistic; he attempted to educate the sons of those suburb-dwellers in the spirit of a missionary; to have liked them as they were would have seemed to him a betrayal of his ideal of 'humanity' as it should be; a perfection as remote and vague as the choruses of *Prometheus Unbound*. When he found that I shared his contempt for the actual, while refusing to dedicate myself to the service of the ideal humanity, he was displeased and troubled. Poetry, too, which he himself had encouraged me to read, was a cause of division; for him a means to an end (the betterment of mankind) for me poetry seemed rather one of the ends to which humanity was perhaps only the means.

In loyalty to his father and his father's father he had remained a

Methodist; and now, instead of the sweet staid sabbaths of Bavington my mother and I were led, she unwillingly but dutiful, I unwillingly and protesting, to the Cranbrook Park Wesleyan Methodist Church (it was not called a chapel, for the Cranbrook Park congregation had aspirations) every Sunday morning and evening. My father never doubted but that in time he would by patience and his own unswerving conviction of what was right, bring my mother to share his dearest beliefs; that I would do so he took for granted. That my mother remained uninterested troubled and puzzled him, but he never for a moment asked himself why this might be so. As for myself, I detested the imprisoned hours spent mentally rearranging the panes in the stained-glass window, suggestive of the Victorian Gothic style which had remotely influenced the design, taken no doubt, from some builder's catalogue. I could never make those little panes come right, alter them about as I would, or the arches and the pillars and the roof-vaulting, among which my mind busily wandered seeking for beauty and symmetry and finding none. I only knew that in the little simple stone kirk at Bavington I had been happier, and the shapes had been right; I was half a lifetime from knowing that its simple proportions were of the eighteenth century, to which architectural rightness came as naturally as wrongness to my own.

The congregation of shopkeepers and commercial travellers were no more my father's kind than they were of my mother's. He missed the warmth of that Methodism Coleridge so well described as 'a stove' ('heat without light', as he said); the revival meetings, the 'speaking with tongues', the 'simple faith'; but this he would never quite admit, for he, too, was trying to keep faith with a vanished past, though one neither my mother nor myself could share with him. He was a 'local preacher', as it was called; and I heard him preach to these people very often, in his beautiful calm voice. On week-nights too he often spoke for the League of Nations Union, which he saw as a practical means of leading the world a little nearer to that heavenly city which was, he believed, already coming down from heaven as an earthly reality as the socialist cause grew in power and numbers. The brotherhood of man of which the Gospel speaks he understood as an egalitarianism based on the abolition of property, a having of 'all things in common', like the first Christians. Communism, to him, was 'true Christianity', about to be realized at last in this world. I remember, soon after the war, his delight when Ramsay MacDonald's socialist government was returned to power. The kingdom seemed to him very near in which all these abstractions, universal brotherhood, peace between the nations, holding of all things in common, and so forth, were to be realized. The sermon I remember most clearly of all I heard him give—for even I was moved by his quiet certainty—was upon that *civitas dei* which Plato saw, and St. John on Patmos, and St. Augustine and Æ and many more, 'the holy Jerusalem descending out of heaven from God'. When my father spoke of that city it was impossible not to believe that many now living would see its walls of jasper, and sapphire, and chalcedony. My father was a pacifist, too; to kill was clearly, and under all circumstances wrong; therefore, war must be so. All his convictions, so calmly certain, were based upon rational over-simplifications of this kind; but for my mother and myself, these were not issues which ever arose; caught in the toils of life, we found no comfort in the generalized solutions of problems which were so remote from any that presented themselves to us. Yet among the precipices of her dreams my mother walked sure-footed; contrary to appearances, hers was a courageous soul caught in the toils; while my father's certainties were those of a natural timidity at home within the secure protection of the Christian virtues he practised and proclaimed. Non-conformist Christianity suited his nature; it did not suit my mother's; her nature craved for wilder, stranger, more beautiful myths. Neither she nor I had any wish to live in my father's ideal society. We would have found it as unendurably boring as the Cranbrook Park Wesleyan Methodist church itself. My father, who had learned pure English only at Durham University and as a foreign speech, spoke it most beautifully. His father's household was, so to say, bilingual; the almost incomprehensible Durham dialect, the speech of childhood and freedom; educated English that of his later life. He had a fine ear both for speech and for music, and a knowledge both of the roots and meanings of words. From him I too learned to speak educated English, relinquishing my Border dialect, in which I had found a kind of freedom from constraint, a naturalness I have never since quite recaptured in the use of language. Between us and the surrounding barbarism of Ilford language was our protecting barrier. My mother's inheritance, her Scotch tongue; my father's command, won by study, of the language (and with the words, the thoughts) of Chaucer and Shakespeare, Milton and Coleridge, Words-worth and Emerson, Shelley, Browning, Tennyson (let me add, lest he should be misjudged, that he detested Dickens; 'a caricaturist', he called him, a vulgarian) and George Bernard Shaw. My father was a good linguist, and knew well both Latin and Anglo-Saxon, which for the sake of Bede, Cuthbert and Durham Cathedral, he loved especially; it was, for him, the speech of his ancestors, both natural and spiritual; his own, not a foreign, speech. In European languages and literature (other than Latin) he had little interest; preacher as he was of 'universal brotherhood' my father was by nature a xenophobe so complete that he was quite unaware of it; the Scotch, the Welsh and the Irish (not to mention the French) he regarded as a matter of course as alien and inferior. As for remoter races—

negroes, Indians and Chinese—these had only a theoretical existence, 'on the mission field'; none of us had met any member of these exotic tribes.

Literacy set us apart, and gave us a sense—perfectly justified, so far as it went—of superiority to those who lacked it, even when, as was often the case, these were materially richer than ourselves; a kind of social isolation characteristic, I dare say, of schoolmasters' families. Poverty never troubled my father at all; he really had no desire for anything this world could offer; not even freedom, for he had that, also, in Heaven. Poverty was not my mother's problem, either (nor mine) but social displacement; many of the people of Bavington were poorer than the people of Ilford (or if rich, without living a kind of life essentially different from that of their poorer neighbours, tenant-farmer or hinds) but their way of life was one in which I could have been happy. My father gave me, instead, books; and with books, access to inner vistas, to the 'realms of gold'. But—this he did not realize—he was all the time, by placing in my hands the means of knowledge of ways of life and thought other than any accessible to me, unfitting me for Ilford, sowing the seeds of unrest, of great unhappiness; for I was developing the ways of thought and modes of feeling of people who had lived in worlds where fine sensibilities were sheltered in walled gardens, and high thoughts in old libraries; where imagination led naturally to action in terms of existing possibilities. Shakespeare may be a fine education for a ruling class, but in the suburbs to think Shakespeare's thoughts is to be filled with energies, desires, impulses, which because they can have no outlets, no expression in the real, generate only fantasies and discontent. It was well I did not then know how far removed I was from those worlds which had created the poetry I fed upon, how many ranges of hills remained to be crossed, or I might have despaired of escape, which seemed to me then an easy matter. I did not know then how small a part of true culture book-learning is. During these years education rather replaced life than enabled me to live it; and the habit then formed, from which I have never since been quite free, of confusing things learned from books with lived experience. Yet where else but in the thoughts of others could I then have lived? Again I realize that, in my flight from a meagre reality into a world of extraneous knowledge, how typical I was of that very class I hated and despised.

Yet not everything in my mental world was of this extraneous kind; not poetry, not Shakespeare; these were as myself, were my life. I resented the intrusion into this world (mine by right of nature, as I felt), of school 'lessons', given by, and shared with, people who did not belong to the world of poetry at all. My unease in the academic world, and with people who have an immense amount, perhaps, of academic knowledge of 'English Literature' (and theirs with me, and with poets in general) is of this same kind: their knowledge is of this extraneous kind, and, however great, is not the same thing at all as the poet's knowledge of poetry; or, for that matter, that of the illiterate country people who found in the songs they learned, as I did, in their grandmothers' kitchens, the expression of their own, albeit collective, identity.

When I was twelve or thirteen, with Rutland Boughton's opera *The Immortal Hour,* the Celtic renaissance penetrated the prison-houses of the suburbs. People went to hear it ten and twenty times. When I heard it, in my turn, it was as if those summoning voices spoke to me. I knew who they were: 'How beautiful they are, the lordly ones, who dwell in the hills, in the hollow hills'. My people were not of this world—and with all my young and naive soul in it I sang over and over to myself 'I will go back to the country of the young, and see again the faces of the Sidhe'. I thought these words held a secret meaning for myself alone; yet there must have been multitudes who, like me, heard those voices summoning back to a lost country. I did not then know that in Fiona Macleod's libretto there was transmitted a faint but authentic echo of a tradition as ancient as Pythagoras, known to Abaris, priest of the Hyperborean Apollo, who travelled on his golden arrow from those western isles which lay somewhere beyond the mean shops and proliferating human wilderness that blotted out the sunset fire from our windows. I did not see in those habitations of the lost yet another symbol of that human condition into which the souls (as Pythagoras taught, and the story of Eochaid embodies the same *gnosis)* 'descend'; the makers of myths had never looked so low; the Ilfords of this world seemed outside any mythological ordering principle which might give them even the dignity that belongs to the hells of traditional cosmogonies; a place and mode of being without symbolic orientation. Ilford had no part in the world of mythology or of a legend, was only its terrible negation; I was ashamed that I must return from Liverpool Street Station, where the world ended and the underworld began, to a place where the lordly ones could never find me, a habitation unvisited by the Gods.

> For this I weep, and oft bewail my woe,
> That e'er my soul such dreary realms should know.

Dispossessed as I was of my paradise I still clung, during my school years, to its receding fringes. There were no rivers or crags or burns any more; no longer even torpid Essex lanes and misty fields and hedgerow elms. I turned then to nature's minute worlds, and botany became a passion. I entered those strange green labyrinths of interior spaces, the cells and tissues of plants, and there my imagination found refuge in a world of form and beauty inviolate. At Bavington I had climbed over the last dyke dividing the human fields from the wild, setting foot on barren moor and stony crag always with a sense of home-coming to the sanctuary of wilderness immaculate. The human burden dropped from me as I dropped over that frontier of rough grey stones. There the wild in me came into its own, with the curlews and the dry polypody fern in the clefts of the rock; free. I entered that freedom as into a kind of ecstasy.

It was the same search for sanctuary which led me to botany. My shrines now were those green inviolate spaces of cell and vein, nucleus and astral body. These too were wildernesses inaccessible to man, outside his narrow territory, untainted by his vulgarity, inaccessible to his stupid destructiveness. Here no building estates could obliterate the delicate order, the harmonious unfolding of living form. In the little lighted circle of the microscope I was in the great universe, not the small human suburb. The stars in the great sky and the smallest particles bear a resemblance often observed; as the sky extends into infinite spaces without, so the microscope is the way by which we may enter spaces within, no less vast. Both are ways to freedom for those who, as I did, feel their own world a prison-house. For how many must science have been, as it was for me, an escape into beauty! It is, besides, the escape most easily accessible, even the only access of escape, precisely for the children of the lower middle classes who have no access to any works of man which may be called beautiful; whose houses are mean and ill-proportioned, whose speech is ugly and inexpressive. Even the gramophone had scarcely yet begun, in those days, to make music available to the dispossessed; and 'wireless' was a primitive device with a piece of crystal and a short length of wire called a 'cat's whisker'. My father was interested in fiddling with this contraption, but I paid little attention to it beyond finding the piece of galena crystal rather beautiful.

The charm of science for me, at all events, was aesthetic; and perhaps metaphysical. The shapes of crystals, grown in saturated solutions of alum, copper-sulphate, potassium permanganate and the rest, each had its mysterious modular controlling its growth along line and plane. The behaviour of images in mirrors, where pins, viewed through lenses, reflected and refracted, multiplied and reversed themselves, appeared to be present where they were not, innumerable where there was but one, enlarged, diminished, transposed or made to vanish, first hinted that all may be illusion. The microscope too presented the living plant as a series of appearances—of worlds, one might say—among which that seen by the naked eye is but one we call more real than the others only from familiarity and because of the form of our organs of vision. Before I had heard of the *Vedas* I knew what is meant by Maya, the ever-fluctuating veil of appearances; I was a Berkeleyan before I knew who Berkeley was. I inhabited those marvellous minute worlds whose *magia* opened in the bright focus of the lenses of my microscope. My grandfather had a set of green-bound volumes of natural history—(superficial enough, as I found to my disappointment when years later I came to look at them; written only for school teachers) which had, to my infant self, been works of pure magic. Each contained a construction like those which so delighted both Blake and Yeats in William Law's Boehme, where 'you lift a flap of paper and see both the human entrails and the starry heavens'. Instead of Boehme's fires and demons, the Garden of Eden, the unregenerate heart and the Divine Name, there was a mollusc whose shell lifted to show first muscle, then viscera, then reproductive system; and a plant and a pigeon anatomy; not the supernatural causes underlying natural effects, but hidden anterior causes whose imaginative character was, to me, the same. These paper revelations had made something a little like what Boehme had meant clear to my infant eye: inexhaustible depth and strangeness and terror of byss and abyss. All things have, as it were—so those flaps of paper demonstrated well enough—only a thin surface in the visible world; arid behind and beyond, mystery within mystery. And I wanted to know what lay at the heart of all.

Yet at every level of the real there is form; indeed—this I learned at the microscope which was, in those days, my most treasured possession—each world has its characteristic aspect, so that we may know, as it were, which forest we are walking in by its trees. The liquid shapes of cells; the network of nuclear structure, the geometry of foraminifera and radiolaria, of cylinder, spiral and cone; the rectilinear shapes of the inorganic, the curvilinear shapes of life; for the moist body, like the soul, seeks always to perfect itself as a sphere. Science is incommunicable in words; like music or painting it is a mode of knowledge in terms only of its own forms, which are non-verbal; natural forms, their relationships and transformations as such.

If, however, my musings over natural forms stirred in my imagination metaphysical apprehensions at variance with the fashionable materialism which claims 'science' as its ground, the remote marvels I beheld in the 'vegetable glass' did nothing to reconcile me with the Christian religion (in the debased form in which I knew it) which disregarded as it seemed to me, the beautifully ordered *gnosis* of a natural, without postulating any higher law, but merely the arbitrary 'Will of God', a person who, having made the universe, could 'prove' his existence only by arbitrary interventions; for such 'miracles' were supposed to be. Had I then known the Areopagite's celestial hierarchies, or the writings of Aquinas; if I had seriously read the Creeds, or discussed these with anyone possessing even the rudiments of a philosophic education I might have been less crude in my notions; but the scientists I read and met at that time were, unfortunately, far more intelligent than the Christians. I was for ever arguing my 'science' against my father's 'simple faith', unmoved by the figure of Jesus Christ, whose sublimity is self-evident to anyone who reads the Gospels with head unturned by the clap-trap of 'education' or perceptions undulled by some sentimental or stupid presentation. Truth to say whatever belonged to 'humanity' was for me, at that time and for long after, for that very reason suspect.

Had I learned Christianity from its art rather than in the pseudo-historical, pseudo-factual mode taught by non-conformists, I might have understood many things of which I had no conception until much later; until perhaps it was too late to make a Christian of me. But Christian art belongs part and parcel to Catholic Christendom; in the eyes of iconoclastic Protestantism, 'idolatry'. Failing to understand that art is the natural expression, as body to soul, the language of spiritual vision, those Protestant sects whose 'simplicity' (they were not really so simple; but their hymns and hymn-tunes and a certain sanctimonious use of language in extempore prayer they did not see, since these were not of 'wood and clay', as idols no less than the Madonna robed and crowned) was an expression of the illiteracy of the class amongst which they propagated themselves, had a horror of Catholic art. Such depictions as I saw at this time of the holy persons of the Christian story were sentimental trash manufactured for Sunday Schools and the mission field; and what they communicated—that effete meekness of the Sunday School Jesus—revolted me. The persons and events of the Christian religion were, so my father insisted, unlike the Greek, the Celtic, the Egyptian, the Indian and all other mythologies, 'true'. Thus, not through my father's neglect but through his zeal I was thrown to the gods of the heathen; for if Christianity belonged to the world of fact, to 'real life', I wanted none of it: the truth I recognized was of quite another kind. The Greek gods (in whom I believed absolutely) were perfectly real because perfectly beautiful, and precisely insofar as they did not resemble 'real life' they possessed that perfection whose reality real life lacked. My early distaste for 'the Jesus of History', who was 'just like us' and who so unaccountably and surely mistakenly loved common men (the more ignorant the better, I was given to understand) has survived the subsequent conviction of reason that I had not understood, but misunderstood, the Christian vision.

I was, besides, given to understand that 'being good' was the essence of my Christian duty. Now I knew perfectly well that when I was 'being good' I was at my worst, like a child sitting still in a stiff chair. Pinned

76

down to so narrow and negative a mode of being, compelled, besides, to pay attention to myself and to this 'being good' instead of to the marvels (whether of nature or of the imagination) which offered a world so much more spacious and more beautiful, I suffered, like my mother, from boredom, lack of interest in means and end alike; that 'good' Kathie who was the only outcome envisaged seemed to have nothing whatever in common with me, or with any of those great things I loved; rather that concentration of attention upon one's self seemed to close those vistas and expanses of nature and of poetry which were my real world.

But in the Greek gods (whose stories I found in my father's bookshelves where for him they formed part of 'the classics') I recognized the numinous principle which seemed to me to be entirely absent from my father's Christianity. I became their secret worshipper, absorbing their stories with the same impassioned delight as I learned the orders of flowers. Not only or principally did I absorb these forms with their myths and divine attributes from simplifications and children's versions *(Tanglewood Tales* and *The Heroes)* but, especially, from Smith's *Classical Dictionary*, which it never occurred to me to find dull; on the contrary, because it contained knowledge for which I at that time craved, I found it absorbing. I recognized, in the simple enumerations of the divine attributes, as in the little line-drawings after gems and sarcophagi (in this respect also like the creatures of nature) essential meaning, intrinsically intelligible, and indescribable otherwise than in those very forms, acts, and symbolic attributes. Useless to tell me that the Sunday School Jesus was a figure to be venerated when from those depictions I was shown of Him I could see that this was not so. Intuition is of complex and subtle totalities, and recognizes wholes before it distinguishes their parts; therefore, simplified for children, the divine figures become not more but less accessible to the imagination of childhood. The soul, which recognizes the gods by what Plato calls anamnesis, the calling to mind of what is written in our nature, was never young and will never be old, but exists in another principle. Children well understand the language of expressive form, and the childish naive is a sophisticated, adult and profoundly unimaginative taste. A child does not make critical comparisons, nor could I have said why I loved a dry-as-dust Classical Dictionary more than sentimental depictions and re-tellings 'for children' of the Christian story; but love itself is a judgement—the only judgement, after all, decisive in the end.

My increasingly inhuman 'scientific' vision had its dark side. At times 'objects' as we normally experience them seemed to lose their firm outline. How arbitrary, it then seemed to me, are those frontiers we choose to draw upon our world; we call this a table or a chair, that a rock or a lake, but what is that to nature? How precariously defined are the objects of our supposed knowledge, the picture of a world we paint upon the whirling shuddering flux of energy that plays before us. Sometimes the picture would disintegrate before my eyes, and all would be unknown and unknowable, without form and void; like so much painting of the present time which reflects that very experience of the dismantling and disintegration of the objects of the human world. Sometimes too I would look at people, seeing them not as people but as strange landscapes in which flowed rivers of blood where cells were living lives as separate as fish in an ocean from anything we call a 'person'. We look at a face and see it as wise, expressive, beautiful, human ; but what is a face, looked at in terms of nature, matter, science, but a cluster of sense-organs gathered for convenience at the top of a spinal cord enlarged and convoluted into what we call a brain? What is it that makes a face a face, more than the chest or the belly, inexpressive and animal? So I would think; and upon the thought would follow the terrible shift of consciousness by which the human image was removed entirely, and I cut off from my kind in a material order uninformed by soul.

Yet my chemistry master it was who first showed me the one face which, even at that time, inscribed itself upon my knowledge in a manner not to be gainsaid; as if, after all, divine foreknowledge had prepared, in terms of those lowest of all 'facts' which convince scientists, a miracle they could not refute. The little booklet on the Holy Shroud he lent me described, if I rightly remember, the chemistry of it; a number of 'scientific' facts about how a linen cloth soaked in aloes and the like, and laid over a human body still warm, a body which had suffered the agony of extreme suffering, might undergo the chemical changes necessary to produce something like a photographic negative. What forger, in the early middle-ages or at some earlier time (the shroud had belonged to the House of Savoy, and its history has long been known) would have thought of forging a negative image before the notion of a photographic negative existed anywhere in the world? But, of course, the scientists have their answers: there is nothing miraculous about the shroud, it is a mere matter of chemistry; what if it did once enfold the body of a man who was crucified, on whose brow are the marks of thorns and the spear-wound in his side? But that is not the miracle: the miracle is the face itself; *in imaginem dei*. The solemnity, the nobility, the peace, the perfect intellectuality and serene dignity of that face, of the tall kingly body, the folded hands, answered my folly, reproached my vanity, and kindled in my consciousness something like awe, recognition of the human mystery; for a face is something altogether other than the clay which bears its imprint.

CHAPTER THREE

A Suburban Idyll

I REVIVE the story of my thirteen-year-old self as if that Kathie, who still wore her light-brown hair hanging loose down her back on Sundays, had never been myself at all; and perhaps she really never was, or only in a certain sense. It is not that I wish to disown her—on the contrary, her story is not without poetry, is perhaps like an old poem found in a drawer and just good enough not to throw away; but I can no longer evoke her as myself, as I can the Kathie of Bavington. She was at best an aspect, not, like that earlier child, the whole of what I was. How seldom indeed does the whole person live and enact the present. However, if I was not wholly present, neither was I, as at later and worse times, wholly absent either.

The story begins by my father's bedside in the new local hospital where he was lying with his leg in plaster; he had been knocked off his bicycle by a tram in Ley Street. I was visiting him on my way home from school at four o'clock; his school-girl daughter, wearing her navy-blue drill-dress over a fairly white blouse, and panama hat encircled with the maroon and white school ribbon and badge; my two plaits of hair wispy and bedraggled at the end of a school day. On this day I found with my father a very tall young man with a bony but pimpled face, green eyes, and strange lips, the upper and the lower the same thickness, two long rectangles meeting in a straight line which was curiously expressive. To say exactly of what that line, well-drawn as by an artist, was expressive, I find extremely difficult; I can evoke the expression, but how put into words that characteristic fastidious look of discrimination, scorn, a sense of form and finesse which are seldom seen on faces in Ilford. That mouth proclaimed a non-participation more positive than reserve; yet the withdrawal was less a personal vanity than an aestheticism at odds with the world; Coriolanus' words to the common cry of curs whose breath he hated, unspoken but not unthought, might have drawn that line's 'I banish you'. This young man—to me he seemed a man—wore his well-cut suit with an air of natural elegance which made up for the pimples. Years later, seeing a portrait of Aubrey Beardsley, I recognized the type to which, both by nature and by imitation, he conformed. He looked like Beardsley; for in the suburbs people only look 'like' some person; the suburbs do not possess originals.

Roland Haye—he had recently added, like Balzac, a particle to his name in the hope of acquiring a little more identity and called himself, to the annoyance of his father, 'de la Haye'—had made some real effort to acquire the mental as well as the physical style of Beardsley, who for him was the type and exemplar of the culture to which he wished to become assimilated. This was the young man who, on my arrival, took his leave with a rather over-elaborate politeness, putting on his bowler hat with deliberate artistry. It was polite and perhaps thoughtful of Roland to have gone to visit my father, who had been his school-master, and who also taught the young men's class at the Cranbrook Park Wesleyan Methodist Church, which Roland's family attended; but I do not think my father liked him, any more than he would have liked Beardsley himself as a visitor. The standards implied by Roland Haye's conscious artistry of dress and manner were no less suspect to him than those green eyes, more proper to goats than to sheep. Yet it was through his devotion to my father that I met the man who destroyed for ever the family life which until then had seemed immutable.

I loved my father, at that time, completely and uncritically. Perhaps, as the best of fathers are, he was a little in love with his beautiful daughter, his only child; a child in whose features he could see himself imaged in my mother's finer substance; a love at once narcissistic and blameless, his only happy love, perhaps. At that fatal meeting—for so it proved—I was entirely without foreknowledge. As for Roland, I must have noticed him, for I can see him clearly, in my mind's eye, more than fifty years after; but if intuition said anything at all, it did not say 'This man is your true love'; nor was he, for first and last he remained a stranger to my soul. There was no recognition of a fatal encounter, none at all, scarcely even a shudder at those repulsive pimples; and I wonder whether the long succeeding story of our first love, so poignant, so enchanting, was not, for me at all events, only a long irrelevance, a detour.

To what does free-will really amount at such times as the gods of life choose to cast us for some part in the immortal play but freedom to say Yes or No to the adventure of our destiny? Once we have said Yes there is little we can do, and the president of the Immortals, in Aeschylean phrase . . . Ah well, I was not Tess, though my imagination at that time had certainly been formed by Hardy. It seemed to me then as if Hardy had written especially for me, that no one could understand, as I understood, passions natural and enduring, whole and unbroken, rooted in the earth itself. The gods may play with Hardy's people as they never could with James's or Proust's, subtle complex conscious beings as these may be, but the less plastic to the great opposeless wills. So at fourteen I was like one of those simple, deep-feeling unreflecting archetypal people who respond totally to the cosmic forces; but the other actors in the play acted from other scripts, or scriptures.

I find it extremely difficult to make a start on the narrative, to bring myself to look at those old photographs stored in my natural memory, but of which my soul has no memory at all. Could I, at the time, ever have believed it possible, that I would turn back so coldly to those once burning images? Yet I can see, written in the record of my life, that Book of Judgement, Roland (my father was home again now) coming through our garden gate, wearing this time (for it was Sunday) a blazer and an elegant straw boater. Elegance my father despised (as in P. G. Wodehouse, or Noël Coward) in part because all those loose locks, long locks, lovelocks, gay gear and going gallant the less Puritanical Gerard Manley Hopkins loved, reminded him, painfully perhaps, of those possibilities of myriadfold life from which the industrial poor must avert their eyes if they are to bear their lot. Those who live, besides, only to be, or to do, good, need (he no doubt would have thought) no elegance.

Was Roland's polite call made, this time, simply and solely on my father? It might have been so, for Roland had in him a deep need for a master whom he could admire and love. He played a little, as I remember, on that hated walnut piano, covered with silver vases and framed photographs, to which my mother drove me so unwillingly to 'practise', tearing me from my books. To my mother Roland appeared as an ally in her continual battle with her disobedient and ungrateful little girl, on whom money was spent which she could ill afford, to give me a 'chance' she never had, of acquiring the one useless accomplishment regarded, in that world, as desirable in a woman, to play the piano. Roland's example might help; he could play really difficult 'pieces', Ravel and Debussy and Chopin; if I would only practise, might not her child too be able to produce those dazzling allegros? In my home education was held to be able to produce anything and everything; heredity was discounted. Heredity was I think obscurely felt to be 'unfair', whereas education gave everyone a 'chance'. My mother was, besides, blind to the fact that I had inherited, not her own exquisitely soft hands with their touch of fairy delicacy, but my father's strong fists with knotted joints; the heritage of generations of coal-miners, the tools of whose craft were the pick and the shovel. When it was that Roland's green Cornish eyes first fell upon me I do not know; but soon after that call, our little family of three people whose lives seemed as one was electrified by an event unprecedented: Roland called to ask if I might go to tea at his house the following Sunday; he would call for me and return me to my parents at the evening chapel service.

I was perhaps flattered at being singled out, but, even more, enchanted by the vista I glimpsed opening from the boredom, the non-life which so long had held me. I saw a path and wanted (of course), to follow it and to see to what marvels it might lead. Certainly love was a thought which never crossed my mind; but thoughts of music, books, and a wonderful young man who knew so much of these things seemed something altogether to be desired. My mother, as innocent as myself, never dreaming that her little girl (for I was still, even physically, a child) could attract a young man who played Chopin and talked of Frazer's *Golden Bough* (not a book known to my father, since it had appeared after his student-days and was not on the school syllabus) otherwise than intellectually, backed me up; nor did I see any reason why my father should not approve of an acquaintance so educational. It was a shock to me when he was angry and troubled, as though I had suggested doing something wrong. Conscious of my innocence, thinking him unjust, I argued and protested like the spoiled child I was; for my parents had always told me that children should be given a reason for obedience, not merely asked to obey. Did not, I argued, the Hayes go to the Cranbrook Park Wesleyan Methodist Church? Were they not, therefore, good people? Why did he not like Roland? And so, against his judgement, my father gave in. It was my first serious disobedience; and even to this day I do not know who was right, my father, acting as he did from his experience, or I, winged with the impulse of life.

Had I obeyed, had I at every stage obeyed my father, I would never, certainly, have become a poet. I would have become, had he had his wish, I suppose, first an English mistress in a good girls' secondary school, and perhaps in the end a headmistress. I would have lived a life of social usefulness, a life dedicated to the service of 'others', my happiness in religion, my relaxation singing, perhaps, in some church choir. I do not think that at any point in my father's ambitions for me marriage would have been thought of; I do not think he had any illusions about marriage; he had seen too much of those weary slaves who

> With one chained friend, perhaps a jealous foe
> The dreariest and the longest journey go.

His own marriage to my mother he would have said was an exceptionally happy one; it would have been worse than useless to think otherwise. He would, I think, have wished me to avoid, if possible, a pitfall which at worst could open into a hell, and at best could lead to—well, not to what the poets have called love.

My mother, for her part, wished me above all to be 'pretty' and happy and to be able to accompany songs on the piano; not to ruin my eyesight over books, but to have 'a husband and children' as was 'natural' for 'young girls'. All these in the abstract, or collective sense. That, on one

82

level; that is what she would have said she wished for me because she knew that 'mothers' (the general term again) did wish just that for their 'daughters'. She very often reproached me for not being like 'other daughters'; but then, was she like 'other mothers'? She would never have confessed, even to herself, the wild aberrances of her true dreams and desires; but I believe that, secretly, she wanted me to live out the myth, to walk with the gods, to explore those long vistas of passions, and dreams and intellections, forbidden to her. I wonder, now, if my life has not been a realization of my mother's most secret dreams. It was she who wrote down, before I could hold a pencil, those first poems so many children make; she, not my father, English master as he was, who treasured my words in her heart.

No doubt my father was right in his sense that the *dharma* of a schoolmaster's daughter was to be a schoolmistress not a poet. He had a strong sense of social order, never realizing that my mother and I had never in fact belonged to the world he served; we were social exiles, no terra firma under our feet, able only to sink or to soar in a great void. This was self-evident to her and to me; but he never knew that in marrying my mother he had married a being of another element. Her seal-skin hidden in the domestic meal chest she never found; never returned to the ocean of her freedom. It was I who found it, I who was set free.

When I overruled my father, and, abetted by my mother, went to tea with Roland, I was at the first parting of the ways. Now, still suffering as I am from the lifelong consequences, still permanently injured from the many wounds I received, and still more by those I gave, because of what followed, I try to remember again what made me choose, what, indeed, I did choose. It was not, certainly, sexual desire, or even sexual vanity. My choice had nothing to do with sex at all. Roland offered, as I immediately sensed, a culture less meagre than that of my home; the living culture of our time, Gilbert Murray and Frazer, Jane Harrison and the Celtic Revival, Flecker and Dowson and the *Testament of Beauty* and Promenade concerts, instead of home, homework and Methodism.

But if I chose rightly the choice had its price; never was the breach between my father and myself quite mended. I rejected, then, his dearest values; and among the gods who judge, if some cast white stones for me, others cast black, and rightly so. I rejected socialism and the greatest good of the greatest number for those values which few can reach, in the belief that the high and beautiful things are of value in themselves; are the true ends of life, which the breeding generations exist only to serve and to realize. I think I already knew all that at the time very clearly. I rejected 'whatsoever thy hand findeth to do . . .' as a principle that can lead to a static and narrow virtue. My mother and I had seen vistas of wonder, the green green ways to fairyland. My mother only saw those vistas; I travelled them. The scale fell as it was loaded, on my mother's side. It was my mother in me who before me had walked on the heather moors, who was always watching for a door to open. What I would find through the door mattered little; there was a door and through it I went on my way, or perhaps my Way.

So I went to tea with Roland Haye on the following Sunday. He arrived to call for me, and we walked, in embarrassed silence, along misty muddy Essex lanes and along by the wooden fence of the Claybury asylum, through a bluebell wood, and so back into suburbia and privet hedges to the Hayes' house; 210 Cranbrook Road; a house in the 'better', and older, part of Ilford, a house with some rudiments of refinement, and maid in cap and apron to open the front door.

Roland and I had in common one passion: our hatred of suburbia, our determination to escape. He like me was in exile. Old Mr. Haye was a Cornishman, from Hale, a grey squirrel in a London office who had never become tamed to his cage; he too loved Hardy's novels with that passion we feel only for works that tell our own story. Hardy held before old Mr. Haye images of that from which he was so bitterly exiled, a life still un-severed from its ancient roots. Mrs. Haye too was an exile, but of another kind; each suffered alone. She had met her true love after the birth of her first child, Roland; whom, in consequence, she never perhaps loved. He, the lover in the world of never-to-be, was I think a doctor; for a large print of *The Doctor* hung on a wall of the living room. Now she was houseproud, her dark oak furniture (replica Jacobean) gleamed and her cakes never failed to rise; yet no one in the house was happy.

Those Sunday visits became habitual. Roland would take me into the little dining-room at the back of the house, where he would sit down at his upright piano, piled high with music. There I would sit beside him on a dining-room chair, and he played Chopin's Nocturnes and Mazurkas and his Ballades, whose language of wild longing spoke for Roland's soul, as Hardy's less passionate nostalgia for his father's; Chopin and Ravel and Debussy. He made me sing, to his accompaniment, the Kennedy Frasers' adaptations of Hebridean songs; the first echo of the Celtic revival to reach me. Afterwards we would walk to the church where I would rejoin my parents in their pew.

Roland was already at cross-purposes with the Methodists, amongst whom he regarded my father as a shining exception. The culture which made my father suspicious of Roland from the beginning was of course bound to make Methodism intolerable to him; 'a veneer of culture', my father contemptuously called it; but what else, after all, could it be, in that world? Roland was bound to the Cranbrook Park church only by being the assistant organist, sitting in the organ loft turning the pages for Mr. Raymond Causer. To have access to an organ was, after all, something; but he had already begun to struggle against the crassness, vulgarity and stupidity of a religion of shopkeepers. Mr. Haye, like my father, was loyal to a Methodism which no longer existed, the revivalism of John Wesley who had preached, bare-headed, to the rough and ignorant men of the Cornish tin-mines as he had preached to the coal-miners of County Durham. Both were for ever deploring the falling-away of Methodism from that early fervour, but without learning the obvious lesson from history.

I cannot suppose that in the silent, light-brown-haired school-girl Roland had divined a kindred rebel. I do not suppose he wished me to have any attributes but those of the mirror of his dreams and longings. I, for him, was to be that which Chopin so mournfully and exquisitely desired, the for-ever-unattainable soul of love. For him I was virginity itself, that infinite potentiality upon which he might project passions erotic and religious at once.

It is false to imagine that 'love' can be considered as something distinct from a culture. The mere animal instinct is less than human unless tinged with some mode of feeling, shone upon by the light of imagination, adorned in some style, humanized and ordered by poetry or music. Our style was the nostalgia of Chopin; nostalgia for a perfection high beyond hope of attainment, for which we would rather live in mourning for ever than once forget. The religious eroticism of Verlaine; 'And behold, a Virgin shall conceive and bear a child' overwhelmed us with its archetypal power in a way almost impossible to convey to those for whom mere carnality had dulled the resonances of the awe-inspiring mystery of the incarnation which lies behind sexual desire, the mournful ecstasy of Rossetti's lovers who with burning eyes gaze upon one another in a still trance that possession itself would break. How precariously such love hung suspended over the sorrowful depths of the Decadence I had not read enough of the literature of the time to know; Roland certainly was haunted by some shadow of Dorian Gray, and of 'that wicked book' *A Rebours* (a very childish book, but then we were children and Huysmans the acme of sophistication to Roland). Yet our love was not without forms and images which gave to it the semblance of a style which we, struggling to rise above an environment devoid of culture, and above all devoid of style, strove with a certain heroism to create. It is true that we dressed our passion in the masks created by others; but for what are the forms of art created unless to enable the *filii et filiae* to live their loves beautifully?

For, before many Sundays had passed, we had been assigned by the immortals the parts they had all along known we would play. I remember the failing afternoon light shining, as in a Rossetti painting, through the west window into the little crowded room. We had not gone with the family to church but remained alone in the house, with the maid. Roland played, and I turned the pages of his music. Perhaps he played only moderately well, but the music spoke to us all its message of Paradise, of a time and a place where we were not but longed to be, as we sat caged in the little suburban back room, our narrow view closed, beyond the William Morris curtains, by Mr. Haye's mown lawn and his chrysan-themum plants tied stiffly to their bamboo canes. We yearned for what Chopin yearned for, but possessed no more than we.

He played the third Ballade; and, like Dante's lovers—Roland must have known them, if only through Rossetti, though I did not—we were entranced by the beauty of what we had heard; or rather, Roland was, for in retrospect I can see that I am telling his story, not my own. His left hand, leaving the keys, he laid on my right hand; his narrow hand, with its 'tied' thumb. I was afraid, though of what I did not know. He could scarcely speak as he asked me to go with him into the front parlour; the room where *The Doctor* hung. He led me to his father's big leather arm-chair, and there he seated me, as on a throne; then with deliberation (how often had he, in fancy, rehearsed this scene?) he placed a brown velvet cushion on the carpet at my feet, and kneeling on it he declared his love; a boy's first love, for the archetypal virgin. He would wait, he said, for five years, for seven years; no matter for how long: 'some day you will be my wife', he said. Someday, someday, that infinite distance between desire and realization which passion peoples with images of the beautiful, with poetry, music and painting; for the distance between a dream and a realization is greater than we knew: nothing less than the distance between Plotinus' here and yonder: a distance in kind. Does not all the poetry of life lie in that enchanted land between our desire and its goal?

I had no thought of love; certainly none for Roland. If in my imagination a lover lay hidden it was not he. That, as I sat enthroned in the Sunday evening fading glow I very well knew; indeed I was about to say so, but was too surprised and too embarrassed to find words. I was a child absolutely, virgin as ignorant as Verlaine himself could have wished. But before I had found those words for which I searched, Roland had said, 'May I kiss you?—only one kiss', and those lips of equal width had touched mine before the shudder of revulsion from the pimples, the bony jaw, the green eyes of the wrong man could form itself into words of refusal. So he kissed my lips, and from one moment to the next I ceased to be a child and knew instantaneously that I was a virgin destined for the wedding night.

As he had placed that brown cushion so deliberately at my feet, I had realized, with odd clarity, that the scene was rehearsed. But after that kiss, he repeated the lines (were they too rehearsed?)

O lyric Love, half angel and half bird
And all a wonder and a wild desire—

—and I was taken and caught. It seemed as though the lines were given to me as faith is plighted with a ring of gold. So our particular selves respond to the universal of the ever repeated story, each saying, in Yeats's words, 'Oh that none ever loved but you and I!' The words were as if spoken by Roland to me alone; the living test of true poetry. To say I loved Roland at that moment would be untrue; I never loved him, perhaps never even liked him. But he awoke in me 'love', impersonal erotic love, and laid claim to it before I could draw breath to refuse; and since he it was who had evoked in me that virgin passion, I could no more escape than the *kore* from Pluto's gloomy palace; indeed I felt myself to be bound by a solemn, sacramental bond to him, a man whom I would not have chosen, did not choose.

Perhaps in a simpler age that great inflowing tide of instinctive life on which we were so ecstatically swept away would have been enough to carry the *filii et filiae* through the stations of puberty and marriage and the bearing of children, upborne on the single long green wave of the life, impersonal and immortal, that lives in us. In Arcadia, youth and maiden are interchangeable, the individual mattering only insofar as he and she can play the parts assigned, embody the genius of the one life; and participation in that impersonal wave of life and all its deep joy and wisdom, which informs now one, now another young and nubile body, is the reward of obedience to the great opposeless wills. I can see why, since natural love is such, marriages may be called indissoluble; if the mystery goes by the pattern there can be but one initiation, and the virgin is bound for ever to the man who with a kiss summons her to the play.

Neither then nor later did Roland attempt to seduce me—the *mores* of our class and generation precluded that no less than did the poem we were living, the music we echoed. Yet in that ill-starred first love I knew and understood all that the mere gods have to reveal, an instantaneous epiphany of the mysteries of womanhood. How awe-inspiring, how sacred it all seemed, as if I had passed through some initiation, as if the parlour in Cranbrook Road had been some *villa dei mysterii*, and *The Doctor* that bull-faced Dionysus whose phallic power makes the little brown-haired virgin weep on the knees of the Pompeian priestess: but I had no priestess to advise or comfort me: all must be kept secret, for what would our parents say? They must not know.

So we set out upon our seven years' waiting. The wedding night was for us to be the realization of the perfection of all the joy, beauty and freedom of which works of art are but a reflection; so we thought. But had we known it, only another symbol of that for which the soul waits, another reflection as 'mirror in mirror mirrored is all the show'. But we never travelled far enough to learn that; the memory of first love remains for ever captured in the amber light of Rossetti's *Beata Beatrice*, the resonance of the third Ballade of Chopin.

But if the two goddesses did not, after all, get my virginity, they exerted all their power to claim what was their due; as, being goddesses, precisely, of the life-cycle, they are bound to do. On those Sunday walks along the asylum fence, Roland's long bony arm would now be round my waist; and in the little wood we would kiss beneath a wild apple-tree and weave dreams of that 'someday'. We would spend the first night of a bliss never-to-be in some Greek temple built in Avalon among the apple-trees, the singing and the gold; or we would change the style and live in a small brown house built for love and us to dwell in, in a forsaken garden where now sleeps the crimson petal now the white, and the rose-red seaweed mocks the rose. The golden world lay, for Roland, west of Cornwall, where sweet gales blew and the pebbles on the strand were all of amethyst. We were much indebted not only to *art nouveau* but also to the Celtic revival for the adornments of our dream house under its *ciel féerique et divin*; or, again, ought I to say that he was; and I, ignorant enough, naive enough, amorous enough, young enough to follow enthralled, trod on his dreams; softly, I hope.

With all this he told me, with much emotion, the facts of sex, exacting a promise that I would bear his child; and I, powerless as a rabbit before a weasel, or like Milton's lady in the chair of another enchanter, had not the power to refuse, though my blood ran cold at the thought, for I did not want any child at all, and certainly not his. The *ciel féerique et divin* was another matter; that I did not see merely as nature's ruse to cheat us into fulfilling her ends. Even then, was I planning in my heart to cheat nature for the sake of poetry?

For although I gave myself so completely to the weaving of a dream, something in me remained aloof. Meanwhile I was content to be the mirror of his dreams, which passed over the surface of my fancy without leaving a trace. Beneath its surface I still kept secret faith with my intention of becoming a poet; the two futures were both too remote for their incompatibility to become a reality to be reckoned with.

And yet in retrospect I realize what golden doors he opened. He took me, on his nineteenth birthday, to the Queen's Hall, to hear Casals play the Bach 'cello suite; my first concert. Afterwards we went to an Italian restaurant in Charlotte Street (among so many I have never found it again) —my first Italian restaurant. With our meal we drank cider; my first alcohol, amber essence of the apple-tree, the singing and the gold. It was with Roland I saw *The Immortal Hour*, with Gwen Ffrangcon-Davies in the part which enchanted my generation. He gave me, on my birthday, a bottle of scent; my first scent, *Trèfle Incarnat*, blown over summer meadows filled with dewy clover. My father, who dearly loved the theatre, had taken me to Shakespeare, to Ibsen, to Galsworthy, to Barrie, to Shaw; I had loved these happy family occasions, but they had not the magic of first love in them; and Roland, besides, was of my generation, and we listened—or he listened and I echoed what he heard—for the new voices that spoke for our time. Never were two star-crossed lovers more athirst for poetry and music which would give us the words and melodies in which our great love could be clothed in forms of beauty worthy of it. If we consumed much bad poetry, we at least kept our souls alive on it.

It was Roland who first quoted Blake to me; the Blake beyond *Songs of Innocence*, that is. He had, I think, read Swinburne's essay on Blake (Swinburne's dead roses and the rose-red seaweed that mocks the rose flourished in the coign of a cliff in our Western paradise, and his asterisks stirred in us strange emotions, for even asterisks can be incitements to carnal desires) and believed, like Swinburne, that Blake was on the side of 'evil'; as, by our parents' standards, so he was. I was much appalled by some of the Proverbs of Hell, with their incitement to a carnality which I knew was, when all was said and done, forbidden fruit.

We would both surely have outgrown that first love; and now I wonder if Roland, as he murmured Dowson's lines,

My heart is sick of an old passion;
I have been faithful to thee, Cynara! in my fashion—

was not already aware of the long vista of a life in which our young love would be something long past. This love, into which he poured the very essence of his soul, and all the words and the music of immortality which he would make his own, he laid down, like wine, to mature perhaps when he was old. It was as if this love, so pure it was, could never again be equalled by anything his life could bring to flower; a love beautiful, sorrowful, renunciatory, a minor poem in the mode of the *Décadence* composed by a strange imaginative exile from a world of art who might, had he not been born in Ilford, have been an original and not a mere replica. When he quoted *Cynara* I too was moved by a strange mournful presentiment. In the moment of intensest life, in the very Now of Arcadia, we seemed almost to foreknow, with a poignancy of pity, the later selves we would be, who would have wandered away from the apple-tree, who would be far from the singing and the gold, the present ecstasy so intense that we could not conceive a state in which it would have been forgotten; and if we could, our grief for that forgetting would have been the stronger. So I remember my Arcadian self wept for what we might become; yet now the exile can look back upon those young lovers in their Arcadia without envy, indeed with another kind of pity, a pity without grief. 'The wind blows the ghosts out of the garden'; when together we read Flecker's *Hassan* we did not know that we were ourselves the ghosts.

But the end, for us, involved more painful and more complex passions than those of the poems on which we fed our dreams.

I told my mother, as I remember, as we walked home together one evening after my weekly piano lesson; Roland, I said, had asked me to marry him, and I had promised: in seven years' time. 'But you are only a bairn', she said. She in her innocence had no more imagined such a possibility than I had myself, and must now have reproached herself bitterly for over-persuading my father, who had proved to be right. I too had a guilty conscience; and so now I made her promise to keep our secret; and I think she did promise. But of course such a promise neither could nor should have been kept; and not long after, the storm broke. It was again a Sunday, as I remember, and I was playing hymns on my unloved piano, singing Wesley's 'Jesu lover of my soul' with the pleasing emotion of one who had never known the rolling of waters or the high tempest outside the words and music of the hymn itself. My parents were upstairs in their bedroom and I could hear them talking. Presently my mother came downstairs, much distressed and weeping; then my father; and the storm of life broke upon me then. He began to question me: what had Roland said, done? He had not seduced me, indeed; but he had kissed me; and he had touched my breast. Never before had I seen my father in a passion of anger, and my soul froze. He did not blame me, but only Roland, using of him words that seared my very soul by the ugliness and obscenity with which they suddenly defiled the texture of our dreams. He forbade me ever to see Roland again. My poor father left the house in grief and rage, saying he was going to kill Roland. I do not blame my father—he after all knew more of 'life' than I, and feared I would be, or had already been, seduced. His one miscalculation was the strength of his own moral influence, not only upon myself but upon Roland as well, who admired my father boundlessly. We were, besides, so young that we thought nothing of waiting five, ten, a thousand years for the realization of the shimmering dream; even, perhaps, it was the dream we wanted, not the realization; but how it might have ended if my father had not intervened it is useless to speculate. Unfortunately he intervened too late, and his prohibition served only to strengthen what we now thought of as our great love. What was worse was the searing by my father's indictment as something obscene of a love that had seemed too pure and beautiful for this earth. From that wound, as it seems to me fifty years later, I never quite recovered.

How long before was it, I wonder—I recall the dream suspended out of time, but it belonged, certainly, still to childhood—that I woke one night from one of my nightmares (I was subject to bloodcurdling nightmares, nearly all now forgotten) and cried out for help? How often had my father's calm and comforting presence driven away my demons! On this night, I saw my bedroom door open, and my father came in; but then his face changed and turned into a demon-face and I screamed again, this time in the very extreme of terror. This time my real father heard me, and came up the stairs, and comforted me; the first awakening had been a dream within a dream. Now the nightmare seemed to enact itself in waking life.

I would not, even now, have for a moment considered disobeying my father; but Roland, whom he had visited and forbidden to see me, and I do not doubt scathed and seared, though of course without doing him any physical violence—for that would have been against his mild Christian code—did disobey; he wrote me a letter asking me to meet him: he would stand, he said, every Sunday at a certain gate into the fields and wait for me. But I gave my father the letter and did not go.

There was, however, one way we could, if not meet, at least see one another, which not even my father could forbid. The Hayes' pew in the Cranbrook Park Wesleyan Methodist Church was at right-angles to ours in the transept under the pulpit. Twice on Sundays and once on Wednesday evenings we could gaze at one another askance, Roland sitting beside his father and mother, sister and brother; and I, my light-brown hair loose on my shoulders under my blue velour hat, between my parents. Nor was it only to see my lover that I insisted on going to all the services, even the week-night evening services, but also, after the first shock of guilt and sorrow, in the hope of finding help in the religion in which my father himself so fervently believed; so mixed are our motives. Perhaps also I wanted to prove to my father, by carrying it into the bosom of his own chapel, the innocence of our great love.

I remember one November night—only a few weeks after our separation—a fog came down so thick that after the Wednesday evening prayer meeting I could scarcely see the road; and then, a little in front of me, I saw Roland, his tall stooping figure darkly wrapped in a grey greatcoat. He did not—faithful to our promise to my father, since I wished to obey—speak to me, but made a sign to me to follow him and, Orpheus-like, he led his Eurydice through the yellow fog, the light of his electric torch showing me the pavement. The nimbus of moisture on the texture of his greatcoat enshrouded him in foggy dew, like those souls who, descending into the

Hades of this world become, so the mythologists tell, 'drenched in moisture'. He led me through the bye-roads of Ilford, and up Cranbrook Road to the garden gate of West View; and only then did he turn, looked at me in a farewell charged with all the nostalgia of the poetry we loved; and we parted, he like Clerk Saunders into a darkness where I might not follow him, I through the gap of the privet hedge, whose each leaf was edged with its rime of cold mist, to our front door where the dim light in the hall was broken into a pattern like a shattered star through the frosted glass of the pane. How clearly the images return, how far and faint the emotions of the actors! After this, I memorized at school the Shakespeare sonnet

> Let me not to the marriage of true minds
> Admit impediments; Love is not love
> Which alters when it alteration finds,
> Or bends with the remover to remove.

This too was an act of defiance against my father's authority, for Shakespeare, like John Wesley, could not be called in question; but I remember how savagely he said to me, 'very well, love in your minds as much as you like, I am only concerned that you do not meet again in the body'. I took up the challenge, and tried, poor child, poor stubborn wilful child, to learn Shakespeare's love of minds; for I did not doubt that Shakespeare and Wesley were at one with my father in their condemnation of the flesh; as perhaps they are.

Religion, then, was for us not so much a source of wisdom, strength or love, as a weapon; to me a defensive shield, but to Roland, more resourceful than I, also of attack. To Methodist fathers only one thing was perhaps worse, in those days, in their young than a love affair, and that was 'going to Rome'. Roland began to show signs of going to Rome.

The signs indeed had already begun to appear before our enforced separation. When I first saw the elegant pimpled youth with the boater, Roland was earning his living as a clerk in the Patents Office by day, and studying medicine at evening classes at King's College in the Strand. Perhaps he was fulfilling his mother's secret instigation, her old love for the nameless one in whose honour *The Doctor* hung in the parlour, whose heavy furniture she so dutifully and so joylessly polished. At about the time we met, Roland had passed his first M.B. examination; and now he must ask his father for the money to continue his studies as a full-time medical student.

No one, not even his mother, knew what his father's salary was; and when the old Cornishman refused, Roland assumed—his mother too, it may be—that his father could have, but would not, pay for his son's training. No one ever knew; but how precariously the respectability of suburban households was suspended over a chasm no one in Ilford could long forget. Only when the circuit-steward of the Cranbrook Park Wesleyan Methodist Church died behind his trim privet hedge was it discovered that months before he had lost his job, and that his widow had not enough money to buy a coffin. And so, one day, entering the office where for thirty years or more he had worked for a city firm of wholesale drapers, the little Cornishman was told that his services were no longer required. He was within a year of pensionable age, and this dishonourable form of economy was well known in the City. The class with whom such risks were taken could not retaliate, lacking the means, or indeed the mentality, to defend themselves; for the shame of letting it be known that they had been 'sacked'. Mr. Haye's story is a typical Ilford tragedy; the shock nearly killed him. But that was some years later.

Who, then, is ever to blame for anything? The father best knew his own insecurity; not a young man when he married he had two children younger than Roland; but the eldest son bitterly blamed his father for debarring him from his dream of becoming a doctor, not knowing over what a void was suspended that neat, restrictive suburban villa with trim maid in white cap and apron.

It was soon, then, after my first visit to the Hayes' house that Roland led me up to his room, pulled open the bottom drawer of his chest, and showed me in it his white overall, folded away. To it was pinned a card on which he had written the word 'forgotten'. This he made me read. How typical that childish histrionic gesture; but only now do I realize that the closing of the career upon which he had set his heart was more than a disappointment; it was a mutilation. His, too, was a typical suburban tragedy.

With medicine, forgotten or no, barred to him, Roland turned to religion; for the bars of Ilford chafed him more painfully than ever now that a way of escape had been closed. He quoted much from *The Hound of Heaven*; I never liked the poem, then or now, a hound pursuing a creature it would presently tear bleeding to pieces seeming to me now, as then, an image singularly inapt for the divine love; besides the inevitable confusion with *The Hound of the Baskervilles*. However, the poem served, for Roland, the double purpose of fitting his mood of religiosity, and of annoying his father. Since the author was a Catholic the plain implication was that Roland was being hounded into the Church of Rome. He began to sneer and jeer at 'Prots'; he would tell, in the same spirit of defiance as I memorized Shakespeare's one-hundred and sixteenth sonnet, the story of some evangelical called Kensit, deservedly killed by a brick heaved at him by an outraged Irish Catholic for 'insulting Our Lady'.

Rome, in Ilford, was known to those of us who had never crossed the forbidden threshold of the Catholic Church in the High Road in the person of Father Palmer; whose aged figure was to be seen in Ilford's older and drabber 'Streets' and 'Roads', and even sometimes in the newer 'Gardens' with their well-kept secrets. His flat, wide clerical hat suggested the alien and ancient faith he represented; nor was it entirely imagination that set him apart from the ministers and even the vicar, who were not 'priests'; a word that still carried, in my childhood, a dread significance, of the fires of the Inquisition. His lined face, as I recall its awful impact upon me, was like a relief-map of the human condition; disturbingly, frighteningly unlike the unwritten, un-made faces of the suburb-dwellers amongst whom we moved. And because I was too young to see it as beautiful the old priest's face seemed to me ugly. His presence amongst us was somehow alarming: 'There's Father Palmer', my mother would say, while he was still a long way off. And his passing would remind us that in our town still dwelt the Scarlet Woman. For Catholics, we knew (and we knew little else), worshipped the Virgin Mary, and were for the most part sinners. They 'went to confession' and were absolved of their sins by the priest, only to commit the very same sins again almost immediately afterwards. To me, brought up in a religion which imposed the simple obligation never to sin, this seemed very strange and shocking; for I had never consciously met any person who had 'sinned', but only 'good' people to whom it never occurred to think of themselves as sinners, or even as potential sinners. Therefore when Father Palmer passed, he brought with him the aura of his unholy holy office of ministering to that unknown, anathematized section of humanity, its sinners.

Just how true this picture was I learned nearly fifty years later, from one who had known Father Palmer better than I. Remembering Ilford and its dire respectability, what more natural than that conversation should turn also to Edith Thompson; who in her tragic story had so poignantly experienced the frustration that world of drab mediocrity imposed upon a dream of love and joy and beauty. She, a dreamer of those dreams which in Ilford belonged to the world of never-to-be, was convicted of the murder her lover committed for her sake. Dreaming a dream like hers, I attempted to make poetry its realization; and Roland—dreamed of becoming the anathematized thing itself and seeking Paradise in the habit of religion. So it was, that, fifty years after, I heard how Edith Thompson, condemned and waiting for her hanging (and how I too had waited with her through that interminable agony of delay) had wished to be received into the Catholic Church; for where else could she have hoped to find refuge? And she had sent for Father Palmer. The English law had not allowed her to receive instruction and baptism from him; for she was recorded in their books as 'C. of E.'; but he did visit and converse with her at the distance prison bars allowed; and after her death her sister had received the baptism Edith Thompson had only desired. There had been another murderer too—the 'taxi-cab' murderer, a young man who had committed a crime of passion (his victim was a Catholic actress) and who, apalled at his own guilt, had likewise sent for Father Palmer. He, more fortunate than Edith Thompson, had been received into the one Refuge of Sinners that suburban Hades knew.

My father, like most of those we knew, had held the sentence upon Edith Thompson to be just; for she had been guilty of a crime only less pardonable than murder—adultery. Whatever might be said of forgiveness, the Puritan morality was in truth that of the Old Testament—'the wages of sin is death'; dread words early making my own heart contract with fear, for all my earnest resolve never to 'sin'. That morality knew nothing of 'sin' as a state of being; only of 'sins', discoverable, specific acts which were at all costs to be avoided. No sacramental forgiveness of sins mitigated that narrow and simple rule. The pity was less that some of its adherents were hypocrites than that so many practised that morality with total and life-destroying sincerity.

It was Roland who had told me that old story about the man who, having committed a murder, rushed in remorse to his Protestant Minister, only to be told never to set foot in chapel again. He then went to the Vicar, who was embarrassed by so ungentlemanly an avowal. He went last of all to the Catholic Priest, and brought out once more his confession, 'Father I have committed murder'. The reply, 'How many times, my son?' was not, for us, a joke; it was too close to the reality in which we were ourselves involved.

Therefore it was that when, in his turn, Roland found himself in the toils of life and accused by my father of 'sin', he too turned to the Church of the Virgin Mary, the Refuge of Sinners; though not to Father Palmer, for Roland's sense of style demanded some more dramatic, more aesthetic setting. It was to Westminster Cathedral (accessible to him from his 'office' in the City) of which another pupil of Father Palmer is now Cardinal Archbishop that he went seeking sanctuary.

Indeed that great building was a vital part of the whole aesthetic network of interwoven strands which made up the culture of those years. From Verlaine to Francis Thompson, from *A Rebours* to *La Cathédrale*, from *La Fille aux cheveux de lin* to *La Cathédrale Engloutie*, from the white overall to soutane and biretta was a modulation of key entirely within the style of the period. The brick walls of the cathedral were still austerely bare, but for the encrusted richness of a few chapels. Eric Gill's Stations of the Cross were new, and no less potent as symbolic embodiments of the aspirations of our age than the Sidhe, or Gilbert Murray's little green-backed volumes of Euripides, or Vaughan Williams's music, or Cecil Sharp's collections of folk-songs. What more natural to a youth hurt, frustrated in his ambition to become a doctor, his texture of love-dreams torn by the conflict of guilt, than to turn to that religion, more authoritative than parents, which can open even in the suburbs a door of escape from meanness of culture and narrowness of life into all the grandeur, beauty, dignity and wisdom of Christian civilization? Perhaps, too, like Poe, Thompson, Huysmans and the rest, there was something of the erotic-sensuous in the spell which drew him to the dull gold of dim mosaic, the wavering candles, the still sanctuary-lamp in dark side-chapel, and that great Byzantine cross which hangs suspended in the incense smoke of Westminster Cathedral.

> Lo, in yon brilliant window-niche
> How statue-like I see thee stand,
> The agate lamp within thy hand,
> Ah! Psyche, from the regions which
> Are holy land.

It was from Roland that I first heard the name of Gerard Manley Hopkins; whose few poems in *The Spirit of Man* he pointed out to me in the little copy of that book he gave me; a poet whom I was to hear later in Cambridge, but in terms how different. For Roland his poems were not 'literature' but words of power, living words, speaking from the heart of Newman's convert to the heart of a semblable and brother, a young man living a similar experience, feeling in himself the desire to go 'where springs not fail'. I, not feeling in myself any response to that call, trembled I think as one might on the edge of a cliff over which one does not wish to throw oneself. But how different—and how much closer to the heart of poetry—was Roland's response to Hopkins than the literary detachment of those Cambridge critics for whom the heart's blood of the poet was colourless, odourless and tasteless. As my grandparents had sung to me the songs of Scotland years before, as if speaking their own immediate feelings, so Roland spoke Hopkins's words as if his own; for they gave utterance to his own being. What a degradation of poetry it is, God knows, that any should dare to speak its words otherwise. The 'detach-ment' of criticism is something monstrous and perverted in comparison with that living utterance, spoken from life to life, and for the living of life. And should a poet set pen to paper who is not prepared to meet that test of speaking for any heart in a situation of vital need of words to give form to some crisis of the life? The critics turn into a dead language the most living language of all; and I am glad that my first encounter with Hopkins's poetry was of a living kind.

The story, then, resumes again when—was it a year after our separation? I do not remember, nor does it matter—when, in the time such events take to ripen, Roland's father came to plead with mine that we be allowed to meet again; for his son had gone into a monastery with the intention of becoming a monk. Not, as it proved, Rome after all; he had so far compromised with his father's strong prejudices as to become an 'Anglo-Catholic'. My father shared Mr. Haye's sense of the gravity of this new threat to the ignorant and narrow sect to which piety towards their ancestors bound them. Perhaps too the continued misery of his daughter inclined my father to lift a ban imposed, as he by now must have seen, too late to undo the harm from which he would have saved me if he could: the harm and pain of sexual awakening. The forces of attack now were more powerful than the demon Eros; the Blessed Virgin and all the saints were a threat more to be feared; 'Mariolatry', as it was called. So it came about that at the end of the school term in which I sat my London Matriculation examination I found myself travelling in the Cornish Riviera Express in a corner seat, with Mrs. Haye and Ernest opposite and little Charity curled on my knee. Mr. Haye was to follow for his brief fortnight a few days later; and Roland. I was happy because I was to see him again, and because our parents were no longer enemies.

The village of Gwithian, not far from Hale, was still, in those days, Cornish. That Celtic race, who felt themselves more akin to the Bretons than to the English, and whose language had died within living memory, were still fighting off the invasion of English summer visitors; money, then, was not the supreme value. Two English maiden ladies who had called their house 'Apple Orchard', and who took summer guests, were persecuted until they left; their laundry would be cut to ribbons on their clothes-line during the night, and the like. Mr. Haye saw himself as the returning native, not the alien invader: and I, a Scottish Separatist at heart, warmed to this race who were making a last stand for Merlin's land, Avalon and the Grail. Among those deep lanes of vervain and marjoram and harts-tongue ferns, where glow-worms shone in the dusk, I felt clean of Ilford. It was Roland's father, I think, whom I really loved; he who treated me always with old-fashioned courtesy, and who loved Hardy as I did. Roland's more urbane literary tastes were, truth to say, beyond my scope; but Mr. Haye's longing to return to his roots was like my own. I smoked my first cigarette with charming Ernest (who went to the Merchant Taylor's School, a 'public school', and who already had the manner of 'a gentleman') in the coign of a cliff between highland and lowland, basking not in tragedy but in the summer sun.

When Roland at last arrived I discovered that I was out of my depth; his fantasies had raced ahead, nourished on books I had not read, drawn from sources unguessed by me. He arrived with characteristic panache, with a rosary ever in his pocket or his hand, and sandals on his bare feet. From me he averted his eyes, to me he addressed no word. I was no longer, it seemed, his lyric love, but temptation itself, the poison apple, the gate of hell. How near young tragedy lies to comedy, comedy to tragedy! But in retrospect I do not laugh, for the tragedy—Roland's not mine—seems to me now both other and greater than I thought it then. Then the tragedy seemed to me our poor broken dreams of love; now, I see a youth struggling to free himself from the underworld, hindered by those who might have helped him, thrown back, after each attempt to escape, into his prison. The sandals and the monk's habit were a last desperate disguise by whose means he hoped to elude his captors. Easy enough to laugh at that pose of mock-mediaevalism, but now I see in all Roland's metamorphoses something heroic, the attempt to impose a style, a form, upon his life in an environment which knew nothing of style or form; an affirmation of the imagination in a world formless, narrow and commonplace. The failure was no less tragic than inevitable; for a style is not to be created in a day by those who inherit none. No doubt the mock-mediaevalism has lent a style to many a young man in like circumstances; and Roland's fine new talk of vestments and ceremonial—so contemptible to my father for whom the embarrassing 'sincerity' of the uncultured working-class Methodists seemed (and was, if Gibbon is to be believed) nearer to the Christianity of the slaves of the Roman catacombs than the civilized and civilizing order of the Catholic religion—expressed a deep nostalgia for human culture, for all that rises above the surface of the bog of animality which we all carry in ourselves, the subsistence level of barbarism.

Within Catholic Christendom, the most ignorant and the most learned, the simplest faith and the most subtle metaphysical understanding rest upon the same mythology, the same liturgy, the same words and signs and symbols. Only the Catholic Church sends (or, in those days, sent) down its emissaries into all places: the civilizing reach of the Church was indeed universal, and Roland's first instinct was doubtless right, to take sanctuary in Westminster Cathedral. Perhaps after the initial shock his father would have minded no more than his son's becoming an Anglican; for he lost him in any case. But John Wesley had been a member of the Church of England, and for an Englishman it is the Church of his ancestors, his language, and the specifically English cultural inheritance. By entering the Orders of the Anglican Church perhaps Roland also hoped to overleap the barrier of class and to mix as an equal with men who shared his taste and knowledge, so far above his station. Taste, even more than knowledge: for Roland had taste. The numberless Noakeses of the universities can absorb unlimited information and remain their own crude selves; but Roland's case was different, by nature he was a man of culture, but born in exile.

Roland had passed out of my ken; but in my young grief I thought only 'Why does he not love me any more? How have I deserved this?' Once, in the kitchen of the cottage, I found myself for a moment alone with him. I thought myself a very Marguerite of injured love, and stretched out my hands to him, I seem to remember, in silent pleading; but he left the room murmuring 'It is the Triple Vow, the Triple Vow'. Dressed still in the literary wardrobe of Huysmans and Patrice de la Tour du Pin, Roland was now a fugitive. In bringing me to Cornwall as a luring-bird to retrieve their Hound-of-Heaven-hunted son, Roland's parents failed and saw me fail. No longer his lyric love, I was a little schoolgirl who had just passed her matriculation examination and who must now decide whether, in the sixth form, she would take 'arts' or 'science'.

How artlessly I played my part without my Svengali I realize as I recall the only notion which entered my head as appropriate to the grief and bewilderment I then felt. I knew that a mile or two along the cliff road towards Portreath there was a steep cliff above rocks which the beautiful green and purple waters moiled in a pool called Hell's Mouth. I chose a beautiful spot for my suicide; for suicide in a spot so beautiful seemed an ending worthy of the dream we had woven. I ran from the cottage, tears streaming from my eyes as I hurried along the cliff-road on a summer evening of perfect beauty; reciting, as I ran, all the poetry I knew. I was miserable enough, to be sure, but only miserable, this time, as a schoolgirl of fifteen. The real mutilation had been the earlier one, when my father had shattered, with such violence, the archetypal flower of love. A few days before I had been happy just because there were flowers and glow-worms in the hedges of Avalon. I had, besides, seen Roland's bony pimpled body for the first and last time in my life, as he bathed with his brother in a certain very beautiful pool among the rocks; and I had shuddered. Such a body was best hidden by a brown habit tied with a girdle of rope knotted thrice. But how face a future without our dreams, without that 'someday', that painted paradise we had built together? So I rushed along that cliff road in childish tears, declaiming

> Treacherous in calm, and terrible in storm,
> Who shall put forth on thee,
> Unfathomable sea?

—feeling that words so beautiful must fit my condition. I lingered above

Hell's Mouth where in the moiling waters the seaweed was purple in the green, uncertain now I had reached the here and now to which I had so fancifully conducted myself, what to do. So I lingered by the place weeping for a while, before I was ignominiously led back by two non-conformist clergymen who happened to be passing. I do not think I would have either jumped or fallen over the cliff if they had not come; but there must have been silly children who have been less sure-footed or more desperate than I was.

Nothing ended cleanly or clearly; Roland gave up the Triple Vow and returned to King's College in the Strand, I think with some grant, to read Theology and become an Anglican clergyman; and we were allowed to meet. He talked to me much of religion but I remember nothing of it; phrases like the 'via media' that gave a new style to his speech suggest to me now that he had been reading Newman. Only one image stands clear; the image of a Roman Missal which Roland gave me. In it he wrote, in that backhand I remember so well, 'To my wife'; reverting to our old plighted troth. One day my father discovered the book; and I opened it to find those words cut out, deeply cut through many pages of the fine India-paper. The savage wound the blade of my father's penknife made in the pages cut something from my soul; something he cut out, once and forever. Marriage, certainly, it has since seemed, has never been possible for me.

I remember my virgin self, on the far side of that blasting of first love, looking down the long sweet vista of a woman's destiny. I remember standing, one day, on the edge of a field of hay-grass, wild roses in the hedge, birds singing, and such heavy richness of love on me that I felt myself transfigured by my womanhood into something more sacred than my mere self. It is the sense of the sacredness of sexual love that I chiefly remember; and once, I remembered Roland told me of a girl who had accosted him; a prostitute. I had not heard of prostitutes until that moment; 'I was sorry for that girl', I remember Roland saying; but as for myself, such a pang went through my heart that sex could ever be so degraded from what I knew it to be, from what our young love knew it to be, the very altar of life, that I pressed my wounded heart with my hand and was speechless with pity and grief. I grieved for days, for ever, feeling in that moment the full distance between what sexual love was meant to be, as in Eden, to use the symbols of that old myth, and what it is in the bitter world of Experience. It seems no less terrible to me now; to the poet who still remembers Eden, long after the woman has left its fields.

Mine, I think, was the normal response of woman, considered as a human and not as an animal being; the 'norm' being a lost human perfection and not the mean or average, which may, unfortunately, be very different. Yet I wonder if every woman in love does not see, as my childish self then saw, with pity and shame and grief the distances we can wander from the perfection all seek but few find in *amor*. Like a maiden in a tapestry field of flowers I for a time found it; my first love was, in its way, an epiphany; an epiphany of human love as it was in the first earthly Paradise.

The magic of first love faded in the changing pattern of our lives. Roland the theological student found new interests and, at last, new friends of the kind he needed most. A distinguished rising Anglican theologian, who was at that time Vicar of Ardeley, befriended him, and he went often for weekends to a vicarage of which he used to speak with the gratitude of a lost traveller who has reached at last a green isle in his storm-tossed voyage. He was invited to take me, one weekend; his lyric love, to be scrutinized by these friends from the world of true culture, the world we had known must exist—for had we not lived upon its images in poetry and in music—but to which we did not belong. Roland was beginning to hope to belong. I went with him—it was autumn, and the hedges were golden and bright red bryony berries trailed among the thorns—and was for the first time a guest in the house of cultured people.

Everything there seemed to me as beautiful, as perfect, as the bedroom of little Miss Ellie seemed to Tom the chimney-sweep. I could not have said what the indefinable differences were between this house and any I had known. These rooms were not much larger than those of West View, yet there was a dimension in them which ours lacked; the dimension of culture, of mental spaces, of which the many books, the blue china, the grand piano were but the outward signature. I did not understand, then, that the windows, which seemed to me so simple and so right, as those of the manse had also seemed, were so not through size but through proportion, through a mathematical secret knowledge. The vicar's wife seemed to me as beautiful as Gwen Ffrangcon-Davies herself, in *The Immortal Hour*, and she sang carols with Latin and French in them, old and lovely cadences that spoke to my imagination as if they were sung by Botticelli's angels. Why was this old furniture (in Ilford 'new' furniture was what everyone admired and wished to possess), the plain linen covers, the simple curtains, so subtly and indefinably right? Qualitative differences which I could not define, I felt. I sensed values I did not understand; I did not judge but felt myself judged, and, like Tom the chimney-sweep, knew myself for an uncouth little ape. Yet, like that same Tom, I loved the beauty in whose light I stood condemned. I was speechless with gauche shyness, and cowered beside Roland on a sofa while the vicar played and his wife sang 'Lullay, Lullay thou little tiny child', and 'I sing of a maiden that is makeless'. Precious, it may be; but to Roland and to me a spring of pure water in our desert.

It was not that the vicar or his wife snubbed me, but that I knew myself wanting by their values. Roland, seeing me in that context, must, with his fastidious eye, have seen it too. How could they have known who or what was still enfolded in the scale-leaves of my young bud? I did not know myself; or if I did, could not have told. They could not have known, even, how beautiful I thought were their house, their rooms, their blue china bowls of autumn berries, their music and their gleaming old oak chests and their books. I knew myself judged and condemned, of course; but by myself. I did not think myself worthy to set foot in their house or their company, because it was quite evident to me that I was not. They saw Roland's *kore* smelling of Hades, but did not know how I mourned in that prison-house. They may have advised Roland—rightly, indeed—not to encumber his future by an engagement with a girl of the Hades from which he hoped to escape; I should advise the same in a like case. So after that humiliating glimpse of a perfection which judged and condemned me, he became, I think, a little more aloof.

But the end, after all, was a dramatic victory for my father. At the time of the General Strike, students of London University volunteered to drive buses and underground trains, and an enjoyable time they must have had. Roland volunteered for the underground, and wrote to tell me of his adventures. But in my father's house the General Strike was viewed very differently. My father hoped passionately for the victory of the strikers; his two brothers, coal-miners, were involved, and all his loyalty was to his people and to their cause. Such was his fervour that he carried me with him; I thought myself then, for the first and last time in my life, an ardent Socialist, reflecting my father's strong feelings without really under-standing them, or knowing, myself, the world of the working class. My mother, with her country roots, and her Scottish pride, naturally shrank, as I did, from crowds and from the proletariat in instinctive aversion from their alien smell. I had seen mean and smelly back-yards and dirty children when visiting my father's brothers, but felt no kinship as with my mother's people. Yet I wrote to Roland an indoctrinated socialist letter telling him that he and his like were the enemies of the cause of the people. He was very much piqued and seized upon the pretext of telling me that we had better stop seeing one another. He was right; for had I not chosen my father rather than my lover?

To console me my parents gave me a tiny box-room as a study; I could furnish it as I liked. I had bookshelves, and an old oak writing-table with a leather top; rather a nice table. But the walls were peacock blue and the curtains of orange velvet, a hideous colour-scheme fashionable at the time. My poor mother also turned out of my bedroom my old white painted chest-of-drawers and the faded flowery cretonne curtains behind which my clothes had hung all these years, and my little white-painted iron bedstead, and the old wooden toy-cupboard, and gave me a hideous new bedroom suite from Harrison Gibson's furniture stores in inlaid mahogany veneer, with sombre mirrors that swallowed up the soul into the lonely prisons of Ilford's coldest hells, reflecting themselves for ever and ever. Yet she meant it kindly, and I did not myself know why these gifts, which had cost her so much, and which I tried to see as wonderful improvements, clenched my heart in a vice of misery and the sense of all hope lost. It was called 'ingratitude'; but if I was cruel, I too suffered.

At the time, and for twenty years after, I thought it impossible to imagine suffering greater than I underwent in those years, in that episode; but now I understand that, but for Roland, I might never have escaped the prison-house. I was fledged for freedom now; Roland had helped me to sever every cord of attachment that held me to that underworld. He had shown me images of intellectual beauty, icons of that perfection for which I might have longed in vain if I had not been put in possession of the keys of freedom, the books and the music he first made known to me. Once these seemed only the adornments of love; now that love is remembered, rather, as an initiation into the music of Chopin. As for Roland, he too had been given his chance of freedom. Through what experiences his way led him before his early death, I do not know; but I hope that for him not all was lost illusions.

CHAPTER FOUR

Here I was happy

'What might have been is an abstraction
Remaining a perpetual possibility
Only in a world of speculation.'

FOR me France has been that perpetual possibility, never realized, but on several significant occasions offering me the choice I did not take; mistakenly, it might be said, for on each occasion the French alternative has been manifestly the better; if better and worse are to be assessed in any terms but the imponderable difference between what is, and what is not, on our way, woven into the pattern of our fate, willed for us by God, or however else one may phrase it. Hardly ever have I wondered, about France, was that the right way I did not take? It might have led me by a very beautiful and enriching detour. I have noticed whenever anyone, friend or stranger, has described to me some significant choice or action in life, they have concluded by saying, 'But what else could I have done?' Nothing else; so we always reply, can only reply; another person might have acted very differently, but that particular 'I'? We act as we must, being what we are.

The beginning of France was before the end of Roland, but I find it possible only to follow the separate threads, not to disentangle chronological order, long forgotten. Chronology has little to do with recollection, which raises up wholes, like separate poems, beautifully coherent and complete. Yet there are strange modulations of theme, not recognized at the time; and only years later did I wonder if an unknown Englishman who carved, in a little sunny cave on one of the sandy beaches of Le Pouldu, the words 'Here I was happy' had been Dowson, his heart at that moment no more sick of an old passion than was mine when I read those words. It was not so very long after he had lived at Le Pouldu, after all, that I followed; for are not poets and painters only the first arrivals of the succeeding swarm? It is bitter, but salutary, for even poets to remember that they carry the infection of the civilization from which they are running to the places to which they run; we leave our intangible litter in the lives of those amongst whom we live.

Yet when I first saw those little secret rocky coves, and the mistletoe-fringed Laéta, and the old cities of Quimper and Quimperlé, the destruction (in which, as part of the influx of alien presences, I played my insignificant part) was not yet apparent to the eye. The maids at our little hotel still wore their beautiful dignified costume; high coifs fluttering with starched bands; a little different in every village, and the essential quality of the beauty of each girl enhanced, not effaced, by the identity of her black dress and a ribboned coif worn 'with a difference'. The little coves and sandy beaches were still secluded and scarcely visited, and only a few of the houses as yet belonged to summer visitors from Paris. We came to visit Le Pouldu through a series of circumstances which deeply affected the course of my life. My father was the agent, yet now I think of it he seems to have been chiefly instrumental on my behalf, and to have benefited very little for himself, though that perhaps through no fault of mine.

My father and mother had spent a fortnight, during a summer vacation, at a teachers' conference held at Girton; a rare emergence, for my father, from the company of his inferiors into that of educated people. There he made one of the few friendships I ever remember him to have formed, with one of the lecturers at the conference, a distinguished teacher of English at a famous school in Paris, who later rose high in the Ministère d'Instruction Générale. M. d'H.'s particle was not, like poor Roland's, a fiction, but inherited from his father, a landowner who had been, so he told us the story, defrauded of his estates by a dishonest factor. I remember he once said, in passing, that the particle would have opened for him 'many doors in Paris' which he did not care to open; and in retrospect I marvel at how little realization I then had of social differentiation or those things upon which it rests; for it seemed to me perfectly natural that he should prefer to converse with my father and myself on English poetry rather than with ducs or marquis on nothing in particular; a very brash opinion, as I now see. But at that time (daughter and grand-daughter of schoolmasters and school ma'ams) I had the notion that education was the only thing that mattered, and that to be 'clever' was more honourable than to be nobly-born.

I have since known a few members even of the aristocracy and it has slowly dawned on me that the reason why the well-bred are not necessarily well-educated, and often seem to find great difficulty with their spelling (at first this surprised and amused me, product as I am of an excellent secondary school and university education) is that when you are the thing itself you do not need to read about it in books. An education comes from books, but a culture is transmitted, in countless imponderable ways, by the people amongst whom we live. Much literature is a mere substitute for direct access to a society with its *mores,* and the richnesses and subtleties of a world where individual consciousness and social relationships are more fully developed than in the Ilfords of the world.

But if I had no realization of how M. d'H. came to be what he was, I did recognize his quality. He was—apart from my one miserable weekend at the vicarage of Ardeley—the first person of culture I had met. As a child I had known, however meagrely, participation in the songs and legends of my Scottish birthright; but these stories of places and persons whose names in Scotland endear them to the singers of their fame by their nearness, in Ilford could not help my mother, still less myself, to live our lives, but only remind us of our remoteness from the places of our ancestors and from those banks and braes of heather and broom, the deer and the laverock, to which the imagination of the race is wedded. In M. d'H. I recognized something at once novel and familiar, an attitude, a relationship with French and European civilization of the same nature, though on a higher cultural level, as my fast-fading participation in my Border birthright.

I saw him for the first time in the drawing-room of our house, standing against the French window, casting a kind of light in the room. He seemed too big for the house. He was not, perhaps, exceptionally tall, but, as at Ardeley the very tables and book-cases seemed to have an added an intangible dimension, so did M. d'H. seem not to be contained in the familiar rooms. The presence of this fair Frenchman with his flashing blue eyes and ironic smile, seemed at once to require, and to affirm, spaces of interior freedom my father's house did not provide. Not only did the rooms, the spindly drawing-room furniture, the dining-table and the side-board with its mahogany knobs and brackets and bevelled pieces of mirror seem suddenly small and cramped and crowded, but so did the accepted values of the house; all, that is, except literature, about which he and my father, schoolmasters both, talked in complete accord. I saw my father, for once, in the company of a man of culture; and wished with all my heart that he could be so always. But it was characteristic of him that, during the war, he refused to apply for any promotion, for the head-mastership of a school, because he would not use the advantage of his position as a civilian to steal an advantage on men at the war. All my father is in that; his unworldly idealism, but also his colossal pride in taking always the lowest place. I had not then read Plato's words about idleness—that not only are those idle who are not employed, but who might employ their talents better—but I felt always that my father wasted his abilities through inverted pride. Very likely I was as wrong by his standards as he seemed by mine.

It was as if my father permitted himself to rise to his full stature only at a remove; when he spoke of Shelley and Coleridge and Wordsworth, he judged them in terms of their own values; yet he lived by those of the Wesleyan Methodists, whose values for him represented a norm above which he might perhaps soar, sometimes, in thought, but which remained, like sea-level, that from which he took his bearings. He was no less aware than I was of the cultural meagreness and general ignorance of the Methodists but as Blake says of Swedenborg (to whom also Protestant clergy represented a norm) 'A man carried a monkey about for a show, and because he was a little wiser than the monkey, grew vain...'—a constant danger when the norm is abnormal. My father's monkeys were so far below M. d'H.'s horizon that for him they were non-existent. I am interpreting in retrospect what I then felt simply as a quality of his presence, a mental spaciousness he brought with him, and in which I too began to feel my wings. He waded like Gulliver among our gimcrack furniture, both tangible and mental. Later he used to describe to me his own education by the Oratorians; the splendours and grandeurs of the Catholic liturgy. He would chant, in his fine voice, those majestic and ancient processional hymns of Holy Week, and describe the Tenebrae and the Vigil and the rite of the Paschal candle, bound by unbreakable bonds of love to the Church in whose doctrines he no longer believed. A year or two later, he took me, on Easter day, to Nantes Cathedral; torturing himself with a beauty he loved but felt himself compelled to reject. My father was I think pained to see his own religion of 'simple faith' swept aside as not for a moment worthy of consideration, let alone comparison with the Catholic faith; held, by the monkeys, to be an idolatrous and superstitious ignorance lingering unaccountably in 'backward' countries like France, Spain, Italy and Ireland. My father encountered in his distinguished friend a respect and devotion for everything about the Catholic Church and its culture and its priests except the one point of agreement my father found in it—the truth of its central teaching and the divinity of its Founder. To him, no less than to any Jesuit, Dominican, Benedictine or Oratorian, the little Protestant sects dear to my father were heresies of the ignorant.

Were there, then, really such men in the world? Or a world in which men were like him? Roland and I had scarcely known enough even to envisage such a possible world. To meet such a man in my father's house was, for me, as if an angelic liberator had come with a key; yet it was all so simple, my liberation, with no battle at all, just the disappearance of the battlefield, which had suddenly become small and remote; even on that single visit M. d'H. made to our house (he never again consented to return among that cramping physical and mental furniture) I sensed freedom.

When first he saw me, so he later told me, coming in by the French window where my mother's tubs of blue agapanthus were in flower, he was wonder-struck to find in that wingless underworld such a being as myself. M. d'H. was, I think, the first human being (except my mother) who ever saw who I was; and that is something far more precious than what the young call 'love'. Between us, in the first exchanged look, there was the mutual recognition of beings of the same species, the same race, who meet in an alien world. I knew instantaneously that this was, for me, a meeting of marvellous promise and inestimable value; a meeting of the imagination, as if with Coleridge himself. (M. d'H. had written a book on Coleridge, whom of all English poets he most admired, and with whose marital miseries he most deeply sympathized.) He became, from that visit, my first teacher, to whom I gave the reverence and love of a disciple. He loved to teach; to him, the communication of knowledge gave, it seemed, as much pleasure as it gave me to absorb it.

He never returned; but he invited my father most pressingly to spend his summer holiday at Le Pouldu.

The first summer holiday after my meeting with Roland had been spent in the company of very different mentors. Two or three Wesleyan

Ministers had set up little wooden holiday bungalows on a stretch of shingle on the south coast, near a Martello tower, which one of them had bought, but not yet converted into a house. There my father was invited to bring his family; and he, my mother and I all slept in one bell-tent, and cooked on a primus stove. This I did not mind, nor the stretch of shingle (which that year became famous for a peculiarly sordid sex-murder), where grew strange maritime plants, which spoke to the botanist in me. But in the company of these Ministers and their families I chafed in cramped mental spaces and longed only to get out, out. These Ministers were the best mentors my father could produce as influences to bring his daughter to that 'conversion' which he felt that I, on the verge of woman-hood, ought to undergo. Sudden conversions make up the romance of the story of John Wesley's preachings on village greens and outside those churches he was banned from entering; and I think Dinah Morris was probably my father's favourite female character in fiction; after Shake-speare's Portia, perhaps, or Cordelia. These dramatic shifts of conscious-ness were considered to be the mark of true religion; and indeed Jung has since, in psychological terms, written of the same kind of re-orientation. But to me nothing of this kind happened. Instead, one of those wearers of celluloid dog-collars, of peculiar physical coarseness, fell furtively in love with me; and another, a man of some spiritual stature, I saw tethered, like Coleridge, by a 'coarse domestic life' and beset, besides, by young women of his congregation pining with repressed sexual desire under the spell of a magnetic physical charm he seemed unable to control. So, taking refuge on the flat roof of the Martello tower, I wrote daily replies to Roland's daily letters (in one a long Proustian description of white water-lilies floating on a still stream; so strangely do certain images emerge at certain times. Long after it was among the letters Roland, at my father's request, returned to me; he did not, of course, return all; but I was hurt that he returned my first exercise in the literary art, for I had taken pains with that piece of fine writing), read the first volumes of *The Golden Bough*, Jane Harrison, and Gilbert Murray's Euripides; all lent me by Roland. I found in the archaic religions a world infinitely more satisfying to my imagi-nation, and my own long thoughts blended and intertwined with cloud and sea and sky undefiled by the stifling human community below. I kept myself proudly apart, reciting to myself Keats and Swinburne. Perhaps my resolute aloofness was a challenge, for the Ministers all in turn by persuasion, pleading and flattery tried to capture me; but it could no more be done than, according to Swedenborg, spirits of different qualities can remain in one another's societies. I knew with the absolute certainty of instinct that I was not of their kind, as a blackbird knows it is not a starling. On the roof of my tower I felt myself protected by the spirits of the poets and by the ancient gods. My father perhaps saw that my books were better company, and let me be.

But in Brittany it was I who, for the first time since Bavington, was in my element, my father out of his. We were only able to afford a holiday really beyond our means and above our station because the rate of exchange that year had made France accessible to the English lower middle class; and we were but three drops in a tidal wave which poured in. There was even, at Le Pouldu, another family from Ilford, a sandy-haired spectacled boy from my father's school, and his parents. My father, who in the world of the d'H.'s and their friends felt, I think, as unprotected and exposed as M. d'H. had felt submerged and hampered in Ilford, sought them out, finding relief in his habitual role of doing good to his inferiors rather than taking pleasure in the company of his equals. To me these people were a humiliating reminder, with their faint cockney voices, of Ilford, which I would have liked to forget into the same non-existence as it had for the d'H.'s. My father, who had called me 'uncharitable' towards the Wesleyans of the Martello tower now called me uncharitable because I would have nothing to do with these (as it seemed to me) underworld people who had followed us up from Hades into the sunlight of France which shone so marvellously for me. Perhaps he was right; but it is not easy for the living to escape from the world of the dead, and it seems to me still that winged souls are more often dragged down by the commonplace herd who, ignorant of the use of wings, clip them and forbid their flight, than the wingless injured by the escape of the winged ones. Who, among the vulgar, heeds the misery of imagination hampered and thwarted? The question of charity cannot be resolved in these terms, nor can talent best 'serve humanity' by renouncing its vocation. To evade a high task by seeking refuge in a low one is not humility but despair, spiritual sloth, even a kind of inverted pride.

But my father handed me over willingly enough to M. d'H. who, from the first, addressed his discourse chiefly to me; glad that I should have this opportunity of improving my French, and of otherwise benefiting from the educational company of the distinguished schoolmaster.

So in aromatic woods, and on cliffs trembling in the haze of Monet's paintings, and on the river Laïta, and in the old streets of Quimperlé, and on the sand-dunes of Morbihan, I rambled with my wonderful mentor and his two little sons in a world apart, while on the *plage* my mother learned the art of filet embroidery from Mme d'H. He discoursed on the habits of birds, as he watched kingfisher, woodpecker and jay; heard me repeat whole memorized pages of Michelet on birds over and over again until my pronunciation pleased his exacting ear; philosophized, as Frenchmen will, on Shelley's view of love, of Renan's view of Christianity, of the cruelty of nature (exemplified in the lives of insects, reptiles and even his beloved birds) incompatible with the belief in a beneficient god. Humanism is a poor philosophy, but at the time he broke for me, cobweb by cobweb, the religious snare in which I had become so agonizingly entangled. As my wings were freed I began to feel again, for the first time since my lost childhood, the strength of my own spirit. With the blithe thoughtlessness of youth I imagined that now I had come into my own, now my long imprisonment was over, now the bright sun would shine on me for ever.

I suppose my mentor spoiled me, for he abetted my rebellion; he saw it as a matter of course that I must get away from Ilford; made me feel that I belonged with the happy few, with Coleridge, with Shelley, with such as he himself was. In his company it did not seem like a flight or a rebellion but like an awakening from some gloomy dream. I had no uncharitable thoughts towards the people of Hades, I only wished to be with those of my own kind; and did not need to be convinced by argument that the beaten road

> Which those poor slaves with weary footsteps tread
> Who travel to their home among the dead
> By the broad highway of the world

was not for me; with him I felt no sense of guilt for being what I was. Nor can I find, if I search my conscience, that the immortal judges have had cause to reproach me for vanity or pride, then or since, but rather for continual doubt and discouragement and evasion of their summons. Over and over again I have been misled by listening to the voices of the world, to my father's voice, persuading me not to listen to my daimon but to devote myself to the routine of lower duties. I have never been able to use my wings but when I could elude my father's moral values, admirable values for those who walk, but irrelevant when I have sought to fly. Perhaps I was a spoiled and selfish only child who expected the indulgence from the world which my mother had given me: yet I accepted my destiny, after all, at a price of suffering which many would be reluctant to pay. Suffering follows automatically for those who take it upon themselves to undergo in full consciousness the experiences of life which happen, indeed, to all, but which the instinct of self-protection induces those whom Blake calls 'sleepers' and Shelley 'the dead' to put from their minds.

Ilford, considered as a spiritual state, is the place of those who do not wish to (or who cannot be) fully conscious, because full consciousness would perhaps make life unendurable. What if some Mr. and Mrs. should wake to find that they are strangers to one another's souls? What if some ambition, 'forgotten', like Roland's doctor's overall, should stir too

painfully into consciousness the desire for some skill or craft or knowledge inaccessible? If the corpse buried in the trim little back garden were
to be resurrected into anguished life, the poor weak weeping ugly
disgraceful Lazarus would only have to be killed and buried once more.
The phrase which describes the state of those who 'cannot call their souls
their own' is not without truth, and often for social and economic reasons
which are beyond the control of the sufferers. To break up a marriage,
however soul-destroying, money is needed; to become a doctor or a
scholar costs money; and the sensibility of an artist or a poet cannot grow
in a mean underworld, and in solitude. It is no wonder that in the Ilfords
there are more who fear than who desire the stirrings of consciousness.
For one who escapes, many more must be thrown back to suffer in a
prison-house made only more intolerable by every glimpse of the world of
unattainable freedom. Brittany was, for me, a mountain-top from which I
was shown, for the first time, the world; and I drank deep draughts of
ecstatic happiness. My life, from there, seemed on winged flight, like that
of Michelet's birds. *'Rêves ailées, ravissements de nuit, si vous êtiez, pour-
tants! Si vraiment vous viviez!*—so I incanted my soaring aspiration, so
M. d'H. summoned me to rise to my destiny, or flattered a child's vanity,
as may be. For one thing I am above all grateful: he had the generosity to
hope, to wish for me a winged destiny. That is a kind of love very different
from turbid *amor*, such as poor Roland had laid at the feet of the object of
his desire and subject of his dreams. For M. d'H. I really was 'half angel
and half bird', for he believed me winged, and summoned me to flight. In
the Virgin blue, hands folded in prayer, who looks always downwards,
beholding only the upturned face of her child, whose image Roland
adored, I never saw an icon of my own soul; but in M. d'H.'s bird-winged
race I did, and secretly rejoiced.

The difference between those lives in Hades and the life I now saw being
lived on all sides was not a matter of being materially richer, or, indeed, of
being happier. The ability to live in, not merely to live through the present,
implies a kind and quality of consciousness, which is, like Blake's little
flower, 'the labour of ages'; and is not this to have a culture? In Ilford all
was provisional, was an 'interim', for the time being, would 'do well
enough for now'. This view of life was implicit also in my father's non-
conformist religion, other-worldly rather than sacramental. To my father
himself the poets he loved seemed dwellers in an Elysium remote from his
own world. Shelley's blue Mediterranean and Baeae's bay, Browning's
gondolas, even Tennyson's Victorian flower-gardens were as remote as
Eden or Xanadu. In the world of Scottish songs and Border-ballads, the
life which nourished the poetry was the very life the poetry celebrated and
enhanced; the poetry wedded, in Yeats's phrase, the imagination of the

race to the land; whereas in Ilford poetry brought not peace but a sword. But here again, in France, I sensed a culture in which the arts were a flower of the quality of life, and life nourished by the arts. M. d'H. was far from happy; his marriage was a battlefield and he spared himself no whit of insight into its complex miseries; but his actual circumstances he regarded, and used, as the instrument, the keyboard and strings, from which he must evoke the full gamut of experience, explore, like Coleridge himself, the mysteries of the soul, its joy and its suffering.

In the Catholic peasant world of Brittany I sensed the same actuality, on a lower octave; the priest blessing the sea from the fishing-boats, the ex-voto tablets in the chapel of some local St. Barbe, bore witness to a spirituality not relegated to an after-life; here the miraculous was a dimension of the here and now, the bread and the wine and the fish in the sea, and no village so small but that some saint in Heaven was its especial guardian. The concreteness of painted madonna and wooden child, the candle-flames of prayer, embodied everywhere the Christian mysteries.

I knew that to write poetry in, from, or for Ilford was impossible; but I was too intent upon escape to ask myself the question, 'from what, and for whom, do you expect to be a poet?'.

Ought I to be ashamed, in retrospect, that I took my escape so lightly? I walked on air upon those cliffs whose irridescent envelope of light Monet painted. I saw sun and shadow swoon into Bonnard's mid-day trance, where Proust's *jeunes filles en fleurs* and Manet's shade their delicate flower-faces with little parasols. I stood dreaming in the shadow of old cathedrals, taking all as my due with no knowledge of the cost at which man has raised himself to the vision of such things. I was a little barbarian marvelling at a civilization whose price was beyond my ken.

To my regret and dismay I lost, within two years, my revered teacher; all was spoiled by his falling in love with me. I do not know whether in Brittany I had any inkling of this; if I had I put the unwelcome intuition from me. But when at Easter I was invited to stay in the château near Paris where he had at that time gone as headmaster to one of those new schools American millionaires were founding in England and France at the time, there was no evasion possible. All the pleasure of spring woods, of air heavy with the scent of chestnut flowers, of waking in a sunny bedroom to walk in glades blue with periwinkle, secluded from the multitude; of visiting the Opéra, of lunching with the millionaire himself in a house looking out upon the garden of M. Poincaré (yes, all these things I did) was spoiled by the intense embarrassment into which I was thrown by this unwanted love. In the spring woods my mentor had kissed me, and informed me that if and when he could free himself from his marriage, he would claim me. It seemed that he had not doubted my willingness; but his kiss filled me with a physical aversion which brought down all my edifice of admiration and friendship. It has often seemed to me since that the intrusion of sexual passion spoils all; and yet, only love casts those iridescent enchantments; had he not fallen in love with me, why should he have troubled with me? From that moment I longed only to escape his presence. I felt greatly to blame, wondering how I had incurred this miserable situation. I had lost, besides, the friend whom of all I had known I had most valued, who had opened my prison door and urged me to use my wings. Once more I was thrown back, confused and rebellious, upon Ilford, the lovely vistas of France closed to me; a spoiled and difficult young girl, now, the task of civilizing me which M. d'H. had undertaken abandoned before it was well begun.

The Land Unknown

(1973)

Thel enter'd in & saw the secrets of the land unknown.
She saw the couches of the dead, & where the fibrous roots
Of every heart on earth infixes deep its restless twists.

The Book of Thel

If you would cleanse your mind of old delusions
From your many sins you would be freed.

Motome-Zuka

CHAPTER ONE

Fool's Paradise

I CHOSE science at that moment when schoolchildren reach the parting of the ways; in part because I found the matter of science enthralling, in part because I felt no need to be 'taught' literature. One had only to read the books after all; to be taught 'about' literature, which is itself the teaching, seemed to me a waste of time which could be better spent in learning what is not to be learned from books. I also chose science because our teacher of botany at that time was one of those rare people whose subject is a passion. She was herself still, at heart, a student (I believe she did, later, return to research), and communicated her enthusiasm to my two companions and myself in the science 'advanced course'. We spent long enchanted hours in the little botany laboratory, learning to cut and stain specimens for the microscope, to make detailed drawings of the marvellous structured beauty of plant-tissues; a world where form and meaning were one and indivisible. My father was satisfied because I had made a decision to work for a scholarship to Cambridge: the first step to a career. I was satisfied because in exploring the inexhaustible and lucid beauty of form and metamorphosis in nature I felt that I was approaching some secret source, or source of some secret. I was in love with the beauty of 'nature' but whether as a poet loves nature or as a scientist was not clear; or rather there seemed no difference, what I loved I loved. The two incompatible plans for my future for the time being coincided, my secret poetic vocation and my immediate delight in biology. When the ways would part I did not know. I worked hard; and with a small College exhibition and a County Major scholarship I was admitted to Girton. My father was satisfied, my school was proud of me. That was to be the last moment, after childhood, when I was not at odds with the world.

At that time, too, my relationship with my father was, for the last time, unimpaired by guilt and remorse. If we were ever to meet in some other world I believe he would remind me of those mornings when, for an hour each day before breakfast, he taught me the rudiments of Latin grammar, and read with me, to our mutual delight, two books of Virgil and Horace's *Odes,* books III and IV. In those days it was necessary for every undergraduate at Cambridge to have passed 'Little Go' in Latin. As I had no Latin, my father taught me all I ever learned in the two or three months between my examination for Girton and the date of the Cambridge Previous Examination. He himself loved Latin only a little less than he loved Anglo-Saxon; loved grammar and the structure of language for its own sake; and he communicated to me some of that love. I remember some of those odes by heart to this day. I knew my father, at that time, at his best; for with how few could he share that love of the ancient speech, the ancient learning, his own participation too seldom activated by the circumstances of his life. We seemed to walk together in an ancient civilized world.

When I passed that simple test I truly pleased him. All that turbid turmoil of religion and first love that had so embittered our relationship was forgotten as he taught me the Greek lyric metres, as Horace had used them; and scanned with me those famous hexameters of Dante's master. How often since, from the turmoil of emotion, I have sought and found sanctuary in the calm regions of the mind; and for this I have my father to thank. If he made that escape necessary he did, also, make it possible.

So little did I know of the world, so boundless were my dreams of what the realms of civilization had to offer, that I never doubted when, for the first time, I breathed the characteristic country-house scent of beeswax, lavender and chrysanthemums in the corridors of Girton that before me lay a future of unbroken happiness and freedom, leading to the realization of every hope. I was for the first time enjoying a little success, and standing in good credit with my elders, and with myself. Cambridge, because it was not Ilford, seemed to me paradise. I would henceforth spend my time among people of culture, in whose life of the mind, delightfully occupied with knowledge for its own sake, I would participate. These cultured companions would be mine; they would share my values and among them I would no longer be alone. Poets too I might meet—had not Milton and Gray and Wordsworth and Coleridge and many more gone up, as I was going now, as students to Cambridge? I had achieved what Jude the Obscure and Sue Bridehead had perished for the want of; I had escaped from the underworld.

With the same ease as that with which as a child I had entered the palaces and sat upon the golden thrones of some fairy-tale in the person of the Princess, and into a like unreality, I now stepped into the enchantment of Girton. From the lowest table in Hall I looked up at those great and learned ladies who, in lustrous Italian silks and velvets, with Victorian smooth-parted hair, seemed, at High Table, high indeed; as some of them really were. Tall, beautiful Miss Allen, then bursar of the College, had once, as a suffragette, been chained, so it was said, to the railings of Hyde Park. Now, as under the rule of some royal Abbess, she and her sister dons enjoyed the fruits of their triumph, that beautiful and happy College. There is a world of difference between the admitting of the sons or daughters of the obscure into court or monastery or college to live among an aristocracy (of learning, of religion, or of some other kind) and to learn its ways, and the looting of palace or abbey or college by the crowd, whose total possession can but be a total dispossesion. For the looted palace is no longer a palace at all, nor colleges places of that learning which revolution sweeps away. There is a great difference between the situation of the poor students of my generation, who really were admitted—albeit to an extent more limited than we ourselves realized—into a higher social class, with a tradition and a culture different from, and superior to, our own, and the present situation of such students (even in Oxford and Cambridge) who, being now in the majority, create their own standards. In my student days we were the exceptions; and we were able to learn, to assimilate something from those—still in the majority—who inherited the old culture of England's educated classes. Young barbarians of talent such as myself could still, at that time, to some extent become assimilated into social structures which, by our very number, we were, within a generation, to destroy. It was not our intention to kill the thing we loved, but by force of number we have done so. Unwittingly, unwillingly, we were the first wave of the deluge.

That is of course a sweeping overstatement; no revolution is ever wholly successful in destroying the older culture, and much, thank God, survives, and much is transmitted still to generations of students in Universities whose brick is even newer and redder than that of Girton. But so much at least is true—that in those days revolution was the last thing we wished for. We respected the inherited standards of excellence with no thought of changing them. The dons of Girton believed no less than did the Masters and Fellows of other colleges in the culture they had fought for women's right to share. We as students believed no less in the value of what they had won for us; perhaps even more, the known being limited, the unknown, boundless. Athens, Rome, Florence, all the glory of learning once contained in the word 'Renaissance', cast their magic on my expectation of what Cambridge would be. All knowledge, I thought, was there; as if knowledge and learning existed in a world of its own, in books and libraries. I did not understand that there is no such immortal being as 'civilization', only civilized people; and the continuance of a culture depends upon those who receive its inheritance.

At Girton, then, I first began to study my part, leaving behind the poor natural maiden who would have been content to be Roland's Lyric Love. Girton was itself the first building in which, by its proportions, its architecture (it was then the fashion to decry Victorian Gothic, but

Girton, as an example of that style, is not without distinction) imposed certain intangible values and standards. On those lawns, in those cool corridors, I found myself conforming my behaviour to the architecture and the spacious scale of buildings and garden; walking with a prouder poise, with a sense of being visible to others of my own kind.

On the pavements of Ilford I had shrunk into myself in shame, physically present there against my will, elsewhere in spirit. Is not the chief pleasure we experience from architecture (and perhaps from all other arts, though in less obvious ways) the change it imposes upon ourselves? The justification of the cost and labour of Gothic cathedrals and Renaissance palazzos is the greatness they confer upon, and demand of, those who come and go in them, inducing in us civilized modes of being and behaviour. The mean streets of the Ilfords of the world impose meanness of thought, make impossible, or all but impossible, certain kinds of feeling, certain modes of consciousness; or drive these into bookish dreams. Conversely, in order to escape the silent demands of dignified and beautiful proportions, barbarians must desecrate and violate, smash the stained glass and deface the statues and paint defiant slogans on walls that tell us too clearly, in their beauty and harmony of proportion, that we might be better than we are.

We lived in an environment still beautiful, still within the fast-vanishing culture that had raised these buildings, the last inheritors of certain moods and modes of consciousness communicated by the very architecture of the colleges and the sound of the English language as spoken by a cultured class. So all Romans continue, in a certain sense, contemporaries of Michelangelo and Bramante because their works have formed an environment which continues to exist. We do not inhabit only the present; yet the forms of the past may conceal from us destructive forces which their own different affirmations have become powerless to negate. Dazzled by the façade of Cambridge I did not perceive that it was the architecture of the Cavendish, not of King's or Trinity Great Court, or even of neo-Gothic Girton, that corresponded to the new standards of quantitative, scientific 'truth', to the Cambridge of the present. I did not realize that the new thought which inhabited the Gibbs Building, the Senate House, the Gothic and Renaissance courts and libraries, the Victorian avenues of elm and lime, was no longer that which had built them and which their forms continued to express and communicate. I sang with the Madrigal Society Vivaldi and Palestrina, with the University Musical Society Vaughan Williams and Bach, without realizing that the opinions I was at the same time imbibing were destructive to the very foundations upon which such beauty rests; for the English language spoken so beautifully by young men from the great Public Schools, acting Shakespeare's plays on summer

Fool's Paradise

evenings in College gardens by the Cam, seemed still the living speech of a living culture.

In the mid-nineteen-twenties revolution was not yet in the air. We did not know, young fresh folk as we were, that we were living in the last years of that European civilization of whose architecture, whose literature, whose thoughts we were the heirs. There was no mention of a 'third world' in those days; and even socialism (like my father's), was liberal; asking not for the destruction of a civilization, but that more people should participate in it. That was what I, and I suppose most of my fellow-students, hoped for, and believed would come about through the spread of education. I had not read Dante then, but such idealists as my father did not need Dante to spell out for them the truth that, whereas material goods are diminished by sharing, the spiritual treasures of knowledge and of beauty, of poetry, music and the rest, by being shared are not diminished but increased. So I then believed, and so I do now. Marxism and other materialist ideologies have coloured current attitudes (I write now in 1974) towards the spiritual heritage of civilization with the same envy (or justifiable sense of injustice) that prevails in the politics of material wealth. The possession of knowledge, of culture, is now under attack as 'privilege', regardless of the fact that it is a privilege none need possess to the exclusion of others. I remember how shocked I was (and this was a theme much discussed among my friends) by Huxley's suggestion, in *Brave New World*, that batches of unintelligent people should be bred, in his Utopia, to perform the duller tasks. Rather, we then thought, technology should remove such tasks altogether, enabling all to live cultured lives. But the irrational tide of revolution is not to be turned; and western civilization—the civilization of the Cambridge I knew—is doomed and already largely gone; with all that subtle beauty and knowledge, the mental spaciousness and freedom, the breadth of humanity, the insights, the never-to-be-repeated quality of life created and enjoyed by the race C. S. Lewis (one of its last representatives, as he told us) called 'old western man'. Revolution follows its own laws; and the new age belongs to races and classes who, because they had no part in Old Western culture, will not inherit but supplant; supplant not because the old culture was good or bad but because it was never theirs.

Meanwhile we children of the *entre-deux-guerres* enjoyed our world without any sense of guilt or doom. The acquiring of its knowledge, the participation in its culture, seemed unquestionably good; as did those standards of excellence inherent in every art or science the self-evident standards set for all those who studied or practised them. No one had as yet called in question, or sought to destroy, or to replace, the values of Virgil, Dante, Spenser and Shakespeare and all that unity of culture that lies between Homer and T. S. Eliot. These, for us, were the norm, the measure and scope of our humanity as such. Eliot indeed was our master, in the late 1920s, and it was he who taught us, precisely, to value, to preserve, to transmit, enriched (if we could) but in no circumstances diminished, our inheritance. He had written: 'Someone said, "The dead writers are remote from us because we *know* so much more than they did." Precisely, and they are that which we know.' He wrote, too, of a new Dark Age approaching; but that thought only made our present seem more joyously bright. Our Age was not dark.

Certainly I took too much for granted, even by the standards of those days. I felt no gratitude, so far as I remember, only delicious pride. I believed I had been admitted to Girton because of my deserts. During our first week the Mistress (a figure much like Queen Victoria in my eyes, and indeed her dumpy figure was of the same unqueenly cast) had told the 'freshers' assembled in the Stanley Library of the great privilege which was ours, of the many called and the few chosen. We were an elect, and of this we were well aware. Every woman admitted to the relatively few available places at the two women's colleges must have reached what was, in the men's colleges, scholarship standard. So it was said and so we willingly believed. It was for us, by our work, to justify our election. Perhaps it was this belief, held rightly or wrongly in the two women's colleges (Girton was, after all, a first triumph of the Victorian feminist movement) which has made my own attitude to men in general one of faint intellectual condescension; an attitude of which I only become aware as I remember that all Girtonians believed themselves the mental equals of the best of the men. So do Etonians and Wykehamists instinctively behave towards the rest of the world. They (like Girtonians) are always prepared to grant that Etonians and Wykehamists are in no way necessarily superior to others; but the unconscious attitude remains, and is based, after all, not on personal vanity but on a justified belief in the excellence of those schools. We who in 1926 went up to our Cambridge colleges believed in the excellence both of the education and the culture transmitted by our University; we did not doubt the social value of an educated élite; nor, for that matter, of a hereditary élite by whose presence among us were transmitted those imponderable qualities of English culture book-learning alone cannot give.

Mine was the Girton of Rosamond Lehmann's novel *Dusty Answer*; published the year I went up. I remember the Mistress asking a group of us (invited, as was the custom, in small batches to take coffee in that elegant sanctum, 'the Mistress's room') whether we thought *Dusty Answer* gave a true picture of life in College. I tactlessly said I thought it did; not an answer to meet with official approval. The Mistress could hardly have seen with Rosamond Lehmann's eyes (or with ours) the 'godlike young men' who in those days when examination requirements were less stringent, adorned the Backs, the river, and the courts of Magdalene, Trinity and King's. The phrase 'godlike young men' was current in Girton; and only half in irony, after all. Neither in Florence nor in Athens, nor in Murasaki's Kyoto, could our young aristocracy have been surpassed in that well-bred grace of good looks enhanced by good manners, and by the possessors' own carefree assurance of their own godlikeness. We loved our lords. Innocent of politics, no sense of guilt clouded our enjoyment; a moment of civilized youth, whose joyous freedom will perhaps never come again.

Now all these values are called in question; and asking myself in all truth what I have to say to the egalitarians, I offer an image. Suppose human society to be a pyramid whose base is everyman's due, and whose apex the highest attainable human excellence. Somewhere between base and apex we each must find our place; but never must the standards of excellence be lost or corrupted, for to realize the highest excellence is perhaps the task of our race in the economy of the universe. Those who give expression, whether in knowledge or in moral or aesthetic beauty, to the highest things, are giving to the world patterns of a perfection to which all must strive, which is latent in all. Through the creations of the few we all live, somewhat, in Genji's court, in Plato's Academy, in Mme. Verdurin's salon. If not to enrich, to cultivate, to extend the scope of knowledge, to refine the perceptions of consciousness; ultimately to attain what in the Far East is called 'enlightenment'—spiritual knowledge— what is the task of life, what its meaning?

I belong to the generation of C. S. Lewis, who wrote 'Human life means to me the life of beings for whom the leisured activities of thought, art, literature, conversation are the end, and the preservation of life merely the means.' I also believe that it is better to admire than to envy; to give honour where honour is due; or even to give honour where no honour is due, since admiration creates the fragile world of beauty, creates our Helens and our Hamlets; perhaps, even (as in India the Guru is honoured for the divine in him, not denigrated for his feet of clay) also our saints and our sages; while envy can only destroy that intangible lost domain of imagined perfection. And what we imagine, we create. It is our own humanity that grows by what we honour, it is the royal image in ourselves that our iconoclasms destroy. Strange (so it seems to me, writing in 1974 of my youth nearly fifty years ago) that the very premises of civilization should stand in need of defence.

Psyche's house did not seem to her more wonderful than did Girton to me, with its lawns and rare Victorian flowers and trees and drifts of Tennysonian violets, its still libraries, where light, as in some pre-

Raphaelite painting or romance, filtered through cedar-boughs and amethyst-tinted panes upon Victorian busts of the learned and the great, and Flaxman's little marble winged figure of Psyche herself. Years later I stayed with my friend Winifred Nicholson at Boothby, the last home of that great feminist the Countess of Carlisle, daughter of Lady Stanley, one of the founders of the College; and I recognized there the same indefinable atmosphere of the life of great Victorian ladies of 'plain living and high thinking' that in my student days I had breathed at Girton. The scent of beeswax and lavender, the immaculate housekeeping, the daily rhythm that gives a sense of timeless present; as if this good way were the only possible way of life from time immemorial. Because of the dreams of Lady Stanley and her friends, that rich heritage of English culture at its finest was thrown open to such unmade creatures as myself, in the hope and belief that we in our turn would carry and transmit that tradition. I hope and believe that even now the transmission continues.

So in my first term, as I sped down Castle Hill on my bicycle, and along Trinity Street and King's Parade on my way to the science buildings of Downing Street, I used to declaim aloud,

> Is it not passing brave to be a king
> And ride in triumph through Persepolis?

The sense of glory was a radiance that cast no shadow. All things were possible, I was free, I was in my own world at last.

My life in College seemed at first like a dream, a painted scene, as if life here were made of a different stuff from any reality I had hitherto known; as in a sense it was, though not in the way I thought. The difference lay in no magic light cast on the scene, but in a kind of consciousness; in what, for educated people, constitutes reality; to what themes, experiences, happenings, the attention of the mind is directed; what is noted, what disregarded. I did not see what were the demands made upon those who, like myself, wished to participate. I thought, paddler that I was, that by merely being among swans I had become one.

It was during the summer term that Virginia Woolf visited Girton—the first famous person with whom I had ever been in the same room. She came—it is all history now—at the invitation of the Girton Literary Society, to give her paper, *A Room of One's Own*. The meeting took place in Girton's reception-room, with its mural panels, the work of a benefactor of the College who, having lived before the benefits of higher education, had devoted those long, idle Victorian hours (what happened to all that abundance of time after the turn of the century?) to embroidering in wool on ivory satin rather heavy foliage and flowers and birds and squirrels for the pleasure of those ladies who were to be educated away from the immemorial and symbolic occupations of Helen, Penelope, Persephone, and Blake's Daughters of Albion. The portrait of Lady Carew herself, in voluminous blue silk, hung over the chimney, reminding us that the eye of the Liberal aristocracy was upon all our comings and goings. The grand piano, draped with a piece of oriental embroidery, was pushed to one side. Outside those tinted neo-Gothic windows cedar and tulip tree spread their branches over the sweep of the lawns upon whose green cedar-shaded carpet I was now no trespasser, but one of the happy and thrice-happy permitted to walk.

In the fairyland of the Girton reception-room, then, members of the Literary Society were gathered for coffee, after Hall; young Eton-cropped hair gleaming, Chinese shawls spread like the plumage of butterflies. (I vainly longed for one of those shawls, fringed with silk and embroidered with silken flowers and birds, fashionable at that time.) With Virginia Woolf had come her friend Victoria Sackville-West: the two most beautiful women I had ever seen. I saw their beauty and their fame entirely removed from the context of what is usually called 'real' life, as if they had descended like goddesses from Olympus, to reascend when at the end of the evening they vanished from our sight. The divine *mana* may belong to certain beings merely by virtue of what they are; but *mana* belongs also to certain offices, royal or priestly; and masters in some art were, in those days, invested with the dignity of their profession. A 'great writer' had about him or about her an inherited glory shed from the greatness of writers of the past; and about Virginia Woolf this glory hovered. Every sacred office can be discredited, and in the present world, in England, the profession of the writer has been brought into disrepute by the same looting of sanctuaries as has taken place in other spheres of life.

I had not read any of Virginia Woolf's novels at the time; a few months before I had not even heard of her. Now from her famous paper I learned for the first time, and with surprise, that the problems of 'a woman writer' were supposed to be different from the problems of a man who writes; that the problem is not one of writing but of living in such a way as to be able to write. *A Room of One's Own* made claims on life far beyond mine: a room and a small unearned income were, to me, luxuries unimaginable. To elude the vigilance of my parents, and to write poems on the marble-topped table of a Lyons' or an ABC tea-shop was all I had at home, or for long after, hoped for. At Girton I had a room of my own; but while feeling it my due, I did not, at the same time, expect it to last, any more than a dream lasts; and yet, within that dream, we accept all that comes as a matter of course.

The pioneers to whom Girton owed its foundation had fought for the freedom I there enjoyed. Even so, I cannot truthfully say that I have ever found that my problems as a writer have been made greater or less by being a woman. The only problem—to write well and to write truly—is the same for either sex. As for time to write, there is always time. Volumes might have been written in the time Lady Carew spent on all that wool embroidery upon satin. But perhaps the embroidery was a wiser choice, after all.

But how I loved my College room of my own—two rooms, in fact, a small bedroom and a little sitting-room in 'Top Old'. In the morning, our 'gyp' brought to each of us a can of hot water, set it in our wash-basin, and covered it with a towel. And we each had a coal-fire (also laid for us daily) and a graceful oval copper kettle, polished on top (the kettles of the dons were polished all over). Each of us had our own desk, writing-chair, arm-chair, and bookshelves, with curtains and covers of fresh clean linen; in many of the rooms still of the original William Morris designs, very old-fashioned it was fashionable to think, in those days when Heal's furniture and the rectilinear style were new. We added, of course, our own touches. We had our toasting-forks, from which we dropped our Matthews' crumpets into the fire; I bought some hand-woven blue material, and put up two rhyme-sheets, one, of William Allingham's 'Four ducks in a pond', the other Blake's 'Never seek to tell thy love'. Some of us had Byron's 'We'll go no more a-roving/ So late into the night'. The choice of rhyme-sheets was restricted.

We considered ourselves emancipated, for the chaperone rules had recently been relaxed; and now two or more students might entertain young men in their rooms, to tea, if permission was obtained in writing, from the Mistress, the names and colleges of all students present being given. We dropped our neatly folded notes into the Mistress's letter box the previous day, and as a matter of course received our permission. This was seen as a great advance. A friend some ten years my senior remembers permission being refused to a friend who had been invited to accompany her father and herself on the river; the friend was a daughter of one of her father's fellow-Ministers in Asquith's Cabinet. Yet another relaxation, new in my year, allowed students to carry their own parcels from Cambridge; mostly, even so, we had our orders from Matthews' cake-shop, or Heffers' book-shop, delivered at the College.

No more than we felt guilt as a privileged élite (words with no anti-social connotations in those days) did we feel ourselves 'victimized' by the strict rules under which we lived and worked. If a few habitually, and most of us once or twice, broke the rule of being in College by 10 p.m., and climbed in through a window into a ground-floor room, that was at our own risk, and for the sake of the adventure. We were only too glad to live in that College, the very realization of Tennyson's *The Princess*; to visit one another's rooms, like schoolgirls, for sophisticated coffee, or homely 'jug' (cocoa at 9 p.m.). Most were still virgins at the end of our three years; nor was it the virgins among us who were neurotic, restless, dissatisfied and liable to breakdowns, but the 'emancipated' minority who were not. As I remember it seems to me that living as a student in Girton was one of the few perfectly happy times of my life; but happy as a dream is happy, as something that had befallen me; not, as my years at Bavington, a time when the world, its hills and skies, its simple tasks and simple people were like a part of myself.

But there was another side to my entry into this world, where most of the students, the women no less than the men, were members of the upper or upper-middle classes. Most had been to public schools or to some of the more famous grammar schools. People like myself were still in a minority, I did not recognize in myself a social phenomenon, the first wave of the 'filthy modern tide'; on the contrary, I thought I had myself escaped drowning and crossed a social barrier because I had passed an examination. The fact that I was in those days considered by some people (including myself) to be beautiful, confused the issue still further for me: I expected to be accepted. I thought myself talented and beautiful; had not M. d'H. seen in me the swan I felt myself to be? But I soon discovered that in Girton I was no swan. Those beautiful well-groomed young women from Cheltenham and St. Leonard's Ladies' College who all seemed to have come up already knowing one another, or with friends in common, with brothers and cousins in the men's colleges, were of another race. They were merely continuing to live within a world which was already theirs; no metamorphosis was demanded of them. From afar I admired these proud creatures who came and went with ease and assurance. I would gladly have resembled them, but I did not; they knew, and I knew.

One, I remember, whose dignified beauty and whose clothes (so simple that I in my naivety could not imagine why my own home-made garments looked so different) I had admired afar off, invited me, with other science students in our first term, to tea; she was herself a medical student. She said, assuming agreement from us all, that she thought it a pity that girls from secondary schools should be admitted to Girton. I blushed so deeply that she became as embarrassed as myself, and apologized; but it had been said. After that I avoided her, and the other bright ones. My friends were therefore, of necessity, the outsiders. I was on surer ground with my fellow-scientists, for in the labs I was accorded my due, no more, no less; but what I really wanted was to meet the other cygnets of the species of which I believed myself an 'ugly duckling'—the writers.

Following a College tradition, first-year students formed themselves into 'families'—small groups of four or five, who were thereafter considered to be the little cell in the College organism to which you belonged during the remainder of your three years. So far as I know no one ever changed her family; the feeling of the College was against this; and so to an arbitrary and premature choice we were thereafter committed. Yet it was, in many ways, a happy arrangement; no one was, at all events, lonely or left out. The most interesting member of my 'family' was the senior scholar of my year, a Jewish moral scientist, the first Marxist I had met. She, as a member of a persecuted race, I an 'outsider' by reason of class, were thrown together. She introduced me to the avant-gardism of the time, to the books of Aldous Huxley, Virginia Woolf, E. M. Forster, Lytton Strachey and the rest of the Bloomsbury school; and to Roger Fry's and Clive Bell's books on painting. I had hitherto supposed that the object of painting was to produce likenesses of beautiful persons and of the beauties of nature; but now I read with wonder of 'significant form'. I remember especially those Giottos illustrating the doubtful theory, and the over-whelming impression they made on me. My friend had a reproduction of the *Pietà* in her study, and with what a sense of liberation I learned to dissociate the aesthetic from the religious content of Giotto's eloquent linear figures. If I have come full circle to the opposite view, that meaning and form are indivisible, 'significant form' was, none the less, at that time a most liberating new way of seeing.

I soon discovered, by the scorn of my new friends, that *The Spirit of Man*, Keats and Shelley, Yeats and the other Irish poets, Walter de la Mare, and Thomas Hardy, my old passions, were not the thing at all; nor my old love Roland's *The Hound of Heaven* and Swinburne and Dowson and Flecker. D. H. Lawrence, I to my astonishment discovered, was in the new pantheon. This greatly surprised me, for in Brittany M. d'H. had lent me *The Captain's Doll*, which I had found both ridiculous and distasteful. I now read *Sons and Lovers* and *The White Peacock*, and found them much inferior to *Jude the Obscure* or *The Return of the Native*. When I later read other of his novels. *Aaron's Rod* and *Women in Love* and the rest, I found Lawrence's ill-mannered and sex-obsessed people coarse and low-class; I could identify myself with Tess or Sue Bridehead, but not with these fleshy Gudruns and gauche Miriams. Why, besides, should I be asked to read books about the very underworld I was struggling to get away from? It was as if the filthy modern tide were wetting my heels as I scrambled to safety. It is true that I had not altogether understood either Hardy or Lawrence; I now realize that, in his essays above all, Lawrence saw and deplored the social displacement he himself at once represented and described, with no less grief than Hardy. Conversely, Hardy, like Lawrence, had foreseen the vanishing of the traditional rural world—the world of my own roots, and my earliest loyalty—and of its people. I now see that Jude and Sue were Lawrence's people, already foreseen, uprooted and lost, living by values new and false; but their false values were at that time so much my own that I was blind to Hardy's meaning. How tragic, I thought, that Jude could not go to Christminster to be educated. I did not see what Hardy saw, that Jude, one of the last stone-masons, belonged far more integrally to the cultural inheritance of England than did the string of nonentities who, for him, represented the Oxford to which he aspired. To me, it seemed perfectly natural that Sue, an 'educated' school-teacher, should cling to those ridiculous plaster statues which for her represented culture; for I had done the same myself, with my Medici prints of *Primavera* and Leonardo's head of Christ. To me the tragedy was not the tearing up of the roots of Jude and Sue, which turned them adrift (always uneasily in the country going for walks or looking for lodgings or selling up the old cottage whose life must now become extinct; and not, like Tess, milking the cows or, like Marty and Giles, planting the trees), but their failure to achieve what they longed for—and I also had longed for, and was now more fortunate than they in achieving: entrance into Christminster. I did not see, as Hardy saw, that the same misguided aspirations (or inevitable process) would turn thousands besides Sue and Jude into displaced persons; into Lawrence's characters, without caste or orientation, who are but Sue and Jude a generation later. I could not see this; for in truth I was myself one of these, an unconscious part of that same social revolution, its dupe and victim as they were. But I did know that Hardy had a vision of the mysterious greatness latent in human beings, and that Lawrence's people lacked that stature imparted by the earth itself to those who have not broken the ancient ties that bind Hardy's people to hill and wood and pasture. Not all my ties of the heart with Northumberland's bleak moors had yet been broken.

With Proust I did better; I read six or seven volumes in the original French, partly as a gesture towards M. d'H. and Brittany, where I had been happy, where I had caught unawares a breath of that quality, that atmosphere of French culture which Proust so nostalgically evokes. The Bay of Concarneau, Pont L'Abbé, and the savage rocks of Penmarch, I too had loved. Because I did not realize how little French I knew, I persisted, and began to learn the language I pretended to know; and also to learn a little about society; for Proust's world seemed to me to be a living society (as, in a simpler mode, Hardy's was); whereas Lawrence seemed to be describing rather a lack than an actuality, less a way of life or a culture, than the embarrassing spectacle of people who have none; a breakdown of social order and orientation, or the rise of the outsiders, as one may choose to look at it.

I also set to work on *Ulysses*, then an exciting banned book. As with Proust, I would not admit, even to myself, that I found much of it incomprehensible; so I persisted from beginning to end. But Joyce I found here and there rewarding and full of a poetry whose beauty moved me. This, I was given to understand, was not at all what I ought to have found in *Ulysses*; what I should have admired was not the refrain of *Liliata rutilantium turba circumdet*, reminiscent of Roland's incense-intoxicated religious enchantment; nor the poignancy of Stephen's mother 'folded away in the memory of nature, with her toys'; no, it was the 'difficulties' of the style (an obstacle-race for clever intellectuals) and the obscenities, which were supposed to 'liberate' us from the restrictions of bourgeois morality, religion the drug of the people, etc., etc., etc. All forms of disintegration of morals, social order, language and religion were indiscriminately acclaimed as progress towards that freedom of anarchy which was the vague utopia of the rebels of my generation. (This programme suited me well enough; I had after all, my private score to settle with Ilford and the Wesleyan Methodists.) Yet I admired in Joyce rather what he had in common with Synge and Colum and Yeats and Æ; the vilanelle *Are you not weary of ardent ways*; the depth of family feeling; the Celtic melancholy music and beauty of language; and the resonances of the great culture of the Catholic religion; the warp of Ireland upon which he wove rather than the woof he wove upon it.

I had hitherto looked in poetry for the sublime, listened for that resonance of 'the eternal, in and through the temporal' of which Coleridge speaks; but I was now entering a world for which there was no eternal; a literature of the temporal was what in Cambridge I encountered, a literature compatible with Wittgenstein's and Russell's new logical positivism, Bloomsbury humanism (represented in King's College by Maynard Keynes and G. Lowes Dickinson) and the materialist science of the Cavendish laboratory, that power-house that dominated all fields of Cambridge. All was of a piece, the new taste and the criticism invented to justify it. There I discovered that the beauties I had hitherto found in Milton and the Romantics were not of the imagination, but imaginary; it was I who had failed to understand that where I had thought I had seen beauty, there was none. I and my simple kind had not the courage to retort that, if this be so, there is more value in the illusion than the reality; still less that to have seen beauty, to have been moved by feeling, is a fact which cannot be argued away. Better to have been moved by a 'bad' poem, a melodramatic or sentimental story, than to have missed the experience of wonder and delight. Holy personages have appeared through the vehicle of ill-painted icons, and worked upon those who so beheld them miracles unknown to those critics who seem to grow, in the long run, incapable of being moved by anything so simple and so beyond reason as beauty of any kind at all. 'The best of this kind are but shadows, and the worst no worse...'

In discarding my own intuitions in order to learn a more 'intelligent' way of reading poetry, I truly thought—or thought I thought—that I was taking the way from ignorance to knowledge. For the intellectuality of the beautiful, as the Platonists have known it, my Cambridge had little regard; taking complexity of wit for depth of meaning. The intricacy of Donne's conceits seemed of greater intellectuality than the music of Shelley. For the poetry itself must conform to the new values of science— the quantitative and the rational. I knew nothing of the alternative and excluded culture of the Platonists; the names of Plotinus and Thomas Taylor the Platonist, not to mention Coomaraswamy, contemporary though he was, were at that time unknown to me. Nor could the crude form of Christianity known to me have withstood the scientific culture of Cambridge, complex, coherent, exciting as it was, even had I been trying as hard to retain it as I did to free myself from it. Yeats's *Autobiographies* I later read with secret joy; but I did not dare to say that his words seemed to me to speak with the voice of life in a world of mechanisms; to admire Yeats was not the thing at all.

It was after I had left Cambridge, but before I had begun to question its values, that I remember T. S. Eliot saying that he greatly admired Yeats's *Autobiographies* because these told of just those things which were important to poetry (or did he say to *the* poetry—Yeats's own. I wish I could be sure, for the difference though slight is important); and that too was one of the moments of intellectual liberation which I remember; my secret, unspoken delight was justified in the judgement of our great poet!

Hopkins too I now encountered for the second time; but how different was this Hopkins of Cambridge, this Hopkins of 'sprung' rhythm and hard-to-decipher syntax from Roland's Hopkins who had swayed a young man with half-morbid religious emotion! With vivid intellectual excitement, Cambridge (dismissing the priest's preoccupations as merely accidental) analysed the structure of verse and image; while I. A. Richards's friend, C. K. Ogden, tried to master the metrics of sprung rhythm. I was taken to visit him (I think in London, but I am not sure) and I remember how Ogden set a great humming-top to spin on the stone floor of the hall of his house until it sounded a level note; to which he chanted, first some odes of Horace (*'Faune nympharum fugientum amator'* was one) and then Hopkins's 'Yes, why do we all, seeing of a soldier, bless him' etc; a fine donnish performance in a vanished fashion. Many years later, during the war, for a third time I was to hear Hopkins read; this time by Robert Speaight, and neither as religious propaganda nor as an exercise in syntax and metrics, but, simply and superbly, as poetry!

The Imagism of the new American poets reached Cambridge in the early works of Eliot and Pound (and also H. D., Richard Aldington, and other forgotten names) and, in the context of the 'scientific' criticism of I. A. Richards, at once helped to create the new taste, and satisfied it. *Haiku*, as it were, without the Zen metaphysics.

I did not myself realize the paradox of my situation; for so strong in me were the associations of the very word 'poetry' that I went on trying to fit myself into that bed of Procrustes, believing that somewhere I should find, in the thought of this new school, what I believed must be there because these writers invoked the magic name. As to my mother the name 'West View' had persuaded her that a miserable building-estate must somehow still be a scene in Paradise, so did the name—'poetry'—mislead me.

Truth to say there was more of what I meant by poetry in my work in the botany and zoology buildings in Downing Street. There, among flasks and retorts, plant-tissues and microscopes and the bones of vertebrates I could still slip off my brave new persona and bathe in nature's healing ˃ stream. The marvels of the universe were there open to me and I contemplated in awe and delight the Book of Nature. I could think my own thoughts, arising unbroken from my childhood's world of the Northumbrian moors, and perhaps from still deeper ground. As an anonymous student of natural sciences I was more a poet than ever among the Cambridge poets. There my experience was at once aesthetic and magical; those life-cycles and transformations, embryology and morphology, that condensation of force into form which produces sensible 'nature' constituted a harmonious world of significant form indeed.

Another world to which Cambridge gave me access—and for the rest of my life I am humbly grateful—was music. I could read music just well enough to enable me to sing among the second sopranos of the University Musical Society (then conducted by Dr. Rootham) Bach's B-Minor Mass; Vaughan Williams's *Sea Symphony*; Kodaly's *King David*. In the Madrigal Society (conducted by 'Boris' Ord) we sang, besides the English madrigals, Monteverdi and Vivaldi. In King's College Chapel mine was one among the young voices whose 'linkèd sweetness long drawn out' was prolonged among the fan-tracery. Even in the Girton choir what exquisite old carols and canticles we sang! It is one of my greatest regrets that after Cambridge I let music go, and relinquished my humble place in that most sublime of all the worlds of imagination.

If Cambridge poetry had no magic in it, my generation found glamour to sustain our imaginations on the stage of Terence Gray's Festival Theatre. It was during my first term that, with my avant-garde friend, I bicycled for the first of many times to that magical place, in Cambridge yet not of it. More remarkable than the romantically dim foyer, the revolving stage, the elaborate lighting was—if memory serves as a guide—the imaginative impulse, strong and authentic, the aesthetic sureness of intent, by whose means, week by week, our own little rockpool was refreshed and replenished by the tides of the great sea. Yeats and Lady Gregory had dreamed of creating in Ireland a sense of national identity by the agency of the Abbey Theatre; and Terence Gray came near to creating, in Cambridge, a colony of what was at that time a living culture throughout Europe. What made the theatre, in those years between the wars, so apt a vehicle for the spirit of the age? In Ireland, in Lorca's Spain, in the Prague of the Capeks, the theatre was sensitive to every tremor, neither commercialism nor inane experimentalism had as yet corrupted the impulse which in those years made drama its vehicle. I knew nothing, of course, of this larger world; but that made our own theatre, for me, so much the more miraculous. I had been used to reading books in solitude, and my poetic dreams too were solitary. Poetic drama revealed unguessed possibilities of shared experience of an imaginative world. My imagination was at that time sustained, more than by any other influence except music, by the Festival Theatre. To this day certain scenes, sequences of dramatic emotion, with all their *duende*, live on in me.

How much of the magic arose from the fact that we of the audience knew one another and shared with one another, not as members of some anonymous 'public' but rather as the élite of our Platonic republic, a collective delight? We up in the gallery were absorbed, like the rest, into the palpable blackness of the auditorium, dimly lit, as in the lodge of some esoteric cult, by green light. We unfolded those programmes on whose cover a futuristic figure in the style of Edmund Dulac reeled backwards as though Atropos had at that very moment snipped with her scissors the invisible thread of Fate. With much rustling we opened the transparent page whereon we were able to read in the dark the names of cast and dramatis personae. As the reverberation of a great gong that announced the onset of the tragedy quivered through our nerves and up our spines, the rustling ceased and the curtains rose on Terence Gray's first production, *The Oresteia*. I do not remember who the actors were. Later many names afterwards famous—Ninette de Valois, Flora Robson, Robert Donat, Joseph Gordon Macleod—were to appear on those transparent rustling pages. But upon me, at that time, the dramatic illusion worked too powerfully to retain any human name. Whatever study producer or maker of masks had made of Greek theatre or modern stage, upon my virgin ignorance the impression was as if that tragedy were enacted before us, the ancient figures, masked and buskined, captured in legendary time, for ever 'thinking the thought and doing the deed'. How much more real they were than any actor! Rupert Doone (later to become director of the Group Theatre) afterwards became a friend; but for me he always remained, somewhat, a young Bacchus in a leopard-skin, newly leaped from Diaghilev's ballet. It was as if everyday dress and appearance were the dissimulation, the mask, and not that infinitely more real figure enacted in a painted scene. If the arts be not more real than 'real life', what is reality?

By whatever stage furniture or contrivance the magic was supported, it was no mechanism, no *trompe-l'oeil* which then enchanted us, nor even the skill of the actors themselves, so much as youth's desire to be so enchanted. For us the stage was a magical space, set apart as a dream is set apart, within which each of us could enter upon some inner world. At the stroke of that resonant gong, as the theatre darkened, we became as uncritical and as absorbed as spectators of a dream. And as in dreams we never know what scene may unfold before us, so, week by week, we were shown in some unforeseen guise, in some new aspect or situation, what riches, what depths, what strange and infinitely varied unguessed regions lay within the dreaming mind. We did not so much feel, 'I would have acted so' or suffered so, as 'I acted so; I suffered so.' For to each it seemed that we alone, in our most intimate self, were the enactor, the conscious being from whose life act proceeded, and word arose to the lips of the figures on the stage. Young as we were, did we divine that our own lives too might be scenes enacted by some caste of mysterious beings manipulating us within the magical space of a human lifetime, set apart for the realizing of some one among the infinite number of the possible stories, the possible acts, of the one humanity? At the time we were not merely one, but all these people of the imagination.

The mysterious beings, certainly, let us guess something of their inexhaustible inventiveness, in character and situation, in humanity's infinitely various response to the few and simple themes of love and death. From week to week we saw, with the inconsequence of dreams, it might be Capek's *The Insect Play*, or the revolutionary Expressionist *R.U.R.*; or *The Hairy Ape*, or *Desire Under the Elms*, or *At the Hawk's Well*; or Lorca's *House of Bernarda Alba*, or *Rosmersholm*; and the gods alone know how many more dramas of passion or protest, anguish or aspiration we felt, for the time being, to be our own. I do not remember that then, as increasingly in later life, I ever refused to give myself to the proffered illusion, refused to feel 'This is I.'

It is sometimes said now that it does not matter what we see enacted on stage or screen, depicted in sculpture or paint or architecture, or sounded on our ears in music, because we can accept or reject at will. But can we? Do we not respond at a level beyond judgement? When we are able to judge, to evaluate by critical intellect, are we not already beyond the power of art? And was it not through the deeper influence of the arts, beyond the reach of critical judgement, that civilizations were created and sustained? To suggest that modern man is impervious to those influences which created Athens and Florence and Thebes and the Imperial cities of Pekin and Kyoto is not to say that we are more 'advanced' but that we can no longer feel, no longer respond to the powers of life. But of course it is not true; the lie is put about lest we should become ashamed of the images we feed upon, in whose likeness we choose to form ourselves. Blake knew that 'we become what we behold'; and week by week, in our little city state of Cambridge, we became, at least for a few days, or even for only a few hours, but in memory for ever, Agamemnon and Orestes; became those laborious dung-beetles with their pile; became the daughters of Bernarda Alba, or Strindberg's Hyacinth girl. Some inner being, thirsting for experience and for self-knowledge, was able to enter into every situation and emotion, while as yet remaining itself cloud-like and without personal identity.

But with the literary friends whom I presently made, the talk was all of technicalities, dry dull talk as it seemed to me, without the sense of wonder or mystery. I had learned at school the basic technicalities of English verse, and from my father of Latin; but these exercises in rhetoric, at which I was passably good, seemed to me unrelated to the living process of writing a poem. I may have made too much of the difference, but I still believe lyric form to be the outcome and sign of poetic exaltation and not a prescribed shape into which words may be fitted—Plato after all, thought the same. It is in the nature of things that the English schools begin with what for the poet is the end of an imaginative process, with the 'words on the page', to use a cliché of a later period. I listened, but not with my poet's ear, to the talk of free-verse and imagism and conceits. I have been comforted to find in the autobiography of Dom Bede Griffiths that there were others as naive as myself, at Oxford if not at Cambridge: 'I had always understood it to be the function of the poet to see beneath the surface of nature and human life and to reveal its inner meaning. The beauty to be found in the poem was the index of the degree of truth and insight to which the poet had attained.' So I too had supposed; and even, in the words of the same writer, that 'the function of art is... to evoke the divine presence'. I now supposed that I must have been wrong. It never crossed my mind that these clever contemporaries might not have seen these things, which to me were self-evident; I therefore supposed that they must have renounced such a view of poetry in the name of some higher truth (that pernicious humanist 'honesty' which mistrusts all knowledge but that of the senses) and were seeing with the eyes of a knowledge greater than my own.

Now I can see that those of my contemporaries who had accepted, implicitly or explicitly, the current positivist philosophy had lost access to the wells and fountains of imagination and were engaged in heaping stones to seal the springs which might, had they overflowed, have swept away that sand-castle. Or were they, too, like myself, engaged in a joyless pretence? Were we all suppressing our better natures in order to impress one another or to conform with current fashion? Feeling was not meaningful within the terms of positivist thought, and must be stifled.

I went to one or two of I. A. Richards's open lectures on Practical Criticism. I was too immature, then, to have benefited from them. I was, I vaguely remember, taken to his house, once, by William Empson; too overawed to take in very much; and remember chiefly the strange impact of the Japanese Noh masks hanging on his walls. I have since come to know Ivor and Dorothea Richards as friends; and we share a love of Coleridge, Plato and Shelley. Ivor is a critic who, falling in love with the texts he studied, took to poetry; a splendid example to set against those poets who, led astray by the magpie criticism, become critics. I remember a lecture he gave, years later, at the Institute of Contemporary Arts, in London, on the *Ode to the West Wind*; ingeniously illustrated, as I remember, with little drawings on the blackboard of electric wires and switches and boxes, meant to represent 'communication'; from, as he said, an unknown source, to an unknown recipient: a process beginning and ending in mystery. Shakespeare would have done it with airy sprites, Blake with angels. The little diagrams were the vestiges of a style by whose disguise, in the 'twenties, it was necessary at least to appear to be 'scientific'. But the thought was metaphysical and Platonic.

Whether Cambridge did me as a poet irremediable harm, or good in the long run, it is futile to ask. I was bound to encounter in some form the climate of opinion, the current beliefs of the world into which I was born. Perhaps I am able now to speak with the more authority on the side of Plato and Plotinus for having lived in, and through, the other culture. Not that I clearly recognized that I was involved in any such conflict of values, felt but not defined. What was at issue was Job's and Oedipus's question, 'What is man?'; and in the Cambridge of those days the materialist view prevailed. With greater knowledge I would have understood that two irreconcilable systems were in conflict; but that realization presupposes greater knowledge of both alternatives than I then possessed. As it was I encountered piecemeal situations in which my foolish head was in conflict with my not yet wholly corrupted intuition. But how else are we ever led, by degrees, by trial and error, to discover and to acquire the knowledge we need?

For the time being, religion and poetry perished together in the same ignorance; an ignorance eagerly adopted as knowledge; I readily believed that such true intimations as I then had were to be suppressed. Besides I was so thankful to be free from Wesleyan Methodism that I was glad to let God and the soul go. I had suffered too much in the name of the former, and thought I should be more free without the latter. This was not a mere kicking over of the traces, for I really did think that in adopting—as I then did—the materialist philosophy which seemed so compatible with the matter of science, that I was being intellectually 'honest'—the supreme virtue in Cambridge. Pavlov's dogs and their conditioned reflexes, Koehler's apes and behaviourism, I imbibed as a part of my scientific studies. To Freud I was attracted in part by the fascination of the idea, new to my generation, of an unconscious; and in part also because in revenge for my earlier sufferings I was willing to see parents put in the wrong. But I must confess that the raw sexual instinct of which Freud wrote seemed to me to have little to do with love, as I had experienced it and continued to conceive it, and to have few attractions. From my Jewish friend I learned that Marx had extended the materialist philosophy also into the field of economics, thus revolutionizing the world. Intellectual 'honesty' for the time overcame intuitive distaste and I swam with the other fish in that medium of Bloomsbury Humanism, Freudianism, Wittgenstein's and Russell's Positivism, Behaviourism, Marxism, Imagism, to which presently was added Le Corbusier's Functionalism. It is easier to acquire the fashionable ideas of the moment than to acquire, by an essential culture or by deep and prolonged study, standards by which to judge fashions. The rootless will always be attracted, as I was, towards avant-gardism.

So I set to work to learn the sour new style. I saw one day on the Girton notice-board that a third-year student who signed herself Queenie Roth had some volumes of modern poetry to sell; I went to her rooms and bought from the future Mrs. Leavis those works she had decided were not worth keeping; rightly on the whole, I am bound to say. She obviously despised me for buying Humbert Woolf, W. J. Turner, Victoria Sackville-West's *A Land*. But I persisted and did better next time; because I was so ill-informed as never to have heard of him I had the pleasure of discovering T. S. Eliot for myself. I picked up a magazine called *The Criterion* on the table of a provincial journalist, whose son's guest I was, and began to read a poem which began 'Lady, three white leopards sat under a juniper tree', and was hypnotized by the strangeness of a new beauty; a lament for beauty defiled and dishonoured and unavailing, 'the single rose with worm-eaten petals', a threnody of renunication, of relinquishment of all the old sanctity and loveliness of the world, affirmed in the poet's sense of loss; in which I recognized my own, in which a generation recognized itself, far more deeply, God knows, than in any of our shallow affirmations. Returning to Cambridge I learned that the poet I had discovered was famous; and I recognized in *The Waste Land* the spiritual state of Ilford given its enduring expression. It was a shock to many of us, who in his *Waste Land* recognized our own world, when it presently began to be whispered that T. S. Eliot was a Christian; what to us was mere reality was to him the hell of Dante, the state and place of those cut off from God. We disregarded his theology; yet a generation saturated in Atheism, Freudianism and Marxism inhabited, as we inhabited no other poem, Eliot's *The Waste Land*.

CHAPTER TWO

Experiment

My Jewish friend was the first to discover the magazine *Experiment*, in whose first number were printed some poems by one of its many Editors, William Empson. I claimed to be a poet? Very well, here I must stand my trial by my generation. Through *Experiment* I entered upon my own literary adventure. I read the Empson poems and found them so extremely difficult to follow that I could be in no doubt that their author was far more intelligent than I was myself; yet to me it seemed strange that what appeared to be a love-poem should open with the line:

And now she cleans her teeth into the lake . . .

I was naive enough to be repelled by this image, with its insistence upon a physical function, animal process, inappropriate (as it still seemed to my eighteen-year-old self) to the theme of love; which to me still seemed to demand some image of the soul's vision of the beautiful as reflected in the person of the beloved. Let me here say, since I use term the 'soul' very often, that I am perfectly aware of the possible alternatives, such as psyche, brain, drive, complex, ego, and the behaviouristic terms. Each of these, like the psychiatric language of neurosis, psychosis, schizophrenia, paranoia and so on, cannot be separated from systems of ideas, ways of regarding things implicit in their use. If I use the Platonic (and Christian) word, 'the soul', that is because for all practical purposes I regard the total view of things implied by this word to be truer, or at all events more humanly rewarding, than the alternatives. If that view is, by the standards of Indian philosophy, perhaps over-simple, it would introduce too many complications to attempt to use Shankara's terms, alien to my culture; even were I able to do so. And the same would be true of Cabbala and many other excellent structures by which we can assess experience. Well, in those days at all events I believed in the soul as that specifically human life in us of which the body is the vehicle. It seemed then self-evident that this represents our 'higher' nature, and no less self-evident that what passes in that living consciousness—that being in us which we immediately feel to be our 'I am'—is of greater import than our physical functions. The experiences of the soul, for good or ill, I still supposed made up the matter of poetry; and indeed of all the arts, these being the expression and the record of the soul's self-knowledge:

> Nor is there singing-school but studying
> Monuments of its own magnificence.

I remember the incredulity with which a Cambridge friend once quoted Alexander the Great (was it?) as saying that man is 'never less human' than in the act of sex. My contemporaries may not have reached the nadir of a later mentality which sees us as never more human than in this act; but were already on the way to that kind of Darwinian orthodoxy which regards man as no more than one of the 'higher animals' and activated by physical stimuli of different kinds both from without and within. I see very well now the force of that argument of Aristotle's pupil; for the 'nature' of man was, for the ancient world, precisely that wherein we differ from animal, plant or stone.*

But Empson's line was indeed a true expression of the new philosophy I was at the same time engaged in imbibing; I had not yet understood that those who adopt some sort of Darwinian positivism must forego such opening lines as:

> Tell me, where is fancy bred
> Or in the heart, or in the head?

or

> Love bade me welcome, but my soul drew back

or

> Rose of all Roses, Rose of all the world

Even Edwin Muir's

> Yes, yours, my love, is the right human face

*(1991) If in other cultures—that of India for example—the art of sex is seen as sacred, that is not as an animal function but by reason of the participation of the divine nature.

would have seemed to us embarrassingly naive. But I was eager to learn; Empson was admired for his resemblance to Donne; he too very modern in mood when it comes to the physicalities of sex:

> Marke but this flea, and marke in this
> How little that which thou deny'st me is.

In this new poetry 'honesty' (in terms of the new premises of science) decrees not love but sex; in place of the dreams of the heart the 'facts' of physiology, these being 'real', the dreams not. But of course sex is itself only incidental to William Empson's theme; or one might say that the incidentalness of sex (or love) and the anguish arising therefrom, *is* his theme. When the beloved is no more than the surface-tensions and viscosities of a chemical compound of 98 per cent water (of which a textbook of the time alleged even the Archbishop of Canterbury to be composed; which being so of course so much for his beliefs—but then why not those of Marx or Bertrand Russell?) so much for that for which the soul pines. The beloved is 'That mud/ I have heard speak, that will not cake or dry.' The scientists of the Cavendish laboratory (so near to King's College Chapel and Trinity Great Court, but in how other a Cambridge) had set the problem the poets must resolve as best they could: to discover the qualitative implications of their new modelled universe. Of the editors of *Experiment*, J. Bronowski, besides (in his first year) William Empson, was reading mathematics; and the writing of poetry had in the Cambridge of the late 'twenties no necessary connection with the English tripos. I. A. Richards's attempt to make his literary criticism a 'science' was perhaps not so much a literary exercise after all as a response to the scientific ambience in which poetic imagination at that time and in that place found its excitement, illumination, or whatever that quickening of the pulse may be that tells the poet that here is matter for poetry. Even I was aware that poetry must take into itself, and so qualify, the knowledge of our time; find for the human spirit its orientation in a scientific universe new and strange, but astonishingly beautiful. In that context I could well understand William Empson's attempts to capture that strange inhuman beauty of the universe which in awe-inspiring recessions leads away from the human world into distances minute or vast. The anguish of that situation which dissolved the beloved into galaxies and surface-tensions was real enough, God knows.

William Empson's 'tracer-photon with a rocket's life-line' plunged into a strange cosmos, accessible only to intellect; and yet exercising upon our young emotions a terrible negative attraction, like a whirlpool or the edge of a cliff. Intellectual honesty seemed to demand that we throw ourselves over, and the rocket's life-line offered little hope of rescue. Empson's tone of despair contained by intellectual stoicism expressed a more than personal predicament. I too was under the spell of the new scientific universe. This seemed to me, at that time, the 'real' world, and the world of Yeats, Shelley and what had hitherto for me been 'poetry', a fairyland which I must relinquish in the name of that reality; the gods of *Hyperion* (I knew the poem by heart) were, I was now told, mere literary furniture, stood for no reality known to my new world; sorrowfully, but in the name of 'honesty', I let them go. For I did not then know the ground of the philosophy of the beautiful and of the soul, and was easily persuaded that those who wrote of such things were only decorating the surface of 'scientific' realities with pretty fancies. I was not blind and deaf to the wordless testimony of the beautiful itself; but what I divined only intuitively, the flat clever voice of Cambridge ('what exactly do you mean by...') could destroy with pseudo-logic.

Only many years later did I learn that Vernon Watkins had come up to Magdalene, William Empson's college; but had quickly realized that the spiritual climate of Cambridge was deadly to his poetry, and had retreated to his native Gower peninsula and the company of that supreme poet of feeling, Dylan Thomas. He had read the signs and made his escape. The Master of Magdalene had told Vernon he would regret his decision for the rest of his life; but he never did: the daimon's advice is never wrong. That is perhaps what I too should have done; but I had nowhere, any longer, to escape to. The 'Kathie' of the Manse had been driven out of her hiding-place in the wilds, and Roland's Lyric Love was now an Eton-cropped eighteen-year-old undergraduate dedicated to a ruthless pursuit of 'scientific', which is to say impersonal and inhuman, truth. The only course open to me was to go on, for I could not go back.

The one or two poems I had written, during my first year at Girton, were of an immature and personal kind, in no way comparable in quality with Empson's already mature and original poetry. However, I sent them to William Empson; and in due course, to my intense joy, I was invited to lunch by the poet himself.

When I saw William for the first time, he was reclining upon a window-sill of his rooms in the first court of Magdalene. I remember the impression he made upon me—as upon all of us—of contained mental energy, as of a flame whose outline remains constant while its substance is undergoing continual transformation at a temperature at which only intellectual salamanders could hope to live. This impression of perpetual self-consuming mental intensity produced a kind of shock; through no intention or will to impress; for William was simply himself at all times. William came down from the window-sill and brought in the College lunch from the window-box where it was keeping cool (or hot). I seem to remember that there was another guest; but in any company William was the one remembered. Never I think had 'Bill' any wish to excel, lead, dominate, involve or otherwise assert power; he was at all times, on the contrary, mild, impersonal, indifferent to the impression he made to the point of absent-mindedness. Nevertheless his presence spellbound us all. His shapely head, his fine features, his eyes, full lustrous poet's eyes but short-sighted behind glasses and nervously evading a direct look (I always mistrust people who look you straight in the face) was the head, in any gathering, that seemed the focus of all eyes. His mannered speech too charmed us; those Wykehamical intonations slurred and stressed into a kind of incantation, even when he was not declaiming poetry; which he did with frightening intensity, like one possessed.

He was beardless that year; but on a long vacation grew his first beard (I think on a skiing holiday in Switzerland) which added to the daimonic energy of his appearance. His mother (I remember his telling us) had offered him ten pounds to remove the beard; and he had written her that 'since no one had offered him a larger sum to keep it on' he was obliged to accept her offer. So the beard went; but not the instinct for that mandarin form of barbarity, which did assert itself later, as we all know.

The Editors of *Experiment* never took me seriously as a poet, of course, although they all, in turn, looked me over. J. Bronowski ('Bruno') invited me to tea in Jesus College, and produced for the occasion a bag of Chelsea buns and James Reeves, another editor. Only a few years ago Bruno (whom I later met again on account of Blake, and saw frequently) asked me, in the friendliest possible way, what I *really* thought of my own poetry; he was paying me the compliment of crediting me with enough Cambridge intelligence to share his own low opinion of my work and giving me the chance to disown it. Not, indeed, that I have any exaggerated notion of my own poems; they fall far short of what I should have written, of what I hoped to write; but had they been better, Bruno might have liked them even less. William Empson reproached me, at a poetry-reading at which, by chance or by the innate pattern of events, he himself, Vernon Watkins and I were reading our poems, with having 'escaped from Cambridge'; as if I were a deserter. I think he was sorry, from pure affection, for my defection; but that ' Cambridge', an imaginative entity so real, to which he himself belonged and had in great part created, was neither my beginning nor my end. Bronowski, in a television interview following a series of broadcasts entitled *The Ascent of Man*, described those years in Cambridge as 'the time of my life'. Bronowski's imagination responded to the new thought which has become, now, a popular orthodoxy, or norm. The received opinion in our little circle, in those days was, in essence, the theme of his broadcast series; even many of the examples, many details, came back to me, as I watched that series with a strange blend of nostalgia for what to me was less 'the time of my life' than a fool's paradise; and realization of how alien those ideas, once so familiar and so zealously accepted, must always have been to me. But at the time I possessed neither the courage, nor the knowledge, of my intuitions.

My first published poems were praised by only two persons. One was Herbert Read, to whom a copy of the second (or was it the third or fourth?) number of *Experiment* was sent, and who, to the surprise of the many editors, singled out my poems as having some quality. This was the first praise I had ever received, and praise to the young is something more than a pleasure, it is as essential as water to seedlings. The other was from the Earl of Listowel, then Lord Ennismore (or was he during that year 'Mr. Hare', as he chose to become for a time?). His letter I remembered often afterwards in moments of discouragement; for he told me he had liked my poems and that I should go on writing in my own way 'and let your friends' advice go to the devil'; a strong and astonishing phrase, to me, thinking, as I thought I did, so much more highly of those friends' judgement than of my own. A heartening phrase.

Sometimes William invited me to meet him in London during the vacation. He probably thought I was pretty. I think he was, besides, quite simply loyal to all his friends in an undemanding, impersonal, quite uncritical way, just because we were there. So, taking the train from Ilford to Liverpool Street, I would meet William on the steps of the National Gallery, or wherever it might be. He took me to the Noël Coward reviews, and to the Diaghilev ballet; *Le Coq d'Or* I remember, and *L'Aprés-midi d'un Faune*. We walked together among the oriental gods in the British Museum. Left to myself I would no doubt have strayed among the Elgin Marbles; certainly never paused before Bill's Oceanic 'supreme god in the Ethnological section'. Those flame-encompassed bronze Shivas, communicating the sense of motion in stillness of a perpetual transmutation, seemed to me then (rather than the more earthly and serene Chinese deities) the very essence of William Empson. I was one of the few to read his manuscript, lost during the blitz (not burnt or bombed but left in a taxi by John Davenport and never found), on *The Faces of the Buddha*. If I remember aright, one of the contrasts made between the figures of Christ and those of the Buddha was that, whereas it demanded supreme artistry to capture the Christ-like aspect, the Buddha's face itself (and not some symbol comparable to the Cross) was the icon of the Buddhist world; an aspect capturable in its mysterious vacancy by even some ignorant village wood-carver. That expression, written upon the void itself, exerted its power upon the poet of the new void of our world of photons. The sense of the relative, the impermanence, the unreality of the appearances opened by the scientific universe, was old in Buddhism before our civilization was born. It seemed to me at that time a perfectly natural extension of William's intellectual passion and intellectual subtlety that led him to consider the face of the Buddha. He was not religious, but then Buddhism is less a religion than a way of apprehending reality. Is it fancy that it was also with William that I visited the Chinese exhibition at Burlington House, the most marvellous art I had hitherto seen? If not in fact, in spirit it was William who led me there, for it was he who opened our eyes to the Far East.

By the time William reached China a newer anti-religion was already rising to power; and as the son of generations of soldiers and administrators, William concerned himself with the political realities of the world, and therefore with Marxism; though his intellectual poise and detachment would of course no more have committed him to the brash Utopianism of Marxism than to the finer subtleties of Buddhism. All the same, it is perhaps necessary to an understanding of his subtle sense of the relative to read his poems in terms not only of a scientific relativity but in the flicker of that everlasting bonfire which gives the same fluidity to the dance of Shiva as to the smile of the Buddha. Unreality itself, after all, is itself only relative:

> Not but they die, the teasers and the dreams;
> Not but they die; and tell the careful flood
> To give them what they clamour for, and why.
>
> Our claims to act appear so small to these,
> Our claims to act
> Colder lunacies...

William was well aware that the answers, no less than the questions, of our sciences were only that rocket life-line of human knowledge thrown out into the void; which he knew (as cruder minds do not) no increase of that knowledge would ever lessen.

Yet I think I learned more, in those years, from the inspired talk of Humphrey Jennings than from any other person. I see him, in memory, as an incarnation of Blake's Los, spirit of prophecy; whom in appearance, with his full flashing eyes and mane of yellow hair, he much resembled. Humphrey used to declaim, with 'the mouth of a true orator', long passages of Blake's prophetic books. Years before he made his war-documentary film of the London fire-service, *Fires were Started*, he would recite the passage which begins: 'I see London, a human awful wonder of God.' Unlike other of my avant-garde contemporaries Humphrey had the sense of wonder and of glory. He talked of Triumphs, of Gray's Progress of Poetry, of Inigo Jones. He designed the costumes and scenery for Purcell's *King Arthur*, one of the most memorable of Cambridge musical productions. While the rest of us were reading Freud, Humphrey was already reading Jung's *Secret of the Golden Flower*; he quoted from Lao Tze, and not only in Arthur Waley's translations. I remember after one vacation returning to Cambridge, having at last made up my mind to put Rosetti and the pre-Raphaelites behind me; to discover that Humphrey was using all his eloquence to reinstate them. His mother was a disciple of Ouspenski; and Humphrey used to say of her, 'My mother thinks she has the key of the universe in her pocket; and perhaps she has.' Of that denigrating rationalist 'honesty' he had not a trace, making whatever his imagination touched seem always more, not less, than it had seemed before. In none of the many arts he attempted (he painted, wrote, made films, designed for the theatre) did he ever succeed in expressing more than a trace of that inspired quality which remains now only in the memory of his friends.

Humphrey was already married, as an undergraduate, to beautiful Cicely Cooper. She was tall, statuesque, and as silent as Humphrey was voluble. She had been a débutante, and her wonderful simple clothes were in the style of *Vogue*; which I first saw on her table. Her little white straw hats shaded her beautiful eloquent grey Irish eyes. She was everywhere accompanied by her fierce Pekinese dog. From Cicely I learned with astonishment that cookery could be an art. When she married Humphrey her parents cut off her allowance, and they lived in poverty in a tiny house in Round Church Street, made elegant by Cicely's taste and Humphrey's skill. Humphrey (partly French) and Cicely, a perfectionist also, had nothing about them which was not beautiful. One basket chair only, but the stripes of the Basque linen of its cushions were right to a hair's breadth. On her small housekeeping allowance Cicely would make not 'rice pudding' but delicious *gâteaux de riz*: no more expensive, but infinitely better. Humphrey painted with the perfectionism of fine art the flimsy walls and doors and the uneven floors of that little house where poverty itself was immaculate.

It was Humphrey who made us aware of contemporary movements in France, who opened to us the pages of *Minotaur* and *Transition*, and *Cahier d'Art*. Later he became involved in the Surrealist movement and the friend of Magritte and Paul Eluard. He held forth on Marcel Duchamps and other makers of the movement of *Surréalisme au service de la révolution*; under whose banner he harangued the young men of our new age. On whatever subject Humphrey held forth he was irresistible. 'You must *be* 1932,' I remember his proclaiming in that year; and indeed he 'was' 1932, following Rimbaud's injunction (often on his lips), *'Il faut être absolument moderne.'* It was from Humphrey we caught that magical awareness of the growing-point of the consciousness of the world, which is (or so we then believed) the poetic vision itself.

I know of no name for the phenomenon by which, in any generation at any University, the young discover and recognize in one another those who make up that mysterious growing-point. It is not necessarily those with the most distinguished academic careers who constitute that 'happy few' (we used Stendhal's phrase unashamedly, for it had not occurred, then, to anyone to call in question the self-evident existence of that élite). Not all its members were friends, or liked one another; but all were aware of one another. What strikes me now is how right were those instinctive recognitions and how many of those of my own generation were to become more or less famous. Aloof, in Trinity, Steven Runciman and Anthony Blunt; in Magdalene, Bill Empson, and the photographer Henri Cartier-Bresson; Michael Redgrave; T. H. White (author of *The Once and Future King),* was already respected, for he had published a little volume of verses, *Loved Helen.* J. Bronowski already spoke in the editorial plural—('we' think, etc., later justified by popular acclaim; to which, neverthelesss, he never sacrificed certain principles of intellectual and moral integrity). James Reeves; George Reavey, Pasternak's first translator; several young Trevelyans (I knew only Julian, the painter, at that time); Robin Darwin; Richard Eberhart, our American poet; in King's Julian Bell, killed in the Spanish Civil War, but not forgotten; Alistair Cooke, elegant with his bow-tie, about to take off for America. What we recognized in one another was not academic distinction, or any tangible achievement, but rather a sense of being involved, individually or collectively, in the advancing frontiers of, not so much knowledge in the abstract, as the consciousness of our generation. We felt ourselves to be a growing-point even when we were in the bud. This must be a natural process, repeated in Athens, Florence, Paris, Nalanda, Kyoto, Boston, wherever the Good City may reappear; as it will always reappear.

We knew fairly accurately how we ourselves and others stood years before we had been put to the proof. But I wonder how many of us realized then that Malcolm Lowry, the only one (besides Humphrey) of my then contemporaries to whom the word genius can be truly applied, possessed that gift of which Cambridge values took little cognizance? True, John Davenport, then as later remarkable for his discernment (he was also one of the first to acclaim Isaak Dinesen and a boon companion of Dylan Thomas), loyally and constantly, if prematurely, proclaimed

Malcolm's greatness. He did indeed publish extracts from his first novel, *Ultramarine*, in *Experiment*; but it was only after many years that *Under the Volcano* showed us who Malcolm really was. Shy, tongue-tied, gauche except when he played and sang to his taropatch, little use at examinations, his gifts were ,of feeling and imagination; aspects of life little valued in our Cambridge. William Empson, among us in the full blaze of his glory, impressed us more, because his gifts were within the range of our understanding. William was able brilliantly to articulate a student's intellectual and emotional experience. As between William's brilliant gift of discursive intellect and Malcolm's inarticulate, profound feeling and intuitive insight, William's, at that time, impressed us more. Or must I say, impressed me more. Impressed me in part because William's brilliance frightened me and made me feel inferior; whereas Malcolm did not frighten; he was too shy, too vulnerable, to overawe; too disarmingly simple when he sang:

> This year, next year
> Sometime, never,
> Love goes on and on for ever.
> What makes the world go ro-ound is love.

Yet the singer of these simple sentiments possessed virtues and qualities of genius that were no part of our Cambridge scheme of things; Bill had no great opinion of him; and, as always, I followed my foolish head instead of the simplicity of that other faculty to whose recognition the head has, in the long run, to bow.

I was in a sense committed to this world whose values and whose philosophy, whose poetry and whose criticism, I have since slowly unlearned. I had eaten in Cambridge the pomegranate seed that in Ilford I had refused, and I was a willing captive—was, indeed, captivated—yet in another sense it was all unreal, my thin brittle new personality playing its part as in a play, or a dream. I played my part but did not live it; yet I assumed it with, I must confess, much enthusiasm. I was not, at that time, anyone or anything except the part. I was I think entirely absent from myself, and lived in my new *persona*; my chief occupation during these years—my chief pleasure as well—was the constructing of one. I was a living example of those theories of behaviourism and conditioning which I studied in my text books. Heaven knows I had need of a mask, if only for the protection of my interior self; but somewhere between Ilford and Cambridge I had lost that self; lost my soul. Yet that mask has remained the only one I ever succeeded in constructing. I wear it, even now, with deceptive ease; for a mask is a protection, a concealment. It is also uncommonly hard to get rid of, like accent in speech, or other marks written on us as we go through the world, which tell strangers where our journey has led us. I have a great dislike of my own mask, whenever I catch a glimpse of it. It fits remarkably ill the person who slips it off whenever solitude permits; yet I cannot disown it, it is what I chose to make of myself, at that time.

I see now that my will and my heart were at fault or I would never have been betrayed into ways of thought so destructive of feeling. Heartless and hard as I was, with my little dangerous knowledge, I was a monster indeed. But what other ground had I, at that time, upon which to build a life? It was by no will of my own that my roots had been torn out of their native soil. There was no turning back.

There is one memory whose reproach has never left me; doubtless it is the symbolic veil of much more that lies behind it. At the end of I think it was my first term at Girton, my Girton friends and I planned to bicycle back to London, leaving our luggage to follow by Carter Paterson. The return to Ilford from Cambridge was, for me, like an extinction. The two worlds, the two lives were, in my experience, utterly unrelated: the one a nightmare which might after all prove real and swallow me back into itself; the other a reality which might prove a dream and elude me. Both could not be true. I do not know how to describe, except to those (and they must be many) who have also known it, the gulf which separated the two worlds between which my life was now divided. To my friends, home and Cambridge were only separate places in the same world, and life; to me they were as removed as the Tower and the Court to Calderon's Segismundo (whose nobility and whose philosophy I, however, lacked). I dreaded the end of term, the vacation which condemned me to become again my Ilford self. And yet my parents looked forward, and especially my mother, to the return of her spoiled beautiful clever daughter, as her own one slender link with the bright world. My mother's life was, I think, vicarious, lived through me; all that I was now living in that remote world she now hoped I would give her; while I, possessing a foothold of escape so precarious, feared above everything the intrusion of my parents upon my new identity, whose separateness from them I was determined this time, and at all costs, to keep. I had not survived without mutilation their destruction of my first love, and this time I was all defence. But to my mother I was herself, an extension of her own life, as Persephone of Demeter; but the roles were reversed, for it was my mother who was imprisoned in Hades, realizing only in me, who lived in a brighter world, her dreams and hopes. But I was neither willing nor able to rescue her from her place of darkness, the scene, for me as for her, of so much sorrow. I feared to be dragged down myself and I saw no possibility of saving her from drowning. Her grief might well have drowned me, had I loved her; but instead, her love, her attempt to enter wholly into my life, I called 'possessiveness'; a fine word, scientific and unfeeling, from my brave new world. I had no mercy.

And so from my bicycle I alighted outside West View in a mood of guarded and resentful hostility. The house seemed smaller and uglier than I had remembered. Between the garden gate and the front door I had to shrink back into those mean dimensions which had once held me, and in which I had so chafed for freedom; to cease to be that wonderful winged creature I thought I had become; to become again my mother's Kathie, my father's daughter. The process was too sudden: the dining-room seemed to me unbelievably small, everything in it ugly, from the net curtains to the roll-top bureau and the black marble clock on the red marble mantelpiece. I looked round the room in vain for some beautiful thing upon which to rest my eye, and found none. But my mother had prepared for my coming; all had been dusted and polished with love. In the middle of the dining-table, on the blue chenille table-cloth, stood a vase, a blue and white vase of cheap Chinese ware; in it was a spray of mimosa. My mother asked me if I did not think it was beautiful; and, God forgive me, I said No. I repulsed her, and refused the flower she offered me. Now I cannot see mimosa or smell its heavenly fragrance, without seeing the blue vase, with my mother's flowers, and knowing that many murders have been less murderous than my cruelty then.

My secret intention, at Cambridge as formerly in childhood, was to be a poet; but what had I to prove my claim? My poetry, as I alone believed, lay in the future. And supposing I had been able to prove myself a poet (as William had already done) what do poets do, on going down from Cambridge? Write poetry? But where, in what circumstances, in what capacity? I had no idea. I saw Julian Trevelyan setting off for Paris to be a painter, and this seemed right and natural. He lived there very simply—or it seemed simple. Julian Bell could live in the country, in his mother's cottage, and 'write'; and this too looked simple; the very name 'cottage' suggested simple poverty. Brought up as I had been to think that money did not matter, it never crossed my mind that the only thing which prevented me from doing likewise was the five hundred pounds a year on which each of these friends could afford to live simply. I early made a vow to myself (I have even kept it with some lapses) never to do for money anything which I would not do for its own sake. I have lived most of my life as if I had an income, without having an income. Most of the poets I have known have done the same, more or less, and survived by miracle. Now, believing as I do that all is miracle, I wish that my faith had been greater.

I had never clearly thought about the difference between a vocation and a career, or the practical problem of how to relate the two. I had not thought about a career at all; I had merely floated on the crest of the waves, never doubting that the world would somehow look after so bright a creature as myself. I had worked hard enough during my first two years and taken my Natural Sciences Tripos, Part I at the end of that time, thus becoming qualified for my honours degree. I had hoped, but not with much confidence for a first, and obtained an honourable enough II.I. I had therefore a year to spare, as it seemed to me; and at this stage the obviously wise thing for me to have done, had I been a sincere scientist, would have been to take Part II in either Zoology or Botany. Ill-advised—unadvised, in fact—I thought I could at this stage best be about my daimon's business by reading Moral Sciences Part II. I imagined, naive as I was, that from 'philosophy' I should learn the deep truth for which I was ever in search. Under the illusion that 'psychology' would unlock to me the secret knowledge of the soul, of consciousness, or at least the material of Freud and Jung, I wasted a year in the Department of Psychology, which was in fact concerned only with the physiology of the sense-organs; I had strayed unawares even deeper into the mirk of behaviourism. I obtained only a third class in this ghastly subject; but I deserved no better, for my third year I devoted, in reality, to my literary education; that is, to the reading of Proust, Joyce, Eliot, Arthur Waley's translations from the Chinese, Greek drama, and a general course of English and French literature, ancient and modern, undertaken by myself with advice from my friends. I have always worked hardest and best at self-imposed tasks. As my father would have no priest between himself and God, so I would have no intermediary between myself and my fellow-writers; for so, from the very outset, I regarded them.

When, therefore, Cambridge came to its sudden end, I had no idea what I would or could do, and had no idea where to turn for advice. This may seem strange; but I had lost touch with those concerned with me as a student of biology, and my adventure into the Department of Psychology had been disastrous. In any case, what really concerned me was neither the one nor the other; and I was too much in awe of all senior members of the University to go for help to any adult. If there was at that time an Appointments Board, I did not know of it—this was not the sort of thing I ever knew. It may seem incredible that a not untalented student, for whom so much had been done, should not have known, at the end of three years in Cambridge, which way to turn; but so it was. My only friends were of my own generation.

Julian Bell took me to see Virginia Woolf to ask her to give me some kind of job at the Hogarth Press; but the tongue-tied, badly dressed, ignorant girl made on her (she looked worn and human at this meeting, without the *mana* of my first sight of her) no impression, and no job was forthcoming. I was interviewed by one or two head-mistresses of girls' schools looking for junior science-mistresses; but to them I was not Kathleen Raine the poet, but a young person most unsuitable for their staff, obviously not a lady, and only moderately well qualified to teach. The unbearable humiliation of these interviews threw me into a panic terror. For my father had meanwhile found a place for me as a teacher in a secondary school a mile or two from Ilford: I could teach there and live at home.

If, now, I were to encounter such a girl as I was then, I think she would inspire in me little confidence. I would not believe her capable of realizing a dream so remote from the circumstances of her birth and upbringing; I would be disgusted by her avant-gardism, would say, like the beautiful medical student of my first year, that is what comes of letting secondary-school girls into Girton: they lose their heads and their bearings. But it was not so simple as that; for most girls, secondary-school or otherwise, who go up to the University want to follow some specific career, and are set on their way to accomplish it; whereas I wanted to soar, to be a poet, to live as a poet, to think the thoughts of a poet. I had not realized that Cambridge was no more a place where such a vocation could be realized than was Ilford. Was I mistaken, has all my life been only a long flight from reality, a refusal of the Darwinian virtue of 'adaptation'? Yes, but to what reality, to what environment, then, ought I to have adapted myself? Should I have been a farmer's wife in Northumberland? I might have been happy if such had been my lot. Or a city clerk's wife in Ilford? The mistress of a distinguished Frenchman? The school-teacher my father always saw in me? Aunty Peggy, dear schoolmistress of the children of Bavington, astonished me once, later, when my life had become even more entangled, by blaming my parents for driving me up the educational ladder; she, at least, knew that the 'Kathie' of Bavington was a simple, happy creature, who might have found her place in that rooted world among my old companions. What good had my education done me? None, in her opinion. But my destiny was otherwise. Those, besides, who, like myself, had seen nothing of 'the world' but its Ilfords are not likely to consent to the curbing of winged dreams to fit such a norm. I was more ignorant than I knew of the world and its many doors, open or closed. To me it seemed like a blank wall of steel, and the thought of going out into it filled me with a nightmare terror which I could never have explained to any of those friends and contemporaries for whom the world was *terra firma* from the outset. I had no place in it save one from which I must escape, as from the City of Destruction; home, my only security, was the place from which, above all, I must escape or perish. Like the legendary martlet, which has wings but no feet, I must fly because I could not come down to earth. Fly or perish; fly and perish.

CHAPTER THREE

'From Fear to Fear Successively Betrayed. . .'

William Empson

PERHAPS I would never have accepted such spurious truths of Cambridge rationalism had I not closed my heart; which could never have been deceived by the new doctrine that 'honesty' consisted in disregard of feeling (which was 'purely subjective') in ourselves and others: a quantitative, positivist honesty. Pithed frogs, a charming dog made to run before Professor Barcroft's class of physiology students with the spleen stitched outside its skin, and many other things of the same kind caused me not a qualm, since the pursuit of that inhuman 'truth' justified all. Feeling is at disadvantage when it argues its truth against that of cold reason. In the Cambridge of the 'twenties this was the more so because the scientific materialism generated in the prestigious Cavendish Laboratory and its encircling power-houses made reason itself serve the quantitatively verifiable. 'We do not cry because we are sorry, we are sorry because we cry'; mind is an epiphenomenon of the brain, love of sex-hormones, and so on. I do not wish to vindicate myself by blaming the mental climate of Cambridge; but I must say that spiritual defences stronger than mine would have been needed to survive. On the one hand the 'logical positivism' Russell and Wittgenstein (then in their meridian glory), on the other the civilized arrogance of the Bloomsbury school, whose atheism was no less assured. And because between my father's unassailable puritanism and Roland's more spurious Anglo-Catholic aesthetic asceticism I had so greatly suffered (so I thought) through religion I was the more willing to join 'The Heretics' who met on Sunday evenings. Disbelief seemed, at that time, to offer a sort of freedom.

It is also true that the cold clear rational faculty, so able to wound, cannot itself be hurt, as feeling can. This, in the Cambridge of the 'twenties, was taken to be a mark of the superiority of rational judgements to those of the heart: the reason sees impartially, and is therefore unprejudiced. That there are matters in which reason cannot see at all nobody—if anyone dared to think so—ventured to say. Jung's *Psychological Types* had been published, but among the Heretics, Freud was orthodox, Jung heretical. I had learned my lesson quickly after making a fool of myself by confessing to a love of Shelley and Keats (William Empson did not approve of Keats) and of the Celtic Twilight. I had given a reading from the Irish poets at a Wesley Guild not long before I went up to Girton, but I soon learned not to mention Æ and Padraic Colum and, for that matter, Yeats, who was held in equally low regard. 'The Early Yeats', they later called him, justifying their own failure to identify him as the greatest poet of this century; as though the author of *All Souls Night* were a different person from the author of *Fergus and the Druid*.

Yet prepared as I was to be heartless and 'scientific' towards others, I was myself agonized, guilt-ridden, and as sensitive as if some vital organ in myself had likewise been exposed to every painful touch. No woman is more dangerous to others than a young girl whose heart has been destroyed; as, between Roland and my father, mine had certainly been. It never occurred to me that I could be dangerous, for I was aware only of my own misery. When we are unhappy it does not occur to us, so much do we feel ourselves to be the victims of the world, the sufferers in every situation, that in our very helplessness lies our power to injure others.

The injury I had myself suffered through my first experience of love was apparent to no one but myself. I came and went in that young world, myself young, with enough natural beauty for my ignorance of how to behave or dress or float or steer myself (between excessive social fear and excessive social elation) not to matter very much, buoyant with the superficial cold excitement of the unfeeling; for I, who had felt too much, now felt nothing, loved no one. I believed I would never love again, believed, in the words of a not-yet-quite-forgotten early influence, Fiona Macleod, that 'there is only the one love'; and for me that one love lay, I thought, in the past.

Yet I can distinctly remember once waking on a May morning in Girton (it must have been May, for the memory brings with it the scent of honeysuckle and the dapple of sun through young leaves) and the sudden surprise in which I said to myself, 'why, I am happy!' The leaden weight had lifted; it did not last, nor have such mornings returned to me so often that the impression of astonishment has ever been effaced.

Yet at the same time I did enjoy the power I knew I possessed; the knowledge that when I entered a college hall for some concert, or the foyer of the Festival Theatre, or bicycled down Trinity Street, or even took my seat in a lecture-room, I would draw, if not all eyes, at least a great many, exalted me the more pleasurably for my own vulnerability. I do not say that I was beautiful (my bone-structure is plebeian and has not stood the test of time), only that undergraduates thought me so. I was told, half a lifetime after, that a little Society was formed to watch for me to pass, whose members counted the score each week of the number of times they had seen me. I do not even know who they were.

There was a time, in my first year, when Denis Arundel, seeing me afar off, was determined to give me the principal role in his production of Purcell's *King Arthur*; and for a moment I enjoyed, in Girton, the infirm glory of being 'the girl Denis Arundel was raving about'. (My father forbade me to take the part, pointing out to me that I was at Cambridge to work, not to waste time in amateur theatricals.) This turned my head completely for a time; for it is hard, at eighteen, to grasp the truth that to be loved for our beauty is not to be loved at all. We expect to be treated as the goddess whose reflected image we bear; we think we are ourselves that goddess. When at the end of my third year I had no idea where to go or what to do, William Empson's idea was that my face would adorn the cinema-screen and he sent photographs of me to his old school friend Anthony Asquith. The photographs were well received, but nothing of course came of it. I may add that I have not a trace of the actor's gift.

I discovered the power of my youthful beauty quite coldly, without happiness; and although I was quite unscrupulous about being admired at a distance, and fed upon such tributes, any closer approach threw me into an excess of guilt. I had brought with me to Cambridge, from my father and the Wesleyan Methodists, nothing of what was best in my father's morality, and may have been Christian in Methodism; but I did retain the strongest possible sense that to attract a man sexually must imply guilt on my part. I judged, besides, all professions of love by what with Roland I had known love to be, as deep as life. I had no other conception of it; that the physical instinct of sex could ever be separated from the depths of feeling with which, for us (and, as I still believe, for all the uncorrupted) it had been associated, I could not so much as imagine. To awaken such love, such tragic possibilities, must indeed be a grave matter. Twice I had brought sorrow upon myself and upon others by the inadvertent exercise of my power to evoke erotic love; and in Cambridge that power was all the more beyond my conscious control because I had become quite frigid; for not only was I pursued by my own heartbreak, by Roland's battles between desire and asceticism, but by my father's religious grief and anger, and my mother's tears—all caused by my fault.

So that, if other young women might enjoy the play of 'laughter-loving Aphrodite', to me it did not seem like play, but deadly earnest, guilt and misery. I tried to avoid and evade any sexual advance or entanglement, keeping the young men I met at the distance of friendship, trying to establish friendship. I was in this successful only with those of my men acquaintances capable of the kind of respect which friendship with a woman implies; or with men whose manners were good, and who therefore would never approach more nearly than they were permitted. It was, therefore, the very men I did not want and whom I liked least, those whose quality of feeling was least fine or who flouted convention, who were able to trip up my unstable balance. I felt myself to be like a creature hunted for its skin. I had lost

> The undaunted courage of a Virgin Mind
> For Early I in love was crost
> Before my flower of love was lost.

I hated and feared my home, I had no one to protect or advise me, my head was full of a confusion of untried opinions, many of them adopted for no better reason than that they seemed to offer me the greatest possibility of freedom from my parents' power over me; a sorry state altogether. Into this lamentable loveless, despairing helpless morass I sank deeper and deeper with every attempt to extricate myself.

For nearly the whole of my first year I kept my precarious balance; but M. d'H. was writing to me, laying his future at my feet and liable at any moment to arrive in Cambridge. This dreadful possibility I did not know how to prevent, for how could I be ruthless to my old mentor, my first philosopher and friend, towards whom I still retained the respect tinged with awe which children feel towards members of their parents' generation? While I was thus racked with anxiety a student many years older than the normal age of undergraduates suddenly 'proposed' to me. This was almost the first conversation we had had, for I had met him only as a member of the small biological tea-club to which I had been so proud to be elected, and so foolish as to imagine that my election had something to do with my promise as a biologist. His proposal took me utterly by surprise, his mature age put me at a disadvantage with him, but I thought I had, however badly, made it clear that I wished to reject his unwelcome offer. But, being extremely naive and maladroit, I confided to this man something of my predicament with M. d'H. This proved fatal; and between my weakness and his want of whichever of the nobler virtues I had hoped or imagined I might have appealed to in him, I found that he had persuaded me into an 'engagement', and on that condition taken it upon himself to 'protect' me against my still honoured friend. What better pretext could I offer M. d'H. for ceasing to correspond with him than that

I was 'engaged'? Thus I placed myself in the predicament of having blindly accepted the protection of a man I scarcely knew against the only wise and mature friend I had, then or for many years to come.

I distinctly recollect the sense of guilt and responsibility I felt at this declaration, although in fact such violent and sudden attractions have no more claim than has the moth to the candle.

My problem at once became how to rid myself of this man into whose power I had, through mere social maladroitness, fallen. He threatened suicide on my attempting to break off the 'engagement'; and I had not the discernment to see that this threat was most unlikely to be carried out. It took me more than a term to free myself; as at last I did by provoking a quarrel in which he himself requested the return of the engagement ring and the string of 'culture pearls' he had given me. I walked away from Emmanuel College, rid of these tokens of my degradation, like an animal which without knowing how or why finds the cage-door open.

It was after that escape from ignominy that I began to make those friendships among my fellow-writers which transformed my life at Cambridge from the obscurity of an anonymous science student from Ilford, to the infirm glory of undergraduate notoriety.

Brief as was that shameful and meaningless engagement, of one memory I cannot free myself: I took that intruder into my destiny to Bavington. In the summer vacation, he was invited by my parents to accompany us to the Manse. No doubt they were thankful, after the sorrows my first love had caused us all, to imagine I had now found happiness, and as unaccountably welcomed this engagement as they had opposed my too early love. Of course he no more visited Bavington, in reality, than he was 'engaged' to me: both events were unrealities (though God knows such unrealities may swallow up a lifetime, not a matter of a few weeks only) for places have their inviolable secret essence, as have human souls. But that visit, in the degradation of that relationship, laid waste my sanctuary; I felt I could never, thereafter, return.

That miserable visit was to be the last time I ever stayed at the Manse; and now I was not able, any longer, to reach across time and what I had myself become and done, to my old companions and play-fellows and the fields and the moors; the well and the burn, the summit of Simonside on the horizon and the liverwort on the stone outcrop, the scent of camomile in the farmyard had, as Blake puts it, 'wandered away into a distant night.' Paradise was lost, but so lost was I myself that I had not even, any longer, as with Roland, the consolation of poetry; not even that grief which is still a mode of love, and a keeping faith with that which is lost. Where once there had been a place, and what once had been my life, had been myself, was only an apathetic negation.

'From Fear to Fear Successively Betrayed . . .'

To those who move from one social setting into another entirely different, the new world must always seem more or less unreal, dream-like; so that the natural proportions of human loves and hates, the sense of who and what we ourselves and others are, and how we stand in relation to them (things known instinctively, from birth, in any village, or in any world which is, village-like, continuous and hereditary) is distorted if not entirely lost. The child who in Northumberland had lived among people who were all, good or bad, clever or half-witted, part of the very texture of life, entered Cambridge after a period in Ilford during which, thread by thread, these natural attachments had been broken. Desperate to replace myself in the human world, I was nevertheless almost incapable of doing so. Intellectually I succeeded, to some extent; but emotional ties are deeper, and do not take root so easily.

If I had not done it myself I would now find it hard to believe that an attractive and intelligent young woman, after spending three years at the most famous of women's colleges, could marry, as I did, without love, without sexual attraction, without any good reason at all. People may say 'but you must have *thought* you were in love'; but I did not: what I thought (if anything) was that I should never love again, so what did it matter? I prided myself upon making no attempt to captivate any of my more distinguished acquaintances—on having, on the contrary, held them at arm's length—the sense of honour of the poor, inherited from my father, and not, perhaps, to be regretted. But, with whatever scruples I had about what I would *not* do, I did far worse; not actively, but passively, in mere weakness; had I been, so to say, 'there', I would not have acted so: in my absence, these things befell me.

Where there is neither love in the heart nor wisdom in the mind, we seem as though involved in that blind mechanism behaviourists take the world to be. The sexual instinct is, when awake and living, vital, bringing together, for its own purposes, those who should be brought together, with much wisdom, so far as those purposes go. The blind passive involvement catches us up in a seemingly mechanical causality when, on the contrary, we are neither spiritually, emotionally, nor even physically alive; when the soul is inert we become like inert matter, driven hither and thither like the legendary atoms, by impulses which seem as if external to ourselves. Purposeless as the little balls that roll down pin-tables we are deflected on our passive, and always downward, course, by every obstacle; coming to rest in some pocket which may score five, or a hundred, or zero. The punishment of those who believe the world to be a mechanism is that, for such, this state exists.

The self-assurance and equilibrium of those who live on the physical plane does not exist in those whom nature designs for another kind of love. If the sexual instinct was at that time my undoing, it was not through its strength but through its weakness; no one who lives much in the physical could have been so overset as I was; what happened to my body did not seem to me greatly to matter, after my early heartbreak. It is not for myself that I am pleading the cause of that long-vanished young woman (for now what does it matter to me?) but for others like myself.

It was not, God knows, in the Christian sense a marriage; it was, rather, an alliance against society made by two young people whose only bond was a rejection of all those old values, good and bad, from which we were both in revolt. It was, one might say, an anti-marriage. I entered it with one secret assurance—that it would not last; it was an emergency measure. Neither believed in that old fiction of life-long marriage. Because of this tacit mutual cynical contempt for the marriage bond, it seemed not altogether like entering a prison, but, rather, like a kind of refuge.

But on my side there were more ignoble ulterior motives; marriage seemed a trivial price to pay in order to stay on in Cambridge, to go on walking among those trees, by that river, those buildings of beauty; and besides, I had no idea where else to go. My motives, then, were the fears and weaknesses of a character whose dread and ignorance of the world were limitless; his perhaps the 'bagging' of the white deer, or white blackbird, admired by many. But such prizes amount to nothing, when the excitement of the hunt is over, but a rotting corpse and a few feathers.

Upon such despicable grounds, then, I married. Love I believed was over; social duty had no meaning for me, since far from wishing to preserve the stability of the family and society from which I was in flight, my only wish was to escape. Despair, besides, does not rest in passive hopelessness, but is active, committing a piece-meal suicide in an impulse of self-destruction (or merely of destruction) which runs its course towards some decisive disaster, which alone can reverse the destructive process. It seems as if we are driven to make of ourselves and of our lives images of the inner grief and self-immolation of a broken love. The tearing of the hair and scratching of the cheeks is as nothing to the worse defacements girls in despair will work upon their lives. Despair is, theologically considered, not only a sin but the greatest of all sins; and yet at the same time there is a sort of pride in it, a pleasure even, as in the only great thing left to us. It is also a kind of revenge on those whom we imagine have driven us to it—in my own case, my poor father and mother, by now so bewildered by me. Their view by then was already that their daughter had broken their hearts and bowed them with shame in the eyes of their neighbours; and the terrible truth is, that this was indeed so.

Yet at this lowest point to which I had yet sunk, I had no conception of the nature or extent of the sin—to use the only true word for it—which I was so joylessly committing.

What we lived in was in truth fornication, not marriage, but just because we both so despised Wesleyan Methodism, because to us it meant so much less than nothing, cynically we made the blasphemous gesture; because a Christian ceremony could not touch such disbelievers, we were married (to placate our parents) by his father (a Methodist minister) in my father's church; in the Cranbrook Park Wesleyan Methodist Church where Roland had practised Bach preludes on the organ, and two star-crossed lovers had gazed at one another entranced, through the sermons of the Rev. Edgar C. Barton. No one was invited: it was not that kind of marriage, there was no joy or love to share; and I went through it all as in a dream. I do not remember that I even thought of Roland; only now in writing of it years after do I feel the pang of grief for the violation of that early love. No one tried to stop me. My father had, I suppose, taken too much to heart the sorrowful consequences of his first interference to attempt a second.

Only one clue even then I did not relinquish: the determination to be a poet. Indeed a common intention to be writers was the only positive ground of our complicity.

The man whose name I so briefly, so inadvertently, and so undeservedly, bore at that time, Hugh Sykes Davies, was a friend of so many members of our Cambridge literary circle that, in the matter of friendships (at that time a bond we probably both felt to be far more binding than that of marriage) our Cambridge life went on somewhat as before. Humphrey and Cicely Jennings were our friends; and Hugh was very close to Malcolm Lowry who came, like himself, from a Methodist background. Both played golf with the detached expertise of the intellectual and I have a vivid picture, more like a photograph than like a memory, of Hugh and Malcolm swimming together in Quy fen, while I, in a complex despair worthy of *Under the Volcano*, looked miserably on.

I had of course read the passages from *Ultramarine* published in *Experiment* and the book itself when it appeared. I was puzzled by Malcolm's evident feeling that the stoke-hole of a tramp-steamer and the brothels of Eastern seaports were somehow closer to 'life' than Monteverdi and Shakespeare played in College halls and the civilized minds of Cambridge. Not the point, of course—I missed the point. I did not understand that Malcolm had taken upon himself an exploration of the whole scope of his world, a quest for paradise which must take into account the hells, 'under the Volcano' on whose green and fertile slopes our Arcadia so precariously lay. We all thought of ourselves as the growing-point of our time; but whereas most of us were only the eternal avant-garde, Malcolm really was open to the suffering and heart-breaking aspirations of humanity's collective mind and most secret thoughts. For genius is not a personal gift but precisely that gift of access to the universal which Malcolm had and we had not.

And yet, though we did not know it, under Malcolm's volcano is precisely where we were, Hugh Sykes and I. I was his faithless 'Yvonne', though I did not, like her, in compassion return when I left him. Malcolm's book has, I now see, mysteriously defined the mental climate in which my first marriage had its brief existence. We were, unawares, experiencing just those underground influences, the subterraneous gathering of catastrophe that Malcolm Lowry so powerfully evokes. The uncharted freedom of a bohemian way of life, just because of its freedom from the ordinary social pressures, reflects, vibrates to, what is 'in the air'.

Hugh, like Malcolm, was very much aware of the Spanish Civil War and was presently to be drawn, like others of that generation (Burgess and Maclean were among his friends, as fellow-members of that élite of élite 'the Apostles') towards Communism. Herbert Read was related to him; and Herbert's gentle and idealistic form of Anarchism was a gleam of light in the sky over Dis, at that time.

But if we were living in the hells we did not know the place by its true name; this, we thought, is the reality of things, this cynical despair is seeing things as they really are. And the hells have their pleasures, if not their joys; not least among these, as Milton knew, the building of Pandemonium, city of those arts and sciences by which the lost adorn their doomed city. To give expression to despair, to uncover, layer upon layer, with the artistry of a Virginia Woolf, bottomless subjectivity; to strike heroic postures of bitterness; to fabricate opinions—these things have their joyless pleasure. We read Petronius and Lautréamont and *Ubu Roi*; and explored our habitation cut off from the light of heaven by the phosphorescence of Surrealism—soon to be *'au service de la révolutiom'*. Only Malcolm saw the hells for what they were; and in so doing—like Dante by the mere change of a point of view, under Satan's hairy thighs— was to be free of them, in the end, the volcano under him and the lovely light of Paradise dawning for him, at last, over the cleansing sea of Dollarton. But all that lay in the future. Neither Hugh Sykes nor I myself knew ourselves in hell, having quite forgotten paradise.

In secret my daimon still reproached me, but indirectly. I remember very little of what I did or thought about at that time, with the exception of the Noh plays of Japan, which seemed to belong, in some profound way, to that which I still was. I read all those translated by Arthur Waley, Pound and Fenollosa, and Marie Stopes. It was among the latter I found the symbol which at that time spoke to me: the play *Motome Zuka (The Maiden's Tomb)*. In that play the confrontation is with the ghost of a young woman who had, in mere vanity, urged her lovers to a rivalry which involved the taking of the life of a mandarin duck. Why this so deeply shook me I did not know; it is when we do not know why they move us that symbols have, indeed, power. There were some mandarin duck in the Cambridge Botanic Gardens; and their strangeness, like the idiom of an unknown, highly subtle and profound Eastern language, I pondered over. I felt the unbounded nature of the maiden's guilt and grief, more deep than that of the mariner for his Albatross, so it seemed to me. What had I killed? I did not know. Perhaps, hating and despising the human kind, including myself, I could be touched only by the innocence of animal nature, made to suffer by the evil of man. Perhaps I had some obscure sense of inadvertent responsibility, of what those do who 'know not what they do': the girl had not intended harm to the creature, yet her heartlessness had started a chain of cause and effect of which the death of that innocent beauty was the term. In her hell she reproached herself less for the rejection and death of her suitors than for the death of the bird. I perhaps sensed in that philosophic play a morality far different from that from which I was in flight, a morality cosmic and inexorable. Sin, in that perspective, does not consist so much in the deliberate act knowingly committed (the Church's 'grave matter, perfect knowledge, full consent') as in the state of ignorance itself. Unawares and even against the conscious intentions such a state of being may—indeed must—set in motion a series of fatal consequences. I did not know why the myth so held me; but I knew in myself those hells of emptiness through which the maiden falls and falls to all eternity. I knew, too, her perverse, despairing refusal of proffered salvation, her remorse which was nevertheless so far from repentance because loveless, self-enclosed, for ever cut off. Her cry 'This too I have done, this too I have done' spoke to me at that time as from the depths of my own life; yet, just as a child does not realize that the power of a fairy-tale lies in its truth to the archetypal nature of childhood itself, so neither did I recognize the power of *The Maiden's Tomb* over me as an identification with the maiden's guilt; still less did I see wherein her guilt (or my own) lay. I pitied and was aghast at her fate.

Only in reviving this memory thirty years after do I recall an earlier mandarin duck. In my first term at Girton I had bought for my mother on her birthday one of those prints sold at the British Museum, a Chinese painting of mandarin ducks and a lotus. (Years later I saw the same, or a very similar print in Mrs. Yeats's house in Palmerston Road in Dublin, and wondered under what circumstances W. B. Yeats—if it was he—had chosen that print.) Was my terrible sense of guilt occasioned by the knowledge that I had destroyed the deepest link of my childhood, that with my mother? That I had betrayed her, perhaps killed her soul, or my own? It may well be so. All that I had from my mother, the flowers of my childhood, Bavington, Scotland, everything I had ever loved and been nourished by I had betrayed and had cut my life off from hers, leaving her, as well I knew, desolate in Ilford. But nothing of that had weighed with me one straw in the balance with my own impulse to escape.

A Chinese poem translated by Ezra Pound I also used to repeat to myself:

> It is said that a certain princess
> When she found she had been married by a demon
> Took a garland of jonquils
> And sent them to her lover of former days.

Yet I no longer loved Roland, he was gone, forgotten, I thought of him without a pang. The charm the poem exerted over me was, so I thought, purely literary.

My despair, if such it was, was painless, for I was at that time dead to all feeling, and saw my guilt and my sorrow alike reflected in the mirror of symbols, as if apart from myself. I coldly watched myself as from a great distance living a life utterly unreal to me; as if I were someone else. I fell very mildly in love with a charming homosexual friend; this sentiment I felt to be innocent because sex and physicality were not involved. It was also a turning towards lost France (he was French). I saw in the kind of Platonic love possible between a homosexual man and a woman a relationship free from the squalor of the body, and vaguely felt that such a love would be appropriate to me. I had always, as a student, been attracted towards such men, who were, indeed, so often physically beautiful, and of a fineness of feeling lacking in the others, at least in their behaviour towards women. They did not hunt me for my skin, and I knew that if they liked me at all it could only be for myself—whoever she was. As to my body (as distinct from my beauty, which I thought of as something apart) my attitude towards it was of contemptuous indifference. It seemed no longer myself, or even mine. Like any prostitute I was able in this respect also to be what I would have called 'detached' —a cardinal virtue of scientific rationalism. Rimbaud's *Je est un autre* was another of the phrases of that time; in a sense, however, far removed from the deeper meaning which I would see in it now. It was, rather, a kind of disclaimer of any responsibility for that detached 'other' who went through the motions of life bearing my name (or not even that, for I bore, then, the name of a stranger). Apathy is a kind of half-suicide, of all the forms of despair the most abject. When I was absent from myself I think I was capable of any degradation, nothing seemed real enough to matter very much at all. I wonder if the worst atrocities have not often—or always—been committed in the absence, so to say, of the person? Whether or not this is so, such absences are extremely dangerous, for those absent from themselves can perform any ruthless or degraded act with complete indifference; even with a kind of masochistic self-pity. 'That I should come to this!' we cry within ourselves, desperately hoping that if things become bad enough some angel or minister of grace will come to our aid. We fling ourselves downwards hoping to find ground if we sink low enough: there must be, we somehow believe, a limit to the fall.

I do not know how we may ever know, in retracing the record of the past, where our responsibility lies, and where we have merely undergone rather than enacted, lived through rather than lived, an event, unless by the sense we have of abiding identity with that past self, or event, or action performed, for better or for worse. I find, for myself, that this sense of identity with past selves is by no means continuous. It is rather as if at times I was present in my life, at other times absent from it altogether; especially after my childhood. The mind which wandered among the structures of mosses and lycopodia in the laboratories of Downing Street was certainly mine; but not the Girton undergraduate whom many of my contemporaries seem to remember better than I remember myself; nor the neurotic bohemian who so dishonourably prolonged her residence in Cambridge, which she dared not leave because she did not know where else to go, by the travesty of a marriage.

Yet up to this point in my life I could perhaps still have pleaded that I had been the victim of circumstances; monstrous as I was, I had in great part been bent and diverted from my true direction by people whose power over me was a part of the given conditions into which I was born, and which were none of my making. Some, even, of my most violent reactions may have been not the least, but the most excusable. But when does responsibility begin? Is it a gradual matter, or are there moments, confrontations with the powers of life, when we make choices by which, because we so deeply made them, we must abide? I believe there are such moments; and marriage ought, of course, to be such a deep choice. In fact this is not always so, and mine was not.

Which of my marriages, if either, the Catholic Church, for instance, would regard as valid, I do not know; it has long ceased to matter. If I were to meet, by the well of life, the Judge, I would say of myself, now as then, 'I have no husband'; and perhaps I should be answered, 'Thou hast well said, I have no husband. For thou hast had five husbands; and he whom thou now hast is not thy husband, in that saidst thou truly.'

I never, as a writer, relinquished the name my parents gave me; 'Kathleen Raine' has been my only enduring identity, yet even that is in some ways accidental; for the poet in me is my mother's daughter, whose name, Jessie, is mine also, although I have never used it; the 'Kathleen' was given to their baby by two young parents who thought it 'sounded better' (with Raine) than Catherine, the name of the aunt after whom I was named. Perhaps I was misnamed at birth; and that secret identity beyond the name? I have at times felt that I have no name, or do not know it.

But that nameless identity I have never relinquished for any man; and had I done so that would have been, I believe, a far deeper betrayal of an original and anterior dedication, one as deep as life, a bond with my daimon not to be broken. No relationship with any man has ever been, for me, of a comparable reality. I mistrust any kind of plea for an exception to the great and abiding laws of life; and yet the vocation of those dedicated to the gods has in all traditional societies been recognized; and the monstrous Medusa was a priestess who broke her vows. Perhaps for many people such questions as these do not arise; but I know that such a predicament as mine does, as a reality, exist. In a simpler world I might have been a nun, or temple virgin, or *devadasi*. I have had to discover, without guidance and with much pain, that my destiny is a solitary one.

Have I merely clung to the illusion that to be a poet was my vocation rather than face the appalling 'realities' of life? M. d'H. had given me a phrase of ancient wisdom which as a schoolgirl and long thereafter I used to repeat to myself, like a *mantram*:'Better to be a crystal and be broken than perfect like a tile upon the housetop.' I never doubted that I was crystal, though to be broken did not seem in any way inevitable; nor did I reflect that tiles are more fragile than diamond, for that matter. In my happier moments I have seen—I still see—the poet's vocation as heaven-sent. But was that compelling imperative secretly implanted in me by my mother who, before I could hold a pencil, wrote down my infant poems? In secret she summoned me to realize her dreams, her unused gifts, her unfulfilled imaginative capacity for experience and expression. She, more naturally gifted than I, was bound by the conventions of her generation, the narrow circumstances of her life, her hawk's eye hooded in her captivity. Was the summoning voice her voice? Perhaps in part this was so. But supposing the sense of vocation—a human experience so universal— to be in part explicable in terms of Freud's 'super-ego', may not this in itself be an aspect, the appointed means, of the process of human aspiration carried on from generation to generation?

Yet in moods of despair, or perhaps of sober realism, a far different voice has mocked me; reminding me that, after all, my poetry has amounted to nothing of value and is no justification for a life whose mere selfishness has masqueraded as vocation. I can make no defence; it may well be so. And yet despair is only another and more destructive sin. Better to try and fail, I try to tell this mocker; better to fail than not to make the attempt. And then the accuser speaks his deadliest word: 'It is not only you yourself who has suffered, you have made others suffer, others pay the price of your poor little vain volumes of verse. I am only', he adds, 'here to open your eyes to the real state of affairs.' And I try to say, Shelley? Coleridge? Milton? Does not the great gift of their poetry to countless lives justify their catastrophic domestic stories? And at that the Devil laughs; for where is my *Prometheus Unbound*, my *Kubla Khan*, my *Lycidas*? Very well, I say, I deplore the failure, the betrayals, through want of courage, through cowardice, through whatever cause, of that clear calling. Was it not the man with one talent only who, in despair, buried his in the ground, to be condemned for his hopelessness? And without trying to write poetry I might have failed just as catastrophically to live a good life, caused and experienced no less suffering. Do only poets fail in the conduct of their lives? And is not every life a vocation (I say, my courage returning), a way to be followed truthfully, come what may, and not only the special case of poet or nun?

Let me, in all humility, own that, as regards marriage, I am of Shelley's party still. Neither the maintenance of social order nor the natural claims of the family have ever seemed to me of the same order of value, or of reality (which is the same thing perhaps) as the soul's pilgrimage, whether the pilgrim be poet or no. I cannot regard a life as a brick in a social structure, but only as a way, which each must follow, out of the mystery, into the mystery again; my most fatal dishonesties, from which have resulted injuries both given and received, have all come from my cowardly attempt to take cover within some social structure or institution. When I have realized my mistake I have without hesitation or remorse set about extricating myself. I never saw any reason to regard a mistake as binding; still less as sacramentally binding, but then sacrament was something, in those years, entirely outside my comprehension or experience. My remorse has been in all cases for entering, not for abandoning, untruthful relationships and situations. Heaven knows what moments of nostalgia I have had for that sweet lost paradise of the love between man and woman, the natural bonds of the family; but of those relationships, as it has proved, I was incapable. Having said all, I cannot justify, but can only affirm, my destiny.

CHAPTER FOUR

The Somnambulist

I ALLOWED myself to be rescued from my first marriage by Charles
Madge; for this I was altogether to blame, for I was older than he, and I
allowed him, in the chivalry of his poetic vision of me, to wreck his
University career for my sake. He had fallen in love with me afar off;
written poems to me. It seemed as if I were summoned by him with the
voice of poetry. Did I love him? God knows; I was too desperate a creature
for any sane or happy love; but I did see, as some Lady of Shallott might
see in her glass, his nobility of character, his rare poetic imagination.
What he saw in me, only God knows too; my delusive and neurotic
beauty, of course; perhaps his poetic muse personified, since he knew me
to be a poet; perhaps some Florimel fleeing through her night-wood of
enchantments (Spenser was the poet he most loved; in appearance he
somewhat resembled him); perhaps, even, a woman of the people, whom
as a Communist (as he had just become at that time) he could fitly idealize.
Our relationship was altogether noble on his side; and even on mine there
was cast a sort of reflected nobility. I remember well the terms in which he
offered himself to me: 'Come with me,' he said, 'and I will give you a cause
to live for.' What he offered me was the cause of Communism; and I,
sickened by cynical hedonism, missing, perhaps, the Christian aspiration
of my father's house, listened.

I was like an invalid paralysed by a mortal illness when he drove me
away from Cambridge in his car; an illness of the will, invisible. I clung to
him in the desperation of weakness, grateful beyond words. Yet I wept
and wept and could not be comforted, imprisoned in my own selfish
shame, as if it were my life and not his which had been ruined by our
elopement. Once he drew a portrait of me on a handkerchief, a sort of
Veronica's napkin on which he depicted a weeping face; which was indeed
the face I turned to him. On the wall of the little room where we lived in
Upper Gloucester Place he painted over the fireplace on the white wall, a
tree with faces in it: the faces of our children, as he imagined them, and
saw them in the glass of the future.

While I clung to him as a drowner to a straw, I was at the same time so
ashamed of my elopement that I would see no one, and would meet
neither my former friends nor his; for many months I hid from my
parents. I seemed to have lost all identity. I would not, then, have dared to
use my Cambridge degree in applying for any kind of post, for I felt I had

forfeited all right to use it. For a while I hawked men's socks in the city; I tried to get a job as a manageress in the Lyons' tea-shops, but was rejected. I cannot remember what I then did it is all too terrible. Once I remember Charles had persuaded me to go with him to a party given by Janet Adam Smith in Ladbroke Square. I remember getting as far as the second floor landing seeing the former and future friends for whose friendship I longed through the door. There was an eight-some reel in progress; the first time I ever saw Edwin and Willa Muir, the merest fleeting impression for I turned back from that innocent happy throng as into the outer darkness of the outcast. On the landing of the stairs I wept, Charles striving to comfort and persuade me to go in with him; but I would not.

Yet his mother heroically accepted me and was more kind than I ever deserved. How she could have endured to let me set foot on the lawns of North End, under her ilex trees and limes, how let me enter that house where all was 'accustomed, ceremonious', in which she, a war-widow, had like a Roman matron brought up her two sons, sent them to Winchester and Cambridge, hoped for them—and of Charles especially— great things, by me laid waste, I cannot now conceive. And yet she did; she must have found my commonness hard to endure, but she never for a moment made me feel that this was so; only once she asked Charles to ask me not to wear a beret for a hat. But I loved her; and this perhaps she knew. Had I been she I could not have behaved towards the intruder, the wrecker of a mother's hopes, as she behaved towards me. To the end of her life, every Christmas, she continued to send me ten shillings to buy some plant in her name. The one I think of as especially hers is a verbena; for in her garden there was a most luxuriant and lovely verbena, wrapped each winter in careful sacking.

Charles, perhaps because of its very perfection, because he had as a child and as a boy been so happy, was in reaction, like Prince Siddartha, against a life too perfect. From Winchester to Magdalene he had gone, the fine product of an old culture. (Charles's father had been one of 'Milner's kindergarten' in South Africa, where until 1914 he remained as a District Commissioner; as Colonel of the Warwicks, he was killed in the trenches early in the first world war.) It takes many generations to produce a house like North End, such women as Mrs. Madge, bred in those austere patrician values he was himself about to abdicate.

Nearly all Charles's Marxist friends were of the upper or upper-middle classes; there was one Honourable, and a number of Wykehamists whom he had magnetized with his own enthusiasm. They were the victims of the conscience of the English ruling class, as was Charles himself, idealists with nothing to gain and everything to lose by the revolution for which they worked all the harder for that, blinded by their own disinterestedness. Charles himself had never seen the working-class until one day the hunger-marchers from the northern coal-mines (my father's Durham) appeared in Cambridge, and he became a convert to the cause of such squalor and misery as he had never dreamed could exist. Charles and his friends in pure disinterested generosity were willing to throw away the heritage of their culture, of all that had gone to create their own sense of *noblesse oblige*. The crowd, 'the workers', they saw from afar off, and in the light of their own high level of culture; and of such idealism as theirs, of course, the real revolutionaries were glad to take advantage. What none of these patricians of the Left understood is that what they were prepared to give and share would not be received but merely cease to exist. It was not a matter of more young men being given the 'opportunities' they had themselves enjoyed, the North Ends, the College cloisters, but the cessation of such things, which after the revolution would simply not exist at all. The masses will not even know what they have destroyed.

Meanwhile Charles conceived that strange half-poetic half-sociological expression of the pre-war years, Mass-Observation; he joined forces with Tom Harrisson, who had been studying the anthropology of Bolton and Blackpool. We lived, then, at Blackheath where we had gone to be near Humphrey and Cicely Jennings. Humphrey was working with the left-wing film-director John Grierson, and another Cambridge friend, Stuart Legg, in the G.P.O. film-unit, which at that time was making documentary films of 'men at work'; a pale reflection of the post-revolutionary Russian films of those years. To Charles, who seemed at the time a man inspired, almost as a medium is inspired or possessed, the idea of Mass-Observation was less sociology than a kind of poetry, akin to Surrealism. He saw the expression of the unconscious collective life of England, literally, in writings on the walls, telling of the hidden thoughts and dreams of the inarticulate masses. In these he read, as the augurs of antiquity read the entrails or the yarrow-stalks, those strange and ominous dreams of the years just before the second world war. This was poetry indeed; but to me the mass and its mind was terrible and deeply antipathetic; was, indeed, that from which I was in flight. During my calamitous 'engagement' I had attended, with that unwanted fiancé, the cup-final match of the Football League. There I had seen the crowd, many-headed and pullulating, its component units seeming scarcely human and its aggregate lacking any feature of the 'human form divine', its only language a roar. But to Charles, as to our as yet unknown contemporary Teilhard de Chardin, the soul of collective man was mysteriously beautiful. Once I remember we were walking together in Kew Gardens, and came upon a waste corner filled with single aster flowers. These flowers, with their many hundreds of solar discs, all turning to the one sun with the heliotropism of Blake's sunflower seeking after that sweet golden clime, seemed a symbol of the crowd, of the innumerable multitude of mankind, anonymous, equal, each imprinted with the same form, yet as a mass, in the mass, possessing a beauty of multitude beyond the beauty of any single flower, though each flower also had its unique and particular beauty. I saw the asters through Charles's eyes; as I did the writings on the walls of the great city, the multitudes of smoking chimneys between Charing Cross and Blackheath, and the rows upon rows of brick back streets all bearing witness to the human mystery. I tried to overcome my instinctive aversion from the Giant Polypus, and to see all this, as he did, not as sordid blind sub-humanity, but as strangely, mysteriously glorified, as if lived by a great life-force immortal beyond all those meagre mortalities in whom its stress and pressure was at work. The crowd Charles saw, as some other Marxist poets have seen it—as Edwin Muir once saw it in a state of visionary exaltation—not with fear and hate but with a participation almost mystical. As Plato describes the communication of poetic enthusiasm by the image of a chain of rings all magnetized, we all caught from Charles (for he was the magnet) a vision both high and prophetic.

Yet at Blackheath I felt always (as I told Gay Taylor at that time, and she later reminded me of the words) as if I were living in someone else's dream; and Charles was the Red King; in his dream I lived in a state of enchanted un-reality. The unreality was not in Charles's dream—which for him was reality itself—but in my own state. I had strayed—trespassed, rather—into the life of another human being, not so much as a person who comes into a room where there are other persons, but rather as a ghost or a somnambulist ('Cesare the Somnambulist' in *The Cabinet of Dr. Caligari* was a potent image of that time doubtless because—and not all of them in Germany—there were many somnambulists) or as a spectre produced by the displacement of an image by mirrors may seem to be in a place where it is not. Never did Charles for one moment give me cause for unhappiness; I felt him then, and in retrospect see him still, as a being of finer quality than myself. As a spectre might truly wish to be part of the world through which it appears to move (if a spectre could wish anything at all) so I could well have wished to be really where I seemed to be.

Often in dreams to this day I find myself back at 6 Grotes Buildings, the beautiful house we then lived in so precariously, between Charles's imaginative poetic exaltation, and my tears and guilt and despair. There was a big almost empty drawing-room where, alone, I used to dance, possessed perhaps by the same daemon that had once possessed Zelda Fitzgerald; for like her I was desperately neurotic and unhappy even while the dream possessed me; and only while I danced did I seem free; 'dying into a dance' from my distraught self. Charles let me dance, let me be free, let me write. We both wrote, though he far better than I; concerned only with our own poetry and one another's and with the imaginative works of our friends, we offered ourselves to the Zeitgeist, dedicated in mediumistic obedience to a mind as it were outside ourselves, the consciousness of that collective animal mankind.

We lived in a state of imaginative exaltation deriving in part from Charles's almost mediumistic visionary sense of the auguries and writings on the walls of those strange years just before the second world war; and in part from the infection of the French equivalent of the same phenomenon of the rising towards the surface of unconscious themes. Through Humphrey flowed the intoxicating obsessive 'paranoiac' images of the *Surréalistes*, the 'possessed' of France. We were (in William Empson's phrase) 'waiting for the end' in a state rather of exaltation than of despair, as if the spectators of an unfolding cosmic drama. Dali seemed to express the unformulated content of our own unconscious state, a blend of brooding dread and somnambulist eroticism, passive, bewitched, yet also seeking, among the wreckage of the outer and inner worlds in which we were astray—worlds which had strangely and ominously converged, as if the outer, instead of offering us protection from our nightmare, had become possessed by it—some pearl beyond price which we felt to be just behind and beyond the veil of each obsessive symbol. In the sea-shell, in the fragment of broken pottery or wave-worn cork (the *object trouvé* attracted towards the waking dreamer as in sleep images less tangible but of a like power of magic arise before us), we hoped to discover this mysterious all-potent and world-transforming talisman.

The veils which concealed this potent marvel were sordid and sorrowful yet obsessively haunting. Mass-Observation, concerned with man, was essentially urban. We hoped to discern on the surfaces of dingy walls, on advertisement hoardings, or written upon the worn stones of pavements, or in the play of light and shadow cast by some street-lamp upon puddles at the corner of a shabby street, traces of the beautiful, degraded, dishonoured, suffering, sorrowful, but still the *deus absconditus*. It was a search for the lost lineaments of the most high in the most low; hence the strange sense of dedication, of quest, in which we walked; anywhere, everywhere, we might receive a sign, that hidden and degraded god might sign to us, reproachful, sorrowful, majestic as the face imprinted upon the Holy Shroud.

On the wall of the Jennings' room in Blackheath, successor to that first Cambridge room, scene of so many marvellous, but unrecorded, monologues, hung a painting by Magritte (I saw it again, after many years, in the Magritte exhibition at the Tate Gallery, in 1972). In the foreground a cannon, emblem of coming war or revolution, was pointed towards a wall or flimsy screen, partitioned into sections. I ought to remember them all, for Heaven knows I gazed at that picture often enough. These were the fragments of a world, not, like Eliot's, 'shored against our ruins', but to be demolished when the cannon fired. There was a section of the façade of a house; a woman's torso; the trunks of some trees; a patch of blue sky with white clouds. Several others escape me—it would be easy to check, but let it serve as an instance of memory's unreliability, its blanks and its blind spots. For all our intoxicating sense of undisclosed marvels under the thin surface of consciousness, we yet saw in that gun pointed at the flimsy fabric of a painted scene the true emblem of the future of our world. It did not dismay us; that is how the spirit of Revolution wanted it to be; the cannon, now about to fire, was our will.

Emptied of this *mana* it is hard to understand, in retrospect, how the lumber of Surrealism once invested a passing host of gods; but the Host was real enough, as the approaching war was presently to show. The strange spirits which were let loose upon our world made their entrance through 'possession' such as ours. Its English form seemed harmless enough; philanthropic, as Charles and his Marxist friends conceived it; yet our possession was akin not only to French *Surréalisme* but to the more violent upsurge of the irrational forces in Nazi Germany. None of those Surrealists or Mass Observers at that time engaged in opening the dungeons of the unconscious and freeing energies imprisoned there had the wisdom to gauge, or the power to control or to transmute what came to light.

Charles had the gift of seeing as pictures in a diviner's crystal glass events forming in that medium (whatever it may be) from which material effects appear to flow from anterior mental causes. Humphrey recognized the signs everywhere, took marvellous photographs of those significant images that seemed to speak to us, as do dream-symbols, from within. But I in that dream was a mere somnambulist, passively possessed though not inspired. As we enjoy our dreams, even our worst nightmares, so fraught are they with that knowledge which is our own being, so I in a sense enjoyed this strange condition, with its intoxicating sense of being in the power of a life beyond my small humanity and, above all, beyond good and evil. 'Ye shall be as gods...'; and so we felt ourselves at that time to be.

The Cambridge word 'detachment' we no longer used: now we were 'observers', God's spies seeing far beneath us the human scene, as if we were ourselves at once spectators and authors of that play but not its enactors.

Just before the outbreak of the second world war, the unreality upon which we were treading rose like a mounting tidal wave; we seemed, straws and corks and drifting fragments that we were, to be soaring to the crest of some strange realization (for we were, God knows, upon a quest, in our *voyage au bout de la nuit*) when the wave broke and crashed us all down. For Charles, I was the wave that broke; for myself, I seemed no more able to alter or stop my course than a breaking wave. I was in the power of unconscious forces stronger than I knew, as I so passively drifted on a dream.

Two terrible images which were certainly not reflected from Charles's dream or the dreams of the mass-mind, haunted me at that time. Launcelot, riding in quest of the Holy Grail, entering a room in a certain castle, sees upon a table, covered with a white cloth, what he believes to be the Grail; but when he lifts the cloth he finds beneath it the body of a dead babe. From the same Arthurian mythology came the other symbol—the knight who watches in the Chapel Perilous before a sanctuary lamp, sees at midnight a black hand come and extinguish the light. I have no words for the dread with which these two symbolic images filled me; nor have I, even now, attempted to analyse the complex of guilt and sorrow, remorse and dread, the life behind those masks. The *objets trouvés* I had hoped to find were not these.

One of those drawn into the net of Mass-Observation was an astrologer, Gay Taylor; and I must truthfully admit that her astrology and other esoteric studies interested me a great deal more than the sociology of leftist idealism which seemed to me (as Blake says of politics) 'something other than human life'. It was doubtless my own despair which made me turn to such things, seeking an escape; but I was surely not alone in my time in my growing inability to continue to live by the values of a materialist philosophy. Even in its most magical and most idealistic form, as Charles embodied it, I found it increasingly claustrophobic, unendurable.

Of all the friends of a lifetime, as in retrospect I understand, Gay was one of the most remarkable, as well as one of the most loved. She understood me better than I did myself; sustained me in times of deepest spiritual danger, never condemned or relinquished me; and besides all that, she was fun to know; she touched in me the springs of laughter, of the life-enhancing absurdity of the near at hand. Under the influence of draught cider (she called it 'the truth drug') what all-embracing conversations did we not have. Yet, like those 'messengers' from Kafka's Castle, her outward aspect gave no clue to her essence. She was among the many 'dotty' correspondents who answered Charles's advertisement for Mass Observers in the *New Statesman*. She volunteered to address envelopes, and came to Blackheath; and although Charles disliked her (perhaps because he sensed in her one of those woman allies of other women who are so dangerous to marriages) remained a Mass Observer long after the movement had ceased to be more than an agency for market research. But market research satisfied something in Gay's nature; she treasured those chance encounters with ordinary, anonymous, and—to use a word she herself often used (verbally underlined) *'odd'* members of the human race. (*'Peculiar'* was another of her underlined words; of possible explanations of any event she preferred always the paranormal.)

Charles observed these odd beings as specimens made remote by the telescope of his 'observation'. Tom Harrisson regarded them as subjects of 'anthropological' interest ('loving' them but as most anthropologists love their primitive tribes, or animal behaviourists their apes). To Gay these were human souls, 'odd' and 'peculiar' as she was herself, but, like her, lost travellers in this most peculiar world. Like some Russian holy beggar she saw her life of odd encounters as fulfilling some unknown but Heaven-directed purpose; because she was a stranger people would talk to her of their troubles, tell her, perhaps, stories long pent up in silence. As a born (if unsuccessful) novelist, these stories satisfied her insatiable curiosity about life and people. But she also prayed for those who asked for her prayers; and when, on her death, I inherited her papers, I found scores of cards, made out in her neat, microscopic hand (reminiscent of Emily Brontë's) filled in with the same meticulous care as the astonishingly accurate horoscopes she used to cast, with the names of people she was praying for during any month: names, reasons for prayer (sickness or some other trouble) and any other relevant matter. Some of these were friends but most were strangers she had met on her travels, or perhaps relatives of these whom she had never seen. On the card by her death-bed, my name was among the rest; and my daughter's.

She kept, besides, a note-book in which she recorded her daily periods of prayer; the time, the depth of concentration, the distractions, or illuminations, or other things to be noted in this, the work of her life. This record took the form of charts, not diary notes. 'Keep your life hidden' was her rule; a phrase taken (was it?) from Lao Tze or some other Chinese sage of the Tao. Only in secret, in hidden lives, she held, is perfect freedom possible, uncorrupted by ambition, undistracted, undismayed by the judgement of others. She aimed at perfect truthfulness, though, God knows, in no sanctimonious way. Indeed when I first knew her perfect truthfulness was perfect truthfulness about sex and her relationships with men; which shocked my ingrained puritanism, even at that time. But it was the same truthfulness that she later brought to her equally difficult relationship with God.

That was long after. At the time I first met Gay her life was as totally catastrophic as my own was fast becoming. She had already published a novel in which she told the story—as it then seemed to her—of her marriage triangle with Hal Taylor (founder of the Golden Cockerel Press, which in the early 'twenties was publishing beautiful hand-printed books) and one of the authors they published, a well-known short-story writer of the time. Her husband had died, leaving his money to relations; and Gay, penniless, soon found herself deserted by her shabby lover. With truly feminine illogic she blamed her husband with unforgiving bitterness, finding every excuse for the lover, and angrily protesting that she had been betrayed by both. Maybe, in the light of inner truth, she was right; or maybe she protested too much. At one time she read every document relating to Mary, Queen of Scots; she was herself a Stuart, but she may have had deeper reasons for seeking to understand the inwardness of Mary's dark and devious marriage entanglements.

Whatever standards of judgement she may have applied they were certainly not those of conventional—or any other—morality, but of a more vital truth. The intangible ambience of her culture was, I think, that of the Powyses, whom she had known; some of their books, also, I have inherited from her. In *Wolf Solent* (annotated in that neat hand, with all the place-names carefully identified) I re-entered, years later, what I recognized, with a pang of nostalgia, as Gay's world. The same half-mystical, half-erotic love of the landscape of the south-west of England—Glastonbury, Gloucester, the Cotswolds—and of certain buildings. Like Thomas Hardy, whose poetry she supremely loved; her father had been a rural architect and restorer of churches. I inherited, too, a great collection of postcards of rustic churches, pagan foliate faces or lewd rustic forms peeping from roof-boss or capital. Not only the interest or the beauty, but, Powys-like, the 'feel', the secret life of places was her secret delight.

Gay's pursuit of 'truth', of reality—of, as it proved, 'God'—was as totally uncommitted to morality as that of John Cowper Powys's Wolf Solent: like Powys's characters she tested every experience, every person on the delicate, subtly responsive, fastidious, but also erotic nerve-endings of her own life. Yet in her appearance she was like a caricature of a lady novelist of the 'twenties with her brow curtained by her long fine fringe, her dangling earrings, her cigarette-holder, her verbal underlinings. Like Dickens's Miss Faversham, she remained as she had been at the time of her great drama; she had enough to do, for the rest of her life, to discover the truth about that one experience. Like many women who live alone she talked non-stop when she was not, with oddities and affectations that were the hardened residue, perhaps, of her once kittenish charm (she adored all cats, and had a series of her own, all people) 'back in the 'twenties', as she often used to say. But even when she was not being witty, the penny-plain world became, in her company, 'twopence coloured'.

In those Blackheath days she pitied my plight and was anxious to extend to me her friendship as to a younger unfortunate, interesting, misunderstood, desperate woman. And God knows every woman needs a woman friend with whom she can be truthful; as it is impossible to be quite truthful or quite at ease, altogether quite naturally oneself, with the opposite sex, in any relationship, however intimate. So it befell at a time when she no more than I had any thought that the journey of life might prove to be a pilgrimage, we became, unawares, what to the end we remained, fellow pilgrims. For we were both on a journey, though at the time with no sense of destination. We were neither of us looking for God, but, much rather, doing our utmost to get away from him. Gay, finer in her responses than I, far less hypocritical, less heavy-handed both in her morality and her immorality, was nevertheless inwardly one of 'God's fools'. She was a mystic; in later years receiving several experiences described in the classics of mystical literature, including the 'sun-flower' (as she called it) of the heart. Of these she felt herself to be so profoundly unworthy that she struggled for years to avoid them. Yet for years I treated her in a most off-hand manner, rather ashamed of her than otherwise among my less eccentric friends.

But once I remember—years later, long after the war—catching, from a bus in the King's Road, a glimpse of Gay, her scarf (as much a part of her habit as a nun's wimple) tied round her head, above the familiar 'fringe', coming from an ironmonger's shop carrying a tin of paraffin for the smelly stove she used for economy. She was very poor indeed, for she refused to take any job more regular than her occasional market-research, because this would have interrupted her thoughts and her meditation; and indeed her incorrigible sloth, as she called it. When she published her second book she took the pseudonym 'Loren Hurnscot', anagram on her two besetting sins, sloth and rancour, so she said.

I doubt if her refusal to do what is ordinarily called work was really sloth, though rancour against the husband who left her penniless may have had some part in it. But in the living of her inner life no one was less slothful; and to Gay the living of that inner life was the important thing, the whole meaning of her existence. 'You see', she once exclaimed to me (it was just by the letter-box at the corner of Paulton's Square and Danvers Street) 'all I *have* is my life.' Again in retrospect I discern an echo of Wolf Solent; or was Gay, rather, among those 'period' people whose way of being, of experiencing, of living a life, gave Powys the matter of his art?

So it was when I caught, as it were, an objective glimpse of her, at a moment when she did not know she was observed, when between us there was no relationship or contact. Carrying the fuel of the poor in her small refined hands, I saw my friend as she was, 'in God's eye', so to say.

Since her death I have been reading the books she left me; Berdyaev and Boehme and Julian of Norwich. I gave away my own Hardy and kept hers, every page lived over, every place identified, every person. The message I had from her through a medium—if she it was—was characteristic of an astrologer who had six planets in air: 'I have adjusted', she said, 'almost *too* (underlined) easily!' Was it really Gay? She herself would certainly have wished me to believe the un-earthly explanation.

It seems inevitable that for a materialist society political ideologies should supplant religion. My father's politics, like Plato's, like Æ's, was conceived as an attempt to make 'the politics of time' conform with 'the politics of eternity', to build the Holy City 'on earth as it is in Heaven'. But what was the holy city of the Marxists and what its laws? To me then, as now, the responsibilities of life seemed personal issues; conscience the arbiter of our acts and aspirations, whether towards ourselves or towards others. It may be said that my life presents a desperately unconvincing argument for that way of life, and that if I had conformed to some rule (Catholic or Marxist) and recognized that what I have called conscience has been mere wilfulness, my daimon a will o' the wisp, I might have done, at least, less harm. But that the assumption of any ideology should replace the perennial task and quest of the soul—should take from us the possibility of damnation or beatitude no social order can confer or take away—is, to me, still unimaginable.

The poetic side of Mass-Observation captivated me; but the political side made me shrink and shudder. There was something in the faces, in the spiritual atmosphere, of some of Charles's Communist friends which I sensed as evil. I remember once some Chinese visited him, whose like I had never imagined to exist, so terrible they were; Marxism had its own style. And yet at that time the Good was identified, in the minds of our generation, with Leftism. Not to be a Marxist then was held to be a mark either of incorrigible selfishness or lack of seriousness. I felt, no less than the Marxists among us, that the current of history which flows in one direction only, flowed the way that they were going; and much of the sense of god-like, invincible power that then possessed us came from this sense of flowing with the tide. To move with that tide seemed even to be a kind of virtue in itself, an implicit faith in the purpose of whatever hidden power conducts the world, even though that power was at the same time denied mind or purpose. Many of us who would not use the word God nevertheless lived by faith in the life-force itself, and to that life-force abandoned ourselves.

I could not go with that mainstream of evolution, if such it was. Of one thing only I was sure, in rejecting Marxism I was putting myself on the losing side.

So to live in Charles's dream, noble though that dream was, I could not have continued: sooner or later the break must have come between two poets each with a daimon to obey. Never was I unhappy through any fault of Charles's, never were my tears caused by him; they came from deeper and more hidden springs than domestic quarrels. That I hurt a man so fine by marrying him for inadequate, indeed for deeply neurotic, reasons, lies heavily on my conscience; but to have remained with him, I being who I was and am, would have been to injure him, so I believe, even more. I did not mean to betray Charles; but those who do not know themselves, who are alienated from themselves, cannot help betraying whether they go or stay. I seemed to love him—thought I loved him, though our love was rather a poetic fantasia than a marriage.

But had I no sense of the responsibilities I had incurred by marriage to Charles, by our children? I had not. As between those duties (which many will say were plainly now those which ought to have come before all else) and the duties which I inwardly still knew I had betrayed before all this tangle began, there was never, for me, any question.

Those who keep those rules of society made to protect human life from unendurable extremes neither inflict nor endure such miseries as I both caused and suffered. By social standards their morality is wise and right, mine insane and indefensible. But, by that morality, was Charles ever my husband? Neither of us, I think, believed in our relationship, whose very essence had been its freedom, from the day it became a marriage; that was not what either of us had meant.

CHAPTER FIVE

The Demon Eros

I LEFT Charles Madge because I fell in love, if Eros be love. I left with no more conflict of conscience than a bird whose wings have been clipped and who one day finds that the pinnae have grown again; or a fish frozen in the ice that finds a river flowing and consciousness restored. Who can withstand the flow of returning life? Those may well condemn me who understand love as *caritas*; but there is only one judge to whose condemnation I must assent, the Judge at the heart of life; a confronation more terrible than with any moral code, but of a different order. If in that Judgement I stand condemned it is more likely to be for heartlessness than for falling in love.

Charles was I think in Bolton with Tom Harrisson, and I was alone; free and alone for the first time since, perhaps, my Cambridge student days. Is there any young woman who does not, when thus for the first time alone, straighten like a sapling long tied down, to the form she had, or should have had? I was invited for a week-end by a friend who had a country cottage; and another guest, whom I had never met, was driving down in his car, and would take me. I had heard his name (he had been a Cambridge contemporary) and that he was astonishingly handsome and something of a Don Juan. He was in fact very shy, and we scarcely found a word to say to one another as we drove first out of London, then into country roads, and at last, leaving the car at the end of a lane, set out to find our host's cottage, hidden in beech-woods which overshadowed us with an older, sweeter world than any I had seen for long. As we walked deeper and deeper into these woods I began to remember; how long how long since I had been in this world of nature which had once been mine! My sophisticated companion too seemed to lose, step by step, his man-of-the-world guise, and trod softly as a deer among the trees. We reached at last the cottage, the archetypal cottage of all fairy-tales, overhung with honeysuckle and sweet roses. There was a huge log-fire in a great chimney where we sat, after our evening meal, drowsed in wood-smoke and the tangible silence of the woods. Our host had filled jugs with great bunches of wild flowers, and we drank water drawn up from an old well. Next day we rode in the woods along bridle-paths; my fellow-guest, as we walked back after leaving our horses, lifted a long straight pine-pole and threw it; he had 'tossed the caber', ancient ancestral skill. His handsome features, his dark hair, white skin and blue eyes, his light tread and his low musical voice suddenly took on a meaning which was not merely that of 'a handsome man'; he was no longer an alien but of my own country, the country lost before all my sorrows began, lost before I began. Yet I had at this time so far forgotten who I was, and everything once dear to me, that his name (a combination of two of those few Highland names which recur in the songs and the history of Scotland) had not even made me think of him as a Scot; I had thought of him as a former student of one of the Cambridge colleges and an acquaintance of this and that Cambridge contemporary; but in that moment the image changed, and I remembered who I was and saw what he was, as in a sudden anamnesis I ceased to be a somnambulist. As he stood among the great beeches he seemed like a messenger; from my childhood, from Bavington, from over the Border; from my ancestors. I felt that they from their long buried dust awoke in the sudden passionate love which the bearer of a name so often loved by them had evoked in me. In falling in love with this Alastair, as at that moment I did, it was not himself alone, or principally, whom I saw and loved, but all those ancestors, and all the echoes and resonances of their lost world and my lost world, and my lost self and perhaps his lost self. To me he was the bearer of the race and its living dust, of the pentatonic and hexatonic melodies of Scotland; he was the bright distant mountains of the imagination, the golden country. The spirits of my mother and my grandmother clamoured in me like ghosts then for the life-blood they had been denied.

My grandmother had ended her life, a very old woman, in a house in a grim industrial town where my widowed Aunt Jean lived on after the death of the husband who had brought her there, among sooty brick streets of back-to-back houses. In a dark and cheerless kitchen the old woman had sat in her dignified old-fashioned black dress with its braided bust and white lace at the neck, her voluminous serge skirt covering her feet, a white Shetland shawl about her shoulders, and a lace cap on her white hair. There she sat remembering things far away and beyond recall. Over the kitchen range hung an oil-painting, brown with age and varnish, of a highland river in spate pouring over its stones; and for her that picture was the gate out of the drab world where she sat a helpless prisoner of bricks and mortar. She told me, so I remember, that often she would look so long at that painted burn that at last it would seem to her real water flowing over real stones, and she there. This Alastair, on that very morning, brought with overwhelming vividness my dead grandmother to mind; I could smell, strongly and unmistakably, her peculiar clean fresh human scent, wafted back from childhood.

It had been Charles's grandmother who had, in a series of terrifying dreams, warned him and raged at him for his union with me, in the very first weeks of it, visiting him night after night and leaving him prostrate. He did not heed her, and still less did I; it seems to me now incredible that we should have dared to go against monitions so unmistakable, whether from the world of spirits in a literal or only in a figurative sense. She had of course been right—that world always is; regarded ancestrally, Charles and I should never have been united. We had defied the ancestors when we entered upon a relationship which they did not sanction.

I conceived, there and then for that incarnation of an ancestral image, a deep and long-enduring passion, for which I would have undergone every traditional ordeal with joy; the symbol of that passion was for me the story of the Black Bull of Norroway, and I the girl who followed her lover to the world's end. It was now my turn to say over the words of the archetypal story. 'The iron shoes I wore for thee, the mountain of ice I clamb for thee, the bluidy sark I wrang for thee, and wilt thou no wauken and turn to me?' Yet in this passion there was nothing personal at all; it was as if the ancestors cried out in my blood that race is all, the individual only a bright ripple upon the ever-flowing river. Swept on like a flake of snow upon the surface of that river (to use an image from the ancestral poetry) we are, for the time, the consciousness of the river itself; and so I felt myself, in this atavistic and ardent passion, to be. All we then experience has the beauty and profound meaning of a unity and a whole-ness, nothing is deformed, broken and fragmentary (as we ourselves are) but all brought to a perfection which is the creation of countless genera-tions. In this collective experience primitive people must surely partici-pate, in a vital current unknown to dispossessed modern man; even perhaps animals—who knows how deep are the currents of life? What else, in the deepest sense, is carnal desire but the will of the ancestors?

At the same moment that I fell passionately in love, I believed in—remembered rather—the divine world. To say 'in God' would be too theological a word for that insight into the sacramental essence of life. My eyes seemed now to behold the earth and sky for the first time, although it was not in fact for the first time, but a re-awakening after a long death or sleep of something I had once and for ever known, and had long for-gotten. Not all my intellectual studies had opened to me the nature of things as did this passionate physical love; and I can only testify to my own experience of the paradox through which the lowest (if physical passion be such) was for me at that time a revelation of the highest. My renewed vision of the holy was in the depths of carnal desire.

I could not have guessed the immense power of the race, had I not experienced it. I had not, after all, any great individual affection for my Scottish ancestors, who now threw my individual identity (which I had so long struggled to preserve) to the winds. I have since seen again that archaic world where the identity of men or women is that of family, scarcely at all of themselves as individuals; this or that Hector or John-Donald or Jessie or Annie, is 'a Macleod' or 'a MacKinnon' or a Campbell or a MacIsaac, and therein lies their sense of identity and dignity; each raised to the stature of a family whose memories and deeds, fading almost imperceptibly from human memory into history, history into legend, are inseparable and indistinguishable from the story of their own lives, whose events are scarcely distinct, in their own minds, from the stories of their forefathers; at best they can add something memorable to the record. The glens and the isles where those same ancestors have lived, and where they live in turn, are their country not by deed of property but by the renewal, again and again, of the covenant of life. In this respect the poorest crofters of the Western Isles are like members of some noble family, Palaeologi or

Howards or Percys, and often of purer blood than these. Their culture too is racial and ancestral; theirs by right of birth, along with their language and their skills; like the skills of their dogs, a race like themselves repeating and transmitting a pure strain, a collective pattern. It is to this racial being, not to anything individual in us, that erotic passion surely belongs, sweeping away all that to friendship matters most, all the shared interests and values of the world we consciously inhabit.

I chanced (long afterwards) to be on one of those isles when an old woman died; poor, almost illiterate, her horizon bounded in the south by Ardnamurchan, in the north by Kyle, and in the west, on a clear day, by South Uist; her pride that she was of the Clanranald. In the small square grave-yard, tangled with bramble and escalonia and overgrown with rank grass and nettles, a hole was dug for her among the bones of former generations; bones of old women and men scarcely yet forgotten were turned up to make a place for her among them. A piece of pasture-land adjoining had been given by the Laird, so dense was the population of the dead in that rank square; but the people would not use it, they would rather return to the hallowed earth of the dead from whose collective and immortal life they had themselves briefly emerged, to be laid back in the ancestral loam with the rites of Catholic burial. There are many such grave-yards in the Isles, scandalous by English notions, but that is how members of an ancient race wish to be buried, in the earth of their own people. My love for Alastair was like their desire to be dug back into ancestral clay.

Conscience never spoke to me one word to suggest it my duty to remain with Charles; 'caught in that sensual music' I was deaf, it may be, to spirits from higher regions who could have taught me another wisdom than that of the flesh, and another love. Perhaps I was, and still am, deeply mistaken, blind to some farther truth which, had I seen it, would have made me stay. Even if that be so, I still would plead that I could not have reached that farther truth without this epiphany of natural love; could not, by remaining a somnambulist in his house, have helped either Charles or myself. I had in Ilford seen too many of the dead living quietly and unobtrusively and respectably, fearing above all else the voices of life which could but disrupt and throw into ruin the false constructions so many build to shelter them from the terrible energies of life. This I could not do, nor force upon Charles a partnership of such a kind. I loved Charles, in one sense, too much to stay with him; in another, not enough. My sense of what was honourable—for I really did think I was acting as in honour bound—must seem strange. I see now that it is possible that I was deceiving myself; I wanted to be free and therefore persuaded myself that this was also the right course. I argued with myself that what is wrong for one must be wrong for the other; that the children of two people mis-allied would also suffer from the continuance of a falsehood. I do not think that for leaving Charles the Judge will condemn me, for I acted in obedience to the most profound truth I at that time knew. For having married him—for that I may indeed stand condemned. The consequences of such a deep untruth must always be, one way or another, terrible.

I had promised, it may be said; but—apart from the fact that, as a Marxist, Charles himself had believed no more than I in the sacramental and binding nature of the marriage contract we had made—the I who had promised had promised in my absence; and this must often be so, even in many formally Christian marriages made in good faith. People do not necessarily know who or what they are, may be dead or asleep at the time a promise is given. And what if the sleeper wake? Those who do not know themselves, the somnambulists, are sure, sooner or later, to betray. A voice did then speak to me, daimon or guardian angel, or ancestral wisdom but not in the name of social duty. It seemed to me then that I was shown the falsehood of years of wandering from the world of living reality; a veil was withdrawn, and behind the outer I saw the inner aspect of my life, and all my edifice crumbled. But does not love consist in mutual tolerance and patience, a compassion for the weaknesses and human limitations of another person, the sharing of the daily tasks of life in kindness? I know, I know; but then I did not know. Besides, all these may be given not in love but in a kind of remorse for not loving. Is not love, upon all planes, a divine energy, a transforming passion, a mystery? It comes not from conscious will but from unconscious depths. Love cannot be domesticated; though, when it is present, perhaps it may enable two people to get somehow through the Heaven knows hard enough ordeal of life. Yet when love is reasonable, is it not because the flames are out?

Is not Eros then more demon than daemon? The story of Phaedra, tortured and driven both to crime and to death excites only pity and horror. Yet her situation is a reality, one of the current predicaments of women struggling in the toils of life. Plato in the *Phaedrus* more light-heartedly lists the anti-social sins of Eros; but he too ends by saying, Heaven forgive those who raise merely social objections against a god, a divine energy.

From the day I left Charles I have never again lived with lover or husband, but carried my burden alone, assumed the consequences of my own acts. With the courage only of my egoism, it may be; but whatever the motive, I have not, from the time of that re-awakening, allowed others to rescue me. I had to get away from the false constructions of years; perhaps I had to release Charles also, whom I had so undeservedly involved in my desperate flight. It may be that I made, into erotic love, a descent, a fall; but even so, I was so strongly summoned to my own place that, up or down, there I had to go.

As for that Alastair, I see now that he was the occasion, not the cause. Even then I never thought of consulting him, for my decision to leave Charles was, it seemed to me, no affair of his. If some part of me wildly longed to be united with his divine beauty, another part knew perfectly well that my passion had nothing to do with such things as marriage and cohabitation. We had absolutely nothing, humanly speaking, in common, upon which we could have built a life. He himself certainly never contemplated any such thing, for he was, I think, cautious and conventional. He probably thought I was making a great a mistake in leaving my husband; 'Such a beautiful sensitive face to go through the world alone,' I remember his saying (indicating, in this phrase, with a remote echo of West Highland tact, that I could look for no support from him). I did not, at this, feel, as might be imagined, self-pity because my lover did not want me; rather I felt something like surprised annoyance that this man should see me as one more attractive conquest of Don Juan (for whom all women are merely variations of Woman) whereas I knew myself a poet, following, however tortuously, a destiny to which Don Juan might himself prove to be the sacrifice. 'The dice are loaded too heavily against you,' he said, when I told him that I intended to make my life as a writer; but destiny is not a cast of the dice ('*Un coup de dés jamais n'abolira l'hazard,*' we had liked to quote) nor does vocation calculate its chances. I felt at last that I was upon my own path again, and that was enough.

What Alastair was like, as a person, I neither knew nor cared. I was not interested in him; a fact which does me no credit. I never noticed what kind of human personality he had; to have done so would have dimmed and obscured the image of the god he for me embodied. It did not then occur to me that this was unkind or unjust, for the miracle of his beauty seemed of far greater value than any merely human attributes he might possess. For his immortal soul I did not care, only for his mortal beauty. Insofar as he departed from 'the beautiful itself' which in him I saw reflected, I would have liked to take a sculptor's mallet and rectify the form. When he was actually present (fortunately that was seldom) I was always strangely put out as if by a double image; for never did the temporal and the eternal quite coincide. It was when he was not there that I most adored his beauty, in the contemplation of his recollected features, rectified by the archetype.

I was led unawares into a kind of asceticism, so far can passionate desire, even in its lowest mode, over-reach any natural mark. But sexual desire is an incandescent state in which we look deep into certain aspects of being. These insights are the fruits of an almost unendurable intensity of passion, a sacrificial immolation of mere carnality. The whole structure of nature which as a child I had innocently lived, as a student intellectually contemplated, now revealed itself to me burning with an interior light and glory, awe-inspiring. This state, known to all lovers, glorifies every blade of grass with a sacramental quality of holiness. Though I longed for the participation of this vision (which is, to the imagination of love, the supreme joy) my lover's actual presence merely dimmed and obliterated this epiphany of creation itself.

In retrospect I wonder if it is not the reflections upon love in the lover's absence that count for most. Gay, in comic vein, used to say that she used to send her lovers away so that she could really *think* about them; an activity the lover's actual presence merely interrupted. Nor did she mean erotic fantasy, but, rather, contemplation, pondering over, the nature and meaning of love. And I wonder if long conversations with Gay on the theme of love were not, in the last instance, far more rewarding than mere 'love'. What was love but the mere *prima materia* of those reflections, ponderings, and indeed occasionally, poems? If I could choose, in Paradise, between the beloved's arms and conversation and cider with Gay, I should not hesitate to choose the Platonic dialogue, and the cider.

I must have divined intuitively that in the sexual mystery the creator is (as the Dance of Shiva expresses and signifies) also the destroyer; for I remember a dream of that time so vivid that I can breathe again its atmosphere as I write. In the meadow opposite West View (restored, in that dream, to its long-lost aspect as in my childhood before its trees were felled and shops were built) I saw Alastair ploughing, walking round the four sides of the sunlit flowering field. My two children were running after him, happily, as it seemed. But the voice which in dreams can speak so clearly and unequivocally then pronounced the words, 'Death, the reaper'; and I recognized in the guise of my lover the figure who on the twenty-first Tarot card wields the scythe, trampling men and women down into the earth, from which hands and crowned heads are seen sprouting only to be lopped off and dug back into the mire. So much for the ancestors and their acre; so much for the process of generation and death. What sex sows, death reaps.

> Whate'er is born of mortal birth
> Must be consumed with the earth.
> To rise from generation free...

It seemed to me then that it was the god of the life-force who had me in his power; but I wonder if after all it was not the poetic daimon who used the lesser deity? I began at last to write poems, a few grains of gold calcinated from all that dross of life in the fires of an overwhelming physical passion. So much anguish for grains of gold so minute! But the daimons do not measure such things by our standards, for their object is to produce the gold and they heap on the fuel until the transmutation is brought about, regardless of suffering. I had never suffered so acutely as at this time when, having left Charles, I waited in vain for word or sign from my demon lover; yet I knew I would rather thus suffer than return to the painless state in which I had formerly been; for now, after long years, I was alive. I endured the endless hours from cup of tea to cigarette, each day a slow ordeal whose end I could not envisage, but which I knew I must undergo. 'It is a terrible thing to fall into the hands of the living God'; for sexual passion is the operation of the living God upon the lowest plane, as it may be, of existence. Yet in that existence, one level cannot be separated from another, and only upon that ground upon which we really stand will we experience the impact of a reality confined to none. If I stood in a low place on the scale of perfection, at that low place at which I then really was I must enter upon the long painful transmutation of love. Sexual love was the best of which I was then capable; it was a reality; it was, for me, at that time, reality itself. I had for too long known what it is to be divorced from reality to doubt or question that light which now shone in my darkness.

Every moment is the consequence of every preceding moment, the sum to which our life, at that moment, adds up; therefore we are grounded in the whole cosmos. In this whole each moment is our location, our standing-place, it is what we have made and what has made us, and therefore is what we are, the only ground upon which we can build; therefore it is exactly what it should be and must be, and exactly appropriate to our condition. In this sense it may well be that a condition of suffering is the best condition in which we can be, the only state of which we are capable; and the most dynamic, the most potent source of transformation and transmutation. I think I drew strength, at this time and for years to come, from my knowledge, for the first time since Bavington, that I was where I should be, that I had come into my own; painful to the extreme limit of endurance as that place and state might be.

Certainly at the outset I had no intention of undergoing suffering of any kind; on the contrary, I wildly dreamed of earthly love; dreamed rather than hoped. A migrant bird sets off to fly across the ocean without the intention of enduring storms; but the impulse to fly is so strong that no storm will turn its flight. I no more calculated than the bird; yet I believe that if I had known in advance all I would have to undergo in poverty, isolation, and the toils of unrequited passion, nothing would have deterred me. Being what I was, I had to go my way; so it is when we begin to live by the energies of life itself. The immense strength of desire seemed to give me a power of achieving and enduring anything and everything. I seemed to myself, then, to be inexhaustible, unconquerable. To poverty and the lonely confrontation with the world I had formerly so feared I now gave no more thought than water fears a waterfall or a meteorite empty space. I suffered, indeed, with unremitting intensity; and yet, like the souls in Purgatory, I threw myself into the flames with joy. Doubtless I had to suffer so intensely because I had so much from which I must be purged; yet even at the lowest level, the pain and the joy of Purgatory are inseparable; and I knew myself to be, now, at last, no longer in Hades but in the holy world of life.

The daimons may have known what they were about; but if I was in their power I was not in their confidence. Yet I obeyed them, after a fashion; collaborated, to some extent; wrote the poems they wrung from me as best I could. It must for them have been like breaking a wild colt, always trying to bolt for freedom; yet in part I was on their side against myself; reluctantly and in tears and anguish I did what they wanted me to do. I did not spare myself, and they did not spare me. I never looked back, even though it was in part illusion, the will o' the wisp of carnal love, that led me on.

Among the threads woven into the pattern, one may have been a curse from whose consequences I could not have hoped to escape. At the cottage in the woods where I fell under the power, for good or evil or both, of the spell of Alastair, I afterwards discovered that my first husband had stayed, after I left him, and when it had belonged to a former owner. Had he called up, then, in his grief and rage, powers in which he doubtless would not have believed, and of which I too was at that time ignorant? I had thought when I left him that I could escape scot-free; but the forces of nature operate whether or not we believe in them or know their laws. If we roll a stone down a slope it will take its course whether we push it deliberately or inadvertently; so, unawares, we may activate daimonic powers, stumbling blindly among them as among rocks on the edge of a precipice. So I believe I fell under a spell worked unwittingly (though not without the will or wish to injure me in revenge for the injury I had done him), when I walked unawares into that deceptively enchanting and enchanted cottage among the old nature-magic of ancient woods. Cause and effect operate on many planes; and there was a pattern in this fatality of which one strand may well have been my first husband's cry for revenge.

Yet the laws of such causes and operations may themselves be subject to other laws. A disaster may by a curse be loosed upon us like an avalanche or a storm at sea; but disaster itself be a means of blessing and turned to good. In any case, whether I was cursed by ill-will or blessed by angels, the suffering would have been the same. Had I been innocent I would have been invulnerable to the curse, or the blessing less painful; in either case I reaped what I had sown, experienced what was my due.

War came, that breaker-up of lives, and Alastair (true to his name and race) immediately enlisted and was soon posted abroad. So that I was providentially saved—and he too—from what might have become a sordid entanglement. I see in retrospect that interruption of an incipient love affair which at the time seemed a most cruel thwarting, as a powerful intervention of the guardian daimons (who make use alike of all conditions of peace or of war) whose protection I at that time scarcely deserved. They made themselves very clear; their purposes were not at one with my carnal desires. I remember still with a kind of pity for the longings and dreams, however vain, however blind, the perfect beauty of an early summer day and myself in the very heart of that summer waiting for my lover, who had promised to come for his last leave before he was sent abroad. On that day I walked not on knives but upon air. The light was of a radiance not of this common earth. Fringing the swift waters of the little beck flowing through my meadow in a dale in Cumberland were marigold and mimulus and anemone and water-avons, and, as I vividly remember, a patch of speedwell of brightest blue. These I remember because they seemed to promise a lover's swift arrival. My white house was swept and garnished and I awaited his coming as that inexpressible and perfect felicity for which all long. The time had almost come; when instead a boy with a telegram: 'All leave cancelled.' I went on blankly looking at the speedwell flowers.

I am glad now that he never came; that no mortal lover entered that valley where for the next years I lived with my children. Indeed for all the time I remained there it was as if guarded by a circle of magic force, a place of refuge, of vision, of poetry, and, the anguish of my unpurged passion notwithstanding, of beatitude.

Even now I find it almost incredible that a life can undergo so many mutations; my one life has been like a series of lives whose stories are like so many reincarnations. I now see that each of these transformations of outer circumstances corresponds to some inner state. It is naïve indeed to suppose ourselves the victims of circumstances, who are continually weaving and fashioning according to our dreams the texture of the solid-seeming world, which reflects back to us what in imagination we generate. Sometimes the plasticity of the world to our states of consciousness seems indeed astonishing. So, my awakening from somnambulism into a natural passion of great purity and intensity, revived the memory of my ancestral roots; and my longing to return to these was almost immediately followed by a period in which I lived in a place in many ways akin to Bavington, yet echoed and repeated on a higher octave, as it were, more luminous, more complex. The natural world was thrown open to me again, and I was permitted to return, for a season, to Paradise. Yet all this came about without any volition of my own; I was led, blindfold, as if by some angelic minister of grace.

CHAPTER SIX

Rescue

To say that this change was the work of my daimon is not to show ingratitude to the friends who were its agents; on the contrary, it is to say that Janet (Adam Smith) and Michael Roberts were to me friends literally Heaven-sent. For what other reason could they have invited me to go with them to Penrith, where the Newcastle Royal Grammar School (on whose staff Michael then was) had been evacuated? Janet and Michael saved me, body and soul, at that time. I had thought of Michael rather as Charles's friend than as mine; for he had included some of Charles's poems in his *New Country* and *Faber Book of Modern Verse*, and befriended him in the days when his attic flat in Fitzroy Square had been a rendezvous for young poets. Janet, as literary editor of *The Listener*, had published the first few poems of mine to appear outside Cambridge but Michael had included none in the Faber book; rightly, for none were good enough, and such qualities as they had potentially were not those of that time, or of the movement whose spokesman he had made himself. For Michael it was who, a few years older than Auden, Spender, Charles and the rest, first presented in his anthologies the poetry of pre-war leftism, an 'engaged' poetry, with its accompanying imagery of an industrial landscape. It was a new vision to which these poets gave expression; and Michael's book on the 'imagist' poetic theory of T. E. Hulme gave definition to an aesthetic which (although nominally Christian) fitted in with the concreteness of the Marxists among them. I was out of my element in that world and began to come into my own only from the time I escaped, not only from Cambridge, but from the literary values of the 'thirties altogether. That kind of poetry was alien to me; yet the poets of Cambridge (and of these

Michael was forerunner) were my first friends. I do not know that
Michael would ever have seen altogether what as a poet I was about, even
though he did like some of the poems I wrote in those Penrith and
Martindale years, and wanted to include them in the revised edition of the
anthology he was planning at the time of his death. Subsequently I
allowed poems of mine to be included, at Janet's request, in the later
edition. For friendship's sake I am glad to be there; but I no more belong
with those contemporaries of the 'thirties, with their political idealism and
social realist imagery, than with William Empson and his 'metaphysical'
(in the literary sense, not the philosophic) positivism; less so, indeed; for
with William—as indeed, with Michael himself, who was, like William, a
mathematician—I did share something of the inscape of science and its
remote images, cold vistas of nature.

Michael saw me differently; he dedicated a poem of his own to me; and
shortly before his death he said to Janet, 'K was our beauty.' Our; for,
whatever I was, I did belong to my friends in a way I certainly never
belonged to husband or lover. I have through 'love' known inspiration
and suffering; through friendship, enduring happiness, unalloyed. I will
do much for my friends just because no submission is involved. Henry
Moore once said to me, in jest, 'I would have made you knuckle under!'—
and what man living has more right to pride in the strength of his genius?
But in fact not Henry Moore, not Yeats himself could have come between
me and that inner companion; no other person's inspiration, however
strong, can take the place of our own inner light. Since my marriage with
Charles, a fellow-poet, I have never for one moment been tempted to
imagine that I could share my interior world in a relationship of marriage,
still less sacrifice my anterior dedication *to* a relationship of marriage.

I did not deserve that rescue; I wish I could believe I have deserved it
since. The transformation of my life began, not through my will but
through Janet's and Michael's kindness, on the night I stepped out of a
dark train into the black-out of Penrith station, with my two weary
children. We had travelled from Devonshire, where in my mother's little
wooden holiday-hut, looking over the blue sea and cloudless sky of
Seaton bay, we had heard Chamberlain's speech declaring this country to
be at war with Germany. From the pitch-black night beyond the dim
platform came the scent of wet fells, and sheep, and the North; and I knew
that after long exile I had come back to my own. The burden and the guilt
of years seemed lifted from my heart by that breath from the hills of my
childhood.

As we walked in the darkness (Michael, like some Mr. Greatheart,
pushing in a perambulator my luggage and my son) I had no idea where
we were going or what we would find; and coming out of the dark

September night into a gas-lit room in Wordsworth Street, where Janet was, and warmth, and light, was strange and inexplicable as a dream. There is no moment of my life for which I am more deeply grateful; for on the night I stepped out of the darkness into that simple north-country room, so reminiscent of the past, with Janet offering cocoa and her welcoming hands, my own life and my freedom truly began. I had returned to my own country, not now as a country child, but under the protecting friendship of two writers of my own generation.

The house in Wordsworth Street belonged to an old Penrith family related to those Hutchinsons who gave Wordsworth his wife and Coleridge his Asra; and some fragrance of that world remained in those rooms; the Wedgwood jug with ferns, the Birket Foster watercolour over the fireplace of children climbing a stile by a bush of wild roses; the faded green serge table-cloth, the Victorian furniture, reticent but cared for. Just as you will find archaic Greece by walking away from the archaeological sites by any mule-track to the nearest village, so the way into the secret world in which Wordsworth and Dorothy and S.T.C. once lived, closed to professors, is known to maiden ladies who live their lives in the house where they were born. But Janet's Aberdeen was a related place, as was my Northumberland; and she set about living in a country town built of the red local granite as to the manner born. Superimposed upon that older world was ours; Michael's books and his typewriter and gramophone, and the late Beethoven quartets he loved; and our children and all their gear. In that house was friendship of the mind, the best of talk, and the shared tasks of the day; the good life, and how sweet it seemed after such an exile as mine had been.

Pipes froze in that bitter winter; that meant we could not use the boiler; and we had to keep all the water needed for our household of infants in the bath, carrying it in buckets from the main tap in Wordsworth Street, turned on for an hour or two every day. Coal was short; Janet and I did the marketing and cooking in alternate weeks, doing our best with the spam and dried eggs. (As cooks we have both improved beyond recognition since that winter.) In the evenings, when the children were disposed of at last, Janet and I would be sitting by the fire darning and mending, and Michael would come down from his attic study with his pipe and two or three pages of his book, *The Recovery of the West*, or a new poem, and we would talk of literature and the war.

My contributions tended to take the form of large ill-informed generalizations; which Michael would cheerfully demolish with a fact or two. I did not believe that the West would recover; and in my sense of the word recover I was perhaps right; but Michael too was right, at least insofar as England did win that particular war, which at the time seemed unlikely to happen. Mankind, Michael used to say, has a heartening way of never fulfilling predictions based upon logical deductions from existing situations; there are always unexpected turns, and only the unpredictable can be predicted with certainty. Michael perhaps felt as I did, but, like all good educators, understood that even when a civilization is in decline, it is possible to make small improvements wherever we may happen to be, and necessary to confine our hopes to attainable and specific ends, towards which it is in our power to work. Now that I am older I admire with greater understanding the stoicism with which Michael concentrated his hopes and fears within the scope of his own field of action. His practical political sense was in this respect altogether unlike my father's; or, indeed, like those University Marxists I had known who had made of the Spanish Civil War a symbol of their vague Utopia.

Sometimes behind the black-out Janet and Michael would talk of climbs in the French Alps, re-living days of freedom above the snowline of human affairs. There were days, too, when Janet and Michael would go off on mountain walks or climbs in the fells; or I myself, with Janet or Michael, and occasionally all three of us. Once we walked to the summit of Fairfield, in February, perhaps, for the wet snow was melting away in the wind. There was a rainbow that day, against the snow, cast by some trick of light from the spray of a little waterfall, and the track of a fox. With Michael, one ice-cold winter's day, I struggled up Blencathra, where, just under the summit, out of the wind which cut like a knife and rattled the wedges of ice which adhered to the underside of every blade of grass, we ate our frozen sardines and Michael smoked his pipe, before we set off for the descent, through sheltering woods, to Keswick. On the New Year's day of a later year, Janet and I, by contrast, basked in the sunshine on the summit of Helvellyn. On another expedition, when our three eldest children could walk, Michael and I took them up Helvellyn, whose summit was a Brocken of swirling mist. Michael I remember saying to me, as the witch's brew of wind and vapour boiled up from below, 'Just look over, K, will you, and see if you can see Striding Edge.' I could; but fortunately only so much of its jagged back as was bearable. Roped, Michael leading, we took our children across. Such days were essentially of Janet's and Michael's creation; they enjoyed the effort and the victory. Left to myself I never wished to struggle, but only to be forever in the places I loved, to sit hour after hour by waterfall or mossy rock; not to visit but to be eternally (at least for the moment eternally) at one with places remote from the human world. I would rather have been one of those hermits who in some cave of the Himalayas meditated upon transience and *nirvana*, than their European 'conquerors'; but Michael was essentially a conqueror of summits. Whenever I see the constellation of Orion, I think of Michael tirelessly striding ahead of whatever party of us lagged behind.

At the end of the first winter of the war the house in Wordsworth Street was sold by its owners and our household had to leave; the Robertses finding another house in Penrith and I to my appointed place. I decided to look for a cottage, and not knowing where to begin I went one late February morning to the bus terminus in Penrith and took a bus to Howtown, on the eastern and wilder side of Ullswater; for at Martindale my Aunt Peggy Black had taught her first school, more than fifty years before. Because of this, taking that way seemed not like a departure but like a return. Crossing to the little hotel I asked if any cottages were to let in the neighbourhood. 'Only the vicarage,' I was told; and when I replied that the vicarage would be much too big for me, was reassured; the vicarage was very small. Over the fell road I walked, the sweet scent of earliest spring poignant in the soft air into which the snow was melting. Martindale vicarage, the most beautiful little white house imaginable, stood in its own field, with a great lime tree at the gate and a beck fringed with birch and alder bounding its little domain. It stood empty, as if waiting for me. The house, which had a certain elegance of proportion above that of a cottage, had a room on each side of the front door and four tiny bedrooms above. Its windows looked south, to Beda Fell and High Street, the frontier never passed by the Roman legions. The garden, enclosed by a stone wall, was sheltered by two spreading yews where a little flock of coal-tits gathered to eat the red berries. On that first sight of it, multitudes of snowdrops were emerging from the melting snow, and the scented buds of the flowering currant bushes were already swelling. A tall window with a semicircular top, of a kind fairly common in Cumberland rose to the whole height of the staircase, looking up the fell-side behind the house where a small rivulet tumbled over its stones and mosses. Often, later, I saw red deer up there, from the Boardale herd, the last in Cumberland.

To the Vicarage I came home to the world I had thought lost to me for ever. It was as if the same multitude of snow-drops had awaited my return, and the sound of the beck that flowed through the field, the sound of the same burn flowing all night that I had heard as I lay in my bed in the blue bedroom at the Manse. Again the evenings were lit with Aladdin lamps, again my field and garden were divided from the wild world only by a stone dyke. The formation of the fells is very unlike the great rising sweep of the Northumbrian moors; in every dale there is a boundary, like the mark of a tide, to which has risen the human world of little fields; above the sinuous line of the last stone dyke rises the world beyond the human, stone and sedge and parsley-fern and fell-sheep, curlew and buzzard; but the wilderness, in a different idiom, tells everywhere of the same nature, still virgin as before the Fall of man. I too felt myself, here, to have escaped from mankind, from all those who had, as it seemed to me, hunted me down. I came like a wounded animal at last into the inviolable safety of my own terrain. Free from Cambridge, from marriage, from Mass-Observation and Marxism, from Ilford, the fell-sheep and the birds spoke my own language and of the things I understood; and I seemed virgin again. It seems to me strange now, in retrospect, that no sense of guilt pursued me there or obscured my vision of the purity of the creation but so it was. Perhaps the world of nature not only protected but absolved me; perhaps the penance was only deferred. Perhaps the deeper truth is that nature does not speak of guilt and remorse, only of that dispassionate mind in whose vast peace an infinite complexity of forms waxes and wanes at every moment, held in perfect equilibrium and perfectly present, as if no evil of past or future had power to mar the perfection of the everlasting Now; a now always immaculate, remembering no sorrow, fearing no dissolution, a virginity for ever renewing itself. Over the dead the grass grows again, and nothing is remembered, no memory hunts down the creatures of that eternal present. Into that Now no Eumenides pursued me.

Some of the farmers and their sisters in the dales had been my Aunty Peggy's pupils and still remembered her. How could I not have felt that I had been led into that valley of refuge, and that it was, for me, under a blessing? A Spanish friend has told me of a word, in his language, which means love of that specific kind which draws us back to that place from which we have come; as old people as they approach death long to return to their native place; or as a mortally wounded bull in the bull-ring will attempt to walk in the direction of the field from which it has been brought: *querencia*. Was it this instinct which led me now to Martindale? I began now to perceive that there is a pattern in life, or rather that a life is such a pattern, however obliterated and spoiled, and I felt for the first time since childhood that I had come into my own.

For many who moved from town to country at the beginning of the war, as I did, the change was only of location; for me it was a change of identity, or rather a return to identity. Even for Janet and Michael the mountains they loved were a relaxation from work; *Mountain Holidays*, Janet entitled her book. But for me, in some obscure sense, to live with the natural creation was, at this time, my work. No less surely than in Ilford, and later in my two marriages, I had known I was not where I should be, at Martindale I felt, each day, each hour, that here I was in my own place. I have often since thought psychiatrists waste much effort in trying to 'adjust' unhappy people to some bed of Procrustes, when all they need is to get away and to find, as I did, their right place and their right work. 'Things move violently to their places, smoothly in their places.'

To an outside observer it might have seemed that my troubles had only begun, the struggle to earn enough money to keep myself and my children (Charles could allow me only a small sum) which I did in part by book-reviewing. I had to cook, clean, saw logs, make fires; look after my children, teach them, carry my marketing once a week from Penrith, grow vegetables in the garden. But to me, free now, and in my own place, all this labour was a joy, whereas the ease and apparent freedom of my former life had been, for all the magic of possession by Charles's dream, a sojourn in Hades. There is a difference in kind between the Hells and the Purgatories, even though in these the effort may be greater and the suffering more acute.

Housework had formerly been to me, as to so many unhappy women, a symbol of enslavement; I had seen my mother all her life hating and resenting what she called the 'drudgery' of housework. This irrational resentment of housework is I believe strongly felt by women whose marriages are unhappy. There is at the same time a compulsion to perform the tasks of enslavement; to leave the furniture undusted might be the first act of freedom. My upbringing had strongly impressed on me the sense that there is some moral virtue attaching to the performance of menial tasks, whereas it is 'selfish' to perform tasks not menial; as if my mother were still accusing me of leaving to her the 'drudgery' of Martha. When at Martindale I had to sweep and clean once more I had a momentary return of the old fear of loss of identity, as if the jaws of Ilford yawned to swallow me back. One day soon after I had gone to Martindale I was scrubbing the stone flags of the larder, on my hands and knees, weighed down by this sense of pursuit; I felt that circumstances were robbing me of my identity, so precarious still, as poet, or as whatever it was I hoped to become. Suddenly, as with the shifting of a *gestalt*, I realized that I was the same person whether scrubbing a floor or writing a poem; that my dignity as a being was in no way dependent upon the role which I had at any moment to assume; for all such roles are merely that, and the person free of them all. I became, from that moment, free of the act; and I have never from that day minded any form of necessary work. Perhaps I have minded too little; to me housework and the like has not been so much a burden as a subtle form of sloth, a temptation to put the less before the more important task. It is all too easy, especially for women, to put the less essential physical task before the more essential intangible work; Martha is always self-righteous in her tyranny over Mary. Thus it was that for so many years, before I permitted myself to write a poem, I would feel compelled to complete all my domestic tasks, even down to darning the last pair of children's socks in my work-basket.

I lived, then, during that summer when France fell, in a state and place where all was radiant with that interior light of which Traherne has written; and beyond the continuous interior illumination of moss and fern, of yellow welsh poppies and water flowing over stones reflecting the glitter of pure. light, the warmth of the sun on the stone seat under the yew-tree, the scent of young birch-leaves and lime-blossom, the line of the fells ever changing in sun and shadow, certain moments there were of another kind of consciousness altogether. Such a state has been often enough described: Tennyson said he could enter it at will; Richard Jefferies and others have known it well. 'Nature mysticism' occupies, it may be, a relatively humble place on the ladder of perfection as compared with those states of consciousness attained by saints and sages; but as compared with normal consciousness the difference is as between the world and paradise, if indeed it be not precisely that. Descriptions of one state of consciousness in terms of another must, to those who have not themselves known the experience, always give the impression of being figurative or poetic; so it always must be when, in whatever field, ignorance passes judgement upon knowledge. But those who know are unanimous in reporting that such changes of consciousness are not of degree, but of kind; not some strong emotion or excitement but a clarity in which all is minutely perceived as if by finer sense.

I kept always on the table where I wrote my poems a bowl with different beautiful kinds of moss and lycopodium and long and deeply did I gaze at those forms, and into their luminous smaragdine green. There was also a hyacinth growing in an amethyst glass; I was sitting alone, in an evening, at my table, the Aladdin lamp lit, the fire of logs burning in the hearth. All was stilled. I was looking at the hyacinth, and as I gazed at the form of its petals and the strength of their curve as they open and curl back to reveal the mysterious flower-centres with their anthers and eye-like hearts, abruptly I found that I was no longer looking *at* it, but *was* it; a distinct, indescribable, but in no way vague, still less emotional, shift of consciousness into the plant itself. Or rather I and the plant were one and indistinguishable; as if the plant were a part of my consciousness. I dared scarcely to breath, held in a kind of fine attention in which I could sense the very flow of life in the cells. I was not perceiving the flower but living it. I was aware of the life of the plant as a slow flow or circulation of a vital current of liquid light of the utmost purity. I could apprehend as a simple essence formal structure and dynamic process. This dynamic form was, as it seemed, of a spiritual not a material order; or of a finer matter, or of matter itself perceived as spirit. There was nothing emotional about this experience which was, on the contrary, an almost mathematical apprehension of a complex and organized whole, apprehended *as* a whole. This whole was living; and as such inspired a sense of immaculate holiness. Living form—that is how I can best name the essence or soul of the plant. By 'living' I do not mean that which distinguishes animal from plant or plant from mineral, but rather a quality possessed by all these in their different degrees. Either everything is, in this sense, living, or nothing is; this negation being the view to which materialism continually tends; for lack, as I now knew, of the immediate apprehension of life, as life. The experience lasted for some time—I have no idea how long—and I returned to dull common consciousness with a sense of diminution. I had never before experienced the like, nor have I since in the same degree; and yet it seemed at the time not strange but infinitely familiar, as if I were experiencing at last things as they are, was where I belonged, where in some sense, I had always been and would always be. That almost continuous sense of exile and incompleteness of experience which is, I suppose, the average human state, was gone like a film from sight. In these matters to know once is to know for ever. My mother when she was over eighty confided to me an experience she had had as a girl. 'I have never told anyone before,' she said, 'but I think you will understand.' It was simply that, one day, sitting among the heather near Kielder 'I saw that the moor was alive.' That was all. But I understood that she had seen what I had seen.

All traditions speak of the greater beauty and clarity of visionary forms; and this must be so, not because these are an 'idealization' of nature, but because souls are those forms of which physical embodiments are but a signature, sometimes almost indecipherable. It is not by chance that the art of a spiritual civilization is characterized by the lucidity of its forms; those six-armed dancing Shivas, rhythmic in every contour, or those sculptured women, perfected in the utmost refinement of eroticism, who keep the doors of Indian temples; or Christian angels with their braided hair and features delicately traced on skies of gold. When natural forms are depicted, as in Gothic foliate sculpture, or the flowers of the Cluny tapestries, or the fish and birds of the Book of Kells, these have the clarity, freshness and perfection of spiritual vision, for it is the souls of plant or animal whose clear lineaments are traced, in all their delicate mathematical intricacy. Paradoxically it is naturalistic art which loses the very form it seeks to copy; materialism makes a chaos of, precisely, the material world.

At about the time of my hyacinth vision I had an immediate experience of what might be the human equivalent of the plant-soul I had perceived. I was lying in bed, thinking, no doubt, of my absent lover. I say this lest it should be thought that my experience was in any way religious or related to prayer or to moral virtue. Abruptly, although my physical body was lying down, I found myself, at the same time, sitting upright, my arms outstretched: but not my physical arms. This body which seemed to have emerged from within the physical envelope like a moth from a chrysalis seemed infinitely more myself than the physical envelope which it had left. It had a sense of lightness, clarity and freedom, a freshness comparable with the flower as I had seen it: not at all like that shadowy tenuous self we are in dreams. All seemed not less but more clear, of a quality more real than the real. So surprised was I to find myself half out of my body that I found myself back in it again. The return to the physical body was like putting on some old sack, rough and crude and barely conscious, constricted and dull; this has never happened to me since, but again, once is enough. 'As dreamers wake from sleep we wake from waking.' So I years later expressed this experience in a line of a poem; words not figurative.

Another insight is more difficult to describe, because it was an intuition purely qualitative; as a thought, most elementary, but as an apprehension, transforming. Truth, truism—words themselves mean nothing, but are only signs pointing to things perceived and experienced. Sometimes in remote places one still meets virtually illiterate people whose words are laden with living content, full of resonances; and the shock throws into contrast the fading of meaning from current language, not so much by the diminishing of vocabulary as by the thinning of the words themselves. Therefore I can only remotely indicate, not define, an apprehension which was transforming. It came from the wind, which blows with such unbroken force down the dales; the incessant rain drifting like a curtain; and along with the flow of wind the flow of water in the beck, swollen with all the rivulets of the fells, pouring itself towards the lake. It was a realization of the *Tao*, one might say, of the power of the elements finding their way not by effort but by effortlessness. I saw that human beings are forever striving against the great current on which we are carried, whose power is so immeasurably great that in resisting we can destroy only ourselves; but if we go witn it, that strength is ours, that energy sustains us.

Perhaps as a corollary to this realization that our only strength is that of the great tides and forces of the cosmos, it occurred to me at about that time that one might pray. My reasoning was simple: if there are no winds and currents of spiritual energy, the attempt could harm no one but would merely be ineffectual; whereas if there are it would be foolish not to take advantage of them. Prayer could only do nothing, or do good: it could do no harm. So simple an empiricism one might expect to have occurred to more people than seems to be the case. Professed agnostics seem not to be experimental, and wait for their doubts to be removed before putting them to the only tests which could remove them.

At Martindale vicarage I shared with my children many things. We lived in the Westmorland of Beatrix Potter, weaving a world of the real and the here and now about our coal-tits and rabbits, our white cat, the dipper's nest under the bridge, the log-fire and bramble-jelly and toast for tea. We had a natural history museum on the landing, where caterpillars, supplied with their food-plant (nettles) presently performed for us their metamorphosis into chrysalides, and later hatched into peacock butter-flies. I shared with them songs from the Baby's Opera, and the Père Castor nature-books, and Edward Thompson Seton and all the old fairy-books and myths. I thought our shared world was a happy one; but my daughter tells me she was never happy as a child. I thought my anxieties and insecurity were hidden from my children, but from childhood nothing is hidden, they see the reality, not the mask we wear, even though it is our love for them that makes us wear the mask. I withheld myself to protect both them and myself from my own secret inner wounds; but also because I was passionately in love with a man other than their father; and by that passion my imagination was absorbed, to their exclusion. This dream nourished my poetry; but it did not nourish Charles's children. To all out-ward appearance I did my best for them; but the inner reality was otherwise. I did not give my children any part of my spiritual life. In this I greatly wronged them, depriving them of what as a child had been given to me so fully in the undivided world of Bavington; I gave part of myself wholly, but it would have been better to give the whole of myself partly. It was as if I were two people, the poet, who existed in solitude, and another person. The habit of keeping hidden all that was vital to the poet had come perhaps from my past, when I had somehow to elude my father's moral and religious dominance, and my mother's hungry emotion, or perish.

Yet in the solitude of my interior world, whose sanctuary I had at last succeeded in securing against those who would, knowingly or un-knowingly, have destroyed it, I lived in continuous delight; the poems I then wrote seem too meagre a gleaning from those fields of paradise. In that interior world my real life was lived; I was almost continuously aware of my daimon, and passing spirits of the elements came and went. It is to me most mysterious that I was permitted, as poet, this vision of paradise, while as a woman I was in so many ways blameworthy. Why was I, absorbed as I was by an illicit and unrequited love, allowed to remain in Eden? Is it possible that a state of passionate love is not only innocent, but a return to the state of innocence itself? I do not know; at the time I had no sense of guilt; I did not think about myself or my moral state at all, but only of what I saw and knew of nature in the deep look I then took into its sanctuaries; and love, even upon the most carnal level, does, it seems, give wings that carry us above the world of guilt into a state of perception in which all is transfigured into the beautiful and the holy. The few poems I then wrote, fragile as they were, reflect, perhaps, an illumination from a world or state which lies beyond and above the egoism of guilt and sorrow. Perhaps a polytheist would have better understood these contradictions; as in the Greek myths some have received the mysteries of Dionysus, frowned on by Hera; or Zeus might bless while Demeter's fields lay barren; or Aphrodite destroy the follower of Artemis the upright. I can see now that I had no right to be so happy; yet I was permitted to be.

Martindale was an experience of solitude; solitude, but not loneliness; for solitude is the most intensely experienced state. Boredom in solitude is to me unimaginable; are we not bored only in the enforced company of the wrong people? People, that is, in whose company we cannot be our true selves? From the intensity of my inner life I had to emerge when human friends visited me.

For into my sanctuary—and during the war the country reverted to what it had been thirty years before, when there were no cars, or few—some friends did penetrate. Janet and Michael of course; and the house in Penrith to which they had now moved (Penrith took on, from my remote dale, the dimensions and qualities of a capital city) was my one point of attachment to the outer world. Once William Empson came with Michael, entirely and in all simplicity as he had been on his window-sill in Magdalene, or in Marchmont Street where, perched on a three-legged chair whose broken fourth was propped by the *Tale of Genji*, he had read me some quotation from a book whose place was marked by a dry kipper-bone. So entirely was he as he would have been anywhere and under any circumstances, that I felt strangely reassured that I myself had not altogether ceased to be the person of my earlier and better Cambridge days. Nature protected me; but I was grateful, also, to my friends for not forgetting me.

William was wearing a strange glossy black waterproof garment, which enhanced that sense of shock which his presence always produced; he had bought it in Hanoi, where he had worn it, very likely, during the great retreat into the interior before the advancing Japanese, in which he had accompanied his students of Pekin University. He was also wearing two left shoes that day, absentmindedly picked up as he dressed for a walk across the fells with Michael (they were going to to climb Great Gable). He confessed to the blisters only afterwards. Not only is William the same against any background, he assumes that his friends are. I could not have explained to him, even had I wished to do so, that in Martindale I was not the girl he had known, for this would have meant nothing to him; and therefore became, in relation to William, untrue. As with my parents I

remained the daughter they saw in me, so with friends I found myself
adopting the *persona* under which they had known me; only alone was I,
at that time, able to be the self I really was. This remained so for many
years to come; may even be so now. The only way to be rid of the disguise
was to be rid of the situation which forced me to adopt it.

William Empson is just the opposite. It was not that he was a townsman
out of place among rocks and stones and trees; he is after all a countryman
born, and had ridden to hounds, so we always understood, in his native
Yorkshire. But environment was indifferent to him, because his mind was
so much its own place that he perhaps never noticed any other; possibly
because he was short-sighted and always wore strong glasses. My
invisible companions, my nature-spirits silently withdrew before William.
Boehme says that spirits of different natures may occupy the same place
but will even so remain invisible to one another, each being in its own
universe; so it was that William never saw my secret world. Nevertheless I
was glad to see William.

I walked with William and Michael by the lake-side as far as Patterdale;
it grew hot, I remember, and I took off my woollen jacket. William offered
to carry it for me, with the simplicity of his good manners; but I,
instinctively too, said no, I could perfectly well carry it myself. 'Of course
that is what you would say,' William remarked with one of his very rare
excursions into the personal. I thought as I walked back alone of
William's picture of me as someone who could carry her own jacket and
refuse the simplest of civilities; out of the pride of the humbly born who
cannot accept favours? Out of mistrust of the slightest gesture which
might arouse my suspicion of the fowler's net? I had been too easily
hunted down; now I had grown wary, adept at evading, like a seed of
thistledown which floats away on the slightest movement of air made by
the motion of the capturing hand.

William's sister-in-law and her two children had rented a house near
Pooley Bridge; and Monica Empson visited me and offered to allow my
daughter to share her children's governess, an act of kindness which I
gratefully did accept. Monica Empson was one of those who, in changing
her location had not changed her world; and I envied her secure place in
the social order; for I had none, not even the magical status of poet—or
scarcely so, for I had barely begun to write and publish. Strong as I felt
myself to be in the company of the birds and weather of the fells, I knew
myself weak and vulnerable in all relationships with my own species. It
was for William's sake that Monica accepted me; William who remained
in his own secure world of the Yorkshire gentry in spite of being a poet.
That world, indeed, tolerates such eccentricities in the family; and I
wished I had such firm ground under my feet. Even in bohemia it

remained firm under William's feet; such as he cannot lose caste.

In order to make ends meet, and also because in those war years accommodation in the country was scarce, I took into the vicarage a mother with two little girls. The arrangement worked well enough; we shared the cooking and the little school (helped by the PNEU syllabus, which we dutifully followed) and one of our pleasant arrangements was that from time to time she or I would take a week-end away. It is hard now to recapture the sense of distance from the world in which we then lived in our valley; war had sealed us off in our pleasant sanctuary, so that Penrith was the only town left in our world; London had vanished over the rim of space. To me this was an unimaginable blessing, as if with London all my unhappy past had disappeared out of the universe. So it was that country neighbours became, as before the motor-car, a closed society, dependent upon one another, and making plans to meet a long time ahead (we had no telephone either) and with a sense of the great importance of small events. Perhaps we touched again, in that isolation, a lost human norm, seeing one another more justly in that oasis of permanence. It was as if we would always be there, like the fells, Janet in Penrith, I at Martindale; and yet we were only there by grace of the abnormal conditions of war.

So it was that my first invitation to visit Cockley Moor was an event almost unimaginable. Martindale had become my whole world; nor did it seem a small world, but rather an infinite one, in which each day was unique, not one moment to be lost; for rain and sunlight came and went, always some tree was budding, some flower opening. To go away even for two days was to miss some event of nature; the house-martins in the eaves leaving their nests, or deer coming down from the fells, or a white luminous ring round the sun, or the first wood-anemones or the last golden day of autumn warm enough for tea on the stone table under the yew.

Through Janet and Michael it was that I first met the friend who from that time to the end of her life was to be my wise counsellor; without whose practical help and charitable forbearance (I use those Christian words for she was a church-woman) I cannot imagine how I could have survived the years that followed. Helen Christian Sutherland, patron of the arts and of artists, Janet had met in Newcastle and visited at Rock Hall. Now she had moved to a new house, at Matterdale; one of the two highest inhabited houses in England, it was said.

The day of my visit to Cockley Moor was one of those days of steady drifting rain that are so beautiful in those hills, enclosing all in still deeper secrecy behind the curtain of falling water. It did not seem to me in any way strange to set out to walk on such a day; for I had been a child in just such a place, and walking still seemed to me the obvious means of coming and going. My father had had no car, nor had Charles after our marriage; I have never had a car, and, apart from the convenience of rapid transport, detest motoring, for, accustomed as I have been to being in places and not merely passing through them, motoring is for me a continual sense of being swept past and away from that in which I would wish to be. To walk in the rain, because this is necessary and natural, because one lives in a world of nature of which rain and snow are as much a part as sun and moon, is part of a lost heritage.

I had packed in my ruck-sack, wrapping it in many layers against the wet, some sort of evening-dress kept from a former life, and dressed myself for the long walk through the drifting incessant curtain of south-westerly rain, soft in my face and bringing out all the delicate scent of the fell, of moss and birch-leaves and sheep, distilled on the tongue like the pure essence of the element of water. As I walked up Boardale and into the loneliness I seemed to have left even Martindale behind me, to be restored to the simplicity of the alone with the Alone; that was the condition I was always seeking, to be cleansed by rain and wind, washed clean of myself; and so, deserved or undeserved, it was; for the elements of nature take no account of moral deserts, refusing none. I seemed, I remember, almost to be walking into the very being of the elementals of the hills and the clouds, out of the human condition altogether; and then, over the pass, to descend again into a world whose frontiers were mysteriously closed, and mud and stone and rain all once again measured by human standards; as cold, inconvenient and dirty.

Helen Sutherland had driven to Patterdale to meet me; and well she might have rejected the shabby figure streaming with wet; but instead she took me into her immaculate car (she was reading the latest volume of the the Faber poets, a translation of Virgil by C. Day Lewis, I seem to remember) and we were driven to Cockley Moor. There, for the first time since the outbreak of war, or indeed long before that, I found myself in a house which seemed to me then more like a place of the imagination—some castle in Spenser (the elegant Spenser rather than the puritan Bunyan), one of those places of arrival where treasures are shown to pilgrim or traveller, and wounds are healed. '*Tout était une rhythme et une rite et une cérémonie, depuis le petit lever,*' so begins the passage of Péguy which hung in the hall (lettered by Helen's god-daughter, Nicolete Gray); I had come from the world of nature into the world of art, another universe. In this house whose very cleanliness was a luxury, whose library of books Victorian and new, whose famous collection of paintings, Seurat and Ben Nicholson, Courbet and Mondrian, David Jones and Christopher Wood and even (in a cupboard for she did not care for them) two Picassos, I was lifted as by a tide above the mean struggle of poverty, to wake next morning in the peace of a spotless white room. Here I was made to feel that the poet in me was a being of worth, of whom much was hoped and expected, who had something to contribute to this world of excellence; whose poems might somehow justify and redeem my existence. Helen Sutherland saved me from bohemia; but for her I should, as a poet, have had no other ground beneath my feet. By her I was given the dignity accorded to poets in former times and in other countries, but seldom in modern England; and access to the great world and its values. For by the measure of perfection all art is finally tested and proved, and not by majority opinion or the fashion of little groups. It is a loss to any artist to have no access to an aristocracy (using the word in Plato's sense), whose function it is to keep alive those values; the pearls and not the acorns, food of natural mankind. The ill effects of this want have disastrously lowered the standards by which works are judged and to which, therefore, they tend to conform, in writers of the post-war generation, less fortunate than mine in the far lower level of culture in the world from which they draw their sustenance and for which they write. 'Conduct and work grow coarse, and coarse the soul' for the lack of a context, an environment of thought and feeling of a certain quality and discrimination which can only be preserved by a class both leisured and learned. For feeling too has its culture. Fineness of feeling requires a freedom and privacy accorded to few in the modern world, to look, to listen, to think without anxiety or self-interest; learning too demands leisure, both to acquire and to disseminate, and the struggle for survival produces many mental distortions.

Of musicians and painters Helen Sutherland had long been a patron; the Bush quartet used to play for her musical parties in London. Vera Moore, the pianist, was her special protégée; from David Jones, from Ben and Winifred Nicholson, from Naum Gabo, long before these were famous (as later from Barbara Hepworth) she had bought their best works; for her judgement of particular works was as discerning as her judgement of the artists themselves. Leslie Martin, then almost unknown, designed the new wing she had added to the old stone farm-house of Cockley Moor. Three generations of Binyons and Bosanquets and Hodgkins had been her friends and many of them her god-children; Lord Gray of Fallodon and Sir William Beveridge among her close friends; these and many more, serious scholars or fine artists. I first met the poet Norman Nicholson at her house, and, nearing the end of her life, she could not refrain from adding one more to the number of her chosen—the poetess Elizabeth Jennings.

Of all these she was more than a purchaser of finished works; David Jones stayed with her at Rock for long periods of work, and painted again—though less happily, for those bare fells were without the dimension of legend or history his imagination needed—at Cockley Moor. Friend, counsellor, perfectionist, she called out in all whom she admitted into her circle of friends in whose work she believed, by a combination of entire imaginative sympathy and exacting attention to detail, their best work, and, upon visits, their best behaviour.

Perhaps only David Jones could in her eyes do no wrong; but it is characteristic of both that even he was on more than one occasion caught in a kind of fatality of mishaps in her house (in the style of P. G. Wodehouse whom she also admired, and allowed to her guests, as she did her good wine, in small amounts, and on proper occasions; for in her library she kept, besides the best and most recent works on history, theology, art, poetry, gardening, and cookery, a chosen shelf of books for pleasure and relaxation).

Once when we were both staying at Cockley Moor David came to find me, much shaken; what should he do, he had spilt a bottle of ink down the immaculate white wall of his bedroom. For a whole day he laid aside the painting on which he was at work to obliterate the damning blot, and late in the afternoon summoned me to see whether any trace could still be detected. He told me how at Rock, perhaps on his first visit, he had, on his arrival in another room whose perfection had reproached him, caught sight of himself in the glass, and had, like Tom the chimney-sweep in Ellie's bedroom, been overcome with shame: obviously his hair must be cut at once. Another guest, a young woman to whom this predicament could be confided, was summoned; she agreed to cut his hair, but how prevent the clippings from falling onto that spotless floor? They arrived at the solution of taking a sheet from the bed to catch the hair, which she then snipped off. But then, how to get rid of it? Together they carried the sheet into the private wood behind the house, only to meet Helen approaching down a walk where she had been feeding her birds. There was nothing to be done but to confess: why had David not told her, the chauffeur could have driven him to the barber, etc., etc. But how well I could understand the paralysing sense of shortcoming that at times I think has overcome us all in Helen's house. I remember Lord Beveridge being scolded most severely for coming in two minutes late for lunch; and there was something about a distinguished Benedictine monk and a hot-water-bottle (Helen often gave to her friends copies of the Rule of St. Benedict, which makes no mention of hot-water-bottles) and Jim Ede picking a forbidden carnation.

Another memory of David Jones comes back to me; in which I seemed to see at once the human vulnerability and the artist's knowledge that his work has moved away from him into a life of its own, into another order of things. Among Helen's collection was David's portrait of Eric Gill's daughter, *Petra in Rosenhag*. It must have been put away (why? Did it speak too clearly and nearly the language of love for Helen's own hurt to be able to sustain it?) for David had got it out, and propped it against a chair in the drawing-room. I remember that I came into the room, and saw David there, alone, looking at the painting. Was he communing with memory or with art? I felt I had intruded, but could not instantly withdraw; and received the pondering sweetness of the look no other person had been meant to see.

Her perfectionism did not begin or end with the fine arts; it was therefore inescapable. Clothes, cookery and domestic economy, wine, textiles, flowers, dog-biscuits, bird-food and the clergy, all must come up to that exacting standard of hers, 'The best *is* the best.' As an Anglican, her only hesitation was as to whether Rome '*is* the best'; but, born to rule, her father's daughter (her father was Sir Arthur Sutherland of the P. and O. Shipping Company) she never submitted to the Bishop of Rome. But she liked others to be Catholics; Nicolete Gray and David Jones were, for her, in this sense, 'the best'. She would have made the greatest of all Tudor monarchs, uniting with the administrative economy of Henry VII the learning of Edward VI, Elizabeth's feminine power of evoking from her courtiers and artists 'the best'; and something of the writing on Mary Tudor's heart.

Helen Sutherland was for me from that time on what better poets than I have often lacked, a friend and protector of whatever small flame was alight in me. There are such things as spiritual friends, friends of the genius rather than of the natural creature it inhabits; and such was Helen Sutherland to me. Because she believed in that small flame of mine she tended and tolerated the rest of me, the wretched young woman whose shortcomings well might have made her reject the whole. This she did with a gentleness which yet never became that facile acceptance of anything and everything, which is the bohemian counterfeit of true kindness. Always she applied (and this with her mind above all) the first principles of Christian morality to each specific situation; having reached a conclusion as to 'the best' in this sense, her counsel or her help would follow. Instinctively she had, besides, a sense of the dimension of time which brings to fruition what is in us; and having decided that poetry was in me, she was prepared to wait, and to tolerate. Never did she reproach me for my sins; only for my faults—for not turning my mattress daily, or for leaving an electric light on in the passage outside my bedroom, or taking too much hot water for my bath; but never for leaving my husband, for my inability to cope with my life, or for being in love.

Her gentleness to suffering, however deserved and self-caused (my own, for instance, but I was not the first of her friends in the world of the arts to have entangled my life), her tolerance of the larger sins and mistakes, was boundless. In some despairing phase I said to her once that I was a failure, and had not and never now would, write the poems I should and could have written; and she replied, gently and severely, 'Well, I have sometimes been told that I am a very good judge, and *I* think you will.' For although she could not help exerting power, she was, at the same time, entirely responsive to whatever each of her friends had to bring. After dinner she would settle in her chair, her dogs at her feet, a piece of embroidery or exquisite mending in her bird-like hands, attentive; if I had new poems, she would listen to them; ask me to re-read, to explain. She would listen, with the same attention, to a young student testing his political or vocational ideas and ideals, as to David Jones or Ben Nicholson. Or she would let us choose some book to read aloud—on consecutive evenings, if we were making a long stay—Dante or Wordsworth, or T. S. Eliot (or sometimes Mrs. Gaskell or P. G. Wodehouse) or Vera Moore would play Mozart and Bach and Couperin.

In how many memories besides mine Helen's drawing-room, designed by Leslie Martin before he became famous (for Helen recognized talent before others did, and was indifferent to reputation, trusting in her own judgement) still exists as it was! It seemed as if, with sun and moon rising and setting over High Street and the sweep of the fells, crossed by moving cloud and cloud-shadows, or sweeping rain, the outer world beyond the uncurtained window that ran the full length of the south-facing wall, was brought within the compass of Helen's civilizing power. To me, the wilds were, and ever will be, places of refuge from the human. But from Helen's drawing-room, thrice distilled, those bare hills and wet clouds, the moon and the stars, became a part of the world of art she had created. Now that room is gone; each thing from its place, where it had seemed to belong as perfectly as every subtle brush-stroke of colour in a painting. Seeing again, long after, on a visit to Edinburgh, two of Helen's Ben Nicholsons in the little museum of modern art in the Botanic Gardens, I was suddenly taken back, in memory, into that vanished room where for so long they hung. The little Seurat too is in Edinburgh; the Winifred Nicholson of Bank's Head in the Kettle's Yard museum in Cambridge; also built by Leslie Martin, and reflecting in its taste much that Helen had originated. I can open the door, in memory, now, and move round that room, touching bookcase, chair and desk; the velvet cloth on the grand piano; the lyre-shaped music-stand; Helen's desk, scattered with her papers, where she wrote to us those inimitable letters in her fine hand, with their added parentheses and insertions and afterthoughts; her own armchair with its reading-lamp with her work-table at hand, and the little pile of *The Times* she never threw away unread, cutting out paragraphs on theology, or nature, or the arts, to send to friends or to keep. The gramophone with its great horn, on which she would sometimes play to us records of Beethoven's or Eliot's quartets; the jars of nuts for the birds and the special dog-biscuits. Over the fire-place the two Persian miniatures that (with her Persian carpets) perhaps celebrated her friendship with Lawrence Binyon; and below them three crystal goblets, and two small Ben Nicholsons; oddly assorted it might seem, but 'the best' of one culture is never out of place beside 'the best' of another. On a round table were displayed the newest books by friends. The very books on the shelves whether history, poetry, theology, cookery or art, their covers immaculate, I could, in memory, still find in their appointed places.

Her pictures, that great, yet most personal collection, still (but for a few donations) intact, belong now to Nicolete Gray; but to Helen's friends they hang, still, in their old places. The great dark Ben Nicholson of interlocking profiles at the end of the room; the romantic early Ben Nicholsons and the later abstracts; the Winifred Nicholson of a white hyacinth against snow; the Cecil Collins pencil drawing; the Italian landscapes by Lelia Caetani, Helen's neighbour since her marriage to Hubert Howard of Lyulph's Tower. Her collection included 'Sunday paintings' by a group of coal-miners in Ashington, valued with the rest; and in valuing their vision and buying their paintings, was she not giving to these also something no social reformer or politician could give? And above all those superb David Joneses, many of them painted at Rock, and some of the fell-side outside the window; and others, of flowers in those very glass vases in which Helen so inimitably arranged winter shoots or spring buds. With its immaculate white walls and the finest works of contemporary artists, that vanished room was the creation of the period and the school of painting of which Helen herself had been the first, as she was to remain the most discriminating, patron. Henry James (her beautiful set of his works is now in the London Library) would have found in her all he most valued. Perhaps he helped to create her.

I saw that room dismantled; first the pictures, then the furniture, piece by piece. I myself heaped on the floor shelf-loads of books, as Helen, confined to her room upstairs, took her leave of them, selecting a few to keep in the nursing home where she went to end her life; relinquishing her possessions with a wave of her hand: 'away, away!' Some went to libraries; some to booksellers; some to friends. I have the set of Balzac that had been her father's; neither library nor bookseller wanted them.

I have written more of my poems on the white window-sill of her little guest-room than in any other house save one. Helen Sutherland was already grey when I met her; and once I saw her on her terrace, leaning on her stick, a bird-like fragile figure of age, and she seemed in that moment an embodiment of the wisdom of time and of all that matures slowly: of all that is comprised in the astrological figure of Saturn who slowly brings all things to their fulfilment. I understood through her that art is the 'foster-child of silence and slow time'; in her house were many clocks and chronometers soberly measuring the hours, but those hours seemed longer than elsewhere, for work and thought, for reading and writing. She loved, too, the great clock-face of the heavens, 'the heavenly bodies', as she liked to call them, who moved so clear and pure over her high sky. Coleridge's moon, Wordsworth's one star that often shines in the morning or evening sky, in the dawn and twilight already in Cumberland gradual and northern, approaching a little the gloaming of Scotland. During the war, too, the stars seemed more in evidence, being the only lights in the night sky; and at Cockley Moor we seemed almost to touch them; not a light in the village or on the road, and nothing above us but Orion and the constellations. Last thing at night Helen would always let the dogs out, and look at the stars, and at the moon. She always knew from *The Times* charts of the heavens which constellation and planets were to be seen in that clear sky, and loved especially the new moon. How often, dressed in hooded cloak and fur-lined boots, a stick so as not to slip on the ice, Helen would lead me out onto her terrace to look up at the new moon, or the Pleiades; and then, returned, she would make me take down Coleridge's diaries, and read to her those passages about the moon as he had, not long before as star-time goes, watched its passing over neighbouring hills.

Yet in Helen's house, nature was outside, valued as a kind of art, a divine art it may be, but yet not as at Martindale, where I lived within its mystery, and not as its spectator. As a country child I had known that *participation mystique*, as perhaps all country people do, or did, or many among them, the very young or the very old, or those gifted with the kind of sensibility which in other classes would lead to learning or the arts. It is my birthright; and at Martindale I resumed what was to me natural, but now with words and some knowledge which might make it possible to express what every hare in its form or curlew in its nest on the moor perhaps knows but does not know it knows.

In Helen Sutherland's house I was in some respects like an amphibious creature breathing air, and needing to plunge back into my own element. I remember the beauty of the New Year's day of 1940 we all spent with her, I and my children and Janet and Michael and their children, and the little evacuated Newcastle boys whom she had with her; turkey and Christmas pudding, golden angels and silver stars, all rare and precious, with that kind of Christian aestheticism associated with the word 'Anglo-Catholic'.

And I remember on another winter day she had given a concert for a pianist also stranded in the North because of the war. It was balm and beatitude to be transported, once again, from cottage to palace, from the world of nature to the world of art, from the struggle to realize anything whatever, to Helen's house of 'the best', where all was achieved, had already undergone its assumption 'out of nature'. Yet of that day of the concert I remember most clearly of all the moment when her car set us down at the gate of the field at Martindale. The moon must have been up, as well as the stars, for there was a birch-tree, entirely encrusted in frozen snow or crystals of ice, and these glittered in the moonlight, green and blue and white. That tree stood in another ground from those forms in which art seeks to embody mere glimpses of a mystery unfathomable; beyond art, so I felt; beyond anything knowable by man. Beyond those limiting frontiers I came into my own again. Returning to that tree I seemed liberated as into a universe upon another scale, beyond all formulations.

Sometimes, too, Helen would visit me, walking along the lake-side path from Patterdale, and I, alone or with my children, would walk to meet her, past the flowering wild-cherry trees of Sandwick, past the slender high waterfall of Scale Howe, past the oak-wood and the birch-wood to the empty fell-side where only juniper bushes grow. There would be a picnic, or return to the vicarage; so on my side of Ullswater I, on behalf of the wild places, received Helen as my guest.

In Helen's house, or with her or through her, I was to meet for the first time many of my most valued friends; David Jones; Hubert and Lelia Howard; Winifred Nicholson who had also been a child of northern hills. She had loved the same wild flowers as I, seen in the hedges of Cumberland the same cranesbill and harebell, scabious and water-avons as I, only a few miles away, in Northumberland. When first I had seen her paintings at an exhibition in London I had wondered how she knew what I thought no one but myself had, in quite that way, seen. When I met her, I understood. From opposite ends of the social scale (she was born in Naworth Castle) we had shared the same beauty, under the same skies. No work could be in greater contrast with Ben Nicholson's abstract period than Winifred's; his with masterly intellectual assurance, hers with the delicate immediacy of feeling; and yet, when he, Winifred and Christopher Wood were working together, there was a quality of feeling in Ben's work which, for all his later mastery, it perhaps later lost. And Winifred, for many years after their separation, could not find the vision those three had shared before Christopher Wood's death, and Ben's departure. Ben (I always thought of him as an elf-man, untouched by human joys and sorrows) was never troubled by remorse, however. When he was about to leave Barbara Hepworth, his second wife, I remember saying to him, in what I intended as reproach, 'You know Ben, you have been married to two very remarkable women.' 'Yes, I know,' said Ben. 'From Winifred I learned a great deal about colour, and from Barbara about form.' So much for marriages. Yet that ruthless integrity of the artist which was for Ben his only law, Helen supremely admired. So, for that matter, did Winifred, for all it had cost her in human sorrow. And so, God knows, do I. I remember when, later, I was wandering in London's hells again, saying to Ben that I could not write, I was too unhappy. He replied, 'When I am happy I use my happiness for my work; when I am unhappy I use my unhappiness.' So surely do all great artists. But I was always too easily overset, falling between the duties of woman and poet and too often failing in both.

To remain for ever, to put down the roots of my life in the place I love, has always been the mirage which I have followed. No more at Martindale than at Bavington did I recognize as a mirage this dream, so securely did the here and now seem to uphold its field and barn, its little parlour and its stone-flagged kitchen, its garden fragrant with flowering-currant and box. I forgot my being there at all was only by grace of an abnormal situation, the war. For the time I remained there my valley had the quality of being for ever, the trees and the beck, the line of hills and the log fire, circumference and centre; and yet the decision to leave was my own.

I began to realize, uneasily, though I was still far from realistic, and still imagined that it must be possible to live by being a poet, that sooner or later I would have to face the problem of earning a living. It seemed to me that in London I could hope to make my way in something I pleased to think of as 'the literary world'; not realizing that the world of those who make a living by writing for the newspapers (whether weekly or daily) has no more to do with the fountains of poetry than has any other profession undertaken in order to make a living. I had, in Janet and Michael, in Helen Sutherland, encountered the values only of 'the best' and because the best valued me, I supposed that to pass muster among the second-best would be easier. What a mistake! I should have been more proud, or more humble; for the only humility I ever had was a false one, an over-whelming diffidence, not in the company of 'the best' (where I have always found understanding) but of the public world, where I have not.

I wonder, now, what I would have done had I possessed even the smallest assured income, the guarantee of the freedom of the merest subsistence? I might have stayed at least a little longer; given to my children a few more years of childhood; possibly; though what is the use of speculating upon hypothetical possibilities? Yet I believe the chief instability of the situation was in myself; the deepest reason for my departure was the unrest which drove me in search of my lover, for whom my passion, in those years of absence, had only increased as it became more imaginary. I was living, in imagination, an ordeal of fidelity, of that keeping faith with the absent which is one of woman's age-old tasks; and as ordeal and task I experienced it, building every day, as a bird builds a nest according to an innate pattern, a beautiful edifice of love, an edifice into which I wove every perception, every thought; which, had it been for a husband whose return I awaited, and not for an empty dream, would have been no different. An instinct of constancy and a strength of something which, if not true love, must surely be one of its components, in me was all misdirected upon a mirage. I explored, in absence, all the imaginative vistas of love. Reading, years after, Lawrence Whistler's idyll of his love and marriage with Jill Furse, I seemed to recognize, in that record of the same years, the same quality of experience as had been mine; for what hair's breadth divides sacred from profane love, perfect realization like theirs from total illusion like mine! Moral or immoral, possible or impossible, the vision love pursues is everywhere and always the same, its source beyond any particular relationship that it may for the time illuminate.

I had not the fortitude to know myself alone. I find it possible, now, to write without turning, in imagination, to some beloved person; but that is because now I know that the only beloved is the living mystery itself. But then, my love was a dream I could not relinquish, for I could not live without the illusion that I was not alone; nor could I have endured the knowledge that I myself was the creator of those situations of unrequited love in which I suffered so much anguish. Yet so, I now understand, it was; my daimon chose for me the inaccessible. Useless to pity Sappho, or Emily Dickinson, or Christina Rossetti, for were not these too under the same compulsion to love only in situations which could not compromise essential solitude, an inner dedication so taken for granted it is not even perceived? I now see, as the type of every woman poet, that half-legendary poetess of Japan, Komachi, who, in her youth a court lady with many lovers, in her old age walked in rags on the roads of enlightenment.

It was not paradise, then, which failed or faded, but I myself who could not pass the test of offered beatitude. Sorrowful, reluctant, the guardians of my place of respite, peace and spiritual restoration, allowed me to sever the ties which bound me and to depart; go, being what I was, I must. I believe I was deeply wrong to go; for with my departure ended my children's brief time of freedom and happiness, their world woven among those fields and streams and magic places on the fell taken away from them, and all the hours and days of blackberrying and toast for tea by our own wood fire.

... every Space that a Man views around his dwelling-place
... such space is his Universe:
And on its verge the Sun rises and sets, the Clouds bow.
In such a world we had lived; and leaving Martindale was like a mutilation;

And if he move his dwelling-place his heavens also move,
Where'er he goes, and all his neighbourhood bewail his loss . . .

It was Helen Sutherland's offer to take my children into her house in order to enable me to seek my fortune in London which made it possible for me to go. Yet I made a fatal mistake; I left my children too young and too soon; and Helen's standards of perfection, which from artists could call out the best, which from me had called out my best, for my children, I realized too late, would be an intolerable burden. I ought to have seen this all along, but I shut my eyes to signs I should have heeded, would have heeded, had I been less bent upon my own ends.

That autumn, day after golden day prolonged the summer. At last the appointed time of departure arrived, and I took my children to Cockley Moor. Only on our arrival did I see, with terrible clarity, what I should have seen before, that my children's freedom was over and Cockley Moor, to me a refuge, would be to them a prison. 'Go back,' my daimon said, 'go back at once, it is not too late even now.' But how could I have explained to Helen, who towards me had been so full of forbearance and understanding, who in kindness had offered to help me? As so often when the daimon speaks, I answered that it was too late, impossible now, my plans made, other people involved, my course set. Ah, the wrong course, my daimon said; and I replied, 'what else can I do?' The daimon said nothing about how to earn a living. Yet the daimon is always right, and this the future always in time reveals. Even money I suppose would have been forthcoming if I had heeded more attentively the warning voices. I might then have been a better poet. I had, at Martindale, made a beginning, but nothing more; and had I followed up the poems of *Stone and Flower* with others—but it is useless now to guess what way my life might then have taken. Had I been offered my chance and proved unworthy of it? Or are such oases only places of respite, not of refuge? If I had, in those years of vision, relinquished carnal desire and the will o' the wisp 'love', might I have been allowed to remain? But that valley was my love; and my love, perhaps, that valley, woven into my dreams and fantasies, and my poems. And yet, someday, somehow, I would have had to go; I was in my early thirties, it was too soon to leave the world; what had seemed home proved to be only a stage in the journey. I remember

William Empson quoting to me, on that walk by the lake-side to
Patterdale,

> Does the road wind uphill all the way?
> Yes, to the very end.

We were both laughing, of course; I did not believe it. I have always been
too ready to believe that the worst was over.

CHAPTER SEVEN

Orpheus in Hell

ST. Teresa was advised by her spiritual directors not to follow her original
intention of confessing, in her *Life*, to her early sins; since from such an
account no good could come to her readers, whereas from her record of
her deepest insights others might learn. Everyone, after all, knows the
banalities of falling short, of our physicality, ignorance and so forth.
Modern practice has tended more and more to reverse this view of what
ought to be told and what withheld. To lay bare base thoughts and actions
is held to be more 'sincere', and in this sense more truthful, than to bear
witness to those glimpses which come only at those moments in which we
seem to transcend our habitual selves. The claim to have seen sublime or
beautiful things, because out of character with our commonplace selves, is
seen as a kind of hypocritical self-aggrandizement; even though in fact it is
only insofar as we all do transcend at moments those vulgar selves that we
can see or know anything of value. One might with no less reason call
musicians hypocrites who, mis-shapen shabby creatures, evoke from
wood and strings and metal and from their own bones and sinews the
music of the spheres. Or what truth can there be in a 'sincere' and 'frank'
wrong solution to a problem in geometry? Only one solution is true, the
rest are not other truths about number, but failures to find it. In an age
when 'the truth' is held to be a mere record of the flux of events, truth itself
is seen as a kind of untruth, because out of the ordinary, above the
ordinary. It was fashionable in my youth to re-write the lives of poets,
saints and others remembered precisely insofar as they at certain moments
transcended their ordinary selves, in terms of a kind of mundane and

animal realism; and this, it is implied is 'the truth' about Milton or Shelley or some other. Yet what such accounts omit is, precisely, the truth grasped by poet or saint in moments of insight, intuition of harmony and meaning, above the animality all share.

I have little, therefore, to tell of the shabby years following my return to London, since these were years of alienation from vision. There is yet another reason for my blanks in the record of this time: the difficulty of reviving the traces of memory. Freudians might say I have repressed things I do not want to remember because too painful or too humiliating; but my own belief is that I cannot remember because the events had so little reality in them: there is no inner content to remember. They were, like so much realistic fiction, uninteresting. Instead of memory there remains a symbol, my own dimly-lit and ill-constructed stage-set of the Hades where Orpheus, singing and playing his lyre (and if that music had ceased he would have been lost) wandering down deeper and deeper among the dead in his search for Eurydice.

The power of this symbol was strong in those war years; Kathleen Ferrier's voice singing *Orfeo*; the dream-like compulsion of Cocteau's Orphée; that dark illusory caverned world (one remembers those sheets of glass, planes of illusion, not stable or fixed, but encountered here or there as they are carried for purposes unknown, by the glazier of windows) express the essence of something undergone by the imagination alienated from the light but not yet dead. In the pre-war days of Mass-Observation we had looked down, like Blake's 'eternals' about to fall into the abyss, on the sorrowful states below; but now I was myself treading paths un-imaginably strange and desolate, no longer an 'observer', but travelling on foot, shelterless. I seemed again, after the sweet refuge of Martindale, to be walking on paths and ways not my own; but whether this was because the tidal wave of events had swept away all individual paths and ways, or because I had lost myself again, I do not know. If I held on to my lyre it was less to play than to hold as a talisman; 'I am a poet,' I believed, 'and therefore the meaning of this experience must be found: for that I am here'.

I made the descent not, now, as a somnambulist but with a sense of quest; I felt it as a task imposed to explore these states, to endure that journey, to discover the limits of those distances. Perhaps it would not have been necessary for me to journey down there, from Martindale where I might have remained with my children, had not the darkness in myself drawn me into dark places; but better one's own nightmare than the shelter of someone else's dream; even our nightmares are expressions of our own reality, stations on our own way; and on that way it is always good to be.

Orpheus in Hell

From that shadow-world the images which return are all unconnected, for there was no form, no story. I cannot remember how I was directed, or by whom, to the furnished room in Percy Street to which I came. Years before, while I was still a schoolgirl, a fortune-teller had told me that I 'would always have a roof over my head'. This had seemed a strange promise, for I had not at that time doubted so ordinary a possibility. 'Honour thy father and thy mother, that thy days may be long in the land that the Lord giveth thee'; these words I had seen and read every morning when I woke in the blue bedroom at the Manse; but I had seen no necessary connection between my flight from my parents (whom I had not honoured) and the ways of the prodigal I now travelled. Now for the first—and by no means the last—time, that meagre promise of the Fates (the same fortune-teller had told me that although I would know true love I would not marry my love) seemed all I had to hold on to, so bottomless seemed the abyss at my feet. 'Time and the hour run through the roughest day' also brought me its arid comfort; but though like him I clung to oracles I lacked Macbeth's fortitude of desperation.

This room, then, was like a piece of wreckage to which I clung. So entirely alien was it, so unrelated to anything in my past, my future, my hopes or expectations, that I found myself invaded again by my old terror of loss of identity, of foundering in the black flood of nonentity which poured like water into a sinking ship. My identity was still a most fragile paper-boat to which to entrust myself; I had become, again, one of the dispossessed, one of the multitude of 'displaced persons' caught up in the great torrent which has in this century swept so many human beings away from all securities, tearing up the roots of lives. I, who longed so much to be rooted for ever in the beloved place (and that place had for a while been Martindale) was by the compulsion both internal and external, torn away once more.

The house in question was let out in rooms to various young women working in war ministries. There is something sordid and vicious in the area of London west of Tottenham Court Road, which yet, like the seamier side of Balzac's Paris, exerts a powerful attraction upon a certain kind of âmes damnées: (phrases from Rimbaud and Baudelaire made our company of the damned into a kind of élite.) The finely proportioned early Georgian houses, running to dry-rot and decay, seemed to lend themselves, like rafts in a storm, to the struggle for survival, for a foothold in 'the world', which is, in those hells, so powerful a mirage; so near did the squalor of lonely back rooms rented by the month lie to the White Tower and the Etoile, to all those favourite fashionable restaurants frequented by the ambitious engaged in using their talents in order to climb to the security of fame. These rooms were not places to be lived in, as the vicarage at Martindale was a place to be lived in (and even now that in retrospect I know what in prospect I did not know, how brief was to be my time there, Martindale seems to have been my home and my children's home for a period not measurable by time, so inexhaustible is it), but only to use as a base, a lair to hunt from and to take cover in. Solitude at Martindale was endlessly rich; but to have nowhere to go out to from those drab rooms, whose very furniture seemed displaced (there was a gate-legged oak table, I remember, to which I looked desperately for comfort and dignity, it and I alike having fallen from the good country world of a solid past) was to have the sense of being banished from existence, with nothing to hold on to beyond a table and a chair and a gas-fire. In Martindale I had my own furniture which, however shabby, lent to me that sense of being mistress in my own house, without which few women can withstand adversity. The very hopes of such rooms as the one I now occupied are desperations, corks and straws tossing on the black gulfs; hope for some scrap of literary work (a book-review or the like) and hope for love, for love the saviour, the rescuer, the end of all sorrow; *Eldorado banal*, but we never think of that on our own *Voyage à Cythére*. And yet I had, of my own volition, exchanged Martindale for this. The world continually reflects back to us our inner states, and this was the aspect of mine. Had I but seen it for what it was; as perhaps in a sense I did, for I did give my inner assent to the experience, I was not, here as at Blackheath, oppressed by the despair of feeling myself passive in the power of others.

> My soul is like a ship in a dark storm
> Blowing I know not whither . . .

was a line which at that time haunted me; and Vittoria Corombona's kind of passion seemed reason enough for any storm and darkness. 'My sin was in my blood, and now my blood pays for't.' With pride, the last refuge of the damned, I made her words my own. Through what hells will we not walk undeterred, to destruction if need be, if passion drives us. In the overcoming of such a passion I could at that time see only a denial of life, and justified myself with Blake's 'those who overcome their desires do so because their desire is weak enough to be overcome'. 'If the fool will persist in his folly he will become wise' might have been more to the point, but I did not see myself as a fool. Webster's *flectere, si nequeo superos, Acheronta movebo* was more in my mood—Webster, who clothed crude and trivial lusts in the trappings of Renaissance splendour.

In the next room lived Sonia Brownell; and in that place of strangers she was the one person who welcomed me as someone whose name she already knew. But instantaneous recognition does not depend on hearsay; and in Sonia I recognized, in the Hades upon whose brink we met, another soul making a journey not unlike my own. Perhaps she would not have used at that time the words of the Order whose nuns had educated her, *magna est veritas*, but such was her faith. In pursuit of that unknown absolute, truth (for her a human truth higher at least than the positivist truth of Cambridge), she was prepared to venture all. Ulysses was her favourite hero because he was guided by intelligence. She always fell in love with intelligent men; and although constantly bedevilled by the current confusion of intelligence with cleverness, she was never long satisfied with the fashionable pseudo-answers the world she moved in offered her. In that world of worldly ambitions and wordly values she was (as my son when he began to read Stendhal said of her) *une âme noble et généreuse*, seeing in the despair into which she so often fell the price that must be paid by seekers after truth who would not be put off with easy answers. Nor was she wrong in regarding the French Existentialists (some of whom were to become later her closest friends) as the most intelligent seekers at that time in the Hades through which we moved.

Sonia may be said to have pursued that quest with more charity and fewer face-saving compromises than I. She has looked into the depths with eyes more merciful than mine, if perhaps a little too long.

Unlike myself Sonia had been educated within the frame-work of Catholic tradition which claims, by tried means, to attain assured ends. But she had rejected her Catholic, as I my Protestant framework, and for reasons in part similar: not from laxity, nor from want of a sense of final ends, but, because foregone conclusions appeared as arbitrary limits imposed upon possibility. Perhaps, since formulations of truth may themselves become opaque objects of idolatry, her rejection was of real falsifications, as mine had been; perhaps unfortunately for herself she retained from her early training in apologetics (years later she confessed to me, late one night, that she had come first in all England in apologetics in her last year at school) the habit of relying upon conceptual thinking in her search for final answers. In this she did constant violence to her own gift of deep and generous feeling, to which such thought often ran counter.

We were both alike under the influence of the spirit of the time, which equated the search for truth in every field (and in the arts especially) with the rejection of all truths of the past. Just because these had already been formulated they could not be that thing beyond, which art at all times seeks to embody. Eliot's insistence on tradition could not arrest the progressive dismantling of civilization (which indeed he himself saw) from the Impressionists to the Cubists, from the Surrealists to the Existentialists; which at that time still seemed exciting enough, a search for new, rather than what in truth it was, a progressive elimination of all possibilities. The writings of Herbert Read embody, in its most serious and responsible terms, what has proved yet another illusion, that the 'freeing' of the artist from tradition can lead to anything except the end of civilization as such. While Churchill conducted his war to save civilization from barbarism encroaching from without, the dismantling proceeded from within.

As with the arts we saw rules not as to be learned but to be broken, so in the conventions of morality we saw only a refusal to confront truthfully the issues of life; in life as in art we must find the answers for ourselves. It had not occurred to my generation that such answers take many thousands of years to find, nor, as Yeats had written, but in a book I had not then read, 'truth cannot be discovered, but may be revealed'. 'The way up is the way down' (T. S. Eliot had lent his authority to these words, written by a mystical theologian besides) is another of those statements which can only be misleading when taken out of context. The only context into which we incorporated any fragment we might discover had been created by ideologies themselves iconoclastic—Marxism, Freudian psychology, Surrealism; a whole within which no fragment of what in another context might be wisdom could keep its virtue. But we did not think the way down an easy way, or for that reason set out to explore the depths; on the contrary we took that journey, without certainty of way or end, as the harder and more heroic way. Conventional virtues seemed, by contrast, the effortless way, or rather a refusal to travel on the Way at all.

The one thing I had retained from my upbringing on the Romantic Poets and the Protestant religion was an absolute belief in the inner light of inspiration as the one sure guide. I found a text in the *Geeta* which says 'It is better to perish in one's own law; it is perilous to follow the law of another; better to fail in one's own way than to succeed in the way of another'. Again I seized upon the words out of context, and supposed the 'law' named the inner light; but the Hindu idea of *dharma* envisages social laws, laws of caste. To me, fugitive as I was from a social order I had never known from within, there was no social *dharma*, only the inner light; I lived as an outcaste. Yet I did believe that every life is a way; that we are given each our own clue to unwind, a clue to lead us through the labyrinth so long as we never lose it, never relinquish the living thread.

The obvious dangers of self-deception, the mistaking, for example, of carnal passion for the inner light (fuel upon which, nevertheless, as every poet has known, that light has often fed) never gave me pause. As for the end to which I might be led, I more than half knew that this could never be anything like marriage, nor even, when it came to the point, a real love affair. For the end to which my love pointed was some absolute beyond these. I cared only for pure love—using the term as one might distinguish between 'pure' and 'applied' mathematics. But, being weak and ignorant, I continued to delude myself for as long as I possibly could, and hoped, somehow, someday, for earthly happiness as well as the other goal.

Even now I cannot think I was mistaken in divining that we can be certain only of our love, must begin where that love is as the only ground on which we stand. If what we love be some Alastair, some mirage, even that mirage has a relative reality, the only reality which we are, at the moment we perceive it, capable of perceiving. To extinguish or deny such love as we have is to be without any light whatsoever; for love, and not that denial of living impulse my father's generation so named, is will. 'Do what thou wilt is the whole of the law', as that lapsed Plymouth Brother, Frater Perdurabo wrote; I too was resolved to 'go through with it'. A difficult, austere and exacting law it proves to be, Crowley had said; and so I too was to find 'the unknown disciplines of the self-imposed task'. These (the phrase is Conrad's) I was to discover in due course.

What I did not know, or would not see, was how high a price others must pay for the way I took; my parents, my children. I see it now being paid still in the third generation, that of my grandchildren. If I had known this, would I have acted differently? I think not; we are all in the inextricable confusion, and grandchildren and great-grand-children must bear their human burden like the rest. The answer may be, after all, an irreducible paradox; as David Lindsay states it in his strange symbolic book *A Voyage to Arcturus*. It is a woman drawn by music away from her family who in that book says 'I am conscious of two worlds. My husband and boys are real to me, and I love them fondly. But there is another world for me... and it makes my real world appear all false and vulgar.' 'But can it be right', the visitor from Earth asks her, 'to satisfy our self-nature at the expense of other people?' 'No, it is not right. It is wrong, and base . . . but in that other world these words have no meaning.' 'In place of a heart you have a wild harp, and that is all I know about you,' the earth-man says. Are heart and harp compatible? So I always hoped, but did not find it so.

People like myself are dangerous to social stability, since we have no loyalties native to us, but only those we ourselves choose; or none at all. And those we are likely to choose, once the simple ties of life are broken, are absolutes and perfectionisms. Social exiles are ruthless perfectionists; and if in the service of these absolutes we do not spare ourselves, neither do we understand compassion for the limitations of others, or that these limits may be bounds set not so much to thwart life as to protect it and make it possible at all.

I believed myself a dedicated poet whose life was, if not a Christian pilgrimage, a legendary quest; but what was I, to the eyes of the world, but a young woman of no social background, who had left her husband, who had no visible means of support and wretchedly shabby clothes? Only my inner pride was equal to the many ordeals and humiliations which I at this time, and most deservedly, underwent. Through Janet I had been offered an obscure job in one of the many proliferating government departments created by the war; a department staffed by ladies of the diplomatic class, one of whom was an Oxford friend of Janet's. Among them I cut a wretched figure; not only because of my shabby and sordid exterior, but from my real ignorance of current affairs. I was, besides, unable to form any inkling of what kind of press-clippings constituted what were known as 'pointers', useful in a way I utterly failed to grasp, towards some end of propaganda or counter-propaganda which was equally dark to me. My clothes, my cough, my misery, my incompetence, my not belonging to their class and caste (and here indeed these women of the legislative or 'ruling' class were engaged in performing their traditional function, in their proper place and doing their proper work, whereas I was not) quickly earned me dismissal. I was passed on, somehow, to another but far more terrible department, connected with market-research, conducted this time by men of neither breeding nor education, where I was even more a misfit, and seemed back in the nightmare of Ilford, swallowed again into the gulf I most feared. What to the ladies of the Ministry, and to the men of the still lower depths, seemed real and important, seemed to me unreal and of no importance; and again I was oppressed by the number against me. Only alone did I still retain any secret refuges of beauty; in the outer world there seemed to be, for me, no place, no *terra firma*, and I found myself sinking and drowning and with no idea of which way to turn.

At Christmas I fled north to Helen Sutherland, to see my children; strangely removed from me they seemed, under her care, our family relationship no longer unbroken. But we went, for a few days, (Helen must have paid for us) to the Howtown Hotel, just over the familiar hill from Martindale; in sight still, but already for ever out of reach. There, snowed up, behind great wind-carved sculptured drifts of snow we were safe from the world for a little while. It was a sweet secret time, shut off from all that lay outside and beyond; and then it was over, and I returned to London with, again, no job and no income. I remember waiting for the night train on blacked-out Carlisle station; waiting interminably in one of those non-places that war seemed to create; filled with people who were, like myself, walking in that grey cold dream. Sitting beside me on a seat on the platform was a young Scotswoman, certainly much younger than I was myself, who might once have been pretty; but now all her hair had fallen out, from some loathsome disease, and she stank; she had no idea of how she was going to reach her destination in London—if she had one—where she was travelling, following up some desperate thread she hoped would lead her to some man or other to whom she was or was not married, but bound by sorrow; she herself hardly expected to find him, but the need to search drove her. 'I was a silly lassie' she said, judging herself more mercifully than I (of whom she seemed a terrible caricature) could judge myself. There is something in that word, 'lassie' (a word my mother had so often used of me and to me) that absolves from all blame, so innocent, so fresh and fair and vulnerable is the young form it evokes. It is a word of endearment; not especially a lover's endearment but the ambient endearment of family love, of village (for it is a folk-word), of a whole environment of belonging. I wished that there was now anyone to use that word of me, and a great nostalgia for that past world from which some dark dirty train was about to carry me away weakened my courage. I gave the poor ruined creature what money I could—very little: a gesture of self-pity.

As for 'the literary world' I had set out to find and conquer, I found myself ill-equipped for the task. I was too proud to serve and too ignorant and inexperienced to be, for example, the literary editor of a weekly newspaper. Sonia, secretary and general assistant on the literary magazine *Horizon* introduced me to Cyril Connolly and Peter Watson. Cyril Connolly once or twice published articles of mine in *Horizon* (none of any merit) and a poem or two; indeed (perhaps for Sonia's sake) he reviewed my first volume of poems with discernment (as it seemed to me, since he praised the poems). But our values were not the same and yet I could not see that, this being so, I could not hope to succeed in the literary *haut monde*. I suffered from a twofold ignorance: of my own strength, as a poet, had I more courageously entrusted myself to it; and of my own limitations. Those who are without a certain range of knowledge or sensibility may be vaguely aware of a lack, but can never form a clear or just estimate of that in which we fall short; because in order to form that just estimate we should have to possess the very knowledge we lack. Thus the uneducated classes see those above them only in terms of such values as they themselves possess; and I still did not possess (my Cambridge years notwithstanding) either the intangible standards, or the exact knowledge, of the élite to which I half aspired. I was still at that time unable to assess those limitations in myself those not in these respects as ignorant as myself could see at a glance. 'Until you have knowledge of a man's ignorance, hold yourself ignorant of his knowledge,' Coleridge wrote; a warning flouted by every rising avant-garde. Such standards as those by which I measured myself then, and by which I was weighed and found wanting, have since all but disappeared; the barbarians now so vastly outnumber people of culture that they themselves now set the standards; with the resulting decadence in every field of art and learning of which it is unnecessary to say more, since it is self-evident to those who are not themselves examples of it, and impossible to grasp by those who are.

I was sure only when I was alone; I wished neither to follow any current fashion, nor to go against; only to write poetry which might reflect some gleam of a beauty of whose vision no one could rob me. I had met most of the writers of my own generation, and many others, yet I remained essentially a solitary, uncommitted. But I wished, at that time, for a word of praise from T. S. Eliot more, I think, than I have ever wished for praise before or since. He had published Charles's poems, and Michael's, and those of other friends and acquaintances; and before I left Martindale I had sent him the manuscript of my first collection of poems; but he returned it. Wait, he said, another two or three years. He may have been right; yet I think he was not looking for such qualities as my poems may have had, but for others which they did not possess. I do not remember how many years later it was that, at a dinner-party, he admitted he had had afterthoughts; though only tacitly, for what he said was, 'Another mistake I made was over David Gascoyne.' (It was indeed.) I do not think he could ever have really liked my poetry, or David Gascoyne's; Edwin Muir was another poet whose work he only slowly came to think well of. We were all alike seeking to express a vision other than his own powerful and potent verse communicated.

Failing to find immediate acceptance in the literary world, or to receive the benediction of the greatest man of letters, I found a true friend of my poetry in Tambimuttu, editor of *Poetry London*. Kafka's Herr K., instructed in advance on how to know by their dress messengers from the Castle, nonetheless unaccountably disregarded the signs because the bearers of them were not the kind of people he had expected, nor did they come in the way he had anticipated. So it was with Tambi; for if many presentable figures in the literary world were shams, Tambi was a rajah in beggar's rags. If for the former, literature was not an end but a means (to wealth, to the pleasure of being famous, and to many more ephemeral vanities and advantages), for Tambi, poetry was the end to which mere wealth, worldly position or power were at best a means. The true aristocrat, St. John Perse's 'free man of high caste', who possesses as by natural right all that the competitive world struggles for, is alone free to renounce all these for intangibles. So it was with Tambi, who valued immaterial above material riches, even though he did not practise the austerities of Prince Siddartha. His bohemianism was extreme, and alarming in its excesses to English eyes unused to so truly Oriental a contempt for even minimal securities. Tambi would have slept, and for all I know did sleep, on the pavements of London without a thought of discomfort, and without loss of some essential dignity. He lived in some squalid room (though sleep seemed to be something he never needed) his clothes were dirty and torn, his fingers, flexible and expressive as those of a dancing Shiva, stained with nicotine; money, when he had it, he spent or gave away with lavish generosity to unworthy recipients overnight without, however, regretting or even remembering it, the next day.

As I was swept along by the turbid river into which I had fallen, it was Tambi who pulled me ashore. I had met him at some time in the past, I suppose; I believe he had come to visit Charles at Blackheath. Now on the pavement of Aldwych Tambi suddenly materialized, like an *avatar* of dancing Shiva, and greeted me, not as a former acquaintance, but as an eternal acquaintance. In such recognitions there is no dissimulation, no possible deception; no ulterior motives are involved. Tambi in his descent into bohemia (and no one ever descended lower and his beautiful features were often disfigured with the scars of drunken fights, usually in the cause of poetry) never lost the power of immediate divination of qualities. He had the gift of instantly recognizing the *rasa* (he himself used that Indian word) of whatever belongs to the imagination.

There may be works of great talent which are nevertheless in a lower plane of intellectuality than seemingly slighter works of imagination. Cyril Connolly recognized talent with as sure an instinct as Tambi recognized imagination; and, naturally enough, had more thanks for it, both from the producers and the consumers of literature. But Tambi knew all the poets, from T. S. Eliot downwards, who had any spark of eternity in them. 'He is really a wild man like me,' he used to say of Mr. Eliot, whom he loved, making a *mudra* with his nicotine-stained fingers; and Mr. Eliot, whose expressions of friendship were most guarded, used to claim to be the only person able correctly to pronounce a Tamil name: 'Not Tambi, *Thumbi.*'

Tambi, then, drew me to land as simply as a fisherman pulls a fish out of the water. I did not particularly want to be landed by Tambi, feeling it beneath my dignity; and I was not as grateful as I should have been. I took it as my due (which it may have been, but why then had I so wanted to be praised by T. S. Eliot or the editor of *Horizon?*) that he said to me repeatedly (like the applause, *baku, baku* of the enraptured auditors of Indian music) 'Kathleen, you are a *great poet*, I will publish your poems, it will be a beautiful book, you will see—'. I did not more than half care; Eliot's rejection had wounded my pride more than Tambi's praise could flatter it. I was, besides, too completely possessed by the passion which drove me through fiery hells, walking on knives after the mirage of love, to care very much for the reality which was, after all, the poetry. Yet at the same time a part of me knew very well that my poetry, and Tambi's praise of it, were a reality, and all that walking on knives, all that anguish, relatively unimportant. Even so, I did not really care; to be rejected by the great and 'discovered' by Tambi I felt to be humiliating rather than flattering; and to my beautiful beloved, my poems had no existence at all. Besides all this, I did not feel that any of the poems I had as yet written were the poems I was capable of writing, and which at that time I still hoped and believed I would someday write.

But Tambi believed both in the poetry I had written, and in the poetry I would write; he believed in me as a poet with unconditional certainty; and my first volume, *Stone and Flower*, together with David Gascoyne's *Poems 1937-42* were published with the *Poetry London* imprint. Both volumes were beautiful, especially David's with its sombre illustrations by Graham Sutherland that so perfectly suited the poems. My own *Stone and Flower* was illustrated by Barbara Hepworth. I had learned to admire, in Helen's house, the perfect taste of Ben Nicholson's abstract forms, discerning in them the kind of detached clarity of mind to which I had myself aspired during an earlier phase, as a student of biology, and again at the time of Mass-Observation. It was Ben who suggested that Barbara should illustrate my poems, from some notion about a woman's painting going with a woman's poetry. If there was an affinity between Barbara Hepworth and myself, it was not I think by reason of our sex, but much more of our period. It seemed to me at the time that what we had in common was a sense of the interior landscape of contemporary science; and so perhaps we had, though it is hardly apparent in my poems. In her work I found the same cool cold quality as in Ben's, the same 'detachment'. Oliver Simon of the Curwen Press printed both David's book and mine. He too cared for poetry for its own sake, and cared enough for mine to introduce me, when *Poetry London* collapsed, to my second publisher, Hamish Hamilton, for whom he designed my second book.

At a time when the fashion was for political writing or for wit, Tambi discerned and valued only imaginative vision. He made remarkably few mistakes, for fashion never distracted him: yet I often wondered how he knew a good poem from a bad, for he never seemed to read them. Typescripts would lie about on his table, for months sometimes, and after a time he would pull one out and say 'This is a *great poem*'; and he would be (allowing for superlatives) right; a poem it would be. The rest he just left to accumulate to mature or fade as the case might be. He never returned these faded manuscripts, which were, for him, simply blank pages. He only noticed, by some kind of supra-sensible radiance they possessed, poems which had imaginative essence. And *Poetry London* made literary history for a while; its Lyrebird covers by Moore, Sutherland, Craxton, Ceri Richards, Cecil Collins, Gerald Wilde, are period pieces. Tambi attempted books in which painter and poet collaborated, and did produce several most beautiful volumes, including my own. That they were uneconomic was, for him, neither here nor there.

Tambi even gave me a niche, for a while, in the *Poetry London* office; which itself was a niche within the offices of the publishers Nicholson and Watson. My duties were indeterminate; but it was a refuge from the terrifying limbo into which I had fallen.

Tambi used to tell me that his uncle was the greatest aesthetician of the century. I did not believe him; but it was true. I had not then read Coomaraswamy's works which, years later, I discovered to contain almost everything I have myself since come to believe about the arts. Coomaraswamy might have deplored the attraction by which Tambi was drawn from Ceylon to London's bohemia; but Tambi, instinctively, looked in poetry for those qualities which were, as Coomaraswamy saw it, its essence: 'Art is expression informed by ideal beauty.' In positivist Cambridge the old notion that some ideas were in themselves of more value as coming from a 'higher' source, than others, had been dismissed. Again with Tambi, and later in my reading of his illustrious uncle's works, I found Dante's truth proclaimed: poetry was not merely to state true things beautifully, but 'beautiful things truly'.

Visiting New York in 1962 I found Tambi living, as usual, in a slum street of peculiar grimness. I made my way there, at dusk, in some fear, for the taxi-driver had deposited me at the wrong address, several blocks away, outside a bar that seemed to be also both a laundry and a brothel or thieves' kitchen; and I made my way on foot, keeping to the middle of the street to avoid the sinister groups on the pavement. Not finding Tambi's name on any door or board, I asked a tiny beautiful star-like dark girl, an Italian probably, if she would take me to her mother so that I could ask; but half-way up the sinister stairs we met three girls who might have come from the film *West Side Story*; the gentleman with long hair? they said; and from their warmth I gathered that here too Tambi inspired affection. Yes, he lived in the basement. So I made my way down among the dust-bins and the electric meters (the stucco, though decayed, was beautiful, and that too was characteristic of Tambi) but when the door opened, there was Tambi wearing an Indian dress of spotless white. His young wife was expecting a baby (my god-daughter) the room had been dis-tempered, and the varnish on the floor was scarcely dry. In my honour Tambi and the son of the former financial supporter of *Poetry London* (Richard March) had worked day and night to finish it. Billy March, on leaving Bryanston, had crossed the Atlantic to be with Tambi, because he had loved him as a child; his own father being dead, he now called Tambi father.

Not only had he splendidly scraped and distempered the walls, but had taken upon his young shoulders the responsibility of Tambi's precarious household. The furniture had been provided by Tambi's cousin, Coomaraswamy's daughter Rohini, the 'cellist. Even her Kshatriya pride and family disapproval had somehow melted into affection before the innocence of bohemianism as extreme as Tambi's to which disapproval seemed no longer applicable, as a curve becomes a straight line at infinity. So some of Coomaraswamy's furniture and fine silk curtains found their way, like other more intangible inheritances, into Tambi's underworld; if underworld it can be called, where so many essential values were preserved.

Tambi's younger brother Augustin, a Jesuit, tried to show him the error of his ways from time to time, and even visited New York in order to do so. I hope he too was disarmed; as I was myself on receiving, in 1967, a letter from Tambi, now the 'guru' in charge of Timothy Leary's 'ashram' in Upper New York State; he offered me honorary membership, adding 'you need not take drugs if you're squeamish.' How trivial my moral disapproval beside Tambi's loyalty!

Among the faces that emerge from the shadows of wartime London David Gascoyne's remains memorable; for he, too, coming, I suppose, into the *Poetry London* office (for I have no memory of place in which to situate my memory of his person) greeted me, as had Tambi, not as an old acquaintance or as a new one, but as an eternal companion met down there in Hades. I remember well how beautiful he was when, before the war, he used to visit Charles and Humphrey at Blackheath, how gentle and defenceless, but, like a wild animal who has never yet had cause to fear man, open and expectant only of receiving the same goodness and out-flowing love that was in him. His fine poet's eyes were full of sensibility and nobility, his eloquent mouth vulnerable; a child of Paradise cast upon our world. Life had not yet hurt him, and he was happy in his early recognition as a poet. He was intoxicated by Surrealism at that time, and he and Humphrey were both active in the Surrealist exhibition. (David I seem to remember escorted in Trafalgar Square a girl whose head was entirely encased in a mask of roses.) He also wrote *A Short History of Surrealism*, since republished. Now meeting him again (he had been living in Paris until the outbreak of war) in wartime London I was shocked by the change in him; for now he looked racked, tormented, his large hands forever moving nervously, twisting a handkerchief, his deer-like eyes haunted; his teeth were decayed, his skin grey. He still had no mask or defensive barricade, and he still had the same sweetness; and where he sensed sympathy he assumed in others a truth of feeling equal to his own. He had now a new volume of poems (*Poems 1937-1942*) ready for publication. Now that these poems have out-lived the moment that produced them, the greatness of some of them apparent to all who care for poetry, I wonder at the miracle by which a sensitivity so vulnerable as his survived and found eloquence in a world so ruinous.

Later, when I was living precariously at 9 Paulton's Square, by all manner of literary hack-work, translations, reviewing and so on (all made infinitely more difficult than it need have been by the interior condition of anguish against which I laboured) David took refuge with me for a while. He was, at that time, even more ill than he had been at the time of Poetry London. He used to say that it was as if his 'brain leaked'; (he later described it as 'like a transistor set inside his head', on which all kinds of voices not his own spoke, wept, declaimed, argued, chanted; while others would say 'we are the gods, the gods'). But he read continuously, widely and deeply in works of mystical philosophy, and existentialism, and talked, rapidly and eloquently, of the divine vision which haunted his darkness like the sun at midnight—an image he himself used—of Boehme, Hölderlin, Kierkegaard, Chestov, all the dark visionaries. He was writing, then, the poems of *A Vagrant* and *Night Thoughts,* and had, besides, a manuscript (never published and now lost) of *pensées* from the philosophers he read. He would lie for hours face downwards on his bed, or wander long in solitary night-walks. To me he turned as a fellow-poet whom he could trust absolutely; trust, for example, not to make emotional demands on him.

Other friends, concerned for the mortal man more perhaps than I was and less for the poet, were eager to put him in the hands of the psychiatrists; but a lyre so finely strung as David Gascoyne's imaginative sensitivity to the invisible currents was not for grosser hands to finger. Although he was, in his natural self, defenceless, to say the least, he had the poet's instinct to protect the lyre. He actually went, one day, to the Tavistock clinic, where, after an interview, the Freudian who saw him said, 'I am afraid I can do nothing for you'; David (his sense of irony was extremely subtle, and played often over his dark landscape) replied, 'then perhaps you will pray for me?' The psychiatrist very stiffly responded, 'I am afraid I do not believe in prayer!' David returned to tell the story which we both thought extremely funny, though (for the Freudian) also sad, and, of course, terrifying, when one recalls that in such hands are the souls of so many. For the rest, the proud Orphic lyre-bearer in him accepted the humiliations of the natural man the daimon so precariously inhabited. It is characteristic of him that he did not fear to speak of God to a professional unbeliever, for he never doubted that in everyone there is the divine light.

Other faces emerged and vanished in that phantasmagoria. Louis MacNeice I did not know very well (indeed I passed as a stranger through those years) but he occasionally took me out to dinner, and gave me odds and ends of writing to do for the BBC; which I did with extreme labour and difficulty, as I did everything except the writing of poetry. Louis was most kind to my struggling and largely worthless efforts. I remember sitting in his company one evening, in the Café Royal probably, and his making up a half-serious fantasy about people who either had, or did not have, 'a little candle' alight in them. He himself still shone, in those days, with a poet's soft interior light which one might imagine coming from the rath of the *Sidhe*. This fine Irish poet, 'baptized with fairy water', was at that time in the 'A.R.P.', and he once described to me how he had, the night before, been shovelling incendiary bombs off the dome of St. Paul's. I saw less of Louis with the years; but the last time was only a few weeks before his death, at a publisher's party given for the American poet Robert Lowell. There were many faces from the past; William Empson was there, and Ivor and Dorothea Richards, and Sonia and Cyril Connolly, and many to whom I could not even give names any more; like figures depicted in some Italian painting, all portraits of faces once known. Louis was there, grey now, but still with something of his former poet's look. To my surprise and pleasure and shame both he, whom I had not seen for years, and William Empson, from whose ways of thought, brilliant but perverse as it has come to seem to me, I had for long been, little by little, dissociating myself, greeted me with the kiss of friendship. Can we resemble Judas in the receiving, as in the giving, of a kiss? I felt this especially in relation to William; who had as good reason, after all, to dissociate himself from me; but it is not in his nature to be disloyal to any once a friend. So I found when an essay I had published on Blake's poems *A Little Girl Lost* and *Found* came under attack by some New Critic, and William rushed (in print) to my defence; as did Sir Geoffrey Keynes, but that was on Blake's behalf, whereas William's defence was on mine. At that same party Sonia whispered aside to me, 'But none of them look in the least like poets!' I pointed out that very few of them wrote like poets either, and that the few who did, looked like poets: William, Louis MacNeice, Robert Lowell, himself, Ivor Richards (wizard of poetry if not quite poet), all these had memorable faces indeed. I have never found that people's looks belie them; David Gascoyne, Edwin Muir, Vernon Watkins, all those who have a daimon have a certain listening look. T. S. Eliot, for all his guarded austerity, had it; and from the eyes of Alexis Léger the diplomat looks St. John Perse the poet; eyes enchanted by '*les merveilles*' which fill his world. (*La terre enfante des merveilles*, he wrote in Anabase.)

Michael Roberts presently came down to London to the European Service of the BBC, and his presence, more than anyone's, gave me a sense of continuing identity; for Janet and Michael were friends not only of the poet but of the poor human creature I was. Michael was always protective towards me, realizing how helplessly lost I was. William Empson, too, broadcasting programmes to the Far East, seemed to think that a poem or two of mine, recorded and transmitted, could help the war-effort; or perhaps that from the waste of effort involved in the war he might retrieve a poem or two. Like all Wykehamists I have ever known (even more than most) William had the gift of resuming anywhere, under any circumstances, in a squalid room in Marchmont Street, in a BBC Canteen, or in a Chinese holy mountain I do not doubt, or in smoking hell itself, a relationship, like an interrupted conversation, exactly where it had last been broken off. But I, unsure of myself, over-sensitive to mental climates and atmospheres created by others, had not that gift of creating everywhere the norm to which any surroundings become peripheral, and became flooded and possessed and overwhelmed by surroundings, from which I suffered unendurably, and from whose overwhelming I could escape only by flight; and I could not always fly. Only alone could I return to my own norm, my interior sanctuary. Alone, some indestructible supernatural strength of imagination sustained me. Alone I could still swing back, like a compass-needle released by other magnets, to my own centre. Never, therefore, so much as in those London years, was I so grateful to the few friends who never deserted me for the assurance their continued existence gave me of my own; for I had no room of my own now, no white house in its garden with coal-tits in the yew-tree, no burn fringed with birch and alder to walk beside where I could listen to my own daimon and to the elemental voices.

Humphrey Jennings too reappeared in London; Cicely, with their two daughters, was in New York, and Humphrey had a room over the Etoile restaurant. That was like Humphrey, who loved good French cooking; in a French, practical way he settled into the best restaurant in Charlotte Street en pension. He was making war documentary films, of which *Fires Were Started*, a film about the London fire service, remains one of the few of the innumerable contemporary works about the working-class which sincerely and convincingly depicts 'the people' in terms of heroic Churchillian glory, without sentimentality and without vulgarity. Such films had been made in Russia, but nothing comparable in England. Humphrey after the war said that it was a sad truth that only the situations of war could give to the common people opportunities to show their finest innate qualities. The war, or perhaps Churchill's eloquence, called to the soul of Albion for the last time, and in those years all kinds of people (the fat red-haired woman who went back to serving vegetables in the greengrocer's, the sweep who lost a finger and won a George Medal rescuing people trapped in a bombed building at the World's End) showed their worth who afterwards merged again into some meaningless background. Humphrey had been closer to Charles and to Mass-Observation than I had ever been, and his war-films were perhaps the fruit of the imaginative moment they had shared and created.

Humphrey was still carrying about with him in a portfolio *Pandaemonium*, his never-completed anthology of the Industrial Revolution, pulling out one page or another descriptive of the impact on the old eighteenth-century pastoral England of the Dark Satanic Mills, declaiming it to such friends as emerged to vanish again into the blackout of our own war-time pandemonium, illuminated by flames not unrelated to Milton's pitch and nitre; for the Royal Society had started the whole terrible process (such was the theme of Humphrey's book) the Mills of Satan appearing first, as Blake had long ago declared, in the mechanistic theorizings of Bacon, Newton and Locke; only later to be reflected in those machines, their expression and image, from whose relentless wheels it seems our world can no longer (whether in peace or in war) extricate itself. Humphrey's anthology was at once an indictment, a lamentation, and a glorification of a race and a nation. For up to the end of the war, for all the multiplication of the dispossessed who have no memory, and who have therefore lost the threads of tradition with which a nation is woven through time, England was still an imaginative as well as an economic entity. Like Churchill, Humphrey saw England's present glory in the light of her past, of Pitt and Nelson, of Stubbs and Gainsborough, of Blake and Gray and Inigo Jones. He himself gave in his war films a last expression of a civilization specifically English. Now the English language has become the *lingua franca* of world barbarism and the landmarks of the past are fast disappearing. I remember walking with Humphrey among the wreckage of houses, where rain dripped down from charred beams and wallpaper hung in tatters, through Blake's Golden Square and the streets of Soho, Humphrey all the time talking of Blake, so that we seemed to be walking within those very blood-vessels of the city to which Blake had likened 'London's darkening streets'.

At the time of Churchill's State funeral I stood my three night hours with the long procession of that English nation, reassembled for the last time; moving—as the cutting East wind blew up the Thames from the docks and warehouses where Humphrey had made his heroic film of the London blitz, from Greenwhich where with him, in the imaginative enchantment of Mass-Observation days, I had so often walked from the

Trafalgar Tavern to the Woolwich tunnel—a few steps at a time from Blake's Lambeth across London's river, and so to Westminster Hall. It was of Humphrey I thought, and of Michael Roberts, who on V-day had come to Chelsea and sought me out, to walk on the embankment and drink in the Black Lion, sharing for once a collective emotion. Our own wartime past seemed to belong to a present continuous with the cold waters of the Thames as they reflected that night the lights of the city, the old dolphin lamp-posts, the glowing face of Big Ben, silent that Friday midnight when I stood with the anonymous English nation, awakened, perhaps for the last time, to a collective imaginative sense of the continuity and glory of the history of its great city.

After the war I saw Humphrey less often; he would re-appear, from time to time, and always with some glory of the world to tell of; but not, any more, of England; he had turned his back upon the industrial modern world, the tragic infernal greatness of Pandemonium; quite lost faith in, and turned away from, the modern West. Once he had just returned from Greece (where he was making a film) and spoke of the life of shepherds and goatherds in the barren hills; the life of Arcadia itself, still to be found in the simplicity of a kind and quality of poverty which in no way destroyed the dignity of illiterate men with half-wild dogs to guard their flocks, women whose houses were beautiful by the very absence of the trash of the machines, 'functional' because in them were only such things as body and soul require: hearth, woollen or goat's hair blankets woven on a loom; figs drying in the sun; a vine with grapes, great loaves of bread baked in an oven built of clay, milk and honey and bread and wine. He did not speak of the continued spirituality of Orthodox Christianity and was, I think, still dreaming of a Socialist Utopia without the machine; a classless anarchy. But, most and last, he was moved by Burma, where he found the human society which to him seemed to come nearest to an ideal perfection: a traditional Buddhist society, where all took its meaning from its orientation towards a spiritual vision. All, as he explained, from the weaving of the basket in which men carried their vegetables to market, to the burial of the dead, was done according to that philosophy which holds in a single thought the impermanence of all things and the existential mystery of the here and now. Years before he had talked of Lao Tze; and now he had found a society which cared nothing for the permanence of things made, because the *Tao* is inexhaustible: 'work it, and more comes out'. He had been present at the cremation of a Buddhist monk, and had, perhaps for the only time in his life, there understood what it is when an entire society is informed by a sublime metaphysical vision; something lost, or all but lost, from the modern West.

But Humphrey's solar hair was white; and my last memory of him is walking across the river from Paulton's Square to visit Battersea Old Church, where Blake had married his Catherine; standing, still, an intelligible though modest expression of classic proportion on its little peninsula of Thames mud where working-class children play. Upstream, the landscape of nineteenth-century industry, trucks clanking across a railway-bridge, beyond the smoking chimneys of Lots Road power-station; downstream, London, its old aspect already changing before the encroachment of office-blocks, inhuman and anonymous. Half-way across Battersea bridge Humphrey paused and raised his arm in the old eighteenth-century orator's gesture; and the Thames, before that gesture (which embraced Dryden's *King Arthur*, the *Triumphs* of Gray and the *Masks* of Inigo Jones, the declamations of Los and the stance of Gainsborough's slender and elegant country gentlemen) became again Spenser's Sweet Thames, now the 'chartered Thames' for so long that its defilement and servitude had become irrevocable. And yet, Humphrey said, in that river, free from pollution, fish might breed again, silver salmon to feed the people of London. All kinds of living silvery shoals once came there; and as he spoke the muddy foul waters flowing under us towards the Tower Bridge, Greenwich, and the docks where Humphrey had made his *Fires Were Started*, became transformed by Humphrey's inimitable magic into Blake's 'spiritual fourfold London Eternal'. The royal swans at least were still there, no less numerous or less beautiful than when Sir Thomas More's gardens ran down to the river at the very place we stood; they were feeding, now, on the waste from the Hovis flour-mills (only a little upstream from the site of Blake's Albion flour-mill) below the Morgan crucible-works; another dark satanic heritage of the triumph of the material interests of industry over the aesthetic idealism of the pre-Raphaelite potter William de Morgan, whose beautiful ceramics could still be seen exhibited in Battersea Old House, and occasionally bought in the antique shops of the King's Road, birds and flowers and Morris willow-leaves in peacock and Persian blues and greens. That was the last of many walks with Humphrey through the streets of London which, in his company, always entered another dimension and became 'ideas of imagination'; as in former days his vision could translate the white wooden palings of Newmarket back into Stubbs' century, or the elms of North Essex into a landscape in China, the tangibility of Constable dissolving at his will into the void which upholds the ten thousand creatures. It seems in retrospect like the valediction of Blake's Los over London's vanished glory. Not long after Humphrey was killed, accidentally falling from a cliff on the island of Poros fatally injuring his head on the rocks below. He is buried in Greece, the country in which he had found 'the good life'.

I did not know of Humphrey's death at the time; but I had a dream on the night he died; the first occasion on which I was certain that some telepathic communication had reached me from the dead. The symbolic dress of such dreams is no doubt given by the dreamer; but the content surely not. This dream was coloured by deep, awe-inspiring emotion. I was in a Gothic cathedral, an immense stone building in which were many sculptured tombs and chantry-chapels. I looked long at the effigies, in stone, of three 'weepers' on a tomb, a woman and her two young daughters (Humphrey did leave a wife and two daughters to mourn him) and as I looked the words 'a rocky death, a rocky death' were repeated, over and over. I then found myself in a chantry-chapel (and were not such shrines devoted to prayers for the dead?) and a voice which I did not recognize, but which I have since believed was Humphrey's, spoke to me of death in a way that brought to my consciousness the very experience of the reality of having to relinquish this life. 'However long you may stay in the sanctuary that protects you now', I was told, 'remember that sooner or later you will have to leave it.' The voice itself was serene, and it was I who trembled because death lay before me, not, as for the happy dead, behind: the 'sanctuary' I knew to be this life, in which I was hiding. The symbol of my dream was one of those small beautiful sixteenth-century chantry-chapels to be seen in the cathedrals of the south of England (in Winchester, for example) but to me the emotion associated with the 'sanctuary' comes from the lion's-head knocker of Durham Cathedral. Now I was made to understand the slightness and impermanence of that shelter; and I was filled with sorrow for myself, and a sort of envy for the speaker, for whom death was not a terror before, but an ordeal already over-passed. And was I, in my low and narrow stone sanctuary, or was the mysterious speaker, among the dead? As the voice ceased I heard the singing of a great choir, and, my voice choked with weeping, I tried to join in the singing—the Gloria of Bach's B-minor Mass. As the voices of the host of heaven and earth rose, the mourners below seemed to be uplifted out of grief on the music of the solemn four-note ascending phrases, carried upward and out of the stone cathedral and into an angelic world of light. Whereupon I awoke. Until I came to write this account I had not remembered that 'angels singing' was, among my father's people, often heard at the time of a death and understood as an omen of death; music being the form under which the human imagination clothes our perception of a sublime harmony. Only two or three days later did I learn of Humphrey's death.

CHAPTER EIGHT

Doors of Sanctuary

Just as Martindale vicarage seemed given rather than found, so did 9 Paulton's Square, which for many years to come was to be my home. It was through Helen Sutherland I came there, and in my worst hour. Returning to London houseless, without any job or source of income, I went, at her suggestion, to her friend Constance (Cooie) Lane, an artist, who also let rooms in her house to friends, and friends of friends. I do not recollect what time of year it was, but my impression is as of spring, early March, perhaps; of sitting in the back of the double room on the ground-floor—then Cooie's studio—with the sun filtering through the branches of the pear-tree in the garden behind. We sat by a little fire we could scarcely see for sunlight, and I poured out to Cooie Lane my troubles; she listened, and took me in, and that night I slept in a room that seemed fresh with the freshness of the trees outside my windows. There were some of Cooie's paintings on the walls—one was of petunias growing in plant-pots on some little balcony in France, or maybe in Italy; some quiet sweet place. All was plain, perhaps even shabby, though it did not seem so, but rather had the air of a house whose chairs and curtains and tables and plants were inhabitants, a group of old friends, well-born but poor. Years later I visited the small Franciscan monastery in Fiesole; there were pots of aspidistra, double daisies in the little formal flower-beds in the cloister, and singing birds, which so vividly recalled to me not so much the outward as the inner aspect of Cooie Lane's house that it was almost hallucinatory. Perhaps it was because in both (though her house was not otherwise obviously like a cloister) all that chanced to come were taken in; and however long or short the time of sojourn of flower-pot, or lodger, or faded linen chair-cover, all were accepted; not necessarily liked (and that too might happen within the cloister) but the disliked person or thing would no more have been banished than creatures from the creation. 'Let all grow together until the harvest' was one of her many sayings. That, perhaps, even more than her artist's poverty, is what Cooie's house had about it that St. Francis' monastery recalled; and, again like a monastery, there was a sense of leisure, of time there being free. Partly it may have been also something Italian in her taste; her Arundel prints, the pieces of green silk, the Florentine pottery and the garden vine. To wake in the cleanness of that room was like waking, healed, after a long illness. I woke there, for the first time since I had left Martindale, with the sense of being once more in my right place and not in a nightmare. Later the house was to become mine; and much of her old furniture, her pear-tree and her vine; yet I could not keep her atmosphere. Her house was what it was because all of a piece, its values, its people, down to its chipped pots and patched linen; what I made never had the Franciscan beauty of what she had made; no parasite can inherit the bee's knowledge or the secret of its honey.

Cooie suffered from a serious heart-disease and one night, soon after my arrival, she had an attack, and I sat up all night with her, comforting her, and holding her hands. I think that was why she gave me her friendship, afterwards, so fully. I tried, certainly, to help her—I could have done no less—and she turned to me as an ally and protector. She talked to me by the hour in her cracked but beautiful contralto voice, with gestures of her dry tapered Holbein fingers. She was full of humour, and a wonderful mimic, especially of cockney; and her characteristic word of advice—she gave it to me but I disregarded it, so diametrically opposite was it to my own natural bent—was *le mieux est l'ennemi du bien*. An old maid herself, she perhaps felt that romantic love had been a will o' the wisp; or perhaps she was trying to tell me (or herself) that her house and its chipped Italian cups and her crayons and work-table was *le bien*, if not Helen Sutherland's 'the best *is* the best'. *Le mieux* for Cooie, was not only rich relations, lords and ladies and lovely cousins who had made distinguished marriages, lived in great houses, had beautiful children; it was also artists more successful than herself—Ben Nicholson was one friend who had surpassed her. Winifred Nicholson (a crayon portrait of her by Cooie hung on the stairs) another. As a young girl and 'poor relation' (her father was a clergyman) she had stayed much at Renishaw and Montegufoni with the Sitwells, and told endless and loving stories of them; of 'Sashie' hiding under her bed from some night-terror, of some godlike young man over whom she and Edith had together sighed. A poet whom I met in London—Keidrich Rhys it was—and who visited me at Cooie's house had recently been 'taken up' by Edith Sitwell, and Cooie asked him to remember her to the poetess. He must have written to her, for he later showed me the letter he had received in reply; one of the unkindest letters I have ever read, saying, in effect, how extraordinary that the creature should still exist, 'like some old nanny or household retainer', I think the phrase was, whom one had forgotten all about long ago. *Le mieux* could be very cruel to *le bien*. I am bound to say that Ben Nicholson was not—that he visited Cooie, enjoyed her humour, and wasn't wanting in gratitude or loyalty for those kindnesses received before fame which are so usually forgotten after.

Her health—and the air-raids—became worse; and Cooie was at last persuaded to go into a nursing-home in the country. I visited her there and was shocked at the change in her: she had the dying look, and although she was talking with eager hope of returning (in the care of a nurse) to her country cottage near her old home in Berkhamsted, she died on the day following her arrival there. Perhaps she had been kept alive only by the longing she had to return to the place of her childhood: *querencia*. That is how her house in Paulton's Square came to be mine; I took over the lease from her executors, and, by small but painful instalments, bought such of her furniture as her heirs did not want. She left me, too, a small Ben Nicholson painting; I sold it later (for too little) to pay my children's school fees. I had to sell everything I ever had of value, from a drawing Henry Moore gave me from his Shelter notebook, down to my last review-copy; indeed I was always utterly lost when it came to earning money. Since the things I wanted to do were not things for which money is paid, I have sometimes, in moments of desperation, had to compromise. But on the whole I have kept my vow to do nothing for money I would not have done for its own sake. I remember once saying something to George Orwell about those with inner wealth not caring so much about the material kind; thinking, no doubt, of my father's people and their unworldly values; and he replied, 'Yes, but those with material wealth don't have the same need of the inner kind.' At the time I saw in this only a paradox of wit; it did not occur to me then, nor for years after, that there could be human beings above the level of the blindest ignorance who could seriously prefer material to immaterial riches. Much later I was struck by an observation in one of Jung's books, that an extrovert in solitary confinement would become in the end an introvert; and an introvert, surrounded by all the pleasant things of life, an extrovert. I wondered then for a moment what I would have become in other circumstances; but then, I made my circumstances by what I was, and chose, from moment to moment and from day to day; as do all.

Cooie's house came to me with her blessing, and the blessing she had herself inherited from those who came before her. The house had belonged to Mrs. Comyns-Carr, friend of Mrs. Patrick Campbell. Henry James, it was said, had stood before the little Georgian fire-place of what was now to be my room; the house had its story and its life. It was my wish and intention to deserve my spiritual inheritance, and the pear-tree and the vine Cooie had loved. Not only was this my intention in what I there should write, but in the blessing I hoped would come to whoever entered under my roof. For, like Martindale vicarage, this house too seemed to me given, by a miracle, and to those from whom it came I felt myself in duty bound to use what they gave as they would have wished.

Very often I would hear the door-bell ring, usually at night, when there was no one there. I thought nothing of it, not even that it was odd; I used

to suppose I had simply been mistaken. It was, all the same, very persist-
ent, as I have realized only since living in another house whose door-bell
does not ring except when someone rings it. If it was Cooie Lane who
visited her old house on those occasions, I never saw her; but a few years
after her death I had a vivid dream of her. In my dream she was in a
charming garden-house or arbour; and, as in life, full of humour, and at
the same time happy with a kind of serene gaiety; she reproached me,
saying 'you have not remembered me for a long time, have you?'—which
was true. The flavour, the atmosphere of the dream was indescribably yet
unmistakably that of Cooie; but this quality, which convinced me that this
was no ordinary dream, I cannot communicate.

Two other dreams of this character I have had. One was of a friend who
had died in the belief that there is no survival; 'when we are dead we are
finished,' I remember his saying to me, bitterly and passionately, not long
before his last illness. In my dream this friend appeared, dreadfully
unhappy, convinced of *being dead:* 'I am *dead,*' he said in the dream; and
believing himself so was confined within this terrible fantasy.

The third dream too was characterized by the quality of the spirit who,
as I supposed, visited me: Edwin Muir. The dream came on Christmas eve,
1960, almost a year after his death. I was a child in a village, wet and
wintry; a dream-village woven no doubt from memories of childhood
winters at the Manse, and also it may be from the village of Swaffham
Prior, where Edwin and Willa Muir were living at the time of his death;
and my knowledge that he like myself had been a country child. I had, in
my dream, to guide Edwin across intricate footpaths and low wire fences,
and other small foot-entangling obstacles; but then he began to lead, and I
followed him to a stone building, a *broch*, or fort, or perhaps only an old
stone barn; yet ancient, with a quality of anonymous ancestral dignity.
Edwin now climbed with ease the stone wall, to enter the upper floor; and
with an effort, I followed him. In front of me he went on into a great
empty loft, without windows or doors, and in darkness. From the far end
of this great hall or loft there blew towards us a warm gentle wind of
indescribable fragrance, and I exclaimed, 'It's the breath of the spirit.'
Edwin went on before me in the direction from which that sweet wind was
blowing, until he came to the far wall which was not, like the others, of
stone, but a thin partition. This he merely touched, and it fell away, and
then he was no longer there; but beyond lay the fields of spring radiant in
the rising sun. I looked into that far-distant sunrise with the knowledge
'there I must also go'; but my time had not come.

At about the same time as I found shelter with Cooie Lane, I also found
a niche in another, and more civilized, wartime department, and if I did
not, here either, quite grasp what I was expected to do (still less know how

to do it) I nevertheless passed unnoticed; perhaps because the head of my department was, this time, a pleasant young man interested in literature, and with some notion of becoming a publisher after the war. Therefore he treated me, as a poet, with a certain respect to which as whatever I was called in his department I certainly had no title. This department was situated in Bush House; but the hierarchies of administration, all those partitions and typing-pools, seemed to me more unreal than any dream. I never believed it to be anything more substantial than a place in some modern allegory—*The Castle*, for example—or rather a non-place, so little did it seem related to the reasons for which human souls enter this world and pass through it; yet down in the canteen in the basement one saw faces (all nullified in the artificial light of that subterranean place) as out of context as my own; Manya Harari, who was later to publish the works of Teilhard de Chardin; Rafael Nadal, who had been Lorca's friend and was, many years later, to become mine. I suppose I must have seen there—though I did not know it—Simone Weil also.

I met there Antonia White; far more experienced in the ways of such non-places than I was, and incomparably more skilled at impersonating the person she was expected to be. She was, I am bound to say, very kind to me; and certainly she, and Graham Greene, who presently also appeared in the Department (for this kind of thing was, as he himself admitted, 'copy' for the books he wrote or might write) influenced the course of my life at that time. If their influence put me off my true course that was my fault, not theirs, for they acted towards me in good faith and with the utmost kindness.

Yet for me that period in Bush House was a betrayal into a most subtle insincerity. Flung into a world where I had to survive not by being what I was but by trying to simulate some other kind of creature than a country child who had grown up into a poet, I panicked; I thought I must play a role, or perish. If the child I was in Northumberland, if the poet of Martindale I may call my real self, that real self, in the years of Bush House, I once again betrayed. Perhaps those years concerned only what Yeats calls the Mask, my outward personality; for when I try to recall them, I do not seem to live or re-live what I remember but rather to see myself as an unreal figure moving among other unreal figures, a shadow among shadows. If any one of those shadowy figures seems real, it is Antonia, not myself.

I had been happy at Martindale because there I had been permitted to be, for that heaven-sent time, simply what I was; and solitude was to me then, and has at all times been, a supreme happiness because only in solitude can I be entirely natural; like some enchanted seal who, alone, can don my seal-skin and bathe in my native element. I have no other milieu in which I can be myself, I am more or less of a stranger (an 'outsider') everywhere. Helen Sutherland it was—and she too had lived much alone—who put into words what few realize about solitude: that it is the most intensely lived of all states. To it belong our deepest thoughts, prayer and poetry are of it; even love; for how seldom, when the real person is present, can we say those things that the heart says to the beloved in solitude?

Hitherto I had supposed myself to be invisible to others; an illusion which had served me well enough; I do not know how well it had served others, for my mantle was not some grey mist of silence, but a curious motley, a patch-work, perhaps the 'cat-skin' of the fairy-tale, made up of scraps taken from the pelts of a multitude of beasts. But now, in London, in order to survive at all, I must simulate some other person, or perish. I had now, so I thought, quickly to make myself into something other than myself, for money-making purposes, since the poet could quite obviously not hope to survive as such; but only by the help of whatever other self I could extemporize. For what, in this world, is weaker than the spirit of poetry? Yet in the end it has been my only strength. I have sometimes wished I had tried less hard to become a beast of burden—been, like David Gascoyne, or like Tambimuttu, unemployable. I was too moral, yet not moral enough; too much a poet, yet not enough a poet; too weak, yet not weak enough to ask, as I could have done, for supernatural help.

Antonia White, sensitive to an extreme degree within and behind it, had a mask which she had, so it seemed to me, cultivated with extreme attention and meticulous care. She seemed to carry it in her hands walking on tip-toe, like a precious piece of glass she was afraid of breaking. She gave thought to how she moved, sat down, got up, crossed a room, like an actress giving careful thought to a part she was learning. All she did was carefully self-conscious to a degree that seemed at times almost perilous, like some delicate feat performed by a juggler. I knew—for David Gascoyne, who was devoted to her, had lent me her *House of Clouds*, and shown me, at the same time, a photograph which caught her off guard— that she was, though a highly trained creature, not a tame one. Behind the mask there was a soul of extreme sensibility.

Antonia was a Catholic; and often she talked of the Church. Of her childhood in a convent of the Sacred Heart (Sonia had been educated at the same school some years later), her lapse, and her return, at last, to the Church, she told me. I listened with a mixture of pity and terror, fascination and incredulity. It was—this much at least I recognized—a real story, a real experience of the soul which she so subtly and minutely had undergone. Different as was her destiny from my own, we were, I recognized, alike in having followed the thread of a destiny, in seeing a life as a quest or pilgrimage. I respected her for living her story, but the story itself was strange to me. I felt about it as about Henry James's novels: what were all these invisible bars? Were these cages of the soul not self-constructed, was it not enough to walk, Bagheera-like, out of the cage into freedom? So naïve was I about the human situation; for, much as I knew about the kingdom of nature, I knew next to nothing about the human world. Yet when I used in my own mind the word 'freedom' I did not mean licentiousness and sloth; I meant what Shelley meant, what Blake meant. The soul, so I believed, has its innate form which must unfold according to its own mysterious inner laws; as in nature plant or animal forms. To interfere, by the imposition of external constraints, with this organic unfolding, was the great sin against life; and the only discipline I could recognize was the necessity of attending scrupulously to the voices of intuition, which guide each aright. And yet I was fascinated by Antonia's sincere, subtle, poignantly truthful story of her return to the Church, her voluntary exchange of her freedom for its rule.

Graham Greene too was a Catholic. I had reviewed books for him at the time he was literary editor of the *Spectator*; and now in the Department it was a pleasure to see him tilting against bureaucracy, a game of skill which he played as others play chess, or poker, perhaps. Graham was, towards both Antonia and myself, invariably chivalrous; like a knight who does battle with every champion, but shows courtesy towards women. I cannot say that I at all understood Graham either; he was not of my own imaginative kindred, but the association was, at the time, a very pleasant one.

To this day I do not know what it was that drove me to take the desperate step of becoming a Catholic convert. It was almost like the impulse to jump down from a giddy height, a loss of nerve. My situation I felt to be desperate; something had to be done, for my love had got out of hand. Since we do, by laws however mysterious, attract to ourselves what is appropriate to our inner disposition, Alastair (who never entered my sanctuary of Martindale) did enter the squalor of Percy Street. How this came about I no longer remember; but I well remember that, in hurrying down the dirty blacked-out stairs, unfamiliar and alien, to open the door to his so long-fantasied presence, I blacked my eye on the newel of the banister and greeted him with the painful disfiguring bruise already spreading; say that my daimon was trying to bring me to my senses by a sharp blow; or that unconsciously I gave myself that unheeded salutary warning.

Yet the habit of being in love with him was too strong. The illumination of this delusive passion had brought the world to life; given me those insights from which I had drawn my poetry. I could not relinquish it; I was rather prepared to follow this love to whatever distant goal it might lead, to lay this useless, unrequited—indeed unrequitable—passion upon the altar of sacrifice. Yet could I do this? I wondered; and I thought I could. Only so, I felt, could use be made of his burning love, so useless on earth, so far in excess of the banal biological purposes of the life-cycle. That it was useless absolutely some sense of economy prevented me from imagining; I could not have endured to live, had I thought so. I must offer myself and my otherwise useless passion, to God. But also—if I am truthful—was I not insuring my pride against the possibility, indeed the probability, the all but certainty, of rejection?

It may be that to those who have never overwhelmingly experienced the power of passionate love such an avowal will seem an incomprehensible exaggeration of a straightforward natural appetite; but those who have will know that I was at that time fighting for my life. Wrong as my course was, I wonder what would have been the right one?

Perhaps, then, as Ulysses had himself tied to the mast as his ship rowed past the sirens (I thought of this comparison at the time) so did I from the Church want only its restraints? I had not in myself the will-power necessary to my own survival; or if I had, needed some outward safeguard of my condition, like a religious habit. Perhaps my hidden motive was defensive, hunted and torn as I was and unable, almost, to live unless I could rid myself of the sexual instinct in one sure and absolute amputation.

But after all, as Antonia so often said, the real question was, did I believe in the truth of Catholic doctrine? She had herself been tormented by innumerable doubts about the truths taught, and had been compelled into faith by her repeated encounters with what seemed sheer miracle. She often amazed me by confessing, for example, her difficulty in believing such stories as that of Genesis, of Adam and Eve and the Tree and the Serpent. Since it would never for a moment have occurred to me to believe in the factual historical truth of this marvellous and inexhaustibly rich mythological narrative, neither would it have occurred to me to doubt it. But, said Antonia, 'we are *supposed* to believe in it as *literal* truth'. This astonished me, as it was so clearly a symbolic allegory, not of the order of historical fact, but of truth of the imagination, expressed figuratively. As a poet this was so self-evident to me that it was impossible for me to become worried about its possible truth or untruth in other senses. Later I went, with Antonia, to a series of lectures on the Apocalypse by a brilliant young Dominican, Father Richard Kehoe; and he defined 'literal truth' as the sense intended by the author of the book, as against personal interpretations. But it was, among my Catholic acquaintance, considered 'brave' to open profound truths where ignorance could at best read a fairy-tale, and at worst, blindly believe nonsense. So it was with the

Immaculate Conception, the Virgin Birth, and so on. When the doctrine of the Assumption of the Virgin was propounded I was surprised to discover the number of my acquaintance, Catholic as well as Protestant, to whom this was a stumbling-block. To me it seemed absurd to find one aspect of a total symbolic event less acceptable than other parts; mythical events (so I thought) are not to be verified (did they or did they not take place) but rather to be understood, as is poetry. If anything I still continued to find the Christian myth, as compared with the pagan richness of symbol, too meagre, and welcomed any addition. If physical fact had been in question—if the Virgin Birth were a parthenogenesis in the sense in which biologists use the term of a phenomenon commonly met with in the reproduction of echinoderms, and occasionally, I seem to remember, recorded of rabbits, why found a religious doctrine upon it? As literal fact such events would have no meaning at all; how deduce the 'divinity' of an incarnation from a biological anomaly? When in antiquity heroes were called the 'sons' of this or that god, the meaning plainly was that they partook of the nature of Apollo or Zeus or Asclepius; and it might indeed be—and so I believed it was—that the nature of the Most High, the Logos, might become incarnate in human form. If a divine order exist at all, such an Incarnation must be possible, once, or many times, as the Indian religions teach; or every time, as Blake believed.

No doubt I misconceived Catholic Christianity altogether, and what I in reality believed was the doctrine of the neo-Platonists, of which, however, I knew at that time very little: I had read Inge on Plotinus, a little of Plato, but not the *Enneads*, and none of the other Platonic philosophers. But I could say the creed, after my fashion; and how else, after all, should a poet believe in symbols?

All these questions were in fact so many irrelevances; for the real lack of realization in me was of quite a different kind:. I had no moral sense, no charity, no 'grace'. Whatever my stupidities may have been, they were not of an intellectual order. On the contrary, my mistake was to imagine that intellectual understanding was all-sufficient, and that nothing more was required. But although I could argue myself into a logical acceptance of Christianity, never could I argue myself into a love for the Christian mythology; even, with sorrow I admit it, for the figure of Jesus as presented by the Church; the dwelling on wounds and mutilations and martyrdoms. So deep was my early distaste for, and fear of, the Christian religion that although my mind could be persuaded, my imagination continued to reject Christianity. Nevertheless, there was no alternative for me, Christianity being the religion of the civilization into which I was fortunate, unfortunate, foolish or wicked enough (all these possibilities are considered both by Plotinus and by the Indian sages) to have been born. Of Catholicism as a culture I may have had some conception; but of Christianity as a way of life, something simple not to be found in books at all—that secret I had not discovered.

Graham Greene too was tormented by 'doubts', though less subtle than Antonia's, for he was a convert, and his mind had been formed, as had mine, on simpler lines than those fine Jesuitical intricacies which James Joyce so nostalgically depicts. I remember his saying to me once (we were walking together through some woods and fields near Berkhamsted and I can remember his voice and his look as he quoted the words, one of my few flashes of imaginative insight into Graham Greene) 'Unless I shall see in His hands the print of the nails, and put my finger into the print of the nails, and thrust my hand into His side, I will not believe.' It was from Graham also that I first heard of Padre Pio, who bore the stigmata. It is obvious that for one of the types of mankind, this proof by physical evidence is crucial; to me, I must confess, it really had no importance whether the Incarnation had, as historical fact, taken place or not.

Graham insisted that Catholicism is essentially a 'magical' religion. I did not quite see what he meant, but had nothing against magic, as such. Transubstantiation, however, did not strike me as a magical, but as a metaphysical doctrine. Again, I regarded with intellectual scorn (in this case surely justified) a certain Anglican bishop much discussed in my childhood who had offered to disprove the doctrine by a chemical analysis of the consecrated bread. What did he expect to find? I preferred an Irishman's answer (it was Louis MacNeice who told me) to the question 'How can bread be God?'—'What else would it be?'

I think my reasons (such as were not downright bad) strangely insufficient. There may have been others of which I was, and remain, unaware; the wish, for example, to please Helen Sutherland. Had I not myself seen and admired David Jones's immersion in Catholic culture? And Eliot, too, not a Catholic but assuredly a Christian. The need, un-confessed and scarcely recognized, of some kind of human context, suddenly felt in the nightmare-world of London; a desperate fear of sinking. For those whom birth and upbringing has predestined to no other, the *civitas dei* is, I suppose, the only society of which we may become members.

Why then did I not embrace some form of Theosophy, or one of the Indian religions? I very much wish I had done so. But—apart from my doubtless neurotic need for self-immolation, my wish to please Helen Sutherland, and my admiration for Antonia and my other new Catholic friends—I must plead in justification for what I knew at the time, and can now see far more clearly, to have been the wrong course, that I lived, as it were, upon the watershed between the Christian era and what is now called the Age of Aquarius. Christendom had inspired all the great art of the civilization to which I belonged; and, God knows, in adopting Catholic so-to-say nationality I was in one respect sincere—in my total rejection of the materialist philosophies. It was less obvious, then, than now, that the Christian era, with all its greatness, was at an end. Yet, as a poet, it was for me to have divined this; and I did know it. David Jones (whom I see as the last artist of Christendom, though not necessarily the last Christian artist, in England) was on one side of that watershed; his love for the traditions, the culture of Christendom was sincere. Mine was not. Yet again I failed to be truthful through cowardice.

Gay Taylor disapproved of my rash and ill-judged, histrionic and insincere 'conversion'. She said my character and my temper became much worse when I was being a Catholic. She herself, keeping the thread of her own 'way' always under her sensitive touch, read the Christian mystics, indeed, far more deeply and constantly than I did; but she also kept the *Tao*, the way of effortless wind and water, the 'way of heaven and earth'. She also said that the Catholic Church had shed too much blood to have remained under any divine blessing; the blood of heretics and of Jews. As in Cambridge I had made the mistake of thinking civilization immutable, so now I made the same mistake, thinking that because the truths of Christianity are eternal, belonging to the nature of things, the Church also must be immutable. Had I attended to the signs how easily I could have seen—indeed I did very clearly see, and yet behaved as though I did not see—that the spirit was moving in other places, not in the old forms any longer.

Gay told me of a 'divine dream' she had had; which, even now, I recall as vividly as if it had been my own. The dreamer—Gay, that is—was struggling across a dark, low tract of country, called in her dream by the Bunyan-like name of 'Broadmarsh'. She toiled on, coming at last to just such a small, low-built but very ancient church as those she loved, in waking life, to visit; for the sake of rustic architecture or (in the vicar's absence) to pray there. She entered the church; where, to her amazement, she found an interior of rich glory of crimson and gold, and a great archangel depicted on the vaulted roof. Overcome with awe she exclaimed, 'it's a *cardinal*'—knowing the word to mean, one of the four archangels who guard the cardinal points or directions of space. The words were then said to her, 'a church in the hearts of men'. This was her 'shewing'; so much deeper, so much truer, than my foolish plunge into the Catholic Church, itself at best only a symbol and a creation of 'the church in the hearts of men'.

Years later, after one of my many periods of vacillation, I went to consult Marco Pallis (himself a Buddhist, but a member of that group

who, following René Guénon and Frithjof Schuon, disseminate the high
doctrine of the transcendent unity of all the 'revealed' religions). Marco
assured me that, distasteful as Christianity might be, none of the other
traditions were in better shape: in the last age of the *kaliyuga*, all were in a
state of decadence. Yet all (and this God knows I have never doubted) do
teach the perennial truth; differently envisaged, each in a manner appropriate to one or another civilization. Born a European, logic (and the
Hindu view of rebirth for that matter, no birth being accidental or out of
place) demanded that, unless for some quite exceptional reason, I should
be a Christian. Reluctantly I accepted Marco's verdict and went, half-
hearted still, once again back to the Church; whose teachings, so far as
that goes, I have never doubted. I have believed too much, not too little,
for Catholic orthodoxy. But no freedom less than absolute is freedom at
all: the poet has no right—no soul has the right—to surrender free-will.

An Indian friend and Vedantist, Dr. Arabinda Basu, from whom I
learned something of Indian thought (an atmosphere in which I have
always been able to breathe, whereas trying to be a Christian is, for me,
like trying to live under water) said to me, just before his return to India
and the *ashram* of his guru Sri Aurobindo, 'Don't let the Church get you
back.' But I did; over and over again I have failed at that test of courage
and honesty. Even now it is almost more than I can do to admit to
myself—as in honesty to those who may read these words I must admit—
that, finally, I have found myself unable to remain in the Church.

I am, of course, looking years ahead. Certainly my true place is with the
esoteric tradition of neo-Platonism, Cabbala, Theosophy. There my heart,
which so sinks in the presence of Christian works of devotion, of most
Christian art, and, alas, most practising Christians, leaps in joyful recognition. No. Every civilization, not excepting European Christendom,
comes to its term. Only the eternal is ever living, not any one of its
expressions in time.

To write this costs me much; not to have written so would have cost me
my integrity; already too often compromised in this matter. For an
unbeliever not to be a Christian is a simple matter, and agnostics and
atheists may well wonder why I have taken so long to make so easy a
rejection; but for the believer—and God knows I have never for a moment
wavered in my belief in a spiritual order—it is not a simple or an easy
thing to say, 'I cannot make a Christian of myself'. Perhaps all I am
revealing is that for all my super-subtleties, I have been loveless and never
found that simple secret known to all loving hearts.

Yet another need may have in part determined my course: the need in
my desperate state to talk to some wise person, some spiritual adviser and
counsellor. The time was past when I would have sought help from any

Freudian; and even had I known any Jungian at that time—which I did not—I would not have accepted any view of suffering or sin which seeks to reduce these aspects of life to terms not of personal responsibility but of 'mental illness'. No, I preferred and I still prefer, the heroic Christian morality which sees in these the stuff of life; in sin, failures for which we are responsible; in suffering, a task, a bearing of the world's burden and a transmutation of its base matter into spiritual gold; a privilege whose purposes are beyond our knowledge which we yet intuitively divine to be of supreme importance in the total spiritual economy of the world. I did not want to rid myself of suffering but to learn how to use it; for above all things I could not bear to suffer in vain. It still seems to me the chief glory of Christianity that it sees in suffering a positive value. Buddhism offers release from suffering; Christianity the Cross, heavy with all the anguish of the world, to be lived and known as the very heart of a Mystery. I wished to understand that mystery, not to be freed from it.

I was told (by Manya Harari, in the canteen of Bush House, it was) that Father Pius Dolin, prior of the Carmelites in Kensington, was a priest of great holiness; and to the obscure door opening onto the pavement of Church Street, symbol of all doors of sanctuary, I went, and was admitted. I remember him as for the first time he entered the little bare parlour where I was received by him for instruction. Father Pius is one of the most beautiful, most spiritually transfigured beings I have ever met. He had a way of entering the parlour with a kind of grace of gesture, like a saint in some Italian painting, yet without himself, so I would suppose, being in the least aware of it; rather as if the painters of those figures had caught the gestures and bodily postures natural to certain states of the human soul; the stillness of those who are, as it were, listening, attending inwardly; a suave grace expressive of calm of mind and charity, the control of a moment by moment dedication and submission of the self to the Self. Those who daily celebrate Mass must come to be aware of the body itself as a kind of living icon, whose gestures are expressive, not only in a general but in a specific way, like the *mudras* of Hindu sculptures and dance; gestures not natural to the once-born, but natural to the twice-born; at the same time beautiful and impersonal, expressive and formal. The natural man has been taken over by the spiritual, the I by the not-I. In Father Pius I for the first time divined—though only dimly, and without realizing the immense significance of what I saw—that the conformity of the natural man, at every moment of a lifetime, to a religious rule, far from destroying a personality, truly creates one; whereas the spontaneity of 'self-expression', the 'natural' behaviour of the undisciplined, does exactly the reverse; as the apparent 'naturalness' of a dancer is the supreme triumph of art over nature. What a barbarian I still was! For with

Father Pius there before my eyes to prove that 'he that loseth his life the same shall find it', I still clung to my notions of freedom, the 'freedom' of the soul to grow in its own way, by its own innate laws. Nor did I yet realize what I have since slowly and painfully been forced to recognize, that the spiritual Way is, like every art, against nature, not with it, upstream against the current, the hard way. But I still had a truly Protestant horror of conforming to an external rule; the self-imposed rule of the dedicated poet, I said to myself, is higher and better than the merely external discipline these Carmelites assume. And so perhaps it is, but, in the long run it, too, no less austere, leads 'out of nature'.

Father Pius was Irish, with a round and (in its physical features) almost comical face; yet he seemed to be over-flowing with the energy of an inward joy, irrepressible; he was habitually at once grave and joyful; and in him I recognized some quality above human intelligence, and far above human knowledge. What he knew, so it seemed to me, was not his own mind, but the 'other' mind, the other Self, which poets know as the imagination, but Christian visionaries call Christ. 'Jesus the Imagination,' Blake writes, boldly equating the two names. Once he told me that the gift God had given him was 'the discernment of spirits', insight into souls.

Just as his understanding seemed to come from another level of mind than his own, so did the continuous sense of joy which his presence communicated, as from some source beyond himself to which he was transparent just insofar as he submitted entirely his human personality to its irradiation. This was a kind of love higher, as I recognized, than earthly eros; and yet, not to have looked down those long vistas of the wonders of creation seemed to me then a pure loss which I could not, for myself, have contemplated. Those other vistas which the saints describe in vain to those who have not themselves seen them, I could not measure. Thus I was in two minds, even in the presence of the freedom and *caritas* of sanctity.

So Father Pius instructed me in the catechism; and how gentle he was with my bruised soul, how charitable, never blaming me, nor condemning the earthly passion which had swept me to the door of the Carmelites. And, talking with this son of perhaps some Irish cabin, how at home I felt, not only with the language of the spirit which he spoke but, no less, with that world from which he had come, the world of country people where, somewhere behind the ascetic life of the monastery, was the sense of home, of the family, brothers and sisters and father and mother, the human pattern somehow, somewhere, right. And how, even though my own life, but for a few years of my childhood, had never run true, I seemed to remember it all, with a nostalgia all the greater for the broken pattern which in imagination I was all the time trying to restore, but which in actuality I never was able to restore. There was something behind the

Carmelite monk which belonged to Bavington, and the Manse kitchen where old copies of *The Northern Presbyter* were kept under the cushion of the rocking-chair; to fetching the milk in the evening, and water from the stone village well in buckets kept in the back kitchen; an earthly restoration of all things to their proper places. How express that sense one has, in the presence of sanctity, of a remembered familiarity, of this being just as it all should have been?

Marco Pallis has somewhere written that the sacramental quality of anything whatsoever is the norm from which creation has fallen with the Fall of man; the change from the sacramental to the profane way of experiencing the whole of the created world being the Fall itself; a narrowing of consciousness, a forgetting. In this sense the holy bread and wine of the Christian Mass are what bread and wine essentially are, unperceived by us. In Father Pius saintliness seemed a return to the lost norm, to things as they truly are. He had a kind of simplicity, remote indeed from the insolent familiarity of the profane world, where the assumption is that our neighbour is as vile as ourselves. On the contrary, he made me feel that nothing can be simpler than to meet all on the ground of the Holy Spirit, the only ground of every being, and therefore more familiar, more native than the world, so strangely alien, in which I lived my outer life. A story I remember his telling me—to illustrate what point I do not know—has strangely impressed itself, for all its simplicity, upon my memory. It communicated to me, in the telling of it, some quality that may elude my re-telling; something which the modern profane world has all but lost. The story was of a nine-or ten-year-old Irish girl whose father was a poor man who sold vegetables from a cart. One day as she was coming to find him, in the market, there was some trouble, and she had to see the police (was it? or other ruffians) beating and striking 'the poor old man, her father. And at that moment, she grew up.' That was all the story; it is the same, with countless variations, that is told and retold in Christian art, of the brutality of the profane world to the human soul, ever defenceless. But what perhaps makes me remember the story when I have forgotten so much else is the fullness of the relationship it implied, in one of the most simple and fundamental of all, that of father and daughter; and the breath it brought from an almost lost world in which a family is a community of human souls, loving one another. The relationship so described was natural, indeed archetypal, but realized to the full in that uncomplicated simplicity in which alone depth of feeling can exist. My own family relationships, complicated and embittered—the uprooting had begun a generation before I was born, many generations perhaps—precluded that simplicity and depth. My own relationship with my father should have been like that, but was not; yet it was not—was it?—only or all my fault that it had been so impaired. When and where had I lost the thread of those simple relationships of love, husband and wife, father and mother and children, brothers and sisters? Of Adam's household, whose natural affections and bonds the Catholic religion has protected through time, in all those countries where its culture has nourished the lives of the people? For—such is the paradox—only in a supernatural context does the natural thrive. True, the story might have been told (but for its ending—the girl became a nun, the obviously most practical thing she could do being to assist by her prayers the souls of mankind, whose bodies must suffer such indignities) of my father's Methodist people, though hardly of the Church of England where the absolute dignity of man is obscured by class-distinction of a rather petty and provincial kind, unknown within the greater Church, accustomed to treating kings and emperors no otherwise than other sons of Adam. Yet, within the Catholic context, it seemed to me to stand out clear of any reformist political sentimentality. No political or social moral was to be drawn; only the naked truth of the human condition, within the context of a religion that protects and saves souls from the world, though it cannot save bodies from the conditions of the world. What the girl had seen in the moment in which, as Father Pius said, she had 'grown up' was the basic truth also of the Buddhist religion, a truth irremovably grounded in the nature of the temporal world, 'Life is suffering'; and with that insight, compassion. Those only who have understood and accepted this truth, and fully felt the violation that cruelty is to those beings who in love's eyes are of infinite value, can be said to have 'grown up'. Many see the suffering without the value, out of context. A strayed Irish bard, from the same world, who about the King's Road was cleaning cars for the price of a drink, asked what he thought of the contemporary English 'angry' social drama replied in a phrase whose roots are in that ancient traditional wisdom, 'Better than anger an elegant sorrow that suffers all'.

But I could only look from afar at the integrity of Adam's family. Had I myself lived by the ancient pattern I would never have come to the door of the Carmelites at all; for to become a Catholic only isolated me still further from the natural bonds and simple relationships of home, and widened every gulf in my life, while at the same time giving me no context, natural or intellectual (since my mind had been formed in other patterns) in which I could live my life more simply. Catholicism was, for me, but one more complication, one more break in the pattern.

On the night before I was to be received into the Church—upon the Feast of the Epiphany—my daimon visited me. I was, so he told me, doing wrong, going against everything he and those greater ones who had at times visited me, had wished for me, demanded of me, given me. I was about to separate myself from the inspirers, from those free spirits of imagination, those intellections who shun prison-bars, and all man-made restrictions and conditions imposed upon the reality which they mediate and express. All this and more my daimon said to me; and can you, he asked, can you really form and fashion your imagination by those symbols to which you are about to bind yourself? And will you part from us, from the elementals who companioned your childhood, from the celestial hierarchies whose natures are free, as you were free in your childhood, and as you are—yes—as the poet in you is free even now? Do you really love those tame saints, so monotonously good, so wingless? Do you not, then, understand what a precious gift is the freedom of the imagination, indeed more than a gift, a sacred trust, given only to chosen ones, and, among these, to the poets? You know—so my daimon continued— that the difference between yourself and your new Catholic friends (not our friends, however, the daimon said) lies precisely in this, that you are one who has been given the freedom of the poet to attend, directly, to our voices. You are betraying us, and you yourself we will leave, we will be compelled to leave you, down there in the world you have chosen. Your humility, not your pride, is false, a cowardly evasion; to rise to what is demanded of you calls for a greater humility, for it demands that you entrust yourself to us; do you suppose that you can do anything, great or small, without our inspiration? In humbling yourself you are an egoist, safe-guarding yourself, through imaginative sloth and moral cowardice, behind a barrier of foregone conclusions, from the holy spirit. When will human beings know that great things are demanded of them, not face-saving conformity?

I knew this was the voice of truth. Not a word did the daimon say about sex or Alastair, one way or the other; it was not upon the issue of passionate love that they admonished me; their words came from a place beyond all that, and this I knew, and mourned with them that last night; the friends and companions of that freedom I was about to forgo, as I then feared, for ever.

And what did I answer? 'Yes, I know,' I said, 'everything you tell me is true. But now I am committed, now I have promised, now it is all arranged.' I had experienced the disastrous consequences of two mistaken marriages, and yet I was prepared, for a third time, to try to deceive the daimon, to go, deliberately and wilfully, against the warning of conscience. 'How,' I continued, 'can I fail Father Pius, that saintly man— even you must admit that.' ('Yes,' said my daimon, 'but that is not *your* way.') What else I said I do not know; I think I raised the subject of Alastair, in a rather overstrained stage-voice telling them of the renunciation I was about to make of my great love; but they were not listening;

and so, all night, I lay awake in the little back bedroom in Paulton's Square, with the pear-tree outside my window in the night, dark and leafless. We mourned together, the inspiring spirits of life and I; I knew they were about to leave me, and could only bid them farewell. But I tempted Providence when I said to them, 'but we will meet again—not now, but someday.'

I went through with it, of course; in a kind of daze; I can scarcely remember the occasion, even though it was Father Pius who received me; Antonia, Graham Greene and Robert Speaight afterwards took me out to lunch; Antonia gave me a mantilla, and Robert Speaight *The Ascent of Mount Carmel.* I was stunned by the strangeness of it all.

For years after I would dream, from time to time, that I was in a prison, sentenced (often for murder) for a term of years, and wake in terror, relieved to find that, in the outer world at all events, this was not so. Sometimes the same nightmare horror would be that, in the dream, I found myself to be married; for marriage was, to me, a symbol of imprisonment. I knew in my heart that freedom is a state, a blessing, a task which I had yet again relinquished, sacrificed.

But Father Pius—that was quite another matter. I recollect that bare parlour, and the Carmelite church itself, as a place permeated by the presence of the spiritual world, a place where prayer had called down that Presence. During an air-raid the church was destroyed by a bomb; I rushed there, in my lunch-hour, this time to offer what comfort my presence could bring to my comforter. There he stood, in his brown habit, among the ruins; where a few others had come, as I had myself. He looked at me, and smiled gravely; grieved, but not at all perturbed to see his church in ruins. I discovered when I attempted to use the symbolic structure provided by the Church that I was, quite simply, unable to project into these outer forms my own inner life. For me it was all a make-believe in which I could not make myself believe; I could not wed the reality of my inner life to the forms; in attempting to use verbal forms of prayer I became unable to pray at all. I know that the great symbols of Christendom still live for many. An English friend, not even a Protestant, not a believer at all, told me how, on a visit to Prague, she had seen, in one of the churches there, an old woman praying. Her eyes were fixed in loving adoration upon some baroque Christ; and my friend saw the lips of the statue move in answer. Another friend—again not a Catholic, though a believer—was given a medal of the Blessed Virgin which had been blessed by a very holy Spanish nun. She was herself at the time in a condition of intense concentration upon a spiritual and emotional problem of her own; and, sitting with the medal and looking at it, she saw, to her astonishment, brownish-red drops running down from the extended hands of the Virgin onto her own fingers which held it. She wiped the drops from her fingers and found that they were blood; and together with this physical manifestation, she seemed to understand some profound mystery of love and suffering. To her the symbol had spoken, the outward form was at one with some interior reality; but for me this has never been so, my relationship with the archetypal world has been something quite apart from the forms of Catholic iconography. Neither have the forms brought me to the archetypes, nor the archetypes to the symbolic forms of the Christian religion. For me they have held no magic—which is to say, have not been animated from within. What this proves I do not know, but truth compels me to record it. I have come more and more to realize that I have to meet these archetypal forms in their interior world, where they are free and mysterious; not in those images, plastic or merely conceptual, in which they are reflected outwardly, be these portraits as life-like as may be. I respect those whose inner life is happily married to some outer pattern; but at the same time, I also accept, finally, with a certain joy, my own imposed conditions, which are different from theirs.

Catholic Christendom, like an ancient vine-stock, may be the enduring root of Western European civilization; and yet a true sense of tradition (in terms of living reality not of merely abstract argument) must include the knowledge of where we ourselves are situated within it, and that is not a matter so much of choice as of fact. An attempt to re-graft ourselves can only produce preciosity of taste, antiquarianism, or the false note struck by Belloc, Chesterton or Evelyn Waugh, conscientious objectors to their own cultural inheritance. Shakespeare and Milton, not Dante, were my ancestors, Shelley and Coleridge my next-of-kin. Yeats was closer to me than Catholic Joyce; for in Yeats, as in the English romantic poets, the poetry is winged towards 'knowledge absolute'; and his great bell-beat stirred in me when I came to read his poetry. As a Catholic convert the first thing I did was to buy Yeats's collected poems, like a sick dog looking for grass.

Truth to say—and to write this confession costs me a great deal—I have never felt complete kinship of spirit with any Christian; though with Indian friends, and with a few others, Platonists like myself, or Buddhists, like Marco Pallis, all that I could never explain to any Christian is taken for granted without any explanation at all. Perhaps my Christian friends find a corresponding lack in me; but in the nature of things I cannot know what it is that they might say to one another 'Kathleen has never understood'.

One day I was in the Farm Street Jesuit church—our department had moved into the neighbourhood of Grosvenor Square, and, coming or going, I often went into that church for a while. On one such occasion I

was simply walking through, when, abruptly, my consciousness underwent a curious shift, so that I seemed, while at the same time remaining
myself, to be a young nun; younger than I was myself at the time, and
standing, so it seemed, in a pleasant sunny garden or orchard of blossoming fruit-trees; in France, as it seemed to me. The nun was wearing a black
habit with a white head-dress, somewhat stiff and projecting; Antonia
thought I had described the dress of the Dominican nuns, but I am not
convinced that this was so, my nun's dress seemed rather different. It was
odd how vividly clear the feeling of the shaped head-dress was to me,
though I could not see it. The young nun was radiantly happy, with a
lightness of heart and uplifting joy. At the same time I was able to
compare from within—to measure, as it were—my own being with hers,
and I knew myself, for all my experience of sorrow and evil, to know
much more, to possess a much greater reach and scope of experience than
she; though I had lost that bird-like innocent joy which she, in her smaller
sphere, had been able to attain or retain. I do not tell this experience as
'evidence' for reincarnation—it might be taken so, but there could be
many other possible explanations; insight, for example, of a telepathic
kind into another soul, of the present or of the past, to whom I was for the
moment attuned, in some respect. Or it could have been simply a symbolic
configuration, a kind of waking dream. I tell it not for its curiosity but for
its content as an experience; for it expressed the plain truth of my real
situation: I was trying to evade, to hide myself in the clothing of a novice,
from my true destiny. We cannot, alas, reverse the direction of growth, try
to make ourselves smaller than we are out of some false sense of humility,
or from cowardice. That young nun's experience of pure joy was not,
now, or ever again, for me: not that joy, that walled garden and those
flowering apple-trees under the sun of France.

Thirty or more years later I unexpectedly 'remembered' (whether the
memory was my own or another's I cannot say, the experience was in
either case the same) the same nun's life. Now she was an old woman,
who needed the support of a stick to walk across her cell; which, on this
occasion, I saw as clearly as I can remember the bedroom I slept in as a
child. I could 'see' on one side, her bed, covered with a white counterpane
of rough texture; opposite, a prayer-desk, and above this a crucifix with a
heavy crown of thorns; a shelf with a few devotional books; on another
wall a picture of the Madonna and the child Jesus, whose halo contained
the form of the equal-armed cross. High up were windows, and the lovely
light in the sky suggested, again, France. There were swifts or swallows
crossing that high glimpse of sky. A door opened into, I think, the
cloisters. And there she had lived her life, and kept her faith. She was not a
rebel; only, ever so little, bored. She had a devotion to the Child Jesus; and

as she crossed her cell, supported by her stick, I knew that her other hand held, in imagination, the hand of the *Puer Eternus*. I do not think she would have wished to be a nun again; am I, is my life, what she wished? If so, I hope she felt—as I feel—that, with all its appalling mistakes my life has been richer than those long sinless cloistered days.

CHAPTER NINE

The End of a Golden String

The years that followed had no radiance in them; but the war was over, and 9 Paulton's Square, with Anna's room, and James's room began to seem like a home. I set to work to earn money in ways that I hoped would allow me to call my soul my own—a freedom purchased at the price of poverty, continual anxiety, and hard ill-paid work; translation, book-reviewing, evening classes at Morley College, all the unusual improvisations. I was not very good at any of these things, and laboured at them all *contre cœur*, like a slave saving up to buy his freedom, but seeming as far from that end as ever. For a short time I had a job in the Publications Department of the British Council but the occupation seemed to me rather less to the point than translations and book-reviews, which were at all events honest toil; so I gave it up. That, at all events, was the form my pride took. I could no more fit myself into the world on its own terms than into the Church. So I remained, poor and proud, as it seemed to myself; to my friends I must have seemed merely poor and incompetent. Nor had I any great cause for pride, for my second volume of poems was much inferior to my first, cut off as I was from my roots, and re-planted in the alien soil of London and the Church. But to me it was obvious that the poems I had at that time written were only a beginning, tentative exercises to keep my hand in; I felt myself to be the poet of my future poems, and under a strong sense of teleological obligation. So a plant in its phase of growth might be said to 'know' that future flower and seed is its purpose, and this irrespective of whether or not the plant ever comes to flower or the poet to realize a potential maturity. And yet I took great risks in continually deferring the work I intended to do, in order merely to keep myself and my children alive. It might be said that this was inevitable; but

254

I do not think so; there is always time if the state of mind is right, and mine was not right; I was incapacitated by a multitude of unhealed wounds, hopes, and despairs. Heaven knows I was not a rebel; I no more embattled myself in unimportant issues than I sold myself; my instinct, after my failure to find a context in the Catholic religion, was to conserve my deepest thoughts in silence, and disguise myself once again in my cat-skin mantle, my *trompe-l'oeil* persona. Yet I felt it all as a battle to defend something of infinite value from the world in which I struggled to survive. Better to struggle than to sell what was above price; to better the woman at the expense of the poet was something I could not have brought myself to do. Gay Taylor was fond of exclaiming that she 'did not know what she had done in a former life' to incur her present troubles; I had no need to look to former lives to see the operation, in my own, of cause and effect: my situation, my troubles, were self-caused.

My house helped me; it was like a friend, its simple and dignified proportions (barely and shabbily furnished as it was) its vine and its pear-tree silently speaking to me of order and dignity and simplicity and by doing so, imposing them. I had planted near the back door some ferns from Martindale; I had inherited from Cooie Lane the blessing of the house with the vine and the pear-tree she had loved, and for long I continued to live in it as under her roof and protection. And Helen Sutherland, and the Robertses (near neighbours again, Michael now Principal of the teachers' training college of St. Mark and St. John, at the World's End) never let me go. I lived on as if provisionally; something, I believed, must changed this long waiting, there must be an end of it. Even now I thought of myself as still a native of Northumberland, of Martindale, of that faraway land where I had not lived as an exile and a stranger. My comfort was the little back garden of my house, its vine, its pear-tree, its jasmine and lily-of-the-valley, its fern from Martindale. The brick wall at the end had been that of Sir Thomas More's garden, so it was said; but the sense of holy ground had little to do with the saint; the tree and the vine and the fern spoke to me not of the English Catholic martyrs, but in the older language of my own lost world of nature. It was the earth itself that was holy. Only alone in my few square yards of London garden could I still, in some measure, become a semblance of myself.

At that time I still thought of my exile not as radical, something which belonged to my nature, or to the human situation as such; still I hoped to find again in this world the here and now of being in my right place that I had known at the Manse; and again, even more briefly and precariously, at Martindale. Because I knew I belonged elsewhere, the present was endurable; for I believed my exile would end, that I would, at last, come to my own. Those who in childhood have known the state of Paradise perhaps always expect to find again what was once so simply there. I recognized the same quality in the poetry of Edwin Muir (and in Edwin himself when later I met him) and, curiously enough—for it takes one child of Paradise to recognize another—appearances notwithstanding, in Herbert Read. In the Herbert Read of the avant-garde I recognized a disguise (albeit a far more convincing one) like my own; Herbert, Edwin Muir and I, none of us had, at heart, ever left our native place.

I remember, too, with deep gratitude how, when I was waiting at 9 Paulton's Square, for Alastair, now returned from the war, and about to visit me, Gay Taylor came to take leave of me, as it almost seemed to both of us. Gay, for many, many years, my fellow-pilgrim, herself by now knew that her journey was towards the Celestial City. At the door she turned to leave me; and said to me, not reproachfully, but lovingly, 'Well, dear Kathleen, good-bye.' And in those words I knew the angels were themselves again taking leave of me. I knew then with absolute clarity that I must not, on any account, marry any Alastair. For once I heeded the message from the Castle.

A friend, having read thus far my story, understandably dissatisfied with so inconclusive a quest, suggested to me that here I ought to pause, to assess my life hitherto. 'So here I was', he would have me say, 'in the middle of my way, in the world of post-war London, having learned...' what? But my record is of rejections; of escapes, as it seemed to me; others might say of disloyalties; abandonments, at all events, of all those refuges, intellectual, moral or domestic, within which, from my student years until now, I had attempted to live. Only in that realm of nature that had been mine in my Northumberland childhood, briefly recaptured at Martindale, did I feel my true place. My wanderings in those other 'states the soul falls into when it leaves Paradise following the serpent' had not given me, in terms of understanding or symbol, the knowledge I had sought through which I might interpret my proper landscape of the soul. One thing at least I had learned in the bitter world of Experience—that everything that befalls us has its cause within ourselves, and is, therefore, and in that sense, be the experience one of joy or of misery, what is our due. If I was impenitent—I had not yet seen myself in the light of the injury I had done to others—neither did I complain. And I had been given, after all, in that world, so much of value, if I could only discover how to use it: the abrasive mental discipline of Cambridge; Mass-Observation's dark visions of the collective mind; Helen Sutherland's aristocratic insistence on 'the best'; and the sanctuary of the Catholic Church, even though that too proved only the brief refuge of Cain the wanderer whose road runs on.

Presently, by another of those seeming miracles by which a change of inner disposition is followed by a corresponding change in the outward course of events, my course became calmer. Blake now became my Virgil and my guide; I took the end of his golden string, and began, with an exhilarating sense of return to duty, to wind it into a ball. Others before and since have found that string longer than they had supposed. As I entered the British Museum each morning, to begin my day's work where Yeats had worked on Blake before me, my heart would give a little leap of pleasure, a sign surely that the work I was doing was the work I was then meant to be doing. I persisted in the winding in of the golden string a great deal more whole-heartedly than I had ever practised the Catholic religion; and felt myself now once again engaged in a serious imaginative task, and no longer play-acting.

Quite early on in my Blake studies Philip Sherrard (who had read a first draft of some of my Blake work, in which I attempted, if I remember rightly, a Jungian interpretation) had lent me the works of René Guénon. These had profoundly changed my outlook; for in Guénon I first found clearly defined that 'knowledge absolute' of which every metaphysical tradition is an expression. From Guénon I went on to discover, with still greater delight, the works of Tambi's uncle; I discovered in Coomaraswamy's writings a view of the arts as the proper language of 'knowledge absolute', a knowledge from which they cannot long be separated and live. I now sought for wisdom not in Academe but 'in Watkins's bookshop', where the legendry Michael Robartes knew he would find Yeats whenever he wished to summon him. Mr. Watkins became my friend; lent me copies of some of his own valuable collection of the works of Thomas Taylor the Platonist. His theosophical bookshop in Cecil Court—that University Library of lost knowledge—became for me, as for others before and since, a shrine of wisdom.

Little by little, I found how great is that literature of exact spiritual knowledge, unheeded by literary critics and literary historians alike; and gradually it become clear to me that not only did Blake possess this knowledge and speak that royal language, but that this learning of the imagination is the mainstream from which poets and artists from Orpheus to W.B. Yeats have drawn life. Proust (in a very different context) uses the image of the way in which letters fall into place as words, words into a sentence, when a clue formerly missing is in our hands which reveals relationships and connections of a kind hitherto unsuspected. The learning of the imagination, I now discovered, is of this kind: it rests upon relationships indiscernible to scholarship as such; which can discover only what it already knows may be there.

With amazement and joy I followed the windings of that mainstream of tradition and some of its tributaries; working upstream, as Yeats had done before me, in the British Museum, where now I spent my days. In the

North Library where I had at that time a desk piled high with strange books, I felt the golden string forming under my writing fingers as they copied wisdom. The clues, once noticed, were everywhere. Through the General Catalogue I tracked Blake's footprints; Hermes Trismegistus, the writings and translations of Taylor the English Pagan, the *Proceedings* of the Calcutta Society of Bengal, Paracelsus and Fludd and Agrippa, Ovid's *Metamorphoses*; Swedenborg, Dante. But if Cabbalism and Alchemy may be called esoteric I was above all surprised to discover how much of this tradition lies plain to view, in the writings of Plato, Proclus, Plotinus, Berkeley's *Siris*; and in the works of the poets themselves. Everywhere evident and accessible this knowledge has at all times been for those who have known how to discern it; hidden it must always remain from those who do not.

When long after I visited Mrs. Yeats in Dublin, she confirmed my view of Blake as a supreme teacher within age-old tradition as that to which Yeats had also come. Works of Thomas Taylor (from whom Blake had learned the doctrine of the Neoplatonists) were still on Yeats's bookshelves; it was she herself who had first possessed them. What a marriage-dowry to bring to a poet! When I left, Mrs. Yeats wanted to make me some gift; she hovered over a pile of recent books, reprints of Yeats's works, books on Yeats. She said she could not imagine what most of Yeats's 'critics' were talking about, however, (and that W.B.Y. would not have known either!) and we left the book-pile. No, I said, not a book. I asked her, instead to give me, from her garden where many rare and beautiful spring flowers were in bloom, an *anemone pulsatilla*; the flower at which Thel, in Blake's title-page, looks so thoughtfully as she considers mutability. This flower is an emblem of Adonis, whose myth is woven into Blake's poem with strands from Ovid, Spenser, and Milton, from Agrippa and Plotinus and the alchemists. It seemed to me fitting that so neo-Platonic a flower should be growing in Mrs. Yeats's garden; so she gave me the flower, and I pressed it carefully. It is now preserved in the pages of my own copy of *The Book of Thel*. With it is a fern-like leaf of the *anemone pulsatilla* which grew on Helen Sutherland's terrace, where so often I have walked and thought, and weeded as well. It was not in a library that the flash of recognition came, but on that terrace where, admiring the curving droop of the leaves, I suddenly recognized them as the same as the leaves on the title-page of *Thel*. Blake too must have loved the real flower, and not the mere emblem.

After Mrs. Yeats's death, Anne Yeats gave me the book which her mother had, after all, left me: Yeats's copy of Denis Saurat's work on Blake, with marginalia in Yeats's hand. Yet I had met Mrs. Yeats only twice; when, emboldened by a research student who had assured me of her willingness to meet me (without which assurance I would never have intruded myself upon her) I had visited the poet's wife and medium, whose hand had written, at the spirits' bidding *A Vision*. She had left me alone, for a time, with Yeats's Blake books; then she had come in, bringing with her, as I remember, in one hand a Cona coffee-machine, in the other a hot-water-bottle. The coffee she placed between us, the hot-water-bottle at her back. She had come to talk to me. 'How long is it', she began, 'since you stopped writing poetry?' I said I had not written for some long time, protesting unhappiness in my private life, or something of the kind. 'A poet has no right not to write,' she said; 'You need a rabbit-bolter.' She explained what she meant—you send a ferret or a terrier down the rabbit-hole to make the rabbit come out. 'I was W.B.Y.'s rabbit-bolter,' she said. It was then she told me that 'Tom' (T.S. Eliot) had first told 'W.B.Y.' (so she called him) to read my poems. So after many years—when I no longer thought of such things—I received Eliot's posthumous acceptance, with Yeats's also.

We talked of Blake; of Thomas Taylor the Platonist. Had I known more, at that time, of those esoteric studies of the Society of the Golden Dawn from which the poet and his wife had drawn their wisdom, how much more I would have asked her! But when, some years later, I had the knowledge, I did not venture to visit her again, hesitating to intrude when I had no longer the pretext of Blake. How wrong I was in this I discovered only too late, by her legacy to me. But to me the greater legacy was that intangible transmission of the sacred trust of the poet. (Later I returned the book to Anne Yeats for the Yeats library; where, I felt, it ought to be.) After all my d*tours I am always brought back to my own task. All my attempts to exchange poetry for religion or to sacrifice it on the altar of human passion have proved in the end to be grandiose evasion.

The Lion's Mouth
(1977)

And last, the rending pain of re-enactment
    Of all that you have done, and been; the shame
    Of motives late revealed, and the awareness
Of things ill done and done to others' harm
    Which once you took for exercise of virtue.

                T. S. Eliot, *Little Gidding*

CHAPTER ONE

The Tree and its Fruit

Io ho tenuto i piedi in quella parte della vita, di là dalla quale non si
puo ire per intendento di ritornare.

Dante: *La vita nuova.*

Too much happens to us in the present world for it to be possible to preserve a sure sense of what is really ours. We think we 'know' what we possess merely by hearsay, or from books, or on the word of other people.
Our lives are encumbered with irrelevancies which we mistake for living
experience, and which in the end come more and more to usurp it. Perhaps we cannot bring ourselves to admit what has at other times been
clearly understood, that one life cannot encompass every possibility but
can realize only one.

What we have lived for may prove to be some few occasions, perhaps
some single event, in which we have known ourselves to be agents of, and
participants in, a life greater than our own. Our deepest realizations,
whether of knowledge or of love, are not our own inventions or dis-
coveries or plans, but come, as it seems, by revelation. Edwin Muir when
he wrote of 'the story' and 'the fable' understood this very well. Our story
is too often—as mine has been—the record of our failure to embody in
our lives the enduring pattern of 'the fable'. But then—and Edwin said
this also—how can we, knowing so little of that lost record of what
should have been, struggling as we are in the dark, hope to do better? And
yet is it not precisely from the dark that we are guided? When for a
moment we succeed in silencing the endless prattle of the conscious mind
and listen, do we not become aware of presences, watching us with rapt
attention, 'full of eyes', as the Bible says of spiritual intelligences? What if
of those beings—and may they not be our true selves—we are but the
instruments? For what purposes how can we know? For to the daimons
our lives are not means to such ends as we might wish. Their ends may
indeed bring us to greater happiness than we could have dreamed; but
equally—perhaps also—those purposes may destroy the mortal actors,
their instruments, in the process, for love and death have always been
their favourite play. Those natural friends who are, according to Blake,
'spiritual enemies', would always save us if they could from the gods; who

have, besides, as Odysseus complained to Athene, a way of absenting themselves at crucial moments, leaving us to our own devices. Very rightly, for the task of life, once assigned, is, after all, our own.

St. Teresa said to her divine lover that it is not surprising He has so few friends, He treats them so badly. 'It is a terrible thing to fall into the hands of the living God.' All have found it so. Yet it is said that none is given a task beyond his strength. If we fail we have no right to complain that what was required of us was too difficult. What is asked, is, always, precisely what is appropriate: it is our own fate and no other that comes to us in our appointed time. For in reality fate is itself a kind of choice; made not consciously but with the whole of our being, which responds only to that to which it is attuned. And of all things the worst is to fail, not in those relationships and activities which were never really ours, but in that inner and predestined calling to which each of us is born. A vocation, surely, always of love, for what is love unless that deep attraction to what is our own?

What brought me to my appointed task was no act of my own will but of those others who for a while unveiled their world and assigned me my part. During the enacting of this, the central event in my life, I seemed to follow the form of an unfolding myth and to embody a meaning which as I lived it I both knew and did not know.

In describing, then, the fate that came, in its appointed time, to me (as it comes to all) I wish neither to expose nor to conceal anything, because mine. I have no right to call 'mine' one more story among the infinite number of stories woven by ever-various life. I wish only to bear witness, for the greater glory of the mystery whose curtain was withdrawn for a moment, so tenuously glimpsed and quickly lost. For I, who had for long periods lived my life in places which were not my place, and among people who were not my people, did come at last to what was my own. There must be some who have never known this happiness; for even if what is ours be some deep suffering or death itself, to miss what is ours is to miss all.

The external events have perhaps little to do with my story; this being the record of an inner experience as it reflected itself in the outer world; as if, for a time, that world itself were a living region of consciousness, like the landscape of dream. The other person who shared these events would have had another story to tell; did in fact tell another story. Yet at the time I thought our two lives part of a single whole greater than either. Was I then blinded to objective truth by self-delusion? Or am I, in now doubting the truth of my own experience, blinded by outer events to the inner and abiding reality?

Eden is rather a state than a place; yet it is a state that makes its own those places in which we have experienced the state. As a child at Bavington I had experienced that happiness of finding in all about me the reflected radiance of what I then still was—myself. At Martindale I had entered it again, as it seems, through the magic of natural love. Now for a third time I was to be allowed to return from exile; and again through love, though in a different mode, as if, at each return, some deeper insight had been given into a reality in itself ever the same.

It seems strange, now I consider it, that in all the years I had lived at Martindale, and even later, when I had stayed so often with Helen Sutherland at Cockley Moor, that I had never once thought of the possibility of going back to Bavington. Doubtless I was right—the distance of Bavington was not a distance of mere miles, but of years, or of something more than years. And yet people do revisit the places they have loved, and such returns have in themselves meaning. Doubtless for me the time had not yet come. I had become another person from that country child who had carried water from the village well and run barefoot about the high pastures. In part I had disinherited myself through estrangement from my family. 'Honour thy father and thy mother that thy days may be long in the land that the Lord thy God giveth thee'; these words had hung above my bed in the blue bedroom of the Manse; and with these words I had broken faith. I seldom saw Aunt Peggy herself, now living in retirement, in the south of England, with my mother's sister Jean. I had moved into another world from theirs; fulfilling too well my parents' ambition for me. In becoming 'educated' I had moved away from those simple things I had loved as a child. But then, they too had moved away, into the world of suburbia and its mass-produced trash, bargain sales in Oxford Street, into new convenient houses furnished from the cheaper department stores, discarding all that at Bavington had seemed so permanent and beautiful. The ground we had shared in common was, but for memory, no longer there. Not only education, but an entire reorientation of my life by ideas and experiences, by music, painting and poetry, by friendships, by a whole range of immeasurable values, had removed me from the simple society of my early Eden.

There were practical reasons too, of course, why I had not returned. I simply had not had the money for the journey, for one thing. There was the war, and people tended not to travel at that time. My children were young, and from Martindale, or from Cockley Moor, Penrith, our market town, seemed at the extreme of traversable distance. Psychologically this was so; and how much there is to be said for those contained worlds in which we at different times ensphere ourselves, lest we become dissolved in a landscape too ever-shifting to gather meaning. But it had been some more positive force which had kept me away, some sense that the gates were closed, that I was forbidden. That child I had been and the world she had inhabited had become for me mere regions of memory; I had not dared to admit to myself how wide the distances that now divided me from my old identity; from my true identity and the only place I had ever felt to be my real home. For me the Manse was still there, as it had been; I knew that to return to Bavington would be to discover that I could not return. Perhaps it was also a sense of guilt for all I had since done and become, or that had befallen me, that kept me away.

But at some time after the war—although the war had nothing to do with that change of inner disposition—I began to hope that I was on the way of return; that all was not lost, or that the lost might still be found again. I could but return as a stranger. Yet now it seemed to me as if, by visiting again those places, a rift might be healed, and I might recover something of that former self and state of being. With astonishment I realized how near, in mere physical distance, those Northumbrian moors were to Martindale, to Cockley Moor, to Lanercost (at the other end of Hadrian's Wall I had once known so well) where Winifred Nicholson lived in her father's house.

Long before I came to know her at Cockley Moor (where many of her paintings hung) I had known Winifred's north-country flowers against north-country skies of luminous grey cloud. How, I had wondered, could she have come to see flowers in that indescribable, especial way that I had known them as a child? Wild flowers I had not seen for years, and country garden-flowers, painted in that especial light—I did not so put it to myself then, but that light is the light of Paradise. I did not see the world as Ben Nicholson saw it; nor—although at Ben's suggestion she illustrated my first book of poems—as Barbara Hepworth saw it. My Cambridge-trained intellect, indeed, understood Barbara's hard crystals and solid geometry. Nor did I quite see nature aflame in the sacramental Christian vision as David Jones saw his Roland's Tree or his Welsh Madonna encircled with native thorns and native roses. A greater painter than Winifred, it may be; but my affinity of seeing was with her.

I was first introduced to her by Henry Moore, at an exhibition in which both had works; and thought her face as lovely as her paintings. When at Cockley Moor I met her again we became friends; and the beginning of my story—for this story has a beginning, a middle, and an end—was a visit to Winifred, then living at her father's manor-house, Boothby near Lanercost.

It was from Boothby that one August day with my two children (they older now than I had been as that former child), I set out to bicycle along the Roman wall. I remember that Winifred had talked to me of Goethe's theory of colour, about which she had been reading in some Anthroposophical book; and I remember how the subtle mauve of the Crane's-bill by the roadside was luminous on that day of our setting out to bicycle from the Banks to Wark; how the yellow of dandelion and mimulus seemed to pour towards us; how the perfect blue of the sky opened great distances. With enhanced senses I was re-entering the landscapes so long ago loved. All seemed to conspire to enhance and brighten that late summer scene into which we that day set forth.

The North Tyne at Wark was just as I had remembered that broad, shallow salmon-river moving with rippling grace over its stones; my grandfather's river, whence he had drawn those flower-fragrant little trout and shining salmon that were for me a memory even earlier than the Manse. But the distance from Wark to Bavington seemed to have shrunk to a few inconspicuous miles. The Manse, though now its trees were felled and its garden ruined and rank was, to my surprise, not smaller than I had remembered; though I did not enter the house. The Lady's Mantle still grew by the kirk wall, the sweet scent of camomile and cow-dung in the farmyard was just as it had been, and the cold, pure water still stirred the sand-grains in the stone well where I had filled my buckets all those years ago. Granny Carr's scarlet tropaeolum still entwined the great yew-tree in her garden; and her son George, as old now as she had been then, still grew, in that fertile earth, sweet-peas, carnations and his own tobacco-crop, all of a luxuriance whose secret died with him. The line of Simonside with its triple summit lay still on the horizon, as once on the periphery of the world; but now I came from beyond the periphery and the centre had become strange. The school was closed now and had become a youth-hostel; and it was there that George Carr, to whom I had written asking him to find us rooms, had put us to sleep; he was now the warden, as formerly his mother had been the school caretaker.

Strange it was to sleep in that room, my children and I on narrow camp-beds, where I had learned to write and figure on a squeaky slate, with a row of friendly faces beside me, lulled by the chanting of multiplication tables. The lattice of roses painted on the wall by my Aunty Peggy's predecessor was still there, and the iron stove and the smell of carbolic soap still lingered in the lobby. It was, I do not know why, one of the worst nights I have ever passed; though what that nightmare was I have not remembered; only a certain atmosphere heavy and oppressive as the spirit of the grave.

Next day I learned that almost every farm I had known was now occupied by the children who had been my school-fellows; all intermarried now, Waltons and Robsons and Thorntons and Scotts. I took my children to Clay Walls, where the younger sister of my old friend

Sally Walton was now married to a schoolfellow; and drying plates in the back-kitchen with her I felt a deep pang of nostalgia, realizing how much happier my own children might have been, had they been born into this or some other of those dignified stone farm-houses that stand so high on the open hills. I had wished for no happier future than to become a farmer's wife, like my schoolfellows; and with a pang I wondered if all my life had not been astray from those simple fields; but that had not, after all, been the land that God had given me.

Next day, in Wark, we supped with my old playfellow herself, now a farmer's wife, living in country abundance. She had remembered me: her daughter was called Kathleen. But when we left after that happy visit I felt ashamed that they had so welcomed me back. Their lives, I felt, had kept faith; and I was not even a prodigal, for I could never return. I felt myself an impostor, guilty of a deception, in pretending to be the Kathie they had known; as if I had been acting a part. Yet who was I? In imagination times and places and people abide for ever as they were; but the reality of this world is also inexorable.

It is hard to recover radical innocence, to be absolved of all we have become, to be as if we had never departed from the abiding ground and centre of the soul of which almost every act is a betrayal; but there are times when, despite all, it is as if lost Paradise might be the end, as it is the beginning, of our journey. For what I did not find at Bavington I found awaiting me on my return to London.

Æ wrote of that lost ground of the soul, 'Just as your will joins your two hands together for one purpose, so the one consciousness which pierces up and down through every plane of being brings you and another together. It is well to know the meaning of the mystic hours as they pass.' For, as the two hands are joined, I was brought together with another person, caught up, as it seemed, in the same swirl and eddy of immortal life.

Within a few days of my return to Paultons Square, Gavin came to my house for the first time. He was brought by Tambimuttu, who had, most characteristically, called some dozen or more times during my absence for the sole purpose of arranging this meeting. I had no great wish to meet the kind of person likely to be brought by Tambi, but then one never knew. Tambi's friends could be (not metaphorically but literally) princes or beggars, distinguished poets or drug addicts. Under persuasion I allowed him to bring Gavin Maxwell who wanted, so Tambi said, to paint my portrait. The idea was entirely Tambi's as it transpired; Gavin, it seems, had lost all his money and was also just recovering from a breakdown; and Tambi was being kind to him, encouraging him to write poems and to take up the career of portrait painting, which at that time seemed his best hope of recovering his fortunes. The thing was, Tambi said, to have an exhibition with paintings of famous people in it, as a kind of bait for custom; and in the warmth of his loyalty Tambi thought of Kathleen, his 'great poet': Gavin should paint her. So Gavin, perhaps as uninterested as I was myself in the meeting, was brought to my door. I took very little notice of him, or he of me; perhaps he was wondering, as I had been of him, what could be wrong with me that I should be a friend of that prince of bohemians. Yet my acquaintance with Tambi was, so to say, legitimate, since I was a poet and he my first publisher; but who was Gavin and how came he to know Tambi? His paintings, when I saw them, were extremely conventional. Yet Tambi was right in discerning, in Gavin, a vein of genius. Tambi's gift was for recognizing people of genius: the work followed.

I can still recall Gavin's appearance on that day, and my own impression of him. He was like some blind bird (perhaps the hawk his own name names), its restless energy a torment to itself for want of sight. It was as if those lids that cover the eyes of nestlings covered the eyes of his spirit. Why Tambi had brought him to me I could not imagine; yet he persisted. He made Gavin set up a camera and take my photograph; then he drove us out into my garden where, under the pear-tree I had inherited from Cooie Lane who had loved it before me, he stood Gavin and myself together, like a reluctant Adam and Eve, and photographed us so. Yet I think both Gavin and myself had quite made up our minds that there it should end. I dislike being photographed or painted, not so much because I dislike my own appearance but because the idea that I am visible at all disturbs me. I do not like to be seen. But then, as Gavin was about to leave, I chanced to say that I had just returned from Northumberland. It then emerged that my places of imagination were his also. It was his grandfather, the Duke of Northumberland, who owned those salmon-waters whence my grandfather had drawn those shining fish; the fir-plantation at Kielder whence had come the pheasant who once had looked at me with jewelled eye; the hill, the heather, the wild thyme, the lichen on the stone, all were his. Gavin was native of my paradise.

Those amongst whom I had lived my adult life had all been strangers to my childhood. They took me for someone who had never been that child. I had been able to survive in exile because I had retained an inviolate sanctuary of imaginative solitude beyond the reach of Cambridge and its destructive cleverness. A part of me had remained, remote and unassailable, in my own country; and by virtue of that inviolate interior world I had been a poet. All my poems that are of any value had come from that solitude. I had believed not only that no other person did share, but that no other person could share, that thrice-encircled place. I had neither the wish nor the expectation of meeting any other living soul who could enter my sanctuary. Now another had crossed the magic threshold; had, it seemed, been there from the beginning. I had met by miracle another person who came from my first world; and because he came from the places where Eden had been, it was as if he came from Eden itself.

Dismissing Tambi with aristocratic adroitness he arranged to meet me the same evening. Then and later we mingled memories. He showed me photographs of the child he had been; and I showed one to him of my infant self standing on the little bridge at Kielder from which he too had looked down into the same swirling burn. All the treasured lore which to my mother's family had made his half legendary, I offered as balm for those wounds and humiliations which had brought him, by ways so devious, to my door. But above all it was in nature, in the wild world above the frontiers of the human, where he and I alike, released from whatever in the human world we were or seemed or were compelled to be, had found our escape and our joy. Both of us in childhood had inhabited that unfallen world; and there the Duke's grandchild and the schoolmaster's met as one. I found in him what I had found in no other person, a knowledge which had always been mine: not a scientist's knowledge of nature (though he was a naturalist of some distinction) but a knowledge by participation, the knowledge nature has of itself; for both of us nature had been, and still was, a region of consciousness. 'We two were born upon the self-same hill'; and there is something in the very light, the taste of wet wind, clouds, moors sweet with heather or white under snow, that in him and me alike had wedded our imaginations to a certain kind of place, and to no other; as curlews will nest only on moors, gull and guillemot on rocky ledges by the sea.

But if his grandfather was of Northumberland Gavin himself was of the country beyond the border, the legendary land of my mother's people: Scotland. The house of his other grandfather (the naturalist Sir Herbert Maxwell), was Monreith, in Wigtownshire; north of the Solway. Why, in the company of Englishmen, had I never felt at ease or among my own? Gavin belonged to my own people in the country lost before I was born. If it was in reality my mother who had secretly implanted in me her own nostalgia, her longing to return to her own country, God knows I experienced that longing as my own.

Was it that very day, or a few days later, that I was standing in my bedroom late at night before going to bed; and I could see, for that time, into two worlds, as if, waking, one were at the same time to explore a dream. But the quality was different from that of all but a few dreams. As I had once held my breath to see the flow of immortal life in a hyacinth, so

The Tree and its Fruit

did I to see the Tree, though it stood in inner space, not in nature. May-tree or Rowan, it bore its clusters of white flowers. In it was a blackbird and at the foot the sleeping figure of a young boy of about twelve years old. The tree was on the summit of a hill, and I was aware of the flow of waters into its roots, gathered from the darkness and cold storms I knew to be raging below. The tree itself, the laden branches, the singing of the bird and the flow of life from chaos and cold to form and flower and fruit was all, I knew, taking place in the mind of the sleeper; all was his thought, his dream raising the tree and its flowers continually into being. I saw neither serpent nor wall round the garden; my tree stood wild and free, uncircumscribed and without any symbol of evil.

What do such visions mean? No explanation could ever 'mean' as much as the experience itself; for such visions are intellections, a mode of knowledge. It seemed an anamnesis of the soul's native place, the immortal world, the reality within and beyond appearances; the same that I had seen in the hyacinth. That is what it seemed to be; a reality glimpsed and lost again when normal consciousness closed in upon me. What I saw did not seem strange, but so deeply familiar that the outer world seems strange in comparison; something at once seen and understood, as a complex yet single thought; that, and the supernatural beauty; for nothing in that world is a mere thing, or object, but sacred; being life itself. I had been taken to the very place I had set out to find when with my children I had returned to Bavington, but had not found there.

Because these things had come to me unsought—the vision of the Tree, the meeting with Gavin like a messenger from home—I thought them Heaven-sent. It was as if the outer event, the meeting with Gavin, belonged to the same order of reality as the vision itself, outer and inner worlds miraculously coinciding. It seemed as if I had, unawares, discovered some lost secret and passed from the unreal into the real. Because Gavin had come from that world I thought that it must be for the purposes of that world that we had met. I never doubted that our meeting was for his good and mine. I had not been looking for a lover—indeed my life at that time was calm and industrious enough—nor indeed was Gavin ever to be my lover. What was between us was something else altogether, though I loved him as much as, being what I am, I am able to use so great a word. The experience had rather, as it seemed, to do with poetry than with any personal fulfilment.

A few days after that first meeting we met at lunch, with Tambi and possibly other people present. I happened to raise my eyes and saw that Gavin was looking at me. The eyes which had formerly seemed closed were now open; and he held mine in a long look, as if testing me; and I saw who he was. In this century it must seem strange to speak of the mystery of

271

the eyes, from which, in former times, it was said that the soul looks out. Dante speaks of beholding, in the eyes of Beatrice, the reflection of the mystery of the two natures of the Divine Humanity; and is not this still the mystery to be read in human eyes? The living light of the eyes is that of the soul's country, not the body's. I tend to avoid looking into people's eyes, or allowing them to look into mine; for those who look into my eyes, so I feel, can see me; and I seldom wish to be seen; but by Gavin I wished to be seen and known.

He told me, early in our acquaintance, that he could not love me with erotic desire, and why; yet in the very telling it seemed to me there was love. He was, he explained to me, homosexual. This did not seem to me to matter, for I understood that I was nevertheless necessary to him; 'Every man needs a woman in his life,' he said; and I thought I was that woman for him. And I, having found the one being in the world who seemed to be of my own lonely species thought that at last all sorrow was over, that I had come at last to that for which I had been born. I too was un-marriageable, though for different reasons, as I had learned to my cost. The poet in me could never marry. Now it seemed that miracle—the operation of some order other than that of this world—had brought together two people who, neither fitting the conventional, or indeed the natural pattern, were perfectly and providentially fitted to one another.

Both pride and the fear of being hurt once more would have made it impossible for me to seek acquaintance with any man; or indeed with anyone at all—I never, in friendship, made the first advance. But it was he who sought me out, he who seemed to need me; for at that time I was strong, he weak; I was happy, he wretched; my life had at last achieved some sort of stability, his was in ruins. Gavin had come to London with the idea of making a career for himself as a painter of portraits after losing all his patrimony on his shark-fishing venture on the Isle of Soay, the little low isle that lies to the south of Skye under the Cuillin. At the same time he had suffered a personal unhappiness. Soon he had told me all the story. My defences were disarmed: I thought I could help him. (And that thought was not all generosity; there was in it both pride and timidity.)

Had Gavin wished to be my lover I would have been happy; but what drew me to him was nothing bodily, but rather the radiance his presence had for me always. He was for me what Gay Taylor used to call 'the man of light' ; seeing him, as I did, with the eyes of my spirit rather than with my bodily eyes. He seemed, besides, a part of myself, as if the 'one consciousness' lived us both. If I were to describe him, as I can describe friends less near, it would not be from that place from which I knew him. I could, of course, do so; but that would be his outward personality. An Indian friend once pointed out to me that in the *Ramayana*, Sita,

questioned about her husband, was silent; from which the querent de-
duced their relationship: he was too near to be described. And for some
such reason, even though I could describe Gavin, I may not do so without
violation of some sacred reticence.

All seemed a miracle, unsought, undeserved, and I vowed deeply to the
world that had drawn aside the veil to keep faith with what I had seen and
known. Seeing his need, I who had at that time strength and no sorrow
offered myself to that world, to take upon myself Gavin's suffering as the
price of his release from it. I was sincere, though I had no idea of the
burden I then took voluntarily upon myself; but had I done so it would
have made no difference, for I knew the task for mine. It is, besides, easy
to make light of pain we have not yet felt.

After my return from Northumberland and my epiphany of the Tree I
felt that I must above all write poems. For a long time I had written none;
but I believed that the 'other' mind, in unveiling a portion of its mystery,
had summoned me to my task. Other and better poets than I—Coleridge in
Kubla Khan, Keats in the *Hyperion* fragments—tell of the awakening of
imaginative recollection, the true poetic initiation, which is the soul's
remembering not of its mortal but of its immortal history; not of individual
knowledge but of the one consciousness, the Platonic anamnesis. Plunged,
therefore, into those living currents and eddies, I thought that I too had
been made an initiate, then, of the immortal world of the imagination, once
and for ever; I thought those doors would stand ever open for me to come
and go at will. I thought that I would live for ever under the branches of
that Tree. Such insights that unite, in Yeats' words, 'for certain moments
the sleeping and the waking mind' are not attained, but given; it was for me
to receive. I thought, then, that I had reached at last the threshold, that here
my task began.

As soon as my children had gone back to school, I went to Helen
Sutherland to write the poems I now felt I must write—the first, as I
believed and hoped, of many more to come from that inexhaustible
source.

It was in the same white room at Cockley Moor, looking over to High
Street, with one small field of Martindale visible among the folds of the
fells; the room where I have written so many poems, the room where I
wrote the poems I called *Northumbrian Sequence*, that I returned to
write, when all was over, this record. I looked back, now, over all that was
still to come, over seven years and more, 'beginning, middle and end,'
those three phases of all completed events. It was another Greek who said
'beginnings are better than endings', but that again is only as it appears to
us: to the divine agents who know the end before the beginning, who
create beginnings for the sake of ends unguessed, it may be otherwise.

I had at this time known Gavin only for two, or at most three, weeks. I had not told him of the Tree, still less of the poems I intended to write; I did not myself know what form they would take. We had indeed spoken of our childhood, his and mine, those worlds so strangely interwoven; of how my mother, in the Kielder kirk, had sat behind his mother, admiring her coils of shining hair; and of the uncle who had died so young, in whose room the birds flew free; and of many things we both had seen and known, though not together. He had restored to me that which in revisiting Bavington I had looked for but not found; and I had perhaps done the like for him, reminding him of a time before his own entangled troubles. While I was in Cumberland, writing my poems, he was visiting friends in the country elsewhere; and he too wrote a poem. We met, after our return to London, and I showed him my *Northumbrian Sequence*; and he then said, 'everyone will think I copied my poem from yours', and showed me what he had written. Neither in metre nor in language did his poem resemble mine, but every image, and the sequence of the images, was the same as in the fifth poem in my own sequence; for he too had described the Tree, as I had also seen it.

Had we evoked, each in the other, the archetype of Eden because the bond between us was the world of childhood? Yet how explain the identity of the images, even when these departed from tradition? How explain why each had chosen a rowan-tree drawing its waters from a dark river, and bearing fruit which was eaten by a bird, whose song then rose from the tree as its highest transformation? Neither Gavin's tree nor mine grew in a walled garden, and in neither was there a serpent, nor any other emblem of evil. The only difference was that in his tree there was no sleeper at the foot, and his bird was not a blackbird but an ousel. As a naturalist he had thought of a bird he knew to haunt the rowan; while my blackbird was perhaps literary, being Merlin; for the vision seemed above all to concern poetry, the oracular bird-voice.

Were the two poems the result of telepathy—'only' telepathy? That would be mysterious enough; but I do not believe this to be so. That place we saw was not of my making, nor of his, as dreams are of our weaving, but one of the archetypal objects of visionary knowledge. How else explain the unvarying character of the elements of that vision, which many have seen, described and painted, differing in this aspect or in that, but in essence always the same? The vision was, besides, so seemingly impersonal, without any bearing on our own concerns, its elements not stitched together, as in ordinary dreams, from daily odds and ends. I thought we had been greatly blessed in meeting on that holy ground, by the Tree of Life.

That either of us should break faith with the mystery which we had shared seemed to me inconceivable; I imagined that we should remain, to the end of our lives, as we were then; and perhaps we should have done so. But one part of the Eden myth I forgot to apply either to Gavin or to myself—the Fall; so inconceivable did it seem that any who had seen the eternal beauty could betray it.

I made a vow that this time I would do nothing wrong, nothing not in obedience to the senders of that vision. I wanted only to give, to pour out upon Gavin the help and consolation for which he at that time turned to me. He once said to me, in those days, 'It is as if a goddess had turned her head and looked at me'; but if there was in my sense of a boundless power of inspiration at that time an element of spiritual pride I was not aware of it, for all seemed to be given from that other kingdom. If I felt in myself goddess-strength, I knew myself to be only instrumental. At that time indeed I seemed to possess a magical power to help Gavin. It was my custom to write small prayers upon slips of paper and place these behind the ear of an Indo-Chinese Buddha; and so many strange and beautiful small miracles seemed at that time to happen that I came to imagine, as I think he did also, that I had a magical power to help him. I seemed to be living rather in that world than in this; and perhaps for a while I really had found unawares some magical secret. Yet in retrospect I see that my belief that I was the giver was all illusion: it was I who through Gavin received riches untold.

As for the painting, that was soon abandoned; I told Gavin that he wrote better than he painted. He talked of Soay and the romance of his disastrous shark-fishery venture, and I said he should write the story. This he did, reading me each section as it was written. He would telephone me at any hour of the day and I would obediently and gladly go, listen, praise, criticize. I was still, for him, sufficiently Tambi's 'great poet' for my encouragement to seem worth having. When as a writer he rose to fame I still saw him as that younger brother, for whose success I was glad; but I always knew myself to be stronger than he, and possessed of greater knowledge and power. I knew, therefore, that the responsibility of our relationship lay principally, if not altogether, with me.

Such was my sense of kinship with him that I sometimes half imagined that we had been in some former life brother and sister, or in some other such close bond of kinship; I never imagined us as having been lovers, much less as married. He told me that in my pride especially I did remind him of his own family. Gavin, at all events, understood that it was pride that had kept me from coming to terms with the world; that it was more fitting to pride to wear shabby clothes and to wonder often enough how the milkman was to be paid than to sell that pride for money to the British Council (for which I had worked for a time) or the like. To Gavin I did not need to explain such things, which for him were self-evident; for he saw, in that respect, who I was. Being himself an aristocrat what others have called my 'arrogance' did not irk him; he felt no reproach in the pride of others.

It is well to know the meaning of the mystic hours; well indeed; but how are mortals to know the meaning of immortal life? When we are awakened to those unguessed depths in ourselves where, it is said, un-fallen man in Eden walked in the divine presence, we are in a world of purposes other than our own; other, at all events, than those of our once-born selves. Supposing it were to be said that so to meet by the Tree of Life is to fall in love, what is love, into which we fall—or rise? Some say that love is always a disguised self-interest; others, that 'God is love'; I do not know which mine was. It was, in either case, the heart of life. What has such love to do with the crude animal instinct by which the species is continued? The soul has other ends, another nature. As an animal, indeed, man is most detestable; yet the real object of Freudianism, behaviourism and the like, is a regression to the animal from which mankind has from the beginning of our humanity struggled to rise. Yet is it not our 'nature' to attempt the supernatural? Whether the *Divina Commedia* be an insight into reality, or a creation of it, such are the realities which belong to man, as man. Alexander the Great who was Aristotle's pupil is said to have said that man was never less human than in the act of sex; and the young world-conqueror returned from India bringing with him a new *guru*, a Brahman forest-dweller, who remained with him until his death; the Rishi is always the last teacher. The human animal may afterwards choose Plato and Plotinus for friend; but the direction of our growth is irreversible; for those who have glimpsed another order, there is scarcely even a question of 'renouncing' carnality: we are drawn by our strongest love, to the most desirable. I, who in my youth was caught up in erotic passion and would have sacrificed all else to it, now thought carnal desire a small thing to forgo for the sake of a deeper love. It seemed to me that to have stood with another soul before that Tree must constitute a sacred bond. Marriage, lacking that dimension, had not seemed to me a binding relationship; but this, rooted in paradisal ground, seemed to me eternally binding; and yet not so much to one another as each of us to that mystery on whose surface individual lives form and vanish. There are those who have travelled farther than I to whom it will be clear that what I took for the end was only the beginning of the journey the soul must take; but I tremble still at the austerities of those for whom all personal ties are renounced; as some (being still as I was in the years of sexual passion) may tremble at the thought of the renunciation of the mere flesh. But I can tell only my own story. By some happy chance we had eluded ourselves, and we were there.

The Tree and its Fruit

The country through the looking-glass is entered, as everybody knows, by walking the other way. But to walk the other way is less easy than it sounds, for who has ever not desired to taste the heavenly fruit with earthly lips? Long ago at Bavington I remember having read, Heaven knows where, a story that must have been written by some theosophist. It told of two people, a man and a woman, who met in dreams. Each set out over the world to find the other and at last they met, married—and lost the vision. Sorrowing they went in search of an Indian sage who said to them 'You were given the seed of the greatest of all trees, but you exchanged it for earthly happiness: you have not been wise.' When I was a child (a colour print of Rossetti's painting of Dante and Beatrice hung in the drawing-room) I used to think 'poor Dante, how sad it was that he could never marry Beatrice whom he loved,' not understanding that he was permitted to meet her in the only country where such lovers can meet. For the life of the soul, its native country is as Boehme says, 'in another principle'; and to enter that principle, and still more to remain in it, is hard. So it was, fallen creatures as we were, that 'we had the experience but missed the meaning'.

For I forgot that it is only as poet that the poet can enter Eden, forgot that the once-born betrays the twice-born, that the mortal self must weep outside the locked gates with the rest of fallen humanity. Coleridge must live on with his sick body and broken heart; Keats, to whom Moneta brought the lyre of Apollo, must die, pining for Fanny Brawne. In Plato's Garden of the Muses, the poets, 'winged, light and volatile' draw honey and milk from divine fountains 'which they cannot do when in their sober minds'. Blake wrote that 'If the Spectator could enter into these Images in his Imagination, approaching them on the Fiery Chariot of his Contemplative Thought...or could make a friend and Companion of one of these Images of wonder, which always intreats him to leave mortal things (as he must know), then he would arise from his Grave, then would he meet the Lord in the Air, and then he would be happy.' Blake's 'as he must know' is not unjustified, since such insights bring their own knowledge with them, tell of their own nature; yet he too knew that 'while we are in the world of mortality, we must suffer'. We are not in Paradise because we have seen one 'image of wonder'. And yet, merely to know that world exists is a happiness so great that the mere knowledge outweighs any possible suffering: and, as another said, 'Life is suffering'.

The once-born have sufferings of their own, because of the inevitable distance between any wish and its fulfilment; yet wish and fulfilment exist within realizable terms: as, when we are hungry, a meal is a possibility, even to the starving. If we starve it is not because this world offers no possible satisfaction for our hunger; and the right conduct of the world of the once-born (the political virtues) consists, precisely, of making bread available to the hungry, shelter to the houseless. But the bread and the wine that feed the body, in whatever abundance we may possess them, cannot satisfy the soul; though positivists believe that this is so. For those who have once seen the world beyond, or within, the world (which is, for humanity, that place or state towards which we are impelled to travel, with an urgency no less than that which, according to the Darwinian mythology, drove amphibians from water to land) there are awakened desires which this world cannot fulfil. Therefore, some starve in the midst of plenty, and some enjoy plenty in the midst of poverty.

Yet suffering was never farther from my thoughts. I wrote many poems and thought to write many more; for I seemed then to stand upon some marvellous threshold. Sorrow seemed something for every past; for who, having once glimpsed the beauty of the world behind the world could ever lose the joy of that knowledge; as such, and irrespective of what might happen to one's self?

Gay Taylor compared Gavin's horoscope with mine and was less confident; certainly there was a bond, but it might prove rather of sorrow than of joy; for the sun of my natal map was in the same degree as Gavin's Saturn; and though I might pour solar beams into his shadow, his shadow obscured my sun. But I did not care, so long as I was to be light to his darkness. I felt then that I had riches inexhaustible to bestow and strength to carry that shadowy burden. As for the possible effects of dark Pluto who, in my natal map, is in conjunction with my sun, little was known, Gay said, about Pluto: she could not tell. I would not have believed that the lonely wanderer in outer darkness could encompass the loss of Paradise both to Gavin and to myself. I had not read the myths attentively enough, or, like Plato's souls when they chose 'patterns of lives', looked into the fate I chose with the caution of Odysseus; but it is too late when fate is already chosen; and that, Plato says, is before we are born.

Meanwhile it seemed that my meeting with Gavin had healed every old wound and made of my fragmented life a whole. My long flight had brought me back at last to all I had ever loved, to the roots from which I had been torn away. The reality of my life, first and last, was my ancestral inheritance: seemingly meagre, it proved now to be richer than I had known. End had met beginning, yet the full circle of return raised past and present onto another plane. For now I had been given back, as an evolved person, what I had as a child lived in country simplicity. Now even the long wanderings seemed to have been not without purpose; the country child, the student of biology, the poet, all in my life that had belonged to what in truth I am, had been restored like a lost kingdom.

Not only the fields of childhood did we seem to share; Gavin was a naturalist, and had taken a way I had once dreamed of following. For him, as for me, such knowledge of nature was less a branch of learning than an experience of imagination. Certain saints have been able to speak to the creatures in their own language, communicating with the one life which is in them as it is in us; St. Francis' birds, or St. Cuthbert's seals. This secret knowledge of nature was Gavin's gift, as poetry was mine; his grey-lag geese, his springer spaniel, Johnnie. As my poetry stemmed from a vision of nature, so was his participation in nature a kind of poetry. He, too, had been brought up on the English poets, and most of Palgrave's *Golden Treasury* he seemed to know by heart.

Martindale too seemed given back; for that also had belonged to the country of imagination which we shared; the same wilderness, the same birds and flowers and brown water flowing over stones under alder and birch, speaking everywhere and always the same language. I was glad, now, that Alastair had never entered that valley, for now that virgin country too I brought to Gavin, bestowing on him all the lands of my imagination. It had been the ancestral voices, then, whose clamour had so summoned me, reminded me, filled me with such overwhelming longing for my own place; but if Alastair was moulded of ancestral clay, Gavin was the spirit of my lost inheritance.

I now understood that there is a fidelity far different from any kind imposed from without, even by the strongest act of resolution. In love it is as if the timeless soul knows all its past and future and what it is. In the light of that knowledge we do not need to promise fidelity, for it is given; we are ourselves the given, not the givers. Because the experience of the Tree, of the shared vision of paradise, had seemed mutual, I thought that Gavin, as well as I, was thus committed. Had Gavin wished to be my lover, I would not have refused; I would not have refused him anything love could ask or give. But since this was not asked I was even glad to make to love the sacrifice of sexual desire; only to love, indeed, can such a sacrifice have any meaning; and this too seemed fitting, and to belong to my fate, as a poet. I was glad, even, to be free of physical involvement, to be among those lovers *che sono gentili, e non sono pure femmine*.

But to every love there are limits; yet since the limit set to mine seemed in no way to conflict with what Gavin asked of me, or with those areas of our lives which we had in common, he never, I think, discerned that limit in me: I would not have married Gavin; for this would have compromised the daimon. I would not, in any case, now, have married anyone; and I thought myself greatly blessed in having been sent, as it seemed by that divine providence that cares for the needs of all, a relationship which was of the only kind of which I was capable. Gavin, too, I believed, had been no less fortunate in finding a woman who, in loving him, was willing to forgo sexual love. Therefore our relationship seemed to me honourable according to the values both of this world and the other. But if I knew what my reservation was, I held it not as a criticism of Gavin but as one more reason for gratitude to the 'one consciousness' who had sent to two unusual people what was exactly according to the need and capacity of each. We had each, besides, our pride of caste: he as an aristocrat, I as a poet; and this, far from impairing our harmony, was an element in it.

For such love there is, besides, none of those pains of separation from which the body suffers; for wherever Gavin might be, or I might be, we were (as it seemed) present to one another. (It is strange that of this aspect of love so little has been written; *Voss*, by Patrick White, is the only novel known to me which makes a love of this kind central.) I had ceased to be alone; for absence was no interruption of the sense of continuous relationship; his thoughts turned towards me as mine to him; we were at all times attuned; or so I thought; for what ground for jealousy could there be in a relationship grounded in reality itself? To be unfaithful in that world is to be unfaithful to that world; and therefore to what we in our essence are.

I was no more blind to Gavin's faults than I was impressed by his skills and talents. Gavin, touchingly humble, perhaps did not understand this. I remember his saying, on one occasion, that he would lose his good looks with age; and on another seeming to think that I valued him for his talents. Heaven knows, on a simple level of companionship to be with him was always a delight. However I might harbour some mistrust or resentment when Gavin was not there, all melted in the joy of being in his company. He was, above all, the best person in the world to laugh with at the happy comedy of life, as two people can who share the little daily things of which relationships are made. How different it had been with Alastair, whom I only imagined I loved when he was *not* there. But no mortal best or worst can be commensurable with what love sees; at best the outer personality can be irradiated by, at worst cut off from, the essence which, in its very nature, we love. The former can cause happiness, the latter pain, or, at worst, grief to the lover; but it cannot in any way disillusion a love that is not in its nature an illusion, but a truer insight. To call love blind is to reverse the truth: which is that only love has insight into another person's essential being. Love is in any case no less a task than a privilege; the task is implicit in the love. It is no one's duty *to* love for no one can at will evoke that mystery; but love is its own duty.

Above all, through Gavin, I could at last make peace with my parents. The long flight from them, the struggle to escape, the sense of being continually dragged back and down into Ilford, had never ceased; there had been times of respite, but always it was there, every new wound reopening the old. In order to survive I had hardened my heart against them. My father I had fought on equal terms, indeed, mind with mind. My mother's weapons had been those of love; her tears had pursued me, the devouring longing she had for me to love her, to be her daughter, to take her into my life. I had fought her off with weapons more deadly than those I had used against my father, hating and fearing her terrible suffering sorrowful unsatisfied love. To have my parents in my life was, defenceless as I had been, more than I could have carried and survived. My father's moral disapproval, however justified, had at all times been at cross-purposes with the deepest springs of my own life; and I could never have satisfied my mother's hunger for all she had been denied—she would have dragged me under with her, like a drowning swimmer. Or so I thought; all who are unhappy must in some measure shrink from their parents' intrusion into the regions of sorrow; and I had never forgiven mine for (as it had seemed to me for so long that the thought had become habitual and all but unalterable), laying a ban on my womanhood, forbidding me to love. Of a Platonic love, my father could not disapprove; and now, my heart being healed, I could forgive them; and also I felt that at last I had gained the victory on behalf of the caged winged spirit which had inhabited my mother and me. The roots of my love for Gavin seemed to go back beyond myself, as if I were enacting a fate laid upon me by my mother, and perhaps by even earlier ancestors, from time immemorial. I understood my mother, now; understood that it was she who had made me a poet, that I was the custodian of all her unenacted possibilities. I understood that her tears and grief from which I had shrunk from my earliest childhood were the measure of those unrealized energies of love and of imagination. I knew that in loving Gavin I loved as she would have wished; even as she might herself once have woven round one or another of those young golden lords whom she had seen so near at hand but yet as far above her as if they had belonged to the race of the gods, her dreams. Even if she had had no such dream, yet it is true that the cement of the feudal world was the people's being as it were in love with the bright illustrious ones whose physical beauty and whose deeds were adorned with poetry. I could see my mother, again, as in her radical nature she was; a hawk with wild bird's eyes, and a wild bird's clipped wings. Gavin himself saw in my mother what I saw; saw the hawk-soul; for he too was one of that winged race. He brought to tea his own mother of the shining coils, and the two old ladies compared memories.

As to all my life between, it fell away from me as if it had never been, or had been a long dream from which I had now awakened. I felt myself absolved of my life, and perhaps was so. I had indeed through weakness or through blind flight injured both myself and others, involved my external life in many falsities; but I had kept faith with some central truth.

For that priceless thing I had torn down my life again and again and been like a sword to all who had come near me. I felt myself absolved because how could a vision of the eternal beauty be given, if not by that world itself? Such things cannot be stolen. The only truth of my life had been the truth of my poetry to the living imagination; and Gavin as it seemed, had come to me as by a miraculous act of the daimons themselves, unsought, not even wished for. How natural, how inevitable does supreme happiness seem, how utterly do we forget all else as if it had never been; whereas sorrow, however long it may continue and with whatever fortitude it may be borne (and I have never lacked fortitude) seems always alien. Never this, the soul cries, not for this was I born. But every joy seems a homecoming, a return to what forever is.

I knew, of course, that Gavin was less committed than I to the inner ground of imagination. We all, insofar as we live in both worlds, are at times more aware of the one or the other, so that the one or the other seems for the time more real. Gavin, I realized, was often intent upon the ends of this world, and was at such times even prepared to use the riches of the other world as a means to trivial ends; a reversal of the due order of values. He had found somewhere a book, made by some Victorian botanist, of red and green seaweeds, beautifully pressed and mounted; each species—some of them rare—identified in a fine old learned script; such a book as I as a botanist would once have wished to make; it had about it the quality which for me belonged to the manuscript books in which my poems are written. It was a book of great imaginative quality, the lovely delicate algae patterns themselves as eloquent as poems. Yet when his first book was about to appear, Gavin ripped the sea-weeds from their pages to make a window-display in a book-shop. I felt as if I had myself been ripped and torn, as if I were those fine learned beautiful pages sacrificed to a hand-to-mouth end, in ignorance. Clearly enough the daimon warned me that I too might be made the means to some trivial end; warned me that the sin, in that case, would be mine no less than this for allowing this to happen; more, indeed, since I had the knowledge he lacked. Yet I believed that because our bond was in the ground of Paradise that never, never could Gavin behave so to me. I believed also that because the world we had seen is more real than this world of shadows, that it must also prevail.

(Now, in 1976, I am revising this record, written fifteen years ago; more than twenty years after the story I am telling. And I can now see many things differently. Love—love, yes, I 'loved' Gavin with my whole soul, but what of that soul? For I recall—why did I not record this when in so white-hot a passion of grief I wrote my story—that Gavin too was warned. He was sitting with me in my room at 9 Paultons Square, that pleasant room with books and a fire in the hearth and a pear-tree outside the window, inherited from Cooie Lane—and there must have been some jar between us; for I remember that over Gavin's face came a cloud of dismay and he said, 'A *spider*, Kathleen!'—a great spider had crawled out from under my chair. A spider, the female devourer.)

As the one consciousness brings about the meeting of persons, so it changes the landscape of our lives in correspondence with interior states; and it was to Gavin that I owed my last return to the earthly paradise.

Gavin, from the wreck of his fortunes, had kept one thing: a small, shepherd's house, on a friend's estate on a wild coast of the Western Highlands; and beyond the house, a group of little islets on the largest of which was a lighthouse.

> . . . an island salt and bare,
> The haunt of orcs and seales and sea-mew's clang.

Into such an isle, so Milton tells, the mount of Paradise was changed when the man and the woman were driven away. Doubtless to Milton, whose own paradise was that Italy he had visited as a young man, such isles must have seemed, as Thule to the Romans, the fittest symbol of uttermost exile. But he wrote more truly than he knew; for the orcs and seals and sea-mews on those salt bare isles live on in the inviolate places. The fine intangible essence of that lost country is in the very air, more sweetly fragrant with the scent of sea-weed, bog myrtle and birch leaves than Milton's

> Groves whose rich trees wept odorous gums and balm.

It is even said by those who live in the Western Isles—and this Milton can scarcely have known—that the Gaelic speech was the language of Eden. Nor could he have known how thin the veil which there divides the visible from the radiant 'other' land whose image is mirrored on those silver seas. The very light is like a quality of the imagination—the same imagination that sings in those ancient pentatonic and hexatonic melodies that seem the pure utterance of the one mind which casts the light on the sea and raises the hills like visions.

Here was the country 'over the border', the boundless country of mountain and sea and isles of which Northumberland and the distant Cheviots had been only a fore-shadowing, a dignity of nature as vast as pride, with yet such tenderness of sheltered glen, of birch and mossy stone, and everywhere the freedom of waters flowing, the freedom of the lives of the wild birds and wild creatures in their sanctuaries. My mother's country, though she had never herself known it.

Is there a spiritual geography, are there certain places upon the earth which are more, or less, attuned to certain modes of consciousness? And if so, do such qualities belong to the earth itself, to certain qualities of light, or sound, or scent, or rock formation? Is there a natural magic, and elemental spirits who inhabit certain places, or kinds of place? Or do people of a certain cast of mind impart to the land their own qualities? It seems not to be true, as Wordsworth sometimes seems to imply, that 'nature' can impart a culture; and the people of Cumberland and Northumberland (whatever they were in the Border Ballad days) are prosaic enough. Hardy's people had a sense of history, yet only Hardy has made poetry of their lives. But in the Highlands I found people who possessed a culture; a culture not only deeper than that of the Northumbrians of my childhood, but also than positivist Cambridge. Oral tradition still transmitted, not merely the history of the race and its memories, but certain ancient attitudes and values lost to the technological present. I was already at this time, though still blindly, seeking for the lost thread of another tradition altogether than the materialist civilization dominant in England; dominant no less in poetry and the arts (as I had discovered to my cost in Cambridge) than in science and technology. My friend Herbert Read continued to believe that its arts can save that civilization; but I had come to see in its arts only another symptom of the spiritual disease of which it is dying.

It was in the June following my meeting with Gavin that Winifred Nicholson and I went for the first time to Eigg; she to paint, I to write. 'You can see the flash of my lighthouse from the *sgur*,' Gavin had said; and for me, Eigg was above all an isle from which I could see the flash of his light. But that is the character of the Isles where summit and skerry are seamarks known to every boatman and shepherd, and the unchanging scene into which life is woven through the generations, from isle to isle, and so is likely to be so long as the mountains of Rhum and Canna's Compass Hill stand against the winds and the seas. Indeed are not all Scots bound into nationhood by a landscape of isles and mountains known to all? And were we not all once so bound to the earth itself, for countless generations before we were driven into the exile of the modern urban scene, ever-shifting and impermanent, where all sense of continuity of the generations is lost? 'I don't know how humanity stands it,' as Ezra Pound said.

On midsummer eve, I remember, we climbed the hill for the first time to the point where the road looks down to Cleadale, the crofters' village facing to the west. The long evening light was magical; Winifred painted a picture of Rhum, which I was not able to see until the paint had dried and the multitudes of adhering midges could be brushed off. From below we heard two girls singing as they gathered up their washing from the machair. Those lovely voices heard in the absence of all mechanical noise, where only the cries of sheep and birds and the sound of the sea accompanied their singing is something not to be heard any more; for the televison sets have reached the outermost isles, and the sounds there now are what they are elsewhere. I did not know then that I was hearing for almost the last time something so simple and so familiar to mankind from the beginning. But it was not so much the past that we seemed there to enter, but the permanent, the enduring norm, the familiar.

We had taken rooms in the somewhat bleak manse; but we were lent an empty house at Kildonan, site of an early monastic settlement. Each day, Winifred painted in one room, while I wrote in the other. Happy, productive days. But whereas for Winifred, whose roots are so deep in the past of Cumberland, it was an adventure into a beautiful strange land, for me it was like a recovery of a lost identity, a re-grafting to an old root, though already long severed when I was born. For our tea we boiled water drawn from the near-by spring on just such a kitchen range as I had known at Bavington. Of course I was not really returning home; it was only as if; yet Gavin's lighthouse flashing its message made it seem so.

On Eigg that summer, and later on the mainland and on other Isles, I came to know people whose simplicity of life was permeated with an essential quality of which poetry is the natural speech; Homer might have sung in those kitchens by turf fires, with shepherds' dogs under the table and the wooden chairs drawn back round the walls. On Eigg there was a bard—Hugh MacKinnon—who composed his verses stretched at length on the kitchen bench, a cap over his eyes; a tradition handed down from the Bardic schools where the *fili* composed their verses lying on their beds and in darkness. In such company I found myself not, as in England, too much a poet, but not poet enough, for I could neither sing nor recite, as all did here, their learning all stored in their memory. I had been away too long by several generations, although indeed in my grandmother's kitchen people had sung—all my mother's sisters had sweet voices and memories stored with the songs of the Lowlands. In the house of Hugh MacKinnon I heard stories of things done and suffered by men and women whose houses now were just green mounds. For the bard is the guardian of memories, and the maker of stories that still brought grief and joy and laughter to the descendants of those vanished ancestors. There were stories, too, that included the inner, the supernatural event; I first met the 'Celtic twilight' not through books but at the source itself; a privilege the more treasured as it was unsought.

If I had not my own story to tell—sadly modern, an outsider's story—I could retell, though with less artistry than he, many of Hugh MacKinnon's stories of people and events of that borderland between memory and history that the imagination of Highland people still inhabits; the borderland, also, between inner and outer worlds. But the telling of such stories is not my purpose, except insofar as they contribute, in some degree, to the picture I have been trying to compose of what a life is, and what a world. I will tell only one, for the story moved me deeply at the time, and seemed to belong, at the time and still more later, to the mystery into which I had entered, to find myself in the deep waters where thoughts are realities.

The story was a recent one, as most stories of the super-natural are; there is no need to go back into the past to find such things, which are common, if not everyday occurrences in the Celtic Twilight. Some cattlemen had been sitting in a bar in Oban, and up to one of the men—who belonged to a certain sept, I think of the Macdonalds—came a grey bitch and stood at his knee. Several men saw the dog; and the man to whom it had come said, 'That is a sign of my death.' He showed no sign of illness at the time, but within a week he was dead. The young priest (now well known and respected from Fort William to Barra and Eriskay) who administered the last rites bore witness to the truth of the story. For it was well known that the grey bitch appears before the death of members of that sept, sometimes to the person about to die, sometimes to a relation. I was told that another man had seen the dog on his doorstep when a brother had died, without his knowledge, in another country; as others will see a white bird, or the death-coach. Thought-forms no doubt; but what is a thought-form?

The story the bard of the Isle of Eigg told of the origin of the grey dog may be a later rationalization of some more ancient belief. It tells of a young Macdonald who went away, like so many impoverished lairds of the seventeenth and eighteenth centuries, to fight as a mercenary in the army of (probably) Gustavus Adolphus. The young man had a grey bitch to whom he was deeply attached; and after his departure the dog grieved and at last left the house altogether. (Here I will add that I have often noticed that dogs, in Highland conversation are treated as persons, their deeds and characters discussed as on a par with human beings; cats are not 'people' in this sense.) After some years the master returned, and asked for his dog. He was told that she was living on a certain islet on the loch, and went to seek her. But the grey bitch had raised, on the island, a brood of puppies. When he came there it so happened that the bitch was (according to Hugh MacKinnon's phrase echoing back to a world that vanished many centuries ago), 'on the hunting-hill'; and the young dogs, being wild, set upon the young man and tore him to pieces. When the bitch came back and found her master dead, 'her heart was broken'; (the phrase as the story was told seemed neither sentimental nor figurative; it is felt to be no less appropriate to dog or bitch than to humanity) and she disappeared never to return to any human dwelling. It is she who appears when a man in that sept is to die.

The frontier melts away in that Twilight between man and animal; mankind and nature altogether. The natural world is presumed to be possessed of life and consciousness similar to our own; never questioned by that part of mankind living close to the natural world. I had come at last to a country where the world is experienced continuously as if informed with life and meaning. All those works of Vedanta and Cabbala and the Neoplatonists that I had been studying in the British Museum saw the nature of things in terms consistent with the experience of these survivors of the archaic Celtic world. Those few who, like myself at odds with current ideologies, have worked our way through Berkeley and Plotinus, Boehme and the alchemists and all the learned books, reach a knowledge which, even so, does not readily transform itself into an experience, informing the whole of life, and embodying itself, as here, in the symbolic images of an unwritten poetry.

For so these stories were to me. But what was I but a stranger and an alien, one of those whose very presence destroys that rare medium in which the thought-forms of a tribe or race form and dissolve? It was Gavin, not I, who belonged to that legendary land.

It was in the early spring of the following year that Gavin first lent me his house. Again, Winifred was my companion. I still have one of the paintings she made there, that I can still enter, sometimes, as if it were the place itself. I first saw that house in the early evening, the sun pouring gold across the sea from beyond Skye into the bay; and the rowan-tree before the house (for there was a rowan) just opening the white of the young leaves that enclose the blossom. Often I have seen the little ferny hill beyond in that peculiar light within the circle of the rainbow which seems to transform earthly green into its unearthly archetype, such beauty does it shed. Primroses grew on that brae, and later in the year heather and thyme and golden asphodel among the bog-myrtle and the gold tormentil. But it is not vegetation that makes Eden, nor the fall of water flowing, nor rowan- nor apple-tree in bloom; it is the power of entering that invisible closed gate which is everywhere and nowhere. I have known the natural world closed, and I have known it open; and perhaps no dust is too mean to shine with that unfallen radiance. Yet I have walked in flowery Italy, in Greece, in the virgin woods of America, and nowhere found that gate.

Many times thereafter I was to live in that house; alone, after that first visit with Winifred. Never was I there with Gavin; yet, living in his house, seeing his sky over me, the spaces of his sea, those near hills and far mountains which were the regions of his imagination; his green linnet in the alder by the burn, his sanderling and plover running on the shore, his tern wheeling over their nests on the furthest rocky islet, his eider floating on the waves, I lived like Psyche in the house of love, alone yet not alone. In the pool of his waterfall I bathed, on his beaches I gathered shells and stones written with the strange language of the sea.

He lent his house, in those years, to none but me; and, as I thought, as if in his absence he wished me to experience his world for him. I saw for him, touched and smelled and heard all as for him, as if every wheeling bird, every radiance of sun or moon on water, every sound of wind or sea or waterfall I was hearing and seeing and touching and knowing for him; or for both of us, perhaps; for the 'one consciousness'. I forgot that his house was not mine, for I was there as it were as an extension of himself, to love all he loved because it was his; was, indeed, himself, a region of his consciousness. I felt it to be my task to enrich and transmute for him his world into poetry.

Near the house, in what had once been a garden (though so long overgrown with fine turf that only the cross made by the intersecting paths could now be seen) there grew the rowan-tree; and I can remember days when I have sat under the blue windy sky, leaning against the silver trunk, looking up into the boundless blue and thinking, what miracle, what unimaginable blessedness to be here and now at the place on earth I most desire to be; by Gavin's rowan.

One midsummer's eve, in the long gloaming, Mary, the wife of the lighthouse-keeper who lived in a cottage on the hill close above the islets, walked with me up the burn, with the setting sun shedding its gold among the birch-leaves as we climbed. By the high waterfall where the burn drops from the treeless level down among the birches that fringe its lower pools and falls, we came suddenly upon a place where not one, nor a few, but many hundreds of globe-flowers were blooming. Each green-gold flower seemed to hold in its sphere of petals the light of that mid-summer evening. Yet had we not been there together, Mary and I, and both seen those golden flowers, I might not have believed after that they had ever been there; for the next year there were none; not even one.

And one day I went to gather rowan-berries, and leaned from a little rocky crag, my head among the branches and leaves; and I saw a black-bird there. It did not move, but remained quiet as if unafraid in its own place; and as at Martindale I had experienced the life of the hyacinth, so—almost—my consciousness seemed one with the bird-thought, the pattern of leaves, the sense of sanctuary where the bird's invisible comings and goings were woven into the tree like a living texture I could sense as some subtle field of vital force; the sense of the bird-soul in the tree, intimate and inviolate sanctuary of the *spiritus mundi*.

I do not know whether such happiness as I then knew is the rarest or the commonest of earthly things; broadcast as the light, as flowers, as leaves, as common as heather, asphodel, bog-cotton and brown butterflies on a moor; for in such things we find it, give and receive it; but like manna it cannot be kept. At the time it seemed in no way strange to be so happy; and yet in retrospect I wonder how such riches could ever have been mine. I planted herbs at Gavin's door and tended the rose that grew against his wall; made him seats from the kipper-boxes cast up on the shore; left for him to find treasures thrown up by the sea, wave-worn wood, scallop-shells, cowries, mussel-pearls; and all his gifts to me were of the same kind, gifts beyond price. Such things were a language in which we communicated—or so I imagined, as I scattered everywhere what Blake calls the 'gold of Eden', hoping that he would gather it. Now I do not know if he ever found that fairy-gold, or if it turned back, as such gold does, to a few withered leaves and worthless pebbles and empty shells.

Because I was so happy to work at his table (I read Law's Boehme there, and Taylor's Plato, and worked on my Blake book, besides the poems I wrote) and to sleep under his roof and to tend his fire and to leave him treasures to find when he came and I left, I never doubted but he shared that felicity. 'Woman', Karen Blixen has written, 'as long as she is free to dwell in the thought of her love, even in the thought of an unhappy and hopeless love, has a home there. If the time ever comes when it is demanded of woman, as of man, that she must forget her love... then she will be driven out on the open, bleak field, without a shelter, exposed to the wind and the weather. Worse than that, she will be running like a mad creature, with dishevelled hair, mocking herself and her own nature.' My home was in my love; to Gavin's house, his earth and sky and sea and the fire on his hearth, I felt that I had come home. Was that so strange a happiness? It is not bodily presence but the presence to one another of two spirits which is the state of love, whether in physical presence or in physical absence. To be alone yet not lonely was to me a happiness I would not have exchanged. It was appropriate to me; for as a poet I inhabited a solitude, while as a woman I felt myself, in those days—and the days became years—invisibly companioned. 'Never again shall I be alone', I thought; for a love which is rooted in holy ground, cannot fail. Gavin had himself once said of our relationship that it would be for all our lives. I thought, besides, that because I had re-entered Eden I must be mysteriously absolved; since how, but by divine permission, could I be there?

During those years I stayed at Sandaig in earliest spring before the snow had melted from the hills; in summer, in autumn: I would go during term, when my children were at school, whenever it so happened that Gavin was not himself there; and he was often abroad at the time. I seemed then to be not so much a person as an eye of the world, a pure consciousness in which the beautiful forms of creation were reflected. Again as at Martindale I could here forget myself, become, as it seemed, invisible, vanish into the elemental world and participate in its freedom and delight. It seemed not so much that Gavin and I were two people in one world, as that one world existed in our two minds, as if earth were a shared vision. So like was nature to imaginative vision that it seemed that Gavin and I had become dwellers in paradise, or paradise proved not, after all, to have vanished from the earth. For the experience was not other-worldly; it was, on the contrary, an epiphany of (so I still believe), the living essence of the natural world. I would sit long by the waterfall merely looking at the sunlight filtering through a green leaf, or bubbles forming and turning and drifting, or elvers ascending against the current; or listen to the wild voices of eider or plover or *gilliebridhe*, or feel with my hand the warmth rising from an eider's nest, or breathe in the sweetness of birch or bog-myrtle, or taste the rain blowing in my face or the berries of the rowan. To perceive, to gather in that beauty, was to me like a task of love; it was as if a river were continually flowing between us, carrying to Gavin all I experienced. As if; for I no longer know whether this was so. But to me it was as if our consciousness were one and indivisible, and that consciousness the world we shared in the 'one mind'.

Certainly the experience owed nothing to whatever in me is peculiar to myself; to my by this time considerable knowledge in many fields, or such small command of language as the poet had by then acquired. Rather I seemed to have recovered a capacity to experience the world as Blake's 'one continued vision of imagination' which is perhaps the lost human norm, that from which we are fallen, a capacity we share with the animals, perhaps with the plants and the rocks themselves. I felt myself, then, to be one of the eyes of earth, Plato's 'happy immortal living creature'; and this knowledge immeasurably greater in kind than any acquired knowledge of my individual experience. Of this I wrote in poems of the time; yet the poems captured, of all that vision, scarcely a glimpse or gleam, so continuous it was, and in itself such a happiness that even the desire to write often left me. There seemed, besides, to be plenty of time; for in the world of nature there is neither past nor future, nothing there has had a beginning nor will have an end; the eider seemed to have all the time in the world. All I saw proclaimed not transcience, but only 'the adorable I AM'. At once creator and creature of the vision it seemed enough merely to see and to live that world; the task assigned alike by love and the daimon of poetry.

I have at times believed, with the Neoplatonists, that the soul sheds its envelope of dust to emerge as moth from chrysalis; but there have been other times—and at Sandaig this was so—when it has seemed possible that what we call nature may prove to be a region of immortal spirit.

> Thought is its cradle and its grave, no less
> The future and the past are idle shadows
> Of thought's eternal flight . . .

At best I saw so imperfectly, so inattentively, so never enough.

I thought to live in that world for ever; and allowed the days and weeks and months and years to pass. But nothing in time, permanent as the present always seems, shares the everlasting quality of those visions we so briefly glimpse between its moments. And I never noticed how, imperceptibly, the other kingdom was withdrawing itself as I grew to love too much those earthly forms in which, even so, it lingered for a very long time before the old story told itself anew; the woman's desire to possess what was given only to the poet; disobedience, anger, remorse, exile, the closed gates; I did not, after all, keep faith with the vision. If the 'one mind' remains for ever, I was not to remain for ever in it, as I had thought. As that mind brought Gavin and myself together, so now in that consciousness we were to be parted, as if by an invisible field of force which in my thoughts I could no longer cross.

For a time it must have given Gavin pleasure to have me in his house. And I believe that pleasure was the knowledge that I was working, upon his world, a kind of transmutation, through the alchemy of imagination. Mere gratitude for such small practical things as I had done for him cannot explain away this opening to me the doors of his world; and when I have heard that 'of course Gavin will always be grateful for the help you gave him by'—introducing him to so-and-so, some publisher, or whatever it was—I have the sense of a deeper betrayal than if I were to be told, 'Gavin hates you.' Yet it came to be as if I had never known Gavin, nor set foot in Sandaig. I could be easily persuaded that I never was there, that the poems I wrote were not mine; driven out of my own memories, 'driven out on the open, bleak field, without a shelter', that I myself had never existed. For those memories were Gavin's domain, and in recalling them I seem, now, to be trespassing in a place I have no right to enter.

How soon did mortality begin to creep in and to obscure an epiphany which, at the time and for long after, I had resolved never to betray, never to fail? The first time Gavin's anger struck at the roots of my life we were on a journey together; he was on his way to Sandaig, and was to take me as far as Boothby, where I was to stay with Winifred Nicholson. His racing-car had broken down near Stamford, which had delayed our journey by many hours; so that—a snow-storm meanwhile had come on—we had to stop for the night somewhere in the Pennines. I am tempted to say that I cannot now remember why we quarrelled; but I remember perfectly well: I had shown Gavin my diary; and such was his dismay that he lashed out at me in anger. To me that journal was a record of sacred things, a search for truth, the bearing witness to a vision. It was—I being a writer by habit my métier to write, and to forbid me to record my thoughts in words—and many of my thoughts concerned himself—must seem like forbidding me to live my life. To him, it was a woman's indiscretion, it was a potential danger, it was a threat to his reputation, a kind of potential blackmail. It was terrible to me to discover that he saw it so.

Years later, after a deeper estrangement, I was to watch all those diaries of Sandaig days turning and turning in the pool below the bridge at Lanercost, until the current caught them and carried them down the river Eden to be drowned somewhere in Solway mud. For long I had stood on that bridge, the parcel of books balanced on the parapet; unable to consign them to the river; for they were myself, a part of my life; it was a kind of suicide; and as I stood by that parapet I was in two minds as to whether to drown my books or myself. It was, in a way, a suicide; or a trial suicide, to see whether I could do it. It could scarcely have cost me more to destroy myself than to destroy for ever the record of my happy years. When the books were caught at last by the current I followed them downstream, watching them until they sank, as the river flowed through pastures towards the summer sunset.

The rift that opened then between us was, I now realize, profound; for me, all life is the raw material of poetry; for him, to write about another person is a betrayal of trust; a reasonable point of view; but one so remote from my own intentions towards Gavin—my love for him, my concern to do him only good—that his seeing me in the light of an injurer (or potential injurer) came as a shock whose violence seemed to tear my heart out by the roots.

That night, sleeping in a strange bed, at the heart of an unknown country of cold storm, I had a dream. I was walking down the familiar path to Sandaig; and when I had crossed the burn I could reach neither the house nor the tree, because a high palisade of wooden palings had been built, ugly and hostile, and the beauty of the place all destroyed. The wooden barricade was a fit symbol of the wall built about the first Eden after the Fall; but—so mysteriously does the outer world mirror inner events—in the end, such a wooden palisade, precisely like the one in my dream, was (through logical sequence of events neither of us could then have foreseen) built; and I could never again return, and the place as I had known it was laid waste. A strange blending of symbolism and precognition; for symbolism might explain the barrier, but only precognition, surely, its precise form, those vertical wooden palings. But then, events of mind will always evolve event in the world; Macbeth's phantom dagger became a real dagger all too soon. We are both the creators and evolvers of our fate. Not only in our conscious acts, but also, above all, in our thoughts and passions, we create the event, though its form we cannot foresee. How uselessly we plead that we did not deserve that this or that should happen; for all that happens, good or bad, is but an enactment of our own deepest reality, a reflection in outer events of the inner pattern.

It is easy to see why, as a poet concerned only with perfection and habitually selecting images and symbols of ordered beauty, I disregarded as non-existent, unimportant, not to the purpose, the imperfect, the distorted, the vulgar, all which falls short and does not bear the stamp and signature for which I looked. That is not to say I do not see such things— on the contrary, I am jarred, bored, or pained as the case may be; but pay only so much attention to such things as is necessary for the putting of them from my mind. My own failures, or actions of which I am ashamed, I also long regarded as irrelevances, as fallings-short; my attention has never been held, like a certain kind of moralist, by evil either in others or in myself. My attention wanders from evil, in a kind of disdain to notice its essentially vulgar and worthless presence. For myself, spiritual effort has lain in the effort to create, or merely to contemplate, some perfection, and has never taken the form of moral self-searchings, battlings with 'temptation' and the like. I think it is true that in my friends I am interested only in what is good in them, whatever it may be, disregarding the rest as irrelevant and not worthy of notice, as failures in them to be what they really are. So we read those poems in which a poet has succeeded in attaining some intended perfection, and not those in which he has failed to do so; to do otherwise would be ridiculous. I have always looked for whatever is best in people not from blindness to flaws and faults (these are self-evident) but because I regard all that baseness which the brilliance of Ivy Compton-Burnett and her many less talented analogues exposes as 'the truth' as, precisely, its absence.

No doubt it is true that I have too much discounted the negative power of evil both in myself and in others. Of this Canetti warned me at the very outset of my relationship with Gavin. He warned me that I was disregarding too much other aspects of Gavin's character than those I chose to see. I replied, with truth, that I saw Gavin's faults and short-comings with perfect clarity, but that these had not a reality comparable with the living essence I had also seen; with deeper insight, so I believed; and since that essential beauty is higher on the scale of reality than any short-comings, so it must also prevail. *Magna est veritas et praevalebit:* there is nothing higher than the truth. Neither Loyola nor Plotinus meant Ivy Compton-Burnett's 'truth', nor the 'truth' of this decade that holds the lowest and worst to be discovered about any human being to be the 'truth', outweighing whatever good they may have done, aspiration they may have followed. Plotinus' truth these would call falsehood; as he would have called their truth, the unreal. Therefore I believed 'the real' Gavin to be that 'man of light' I had at certain moments beheld, and not the mire and clay which obscure the incorruptible gold of the soul. I argued that, since Gavin had been brought to me by that immortal world, he was the task assigned me; and that, with the help of those powers who had brought him to my door, I could not fail. I did not doubt that with such help I could, if need were, rescue Gavin from the abyss; such was my phrase; and I remember Canetti's words, spoken most gravely outside 9 Paultons Square, as he was taking leave of me at my door, 'Gavin for you *is* the abyss.'

Of course the evil I could not see was above all in myself. And it is also true that while I was willing and happy to accept my relationship with Gavin as a Platonic love, I never really at heart accepted his homosexuality. Perhaps I was not so naïve as to suppose that I could physically change him; yet I did think that on another level I could win his love. Was I too much my father's daughter, applying that puritan morality in which I had been brought up? Or was I, simply, too much a woman to accept what is 'against nature'? At heart I thought homosexuality to be wrong; though often enough excusable because of some early wound which had been its cause. Gavin had all my compassion. His mother, too, was a puritan; a devoted member of the 'Apostolic Church' founded by Irving (a friend of Jane Welsh Carlyle) of which her parents, the Duke and Duchess of Northumberland, had been prominent supporters, and the Maxwell family also. Had not a combination of family pride and puritanism too harshly restrained her much-loved youngest son; born, besides, after the death of his father, killed early in the first World War? At the dawn of adolescence he had, besides, suffered an illness so grave that his life had been despaired of; and so, thrown back into the power of his mother just at a time when he would naturally have been asserting his independence, was it not understandable that the real 'woman in his life' should be that mother, so devoted, so full of many admirable qualities? It was she who had taught him his love of poetry, encouraged his enthusiasms and protected his sanctuaries. So that other women, had, for him, become forbidden. That I could understand, for that I could feel compassion. Once he said to me that he thought his mother could more easily accept that he had a homosexual relationship than a relationship with a married woman; 'or any woman', he sadly added.

But that homosexuality was either normal or good, that I could not accept. Insofar as I knew of such relationships I pulled against them. And I attributed to unquestionable morality an attitude that anyone but myself must surely have seen was vitiated by my own wish to possess Gavin for myself. He himself must have seen that very clearly. But I was so blinded by foolish pride in my renunciation of the flesh that I was blind to the emotional demands I made upon him.

I have always tended to like homosexual men, in part because of a certain 'feminine' sensibility of mind they so often possess; and Gavin did so beautifully possess that gift of compassionate understanding. 'I have not wisdom', he once said, 'but I have understanding.' He was a very humble person; and what he said was truly and humbly said. I also remember his quoting Traherne's words, 'No creature was ever loved too much, but some in a wrong way, and all in too short a measure.' Beautiful words. Gavin, unlike myself, was generous and humble in his love.

I had also liked the company of homosexual men because they made no physical demands upon me. I had been wounded in the sexual hunt when I was young and had by now become wary at evading any sexual approach. If a homosexual man likes the company of a woman it is for other (and better?) reasons. But with Gavin I was in love; another matter altogether.

Perhaps what Canetti meant was that although to me Gavin presented a sexless image, as if from that childhood where in truth we met, there was another side of his life that was not sexless. I saw him, perhaps, as I would have seen a priest, or a member of a religious order who had renounced the sexual nature; but of course that was not really the case. While I imagined a relationship transcending the flesh, Gavin did not really believe in that kind of thing at all. On the one hand, physical attraction drew him elsewhere; on the other, he probably had grave doubts about my own motives. Was he right? Yes, and no. The poet was sincerely capable of Platonic love; and I believe that to that sincerity Gavin did respond. There was, after all, a bond between us. To the insincerity of the woman—the shadow the poet could not throw off—he responded differently; for that shadow was the devouring spider, the dark side of the woman, destructive, and the more dangerous for my unawareness of its presence.

Canetti had studied evil more closely than I; one might say he had specialized in it; he missed Vienna especially, so he used to say, because the English are 'not wicked enough', and this he found boring. When he warned me that Gavin was for me the abyss, and that I too much disregarded other aspects of his nature, he might have pointed out that the abyss opened also in myself, but he did not; and I was quite unaware of my own shortcomings at that time, as those who are filled with love are unaware of evil in themselves, since love intends none, intends such boundless good. We cannot ever measure that which we lack, wherein we fall short.

I have spoken of Canetti; and I cannot continue without at this point saying more about the friend to whom Gavin's brother first, I think (in affection and in only superficial irony), gave the name of 'the Master'. In the cafés where he sits (trying to recapture a lost Vienna) he is I believe known as 'the Professor'; though he is in fact one of the few among my friends who has at no time been involved with Academe. Both names are appropriate; which is not to say that the Master is infallible, or the Professor omniscient; he is indeed fated, like a character in one of his own novels, always to fail in his attempts to save from themselves those upon whom he expends so prodigally his intelligence, his compassion, his time; I am myself one of Canetti's failures. His novels, indeed, I find distasteful, for all their probing of the mortal worms his characters are. Man is not, after all, a mortal worm, but an immortal soul, and to present humanity otherwise is to degrade, to caricature, to destroy the 'image of God' which the prophets of his own race beheld in us. Iris Murdoch put Canetti (or someone uncommonly like him) in one of her novels; a context not altogether inappropriate.

Canetti is quite possibly the most widely learned man I have ever met; perhaps he is the most intelligent. Yet it was neither for his learning, his intelligence nor his kindness that Socrates by his friends was called 'the best of men'. Perhaps the quality involved is wisdom; and Canetti's wisdom was of that specific kind Socrates claimed for himself: 'human wisdom'. Like Socrates Canetti is unimaginable away from the city; for him, as for Socrates, the human is his field of knowledge, the human experience at once his study and the medium of his creation. There are so-called 'humanitarians' who, filled with some Utopian dream, desire (like my father) to 'serve mankind'; but very few have any talent in the supreme art of the *comédie humaine*. Canetti has the genius of a Balzac for human beings; a genius which is at once a kind of intelligence and a kind of compassion, but is perhaps above all a love for the matter of his knowledge, as such. I am not alone in having felt that there is absolutely nothing of which I, in my highest or my lowest moments, might be capable of thinking or doing, that Canetti would not comprehend, imaginatively explore, make his own, know. There is a story (which profoundly shocked him, which surprised me, in view of his own low view of God) of Frederica Rose saying to Mme. Mayer, wife of the then French Cultural Attaché, 'Don't you think Canetti is exactly like God?'; to which Mme. Mayer replied, 'Yes, but is God like Canetti?' That remains, always, an anxious question; 'The son, how unlike the Father' Blake said, 'first God comes with a Thump on the head, and then the Son with balm to heal it.' So it is with Canetti, who, as a Jew, feels himself personally so to say responsible for that 'tiger-volcano', as I have heard him describe the god of the Jews, always ready to pounce or erupt. 'If I believed in one God, I should be obliged to hate him,' I have heard Canetti say; he is, however, a polytheist, whose pantheon is all the gods of the world, and more than have ever yet, or ever will be, known or named; in their multitude is his faith; in the inexhaustible and incredible riches of possibility, in whose grotesque improbabilities, self-contradictions, marvels and absurdities he delights. 'Behold Behemoth whom I have made'; what the God beyond reason revealed to Job in nature, Canetti beholds in that region of human thought in which abide the irrational forms of the gods. Unlike those psychologists who, blinkered by some theory or made impotent by 'detachment', or perhaps simply frightened by a world too full of things beyond reason, seek to reduce the teeming fertility of the imagination (or the Imagination) to some banality, Canetti lets things be. He would rather watch *supernatura supernaturans*, than relegate the supreme gods of all the ages from gold or stone to iron and the machine, to the ethnological section of any museum, or the files of case-histories. If there be insanity it is at large, and far exceeds the pathetic tentatives to be found in the wards of lunatic asylums. He loves the masks of the shape-shifters not for anything these might 'prove' to psychologist or theologian, but for their own sakes. What shocked him in the story I have told above was I suppose that he would not wish to be thought like the Jewish tiger-volcano. (But to the second question, now, in 1976, I know the answer to be—No, God is not like Canetti. More, indeed, like Gavin, whose compassion and human understanding was not unChrist-like; not, certainly proceeding from some high-place of intellectual pride that set him, in his own mind, above other poor suffering sinners.)

It was at one of William Empson's parties at Hampstead I first met Canetti; sometime during the war. I had never before seen anyone quite like him; as if tremendous energy had been compacted into his small but dynamic person. 'He is like a little lion,' that same Frederica said; but with all the energy of a large lion, or a whole pride of lions concentrated in his immense mental vitality. It was this vitality, coupled with an equally immense interest in people, which first impressed me in him; and no doubt I, like many others, found irresistible his evident interest in what I thought, did, was; an interest at once concerned and disinterested; for Canetti's concern (again like Socrates) is with the discovery and evocation of the essence of each person, with what Ibsen calls the vital illusion; only Canetti is not so cynical as to call anything which lives an illusion, seeing each as one more manifestation of the variousness of life. For those who want simple answers Canetti has none to give; he was essentially 'the Master' for those who wanted complex answers. Those who conversed with Socrates must all have left him not only with a clearer, but with an essentially more interesting notion of who and what they themselves were; and so it was with Canetti. Are we not most indebted to those masters who chip our statues out of our marble? So, as with Socrates, those who loved him did so principally for our own sakes, because he had the magical power of evoking from us, ourselves. Yet the converse is, perhaps, also true; as Gavin once said, 'none of us needs Canetti as much as Canetti needs us'. We were, indeed, his raw material, which every artist needs supremely; even though perhaps among his wide circle he has found some blocks of wood or stone or kinds of clay more to his purpose than others.

I had long thought of him as like Socrates in more essential respects before (I am reticent about even noticing people's physical appearance) I one day ventured to say to him (for the remark might not, after all, have been well received), 'Canetti, has anyone ever said that you look exactly like Socrates?' The Master, however, was already there: 'Yes, of course, it was my nick-name at school.' And to be sure he resembles exactly, as his loving and disrespectful disciples said of Socrates, one of those pottery figurines whose hollow interior is filled with little effigies of the gods. Balzac would have drawn from this physiognomical resemblance some long conclusion about the correlation of mental chracteristics with physical types: why was that wisest and best of men of an appearance which to the beauty-loving Greeks appeared ridiculous? And why do those who know Canetti best take more pleasure in his Socratic features, alive with intelligence and kindness, than in beauty itself? *Qu'est-ce qui est plus beau que la beauté*? To ask the question of Canetti is to ask it about the cosmos itself. I, by nature a Platonist, drawn to beauty and perfection, yet recognized in Canetti a principle beyond the beautiful; as in the sublime religion of the Jews I recognize a principle which transcends that of the Greeks. Beyond perfection itself there is marvel, there is inexhaustible possibility. 'The world is full of Gods' was said by a Greek, but could any Greek (for perfection tends to simplification and abstraction) have known how full? Would Socrates himself have tolerated even those neighbouring barbaric gods Aristophanes laughed at in *The Birds*?

But Canetti delighted in the churinga stones of the Australian aborigines, fraught with the power of the ancestors; shape-shifters and devourers, maggot-gods, totems and demons. Yet in his room hung photographs of the sculptured saints of Chartres, and a post-card of Delphi showing that wisp of smoke which issues from its cleft in the rock as once from the Sibyl's cave; he would contain even the beautiful.

Once he said to me that it would be his wish, if that were possible, to experience the being of every creature in creation; for one whole day he said, he would like to be a worm—to know what it is to be that worm, so limited and inexpressive.

Loving in Canetti, as I did, a peculiar greatness, I was perhaps seeing in him an aspect of the race which was, and remains, in a special sense 'chosen' by that God of whom Canetti demands an answer to the predicament of his creature man beyond any the churches (including the synagogues) can give. Blake went to the heart of the matter, as always, when he saw that the god of the Jews, who spoke by the prophets and was incarnated in the Son of Man was the divine Imagination itself; and that therefore in time the whole world must come to 'worship the Jews' god'. If God chose to become incarnate in the Jewish race (as Christians are by their faith bound to believe) it was not, presumably, by one of those caprices which Canetti might attribute to the divine shape-shifter, but because of the natural aptness of the vehicle.

Other races have perhaps a greater metaphysical sense; Indians in particular. But in Canetti I recognized and valued a quality I have never found in even my perhaps more spiritually translucent Indian friends; that tendency implicit in the doctrine of the Incarnation of the Messiah, to a boundless concern for the weakest and the worst, a willingness to pay the ransom for the worm, which at the nadir of creation cries out to God to justify what there it must endure through its remoteness from the glory of a Heaven which is all wisdom and power. Defending God on one occasion I said that He did, after all, become Man in order to redeem man; and Canetti replied with unusual gravity, 'He could do no less.' To have taken on, as Canetti thinks he has done, the task of saving men from a relentless God is in the tradition of Abraham pleading for Sodom, or Ezekiel, or Jacob whose thigh-bone was dislocated in his struggle with the Most High; for if towards the rest of mankind Canetti had that compassion which he would feel towards the worm, upon himself he took divine responsibility. In this losing battle there was doubtless an immense pride, and yet he was within the tradition against whose God he so fought. Like the prophets before him he pleaded the cause of the worm before the Most High who created him, and whose sufferings, ignorance and, ultimately, his sins, must lie at the charge of his Creator.

If I noticed evil too little, Canetti explored its full extent, all its devious imaginings. At times he wearied of the task like the god who 'repented him that he had made man'; wondering at times how much further down is the bottom to which he has taken upon himself to go?

As a prophet of the *nadir* he was a mind of his time. To Canetti there is nothing in the unfathomable stupidities of evil which he likes or admires; if he was concerned with the lowest places it was not, as with some of the literary company he may find there, as a propagandist for human vileness.

With Canetti I at times felt that the vision of the beautiful, of ideal perfection as the Greek philosophers have understood it, lacks some other quality without which all the outpoured abundance of the marvels would come to a standstill. Beauty has a marmoreal finality; if it be achieved, all ends there: is the lack we discover in perfection, imperfection? Creation is after all a flux away from, not towards, the still perfection of the One we call beauty, a fanning-out into a multiplicity of shapes and forms. The grotesque and the ugly are aspects of infinite possibility; and this too the Jewish genius has at all times best understood. We think of no single type of Jewish beauty, as we do of the Greek; rather the Jewish race runs to extremes, exemplifying, besides men and women of dazzling, almost excessive beauty, all manner of the grotesque and the ugly, and is not least within its genius (that genius being a fertile creative abundance of imagination) in the descending spirit which flows down into the lowest effects and into 'the many'; whereas the Greek genius tends always to ascend towards the highest causes, and towards 'the One' and 'the All', and the beauty of some norm.

Sitting with Canetti at the table of some shabby café open all night, he once remarked to me, I remember, that he came to such places 'to get clean', after any form of social pretence; finding in the shabby depths, among professional thieves and prostitutes, a kind of truth to the nature of things. The Greek philosophers call this world 'the dregs of the universe'; but just in those dregs the Jewish genius comes into its own; for it is to this point God must descend if descend He will. Canetti at least would not spare Jehovah one atom of the mire and misery, the ignorance and depravity into which man, his creature, whom having made He must know is weak and foolish, has fallen. I remember how he pointed to the stains on the tablecloth between us, and said it was this, this with which he felt he must keep faith, which he must understand, towards which he was responsible; for in conversations with Canetti it is sometimes difficult to discover where he thinks his own responsibilities end, and those of the God whom he so relentlessly confronts with his evil deeds towards man, begins. Yet at times he has admitted that there may be 'the good God' somewhere beyond the cruel demiurge. Anyone who felt it necessary to define precisely Canetti's heresies would find abundance of material; but to argue whether he is right or wrong is a dead occupation; his own intense concern, comprehension, his genius for seeing into remote places of the soul's experience, and from points of view as strange as the eyes of bees or the tactile blindness of the Biblical worm, or Kafka's beetle, is more imaginatively, revealing than anything that might be gained by placing him on a theologian's bed of Procrustes.

Canetti was not, however, without critics whose authority he himself acknowledged. Sometimes in his dreams, so he once told me, he would find himself in the presence of very old men, thousands of years old, far wiser than he himself; Chinese sages, perhaps, or simply sages. These very old men are to Canetti what Canetti himself was to those who thought of him as 'the Master': they laughed at him and his notions, and mocked him as a child.

'Christianity', I remember his once saying (very late at night when we had been talking for hours), 'is so vulgar'; I knew at the time what he meant, though I now find it difficult to put into words. He meant, amongst other things, that Christianity accepts with too easy a facility the answer to what seems to him God's worst outrage against man: death. To accept with facility, complacency, or sentimentality, the redemption of man from his mortal predicament, is to fail to confront the predicament itself. It is death, to Canetti, which is God's unforgivable crime against his creature man.

Sometimes it seems to me that there is something willed and put on about Canetti's way of seeing death, as of a false supposition followed up to see where it will lead. To the Platonist, the Buddhist or the Hindu death is nothing worse than the pain involved in dying (not so great, as a rule, as the pain involved in living) for the soul after death finds itself precisely where its actions have placed it, to reassume its task in this or some other world or situation; at worst to linger in those hells or purgatories of the soul which we travel here no less than there; and at best death is a homecoming of the soul to its own place. To the Christian death is more to be feared because it is believed that this one life determines for ever the situation of the soul in eternity. I myself greatly fear the Judgement (a reality understood alike by Christian, Platonist and Buddhist), the soul's confrontation with all that it most wishes to forget, the anamnesis of every shameful and cruel act, every betrayal of love, every baseness; everything I have forgotten because I dare not remember it; if I fear death it is not as extinction, but because it is not extinction. Death as such does not seem to me an ultimate issue at all; and the Judgement is already present, here and now, and at moments we tremble before the silent reproach of the 'God within'.

Neither presumably can death seem an outrage to a simple-minded positivist; for if the soul be not immortal, there is no mystery in the dissolution of a creature who is, like the Archbishop of Canterbury in the primer of zoology, ninety-something percent water. Only from Canetti have I caught even a glimpse of what the issue at stake was, on the Cross: death as such. If the souls are immortal, as the Pythagoreans and the Indian metaphysicians believe, in what sense had man to be 'saved' from death, or death 'overcome'? If there be such a question, the answer to it (the answer imprinted on the Holy Shroud) could only have been found by a man of Canetti's race; not by a Father Pius, believing implicitly in the immortality of the soul, or any visionary who has gazed into the Christian heavens, or any heavens at all; for death is the tragedy specifically and only of earth, of the mortal worm, of the human condition as it is in this world. Therefore the question is not, for Canetti, to be evaded by the postulation of other worlds or other states of being; these may or may not be; but the mere fact of this world, of this state, that such a world can exist at all, anywhere in the universe, he sees as a reproach to to God so great that he cannot forgive the creator of mortal man who has to endure, in this world, his mortality. In what way can the heaven of heavens obliterate the reproach of the everlasting Belsen? Therefore if death is to be conquered it must be in this world, for the reality exists in no other.

'If I could really believe that Jesus had conquered death I would become a Christian tomorrow,' he once said; for what seems to him 'vulgar' in Christians is, precisely, their complacency, the facility with which they are willing to accept a promise so immense. If it were true that Jesus on the Cross conquered death, then, Canetti felt, all that human suffering, that innocent blood which beneath the altar of a relentless Creator cries out for vengeance, might be atoned for by the god who shed it; for it is not what man has done to God, but God to man, which seems to him to cry out for atonement.

In saying I really do believe the soul to be immortal (and not only on the testimony of Plato and Plotinus, but from such insights as have been mine) I have felt, in Canetti's presence, ashamed, because I have never, as he has, known or envisaged the darkness of the farthest places of the universe, into which (according to Islam) the Angel of Death, looking once on every day of Allah, asks, if God has created anywhere a world more terrible than this; not terrible because of rectifiable injustices, but as such. Such is the dark reverse of the other truth, Plotinus' saying that no world could be more beautiful than this, except that Other.

I have, all in all, admired Canetti more unreservedly, taken more pleasure in the riches of his imagination, that inexhaustible robber's-den of treasures that reveals itself to those who possess the *open, sesame*, than in the mind of any other person I have known well; and yet I have adopted none of his ideas; on the contrary it would be hard to find anyone more naturally remote from his kind of thought, his way of experiencing, from his self-chosen vocation as the advocate of the mortal worm, than I am. I love the order of nature and shun the chaos of cities; I am always looking for a way out from what Canetti travels always more deeply into, the chaos and the ignorance of the human condition. I desire the perfection of eternity and the beauty of the gods; he, like a Boddhisattva, would not permit himself such a luxury as beatitude, or escape from the human condition before the last blade of grass has attained salvation; and if he has contempt for any human being, it is for those who would do so. In Canetti's presence I feel myself condemned as imperfect just because I have sought perfection. Only, I have come to realize, a Jew can really understand Christianity.

All the same (for after all, in my apologia I may surely speak for myself), I am too proud (and so, for that matter, is Canetti) to join the universal whine of the plebeian sense of grievance which blames God, the Government, the state of society, etc., etc., for the existence of suffering; or the plaint of self-pity which lays our unhappiness or failure to the charge of parents, marriage-partners and other people in general. I do not know what those mean who speak of 'rights' which are somehow due to us: have we any, within this mysterious universe? We are all, besides, very good at pitying the hypothetical and remote situations of others, even while knowing very well our own capacity to endure, when it comes to the point, whatever has to be endured. To suppose others lacking in this after all primary human quality seems to me to deny the mortal condition its single dignity—the human capacity to sustain it; not, after all, for very long.

'We met at last in the heart of an otter'; so he inscribed my copy of his first book, *Harpoon at a Venture*; the book I used to be called to listen to at all hours. He wrote the inscription in Italian; easier to say such things in a foreign language; for it was, in its way, perhaps, an admission of something which can only be described as love; if two things equal to the same thing (Mij's heart) are equal to one another.

For Mijbil was the bond that united us. 'May I be his godmother?' I had said to Gavin, as we sat, side by side, watching that enchanting living being swimming in my bath at No. 9 Paultons Square, where he had been brought to call on me. And so it was.

Gavin had brought Mij back from an expedition to one of the four legendary rivers of Paradise (the Euphrates); it is all told in *Ring of Bright Water*. But what he did not tell—at my own wish did not tell—was that whenever he went away for a time he would leave his otter cub in my care, sometimes in London, sometimes at Sandaig; and Mijbil was attached to us equally and alike. It may sometimes be that the love of animals is a substitute for some human love; but for us it was precisely its not being human which made this bond so magical. In the heart of this creature we both loved, warm with the one life-blood of the earth, Gavin and I were united indeed. Mij was a gate-keeper who allowed us to pass, through his life, into the unfallen world of those who there play in the everlasting play of life without guilt or sorrow. It was as if we had been released from our fallen humanity and allowed to return among those still innocent children of paradise.

Not only to love nature but to be loved by nature; to understand the language of the birds, the wordless language of animals. It was given us to enter the fragile essential life sheltered within that warm sleep of an animal curled up, making of itself the closed circle of a microcosm, and at the invisible centre of the body which so precariously guards and shelters it, a spark of immemorial life, a star of life that has travelled in unbroken succession from the beginning, the source. By the protecting, the preserving grace of nature, there it sleeps, black nose hidden in warmth of fur, all the delicate senses sealed in a magical sleep as secure as the circulation of the stars in the night-sky; a darkness no less spacious and still than that into which sleeping life withdraws. On my bed he slept, secure and fragrant, entrusting to me his sleep in the sympathy of that one life we shared; his paws encircling my ankle, or his breathing mound fitted to my shape. On barren rock by barren sea that living creature has lain curled on my knee asleep, microcosm warm with life and warm in the sun, marvel of the animal, so vulnerable to the pounding of water, the cold of wind and rain, the destructive teeth of rock; breathing the violent air so softly in and out of its small lungs; an organism so complex, so vulnerable, raising into existence, at the heart of that desert of rock and wind and water, a consciousness so delicate, so boundless a joy.

Through that magical participation Gavin and I entered the world of the animal itself; for it was not in our world, not a domesticated pet, but wild and free. Each morning he woke into his joy, bounding over the grass to dive and play in the reaches of the burn, calling me to follow, to share his delight in the little fish he found under stones and ate alive with such simplicity of innocence; his delight as he dried his coat in the hot sand. To me he would come bounding, streaming with salt water, to wreathe himself round my neck, whistling with joy and summoning me to join him in that unending play; tugging at the corner of my coat with his teeth to make me follow him into those lovely pools. Up the stream I would follow him, or round the shore; and always he would rejoin me, racing back to me in a rapture of re-union that was always new. He did not obey me; rather the reverse, it was I who followed his wild pleasure into a world where there was always time enough; or no time at all, for every moment was a present without beginning or end.

The only bond between us was love; I was bitten once or twice, and carry those little white scars as the only evidence I ever walked in that unfallen world with Gavin's animal-angel. I did not seek to impose any human obedience upon his wildness; but we had charmed one another into a devotion that was a tie, as I thought, more secure.

Such was my precarious happiness; for if our loving animal belonged, properly speaking, to Gavin, in Mij's unawareness of such a distinction I forgot that he was not mine too. Once I remember Gavin arriving at Sandaig to take over his domain and his water-baby from me; we were by the burn; and Mij bounded first to his master, then to me, racing back and forth, sharing an equal allegiance, in a wild, unbounded joy.

Out of what far-back roots, then, did the destructive forces grow? Resentment and pride, where did they begin? Far back, all through my life, acts of cruelty, ruthless indifference, neglect, wilfulness, blindness; all these had made me what I now was; and from what I was, not from what I intended, came the consequences. Of course Gavin also had faults and behaved very badly towards me in many ways (I have now forgotten in what ways, but at the time he caused me much suffering, which was not, presumably, all my fault). For if the world of the Logos, of the imagination, is our meeting-place, its landscape that native country of which all poetry tells, its life the one love all creatures give and receive, our human selves are peculiar to ourselves, each a different lonely prison-cell, alike only in limitation, imperfection, in being cut off and solitary. We do not know what goes on in others' lives immediately by participation (as in the world of imagination) but by guess and deduction, often false. Pride, Gavin said, was my especial fault; and through a perfectionism more Platonic than Christian, I lacked, perhaps, compassion for the prisoners in the prison-cells; while he, more Freudian than Platonist, seemed to me often not to understand the value of pearls, taking them for diseased acorns. At all events he often turned and rent me; or so it seemed to me. But I do not know how it seemed to Gavin—how Gavin saw me; for that is the one thing no person can know of another, once we stray outside that self-forgetful love that never asks such things, or doubts that self-delighting life is lovable. So it was with our loving otter, so it is with little children. Being what I was, I think I could not have loved Gavin more; but the love of an imperfect fallen creature, to what does that amount? My unbounded sense of giving blinded me to the truth that, giving ourselves, we give the bad with the good.

Self-accusation is too facile a kind of truth-telling, only one degree less false than the first instinctive response of our natural humanity, the blaming of the other person the world at large and even *(pace* Canetti) 'God'. For all the time we were, Gavin and I alike (as all are), standing our judgement in the light of the world we had each momentarily glimpsed. Of this I was—I cannot in false humility deny even now—mindful at all times; of my vow of obedience to that vision to which I remained, to the end, oriented even when only to know myself thereby condemned. I was (to speak now of the heart of love, which lies beyond the frontiers of egoism) prepared to do and suffer anything and everything for Gavin's sake; I felt my love to be a kind of Atlas upholding the heavens and in this arduous interior labour I felt myself privileged, dedicated, blessed. Whatever Gavin asked of me I did; he was at all times in my thoughts and in my prayers. Afterwards people would say—even Gavin's mother, and his brother, 'Kathleen helped him, she introduced him to X and Y,' who found him a publisher, or reviewed his first book favourably or some such negligible thing; Gavin himself might later have said so, thereby putting our relationship into a category of an external kind. I have 'helped' many people in that kind of way, but to Gavin I gave not 'help' but something infinitely more dangerous and incalculable, myself.

Unfortunately it is in virtues and good intentions that egoism most securely entrenches itself; we like to see ourselves in a good light, and in our ostensible good-doing self-criticism is silenced. Having thought—perhaps truly—that Gavin had been brought to my door by divine providence in order that I should help to draw him up out of the complex troubles into which he, a companion so dear, had fallen, I did not notice where selfless instrumentality ended and egoism began; when I ceased to be the agent of the 'one consciousness' and became mere woman, trying to purchase a continuance of Gavin's affection by loading him with superfluous benefactions, in order to extort from him gratitude. Imperceptibly our roles were reversed; it was no longer he who needed me, but I who needed him; I could no longer contemplate my life without Gavin, nor did it occur to me that Gavin might feel otherwise. For in that other kingdom love is given and received; there is no thought of 'possessiveness' and the like except where there is no longer any love. I cannot even imagine, now, what my supposed benefactions were, when I was in fact his debtor, he having opened to me his world, lent me his house, allowed me to participate in the love of his so much loved Mijbil, bestowed on me the lost domain of paradise. But I felt myself the giver because I loved him, and love's desire to give and illusion of giving is boundless.

In the two kingdoms there are two realities, and these seldom at one.

Whereas I continued to remember the world which had brought us together, Gavin, I began obscurely to realize, no longer saw in me anything but my shabby human self.

To my own shabby exterior, my bodily appearance, my human personality, such as it is, that bearer of daimonic burdens, I had never throughout my life given much thought; knowing myself only as an invisible consciousness; surprised and even resentful when I have seen a photograph of myself, so little has the person who can be photographed seemed related to that invisible self. I have always imagined myself as coming and going unseen in the world, feeling a shock of surprise, indeed of panic, when I am told I have been 'seen' in some place by some person of whose presence I was not aware. There is something deeply disquieting in the knowledge that we are at all times involuntarily present and visible. Perhaps I have been unwise so to disregard the shadowy image for which I am, after all, responsible, since it is I who cast it. I might have understood, had I looked at that shadow, how I must have appeared to Gavin; and to his mother, who saw in me the granddaughter of the Kielder schoolmaster, a divorced woman, an associate not to be desired for her son. But I thought Gavin had seen my invisible self, the poet, the chosen one of the daimon.

As I began more and more to sense that in Gavin's eyes I was of little worth, the being who wears me like a shabby disguise made no protest, though she saw, and suffered; for we cannot make ourselves known unless the eye of love can discern that hidden being we each of us are. I had thought Gavin had seen in me, as I had seen in him 'the face I had before the world was made'; now my disquiet came from the sense of some incalculable misunderstanding; and if my tears were one part mortal, they came, too, from the grief of the imagination at the betrayal of the immortal. Perhaps the truth was too simple for me to realize; as Canetti once said to me (I did not believe him) 'You must understand, Kathleen, that Gavin does not love you.'

But that was to me inconceivable. Love has a meaning, a reality; but to not love is, in 'the kingdom not of this world', something without meaning, unimaginable. Yet I was aware of a growing sense of cross-purposes; which, since I was at that time incapable of realizing Canetti's simple fact, 'Gavin does not love you,' seemed to me a betrayal by Gavin of a sacred bond. I was willing to do anything for Gavin in the name of that bond, but increasingly I felt that I was being made use of for trivial ends. My pride, certainly, was not that of the woman. Just because the woman seemed to me instrumental, I felt nothing to be beneath her; the woman did not stand on her dignity (upon what dignity could she have stood?) but because I regarded myself as instrumental I was not prepared to find that Gavin regarded the slave of the lamp as an ordinary slave.

But I sensed more and more that in Gavin's eyes I was only my mortal self. 'Poor old Kathleen, you look like a fat squaw', he once said to me, when he had reduced me to tears. I did not even feel this as an insult; the poet in me was too proud, the woman too unconcerned, for the shaft to wound me; but I did mind for Gavin's sake, and my grief was for him, for what seemed to me his inability to see any longer the fairy-gold I offered. So, bewildered, I endured much silent grief; and the sea within, the sea from which that visionary blossoming tree had arisen, at first blue as heaven, became yellow and green, then purple and black, and the water began to seethe below.

So far I had written. Now on this January morning of 1976, I write in my own hide-away cottage in Cumberland; not many miles from Bavington across the Northumbrian border; nor many miles from my mother's birthplace (Longtown) nor from Kielder, where the lives of our parents and grandparents crossed so long ago. In spring and autumn I see the grey-lag geese fly towards the sun setting over the Solway, and Gavin's childhood home. Can I be more truthful now? Do I know more of 'the truth?' For, as Gavin once said, there is no such thing as 'the truth'; only a different story, experienced by each of the participants. But if I tell my truth, I must include in it a confession of my culpable disregard of Gavin's point of view. If I felt, as oftener and oftener I did feel, aggrieved and resentful towards Gavin, this was on no better grounds, as it now seems to me, than that I suffered. Because I suffered I supposed that he had hurt me. That is an instinctive reaction, but both stupid and unjust; for most often we hurt ourselves, whether by imagining non-existent wrongs, or in persistence in some mistake we cannot or will not see. I can no longer even remember what my supposed grievances were or why I suffered; I can remember the stab of suffering well enough, that seemed like a dagger in my solar plexus often for days or weeks on end; but when I ask myself, what did Gavin do to cause that pain, I am compelled to admit that I can't remember that he did anything at all. I think I lost Gavin's affection not through his breaking faith, but through my own. If I had remained the poet, if I had not slipped so imperceptibly into demanding emotionality, he would not have broken faith with me. I became the spider, and he knew it.

It would be all too easy to say that Gavin's homosexuality lay between us; yet I do not think this need have been so but for my emotional possessiveness, and but for my continuous silent disapproval of his homosexual relationships. And I doubt whether any woman can ever feel otherwise, however much we may make an effort, on principle, to do so. Yet I was content to believe myself 'the woman in his life'; bewildered as I was, once, when he escorted Princess Margaret on a few occasions I told myself that this might well have been in order to please or simply to impress his mother, who would have seen such a match as altogether appropriate for her son, as, of course, in respect of birth it would have been. But I did not take the episode seriously, and it was, besides, very brief.

Then, again, there had been an evening when I fled from Gavin's studio on finding there a pair of gloves left, as he said, the previous evening by a woman friend he had met through me—a slight acquaintance of mine. My flight, unreasonable and instinctive, was an act of what must have seemed to Gavin emotional possessiveness. Yet I would not have felt this had the gloves been (say) Janet Adam Smith's (whom he also met through me) and later events proved my instinct correct. When soon afterwards Gavin took the owner of the gloves to stay with his brother at Monreith, I felt both hurt and slighted. My Achilles' heel of vulnerability was Ilford; and whereas the poet is classless, I had a momentary clear realization that to Gavin and his family I was, poet or no poet, Ilford; and not socially acceptable in their own world. There I think I was unjust to Gavin who did respect the poet when I *was* the poet; and if I insisted on playing the woman, that was my fault. Again, the handsome friend he took to Monreith was far more 'permissive' than I in the matter of his homosexual relations. Very much so, indeed.

In the event she became for a short time engaged to his brother; and once again my fears subsided, and I was only too glad to tell myself that they had been unfounded.

However, Gavin's possible social estimate of me troubled me the less because my own circle of friends were, after all, in their own right, distinguished. Helen Sutherland, whose house had become to me a second home, judged on a different scale. Gavin's painting she would not have taken seriously at all; his books she might have read; but as light reading, not as she read David Jones, or Eliot, or Herbert Read, or even as she read my own poems. To her Gavin and his world would have appeared philistine; though she did think Gavin charming: 'like a sword—or a lily', was her phrase; 'a fleur-de-lys'. So that while Gavin may have held social reservations about myself, I, by other standards, had similar reservations about him. Every art or science has its own standards of excellence and its own aristocracy. That, after all, is what aristocracy, for Plato, is. And that, surely, was why Gavin and I could meet on equal terms at all. He respected my values, when I lived by them; and I his, for I saw in his freedom, his disregard of cautious self-interest and all practical obstacles when there was an adventure in question, something that characterizes a hereditary aristocracy, and is in itself admirable, and without which the world is likely to be the poorer. Truth to say neither Gavin nor I acted from self-interest of that kind in matters that concerned our self-appointed tasks. Both of us alike knew what Conrad calls 'the unknown discipline of the self-imposed task'.

Gavin had another quality which likewise he owed, no doubt, to his birth: he had the gift of making us all his slaves. It came naturally to Gavin to initiate adventure, and to assign the parts to those who gladly joined him. He had also—less admirable—a way as I think all his friends would agree—it was perhaps quite unconscious—of confiding in each of us as though we alone were the one confidante, the one friend upon whom he could rely, to whom he could turn for help. He would summon me at all kinds of times—I must go round now, at once, to resolve some crisis, to advise him on what he was writing or on some other matter; and, of course, I always went, happy to be asked, to be needed; as women always are when we love. Gavin avoided the social scene, he was happiest in these intimate meetings, preferring, too, his own surroundings to going out; although he did often come to me, saying that in my room he found an atmosphere of peace always. Only long after did I realize to how many others he had behaved just so; and they too doubtless were misled, as I was, into believing that they alone were needed. If misled is the right word.

So, with or without reason, I suffered. How vulnerable we are when it is we who love; indeed to love is to allow ourselves to be vulnerable. How heartless we are to those who love us! I do not mean sexual love, for I am inclined to think that, in matters of sex all's fair, whatever may be the case in war. The raw instinct has its own laws which are those of 'nature'. I think I suffered, when I was young, too many scruples in the matter of sex, and God knows too few in the far more humanly significant matter of love. I think, now, of my mother, whose boundless love for me over all these years I had called 'emotional possessiveness' and closed myself against as if it would destroy me. Yet now, myself the lover against whose emotional possessiveness Gavin had perhaps closed himself in a like fear, I knew how little, really, love asks; just that the other person should be open to us, should receive the love we give. Then, the demon-face they fear would be transformed to beauty. If I had only received and valued my mother's love, how little she would have asked; and was not I the loser who for long years kept her at a distance, offering her, as now I began to feel that Gavin offered me, only the exterior self? I hated and feared her tears, that I could so easily have wiped away. There is a law in these things and was I not now reaping what I had myself sown? Now it was I whose love was met with something that was not love. Whatever God may be—the 'one consciousness', the law of Karma, the ground of reality in which we live, move and have our being, that reality is not mocked, the law is both just and inexorable. All our debts must be paid.

Only once did I pass a night with Gavin. He had been desperately wretched and asked me if I would so stay; on the understanding, of course, that there should be no sexual contact between us. And to that I gladly agreed. Yet to me that act was binding as no marriage had ever bound me. When we remove our clothes we remove, as it were, an armour, a disguise. The poor physical body, so defenceless, so vulnerable in its nakedness, can communicate more than any words. We come from the womb, the breast that comforts us is mortal flesh. But how could Gavin, who must have shared his bed with so many, have imagined that to me, twice married and with two children, that simple act was total commitment? Every night of my life, since then, I have spent alone. This has troubled me but little for, increasingly of late years, I have come to realize that we are always, at all times and places, in the total embrace of God. Whoever knows this is never lonely.

At last, one evening at Sandaig, the storm broke. I had been staying at Sandaig, as usual, with Mij; and Gavin was to come, that day, to take over from me. I was about to leave our paradise where for so many weeks I had wandered by the shore and up the burn with our beloved otter. Like some shrine I had tended Gavin's house, happy to be there and to scatter, as I thought, fairy-gold for him to find; shells, and stones from the shore, things I had made or done for him. I was to sleep, that last night, at Mary and John-Donald's cottage, as usual; Gavin was bringing a friend with him.

I do not know whether, then, in feeling myself unwanted when Gavin came I reacted to his real thoughts; I would like to believe I misconstrued them. But the sense of some invisible, intangible outrage not so much against myself as against that of which I had thought myself the guardian, seemed as clear as a scene momentarily lit by lightning. All that intangible web of love I had woven I felt was brushed aside as if it was nothing to him.

For whatever reason, or unreason, I left the house in all the anguish of my real or imagined rejection, and went to the rowan-tree we both loved; the tree I had freed from the tangle of old wire that had cut into its bark, the tree where I had thought 'here and now I am in the place on earth I would most wish to be'. Weeping I laid my hands upon the trunk, calling upon the tree for justice: 'Let Gavin suffer, in this place, as I am suffering now.' I was at that moment beside myself, as one-pointed and as blazingly clear as a streak of lightning as I spoke aloud my terrible invocation. And I went up the hill to Mary and John-Donald with the dagger of anguish turning in my heart.

Two days later my white-hot grief had died down; but the anger and anguish I then had felt had risen from the depths. No less than the vision of the Tree in its living beauty, those words came from beyond myself. Happy are those who do not understand the power of thought to accomplish events.

It is said that a curse always recoils upon the person who utters it; and mine was to take full effect, both upon Gavin and upon myself. Such an invocation cannot be revoked by the mere recovery of temper and good-will towards the person against whom it is uttered. It has a life of its own; when a passion is so powerful as to stir those depths, we awaken forces beyond human control. But for a year all went on outwardly as before; Gavin leaving Mij in my care, as always, when he was away or abroad. He never knew of my invocation of the hidden lightning, and I thought the curse had died with my anger.

Easter came round, and again I was to take Mijbil to Sandaig. All seemed peaceful and my anger forgotten, yet on the day before I left London Gavin had spoken some words that had stirred my sleeping resentment; and again I cannot recall what cause I had, or thought I had, to feel again that anguished sense of inner betrayal. Perhaps I had none; that only he can ever know. But again it passed; I was only too willing to think I had been wrong. When I stepped out of Bruce Watt's boat onto that well-loved strand, that joyful otter-cub tugging at my wrist in the delight of his return to freedom, never had Sandaig seemed more beautiful, never had I felt more deeply the sense of home-coming. Never had I come with a more profound resolve to do all well, all right.

I had for a long time been writing no poetry; for my poetry had come to depend upon Gavin, upon some word that I wanted him to speak. But the word had not been said, and the springs were frozen. Now I had begun to wonder if perhaps my relationship with Gavin depended, rather, on the poetry than the poetry upon that relationship; if perhaps I, closing the gates of my injured heart against my daimon, and refusing to write, were to blame; seeking to force from Gavin the word love would not speak, for poetry's sake; for I knew that, little enough as Gavin might care for me, he cared a little for my poetry. But now I had made one of my periodic resolutions to seek again the threshold of the gods within if purity of intention could raise me there. I knew that, for me, poetry is my only way to travel that spiritual journey; and my poetry has at all times been the expression of such intuitions as have come to me from that world. All other ways and means have, I have always known, been evasions of my task; and attempts to follow techniques of meditation and the like I have always in the end been forced to admit were make-believe. Nevertheless I had, besides intending to write poetry, asked an Indian friend to give me a *mantram*; and each day I rose in the morning and for an hour walked with my animal companion by the burn or on the strand, my will turned towards that steep ascent to whose foothills I thought I had at last come with the intention of never turning back. Never had I been so happy; never had my joyous companion been so happy; every hour of every day was filled with beauty; and I did not guess that these days of such strange exalted happiness were to be my last. I invoked the spiritual world, repeating aloud my *mantram*, and thought by so doing to call down only good upon Gavin, upon my own work, and upon the living creature whose love united us; for I could not imagine any good in which Gavin and I were not in harmony. I asked at the tree that my anger should be forgotten; and in the joy of my magical companionship, and all the poignant beauty of early spring, the scent of the young birch-leaves while there is still melting snow in the air; primrose and anemone and golden saxifrage, the green linnet singing on the budding alder, it seemed that innocence and beauty outweighed all evil.

But for all the radiance that streamed continually from the world within and behind nature, there was a continual undercurrent of anxiety, a daily realization of the hazards of a relationship with a young animal essentially wild, bound to me by bonds only of love. For he could climb cliffs where I could not; bound up the wet precarious stone ledges behind the waterfall where I could not follow; swim round rocky headlands at high tide, that I could not pass; nor would he always answer my call. There were alternations of wildness, which called him away; and love, which drew him back: he was not subject to human will. There were times when I scrambled up cliffs to meet at the summit my loving animal bounding to meet me with all the delight of re-union after separation, to follow me home at my heels like a dog. There were days when I would follow wet foot-marks on the dry stones up the burn, only to lose the track at last and return home in desperation, to find a breathing mound curled up on my bed, under the blanket. Worst of all were the times when he would swim round the headland; then I would follow in a little rowing-boat, coasting the rocks where the beautiful weed and anemones and sea-urchins grow, the sea-garden where he loved to play; watching for his little black head to break the surface of the water, and calling and calling. Most often I returned alone; and once he stayed away all night, and all the neighbourhood was aroused to watch for him; news came that he had been seen, more than a mile down the coast; but when I went rowing round by the loch and calling, he was not there; but, again, there was the joy of returning to hear his whistle of welcome as I entered the house all but desperate. He always came back of his own accord; would always have come back.

Yet there were so many dangers to threaten his life. He had a little harness, and a lead could be attached—very necessary in London, or in travelling. Gavin told me it was unwise, even at Sandaig, to let him run without his harness. But I thought I knew better, imagining every possible accident: what if his harness should be caught in some snag? Some tangle of wire? Worst of all, what if this were to happen under water and he be drowned? When he was lost I would imagine him thus trapped somewhere, unable to return. This had happened more than once when he was with Gavin and he had returned with the harness broken, after some long struggle to free himself. I disobeyed and allowed him to run without his harness; I thought it was safer so.

Another instruction Gavin had given: he could be taken south, down the shore, but it was unsafe to take him north, for in that direction lay the nearest village, and danger. Again, I thought I knew better. Day after day I took him south; but what was the way of that perilous headland where at high tide he used to disappear, leaving me helpless to follow; and of that cliff where I so perilously had climbed after him; and in this too I disobeyed Gavin. Knowingly I disobeyed; I thought I knew best; I forgot that the responsibility lay, finally, with Gavin, forgetting that the little animal who loved me, and whom I loved, was not mine, nor Sandaig, nor all that world to which my love was so wholly and irrevocably given. Love does not think in such terms; if these belonged to Gavin, so did I. I had nothing that was not his, not even my poetry, for that too came from the ground upon which we were, as I believed, as one.

I say that I acted as I thought best; but again I must be truthful: again some small thing in a letter had wounded me, and stirred that sleeping interior sea. Was it, in part, this pain of resentment which inclined me, in the last days at Sandaig, to disobey Gavin? Step by step, not realizing what I did even while I did it, I myself became the agent of the vengeance I had invoked.

More and more, each day of that last month of lovely spring, I realized the danger. Sometimes it seemed an open secret between Mijbil and myself; as if he was, or I was, fey; and I would talk to him, begging him not to find his death. Sometimes I prayed that he might at all events remain safe, until I could hand over my charge to Gavin. I seemed to know that his life was every moment hanging on a thread But where I ought to have obeyed Gavin and put on his harness, I relied upon prayer; I could not believe that the daimons and the elementals, the guardians and the invisible agencies of the world behind the world, of which all this seemed an embodiment, would fail me, if with them I kept faith.

Even so there was an evening—three days before Gavin was to come—when I even got out the harness, intending to put it on; but it was so difficult to put a harness on that slippery limber form, and one was liable to get bitten in the process; so I deferred it.

Next day, at the time of our evening walk, the tide was in; and I feared to risk again that headland where so often before my charge had eluded me; and when we came to the mouth of the burn, I remembered Gavin's instructions, never to turn north; instructions I had hitherto strictly obeyed. But now I argued with myself that to do so was safer than the risk of losing my animal at the point, at high-tide. I disobeyed Gavin and turned north. And in that direction I saw growing, no doubt from some packet of bulbs washed up on that desert shore from a passing boat, a many-headed clump of golden narcissi; but their warning I did not heed: like Persephone those golden flowers lured me in the forbidden and fateful way.

After a few wild joyous comings and goings my animal companion swam out to sea, suddenly wild, and deaf to my call; and he eluded me. The animal-soul of our strange, magical, but doomed relationship swam away for the last time. At its appointed hour—and how far back, in the origins, was that hour appointed—for all my prayer, my love, my desperate desire to avert and avoid disaster, the lightning struck; and Gavin, through my thought and through my deed, though against my conscious will and knowledge, suffered at my hands the worst bereavement it was possible for him to suffer; a lonely man, his love was all given to his little otter. To Gavin and to me, he was more than an animal; a creature of paradise, a part of ourselves. In him I loved Gavin; in his love, a part of Gavin loved me, and Gavin through him accepted a part of my love.

What consolation could it be to either of us that I suffered no less than Gavin? For besides grief I must endure remorse.

That night I did not sleep; I hoped against hope that in the morning I would hear Mij whistling again at the door, left open for him. I lay in anguish, listening to a storm the like of which I seemed never before to have heard, the wind full of lamenting voices as the ragged cloud flew over the moon from the south-west as the gale raged. Anger and grief were in the wind; and though I did not yet know it, all was over, Eden lost, its gates closed against me for ever. With sick hope I awaited the dull morning of the day, and renewed my fruitless search; and at last I heard that an otter had been killed by a workman on the road; yet even then it seemed impossible, unimaginable; it might have been some other otter; I watched the sea still for that little black head, long after I knew.

It seemed incredible that he should have gone, should be dead, not for that day only, but for the next and the next, and all possible days; that there should not be, in all the future, a day to hope for, when he would return. I have much fortitude, and have spent months and years of my life waiting and hoping; never before had I been compelled to forgo hope. But why say more? That finality of death needs no telling of mine. But mourning at last may find comfort in the very love that is its source; remorse never.

I had looked forward with so much joy to the day of Gavin's arrival that, all that cold empty day, there was in my mind a double image, as on a photographic plate: of the reunion I had hoped for, of Gavin and our loving otter; I had pictured the wild loving joy and the laughter of that reunion; and the many things I would have to tell, of the comings and goings and doings, of the anxieties and the happy returns of my animal companion, restored again to Gavin with the addition of so much of my love as he could be the bearer of. And another image, still unfamiliar, strange and blank in its features, not yet lived-with like the image of joy that had accompanied me on all those mornings and evenings up and down the burn and across the strand and by the rocky shore. Death had not yet revealed its full extent, so small it still looked, less than a day old, it shadow covering less than a day of my life; and yet its sorrow was to grow and grow as far as the future should extend.

The day cleared in the afternoon and the wind dropped; and against the empty horizon I saw at last Gavin's boat nearing the shore. It slowly grew and grew, like a death-ship in a dream; and at last the dinghy was lowered that brought him to the strand. He already knew; and, bowed with a single grief, we sat side by side beside the dark brown waters of the empty burn where no animal companion delighted us with his greeting. Neither Gavin nor I had yet realized that the blow so suddenly struck had ended a world; nor that the very grief we at that moment shared was to divide us.

From that time when we sat by the burn together our roles (as I had conceived them) were reversed; it was I who was abased, humiliated, exposed, shamed, Gavin who was the giver; and with a magnanimity the situation evoked from him, he offered me forgiveness, compassion, he accepted a part of the blame; he showed in himself, in this shadowy enactment of the old story of the lost garden, the innate nobility of Adam, as like Eve I wept. But I could not sustain my abasement; my pride in having been, as I had thought, the doer of good towards Gavin, blinded me now to the truth, that it lay in my power to do him a greater good, by accepting a humiliation, in allowing him to take from me the part on which I had so prided myself. I could not abdicate, I could not endure my new role as the blameworthy and the weak; I could not help Gavin any more because I could not let him help me.

Neither then nor thereafter, neither from Gavin, from myself, nor from the divine world, could I accept forgiveness. Refusing forgiveness I refused love. I chose punishment because I could not bear to be forgiven. I had tried to win love by deserving it, but I could not accept it on the only terms reality permits, as something which can be given but never deserved. I felt safer with punishment; for retribution belongs to the order of cause and effect, the law of karma, which gives us our deserts.

'God is love,' Gavin had once said to me, calling me to task for some hardening of the heart against the pain of wounded pride. And now my pride finally chose the way of remorse because I could not endure the other. So I went away burdened by the guilt of my deed; on my head Gavin's life-blood with the blood of his animal soul; for perhaps I did him an injury from which he could not ever wholly recover. I do not know what expiation I imagined could ever free me from such guilt; but knew that whatever punishment should be laid on me I must bear. It seemed to me mere sentimentality to seek exoneration by imagining I might be 'forgiven' by God or man for evil brings its inevitable consequences, and so long as these continue to operate we cannot be freed. By these consequences we must abide, as effect follows cause; endeavouring, at all events, to weave no more spells, to set in operation no more causes whose effects may extend beyond our power to undo what we have done. I could only accept as just my banishment, and bear the consequences of past actions, my own and those of others (who like myself had set in motion chains of causality which would break their hearts too were they to know their progressions) without complaint.

Perhaps the guilt I incurred towards Gavin is not the greatest of the evils of which I am guilty; but, unlike other chains of causality which I may have set in motion, this one was plain to be seen, and had come about in spite of the greatest effort of which I was capable, to do all right in a relationship which I valued supremely.

Many years later I had a dream that in the garden of the new house I had just taken was 'the ancestral fountain'. It was like the well at Bavington, but choked with dead leaves, and with living weeds. The dead leaves I removed easily, but the weeds were so deeply rooted I could not tear them out. Nevertheless the water that rose continually from its hidden source was pure; and in it I washed a new-born child. How many myths tell of the same reality as that dream I have since realized; Porphyry's cave of the nymphs, where the waters of generation rise in the inaccessible darkness of the world-cave; Spenser's spring of sorrow where a nymph of stone pours water which cannot wash the blood from the hands of the new-born infant of Mordant and Amavia; the Christian font and the mysterious rite of baptism. The symbol of my dream was realized when my grandson was baptized; and in the garden where in my dream I had seen the fountain, all his living ancestors were gathered; my parents, and my children and other grandparents bringing other chains of causality unknown; all those whose failures and misdeeds, whose unrealized aspirations and stifled desires he must inherit; a burden unknown to him that he must carry, and of which a part is mine. And the new-born child was held in the arms of the old, who wished him only some unknown good, beyond whatever portion each must pass on to him of original sin. Which is the stronger, the tangled weaving of destiny, the navel cord, cause and effect and inheritance, or the grace of that water rising always pure from a source deeper than the roots of those weeds?

Not the least terrible aspect of that disaster was, to me, that catastrophe had struck at the time when at every moment of every hour of those last days at Sandaig, all my thought was turned towards the source: was that catastrophe an answer to my prayer, or a rejection of it? Was the answer to my invocation of that world the destruction of an earthly paradise? But it was not mine only, but Gavin's that had been destroyed. It is pleasant to do good to others, terrible to see ourselves as the causes of suffering, but is not that too a kind of pride? As to the catastrophe to Gavin, for that too my pride assumed perhaps a responsibility which was inordinate; forgetting that his destiny too must lie in God's hands and not (for all the instrumental part, both for good and ill that I had played in it) in mine. Or was I in fact rejected at that gate because, giving all my love and all my thought to Gavin I was neglecting other duties? Putting that love before my children's good? Before my duty to my parents? The truth is never simple; of all these threads, and others unknown to me, my fate was woven. But at the time and for years after I could see only desolation and remorse, and I turned away from the interior world in a mechanical stupor of misery.

Exile, then, began; for Gavin, I believe, as well as for myself. Did the first man and woman know the very instant at which the gates of Paradise were closed against them? Could they at first believe they were closed for ever? For those gates are invisible to the eye; all looked as it had done the day before, every intricate form of leaf and tree, cloud and island, bird and beast. The burn flowed on, its brown water dancing as before, and the silver ring of the sea still shone as brightly as always. The golden flowers bloomed still, and the scent of the young birch-leaves was sweet on the air. Only the gates were closed that shut the spiritual world off from nature, empty now of life and sweetness. And yet, sitting with Gavin by the burn, I was still incredulous; it could not be that a world was so suddenly gone. Nor could I realize that I had myself brought all this about—for how easily could I justify each act, invoke chance or accident, and disclaim responsibility! But knowing as I did that thoughts are agents of power, whose tides and currents ebb and flow invisibly, I knew that what had come about was fate not chance;

yet still I could not believe that never again would that loved place be Eden.

> Push'd by the horned flood, and all its trees adrift,
> The haunt of orcs and seales and sea-mew's clang
> To teach man that God attributes to place
> No sanctity, if none be thither brought.

*

I think I forfeited my relationship with Gavin not with my heart's cry, or curse, whichever it may have been; nor even when I lost Mij. It was when I refused—when in pride I could not accept—his forgiveness. I had become habituated to thinking of myself in the role of the giver, the helper. I clung to that role in part from self-righteousness, in part from fear of losing him; only by being needed, I thought, could I hope to be wanted. That, of course, is one of the dangers of a relationship in which physical attraction plays no part; and any woman in a similar situation should guard against it. How blind I was! How it must have irked him to see in me the resolute, the over-strained determination always to be the giver, always to be the strong one! My pride and my self-righteousness, of which I was so culpably oblivious, how clear to him! And perhaps equally if I had helped him really, must he have felt at a disadvantage. For we love those to whom we give, not those who are forever giving to us; for one very obvious reason, that in giving we see ourselves in so flattering a light. And is that not one reason why selfish people are so attractive? Less cynically said, they bring out the best in ourselves. But now it was for me to say 'Gavin forgive me' and to accept in our relationship the part of the guilty one, the needy one, open to his compassion and his pardon; that he had been, by the burn that day, so generously ready to give. But I could not play that part; I was prostrated with remorse, bewildered and paralysed. In my remorse I could see no way of helping Gavin or doing him any good again. And yet in letting him forgive me and responding to that forgiveness I might have given him a gift of more value than all my supposed 'help'.

Anna was now at Cambridge, James doing his National Service; and I had arranged with Gavin that he should rent the two lower floors of 9 Paultons Square; there Mij would have had access to the garden; Gavin had already built a tank for him. But that plan, made in happiness, was fulfilled in sorrow. When Gavin moved into my house Mij was already dead.

For the next year Gavin and I, stunned though we both were, tried to remain as if friends; learning only little by little the extent of our devastation. I had no longer the power to comfort him and lived only in remorse; not daring even to pray, since disaster had come at a time when I had turned my thoughts so sincerely—I must even now say I was sincere— to a renewal of my determination to live my life according to the divine will. But now, to see Gavin was to weep; not a few tears, but streaming rivers of tears that would not stop, that I could no more control than the waters of a swollen burn. And that no man can bear. I who formerly had, or seemed to have, so magical a power to succour Gavin, now had no power at all.

One thing I did not tell—could not bring myself to tell—when I wrote this record of old sorrows. But now a memory rises from its grave and returns to me. I was still, then, living in the top flat of 9 Paultons Square, and Gavin and I had not quite lost hope that something might remain. I had been sitting with him in the room that was now his; sadly conversing, it must have been, like Adam and Eve after the Fall. It comes to my mind that he asked me, then, to share his bed with him, as once before; to cast off our defensive armour, to lay down our weapons. And I did not do so. Sadly, slowly, I climbed the stairs to my own lonely bed, leaving him to his own. Knowing that I could no longer, now, give him either help or comfort.

I was at that time living, during term, at Girton; and when on Muriel Bradbrook's invitation, I took up my modest Research Fellowship at my old College, it had seemed no longer necessary to keep the whole of 9 Paultons Square. Now it seemed the same inevitability that had formerly brought us together was to divide us; and all our plans and good intentions were whirled away like bubbles on that dark stream which was sweeping us apart.

I do not know—I shall never know—what Gavin's truth was, nor how long before I realized it he had shut the invisible gates of his life against me, presenting to me, instead, a merely external and social mask. Perhaps there was no absolute moment at which this was so. But I could no longer continue to deceive myself after a certain evening we spent together once when I had come up from Cambridge. How the storm came to break I do not remember, nor does the occasion matter. But I do remember how, sitting in the Berkeley buttery, Gavin laid at my charge fault after fault (including my dress and my physical appearance), blameworthy action upon blameworthy action; most with enough semblance of justification to leave me stripped of every defence; and yet blind love had seen another truth, or those truths otherwise. Against such a presentation of truth as falsehood, or falsehood as truth, or simply of another truth than mine, I was defenceless, and unstanchable tears poured from my eyes (another fault unpardonable by Gavin's code) making me loathsome to behold. The truth of the heart only God can judge; I remember saying this to Gavin at last—that he and I would have to stand the judgement of the God within. Certainly I did not defend myself; for 'the truth' is not an abstract proposition which can be reached by argument but only the aspect persons and events have in living minds.

He left me, at last, at the door of the friend's house with whom I was spending the night. He so far realized my extremity on that occasion as to telephone Canetti and say, 'If Kathleen has killed herself, I shall never forgive her.' But Kathleen has neither the courage nor, ultimately, the despair of the suicide. Fortitude is to me second nature; even, an excess, a kind of outer insensibility, a false strength assumed when weakness might have been better.

But I saw Gavin the next day; and he assured me he had not meant one half of what he had said; and I replied that of course I had never supposed that he had. But, again, his words had come up from the depths, the fiery pits and deserts which lie as far beyond our everyday selves as does Paradise. Both of us were glad enough to rest in the everyday, like dreamers who return to prosaic morning from places of experience too terrible to contemplate. But these things had been said; and I began to wonder—the thought came to me first as a hypothesis which I did not expect to see proved—rather the reverse—whether I ought to withdraw from Gavin's life; to discover, at least, if he wished me to do so. I therefore pretended to Gavin that I was thinking of giving up 9 Paultons Square altogether. This was plausible enough; for now that I had rooms in College I could say that (my son being on the point of marrying), I no longer needed a house at all. I thought he would say 'No, no, please don't leave London altogether, I need·you.' But he did not say it. Then I began, as it were, to pay out more rope; asked if he would like to take over the lease of my house; I doubted, I said, whether I could afford to renew it. (I had at that time the new lease in my hands, made out in my name and ready to sign.) He said he would like it. I expected him to say, 'But where will you live? You cannot bury yourself in a women's College.' ('It was like seeing Achilles in Hades, finding you here' was Stanley Spencer's remark to me when he came to paint his portrait of the Mistress of Girton.) But Gavin did not say it. I paid out all the rope I had; and such was my grief that he took it all that I had no heart to wish to keep anything for myself; I could not defend myself against him, for I had made his interest my own even against myself. My sense of guilt towards Gavin for the loss of our beloved Mij was so great that I felt a certain respite from remorse in whatever restitution it was in my power to make; and all I had was my precarious tenancy of the house which had come to me with a friend's blessing. Even so, at the last moment, when it had been agreed that Gavin, not I, should take over the house, and a new lease was to be made out in his name, I suddenly thought that it was too much, that it was as unfitting that I should give, as that Gavin should take, all I had in the world. I wrote to him asking if, instead of his being my tenant, I could be his: could I keep the little flat at the top of the house? But to that letter I received no answer.

If I had read Aristotle's *Ethics* at that time, I would have understood that, in bringing about a situation in which Gavin behaved badly towards me I was in fact not preserving, as I had despairingly hoped, whatever remained of a friendship in decline, but making it impossible for any friendship to exist at all; for countless instances have proved the philosopher right when he says we can forgive those who have injured us, but never those whom we have injured; since the former enable us to see ourselves in a favourable light, the latter force us to see ourselves unfavourably.

All this Canetti knew, step by step; my motives, my hopes and fears, I told him all as it befell and showed him the letters I received from Gavin. He was much concerned about what I was doing: probably he tried to dissuade me; but I could not defend myself against Gavin when I was myself fighting on his side. Even from Canetti I probably disguised (speaking plausibly enough of economy) the fact that to give up 9 Paultons Square was the thing I least wanted to do in the world. I could not even now relinquish the belief that at some point Gavin would say, 'You have gone far enough away now, don't go out of my life altogether.' But at no point did he call me back, or so much as ask me what I would do; this, it seemed, did not any longer concern him. Still, he invited me to visit him, when the house was no longer mine but his, and asked me to admire his alterations and furniture. It was too much, and those unstanchable tears flowed again so that I had to go away. I sat alone in a corner of the Blue Cockatoo restaurant, where there were candles on the tables, and dark shadows, and tried to regain command of myself before returning by a late train to Cambridge. Gavin had rid himself of me; with my own co-operation and help, be it said—the last good it lay in my power to do him.

One might suppose that by now I had understood that Gavin wished me out of his life altogether. But love is slow to understand such simple, self-evident things. Because the truth of the vision I had seen possessed a reality incommensurable with this shadow-world in which Gavin and I now seemed to struggle as in a dream, I believed that, if I could only somehow get back to that truth, it must prevail; for I had never forgotten that anamnesis, nor could I believe that Gavin, either, could forget what once we had seemed to share.

Once more, and for the last time, I visited Gavin in the room where Cooie Lane had first taken me into the protection of her house; the room that had been mine, where I had lived and written and that had been my children's home. There the superimposed images of memory were all adrift; for it was to this room, too, that Tambi had first brought Gavin to visit me, and where Gavin had said, 'It is as if a goddess had turned her head and looked at me.' There my life, such as it was, had been lived. How it was, on this occasion, that I broke my bitter silence and spoke of the unanswered letter in which I had asked Gavin if I could keep, as his tenant, the two small top rooms, I do not know; but when I did so, he exclaimed, 'The unposted letter!' For his reply, written months before, had just been found by Mary, at Sandaig, unposted, in the jacket pocket of the boy to whom it had been entrusted. Gavin had, of course, said that I could keep the flat. 'But what else could I have said?' he exclaimed. 'After all, I am a gentleman.' Not a very warm reply, I realized, upon reflection; but at the time I laughed and said, 'I thought you *capable de tout!*' and hope rose again.

And those missing letters—Tess of the d'Urberville's, pushed under the carpet, and all those others whose miscarriage seems to have changed lives, are not they too mislaid by the daimons? I had been glad enough to cry miracle when the two hands were joined together; but when by those same hands we were torn apart, I was reluctant to see the same mind, the same purpose at work. I wrote to Gavin from Cambridge, saying how infinitely rather I would lose my house than lose his friendship. I desperately believed that, since that lost letter had been written, every wound was healed, every rift mended. Perhaps even I thought I had by now bought, at the price of my house, at the price of the discretion of my withdrawal, a renewed lease of friendship.

I see now that it was because of Gavin's desire that I should not remain at 9 Paultons Square that I left, and not because of a missing letter. Who knows how such losses come about; just as, step by step, I acted in such a way as to bring about the death of Mij, whom Gavin and I equally loved, perhaps Gavin also brought it about that the letter was lost. Message-bearers are quick to act upon almost imperceptible signs, expressions, moods which communicate that a letter is tiresome, written reluctantly; or urgent, vital. Had Gavin been anxious I should receive it he would have impressed upon his messenger that it was an important letter and must go off at once. There had been a time when he would have telephoned; the cost of trunk-calls from Scotland to Cambridge would never, for Gavin, have been a reason for writing a letter instead.

Perhaps Gavin was embarrassed by the coming to light of the letter and by my boundless joy and relief at the possibility of still continuing to imagine that all had not been lost; for he asked me, once again, to revisit Sandaig. Or perhaps he too hoped that all might not be lost; for I never yet knew Gavin to do anything except because he wanted to do it. In that lay a great part of his charm, for it gave to all his actions an authenticity, an absence of pretence or hypocrisy. When, long before, he had sent me to his house I had known, being there, that he had wanted me to be there; when he no longer wanted me he could make that, too, perfectly clear. And so, hoping perhaps against hope that from the wreckage and desolation something might yet be saved, I went for the last time down the familiar path which for me led to that centre which unreason still called home when reason knew it was not so. So a bird will fly to the place where a felled tree stood. There is for each creature an invisible thread, or beam, which draws it home; and for me the thread drew me still to Gavin's rowan-tree between the waterfall of the burn with its fringe of birch and alder, and the strand where plover and sanderling ran on their rapid feet. But now I found that Gavin had built about his house that palisade of high wooden palings of which I had dreamed years before; it had been built to keep in the other otters he now had at Sandaig. I went through the visible gate, indeed; but by invisible gates I was barred out; a gate was closed within every bud on every twig of birch and alder, closed in rock and water and fern and heather-sweet air, closed in sky and sea and the line of the hills of Skye, in the grey rocks by the shore where I went alone to weep comfortless tears near the last place where I had seen our dear animal angel swim away.

It is said in Celtic countries that a death appears first in the sky, then little by little its darkness descends until at last it touches the earth, and becomes a reality in this world. In the invisible air it gathers, to rain down its shower of blood. When I left Mary's cottage where I was to sleep, to go down the track to Gavin's house, I seemed to be repelled as by the intangible negative force of a magnetic field. I seemed to wade through lead, as in a dream; to be enveloped in a heavy darkness, as if the death I had caused still hung there, or some greater evil to come. Through that repelling cloud I forced my way; and again, for the last time, Gavin tried, I think, to comfort me; not any more as someone in his life, but just because my grief remained as a last bond, which he would gladly break. Yet there was, even so, for one last moment a return of old love; walking back with me as far as the bridge over the burn, he said, 'We will never doubt one another again, never, never;' and I replied, 'Never, never.' Yet the very next day, the tension grown too great for either of us to bear, we parted in anger, each knowing there could be no return, that we had both been hurt too deeply. As I left the house I had said I would not communicate with him again. 'Oh yes you will,' he had said; 'you will write me yet another letter of reconciliation.' For that is what I had done, from Girton, after the discovery of the missing letter had seemed in a gleam of false hope to promise that all might yet be well. It seems that my letter had served only to put Gavin into the embarrassing position of having to respond; now his words made it impossible for me ever to write to him again.

My last memory of Sandaig is one of an overwhelming woe, not for myself but because I seemed to see Gavin, without me, abandoned to a losing battle against circumstances already so weighted against him—otter-boys unreliable if only because they were young; loneliness in that region of imagination we had shared. I knew that I could have—should have—been able to help him to turn these desperate odds; that I still could have done so. If only I could have somehow brushed away some invisible cobweb of illusion and misunderstanding, we should still have been companions, bearing one another's burdens. For we both had heavy burdens to carry, lonely lives to lead. Yet though I felt so desperate and so clear-sighted a pity, I could not speak. Did I lack the courage? Or did I know, then, with the same clairvoyance, that it would be useless? I do not know. Perhaps it was pride, perhaps despair that kept me silent, then and on other occasions when I longed to speak the words that were in my heart. 'Gavin, I love you, let me stay in your life, let me share your burdens, even now, as I long to do.' Why does love keep silent when it should speak? But I have been able to speak from my heart only in my poems.

Gavin had, on that last visit of mine to Sandaig, another otter, Edal; not so dear as Mijbil, but at all events an otter. Now she was ill, so gravely ill that he thought her dying. My last act before I left was an attempt towards expiation. One practical thing I did, which I hoped and believed might help her recover; and in the night after our last parting, as I lay in Mary's cottage in grief, I made one last bargain with the dark angel at the barred gate. 'Let her recover,' I said 'and I will never seek to see Gavin again.' It is certain she recovered; far from certain that my prayer had anything to do with it. Yet at the time it was as if dark wings had taken it and carried it from me, like the beating, living heart of those sacrificed to the gods. To give one's heart to be torn out can comfort when comfort cannot. To the lost, mercy, human or divine, is of all things the most unendurable. I asked for none, and had none on myself.

I kept my vow; hoping still that Gavin might again seek me out, or the one mind bring us together again. That mind can play strange tricks; for when I went to order a name-plate for my new house (for I had taken a house again, in Paultons Square, in the brief period of hope, after learning about the missing letter, that Gavin and I might be friends again, as formerly), the ironmonger from a box of samples drew a brass plate on which his name was engraved: Gavin Maxwell; as if the living bond between us could still unerringly seek out such fragments of a broken world. I heard from him at last; he wrote to tell me he was getting married. When I read that letter I had no longer anything to hope or fear in this world. From that time I felt only one compelling need—to see my life as a whole, to read the pages of my own Book of Judgement; to understand, perhaps, what is written there. Then, perhaps, I might be free.

I can call one witness in my defence: Helen Sutherland, when I read to her the passage about the curse evoked by the Tree—if curse it was, for I did not see it as such, it was a desperate heart's cry for truth—understood. 'You wanted him to *see*,' she said. I had written the story in her house, in the little white bedroom that was for me in all these years a sanctuary in the house of a friend who did value me, who would not have recognized in me the image that I had begun to feel, obscurely, that Gavin had of me. Which is not of course to say that he was entirely wrong. Yet Helen, with her great intelligence, her sense of Christian justice and mercy, and her respect for the best in all of us who were her friends, did see.

When I called for the loosing of the lightning from the tree, I was in a state of unreasoning anguish; yet as I look back now on the flaming anger of that evening when I cried out for the Eumenides, it was, I know, a last and desperate cry for the triumph of the holy and the beautiful world over the vulgar and the superficial. As I stand before those immortal living presences, both the dark and the bright, I would plead that the root of my anger was a desire for the holy reality to prevail. The psalmist was not afraid to invoke the divine justice in its terrible aspect; 'Let God arise and let his enemies be scattered' is a prayer that arises from the depths of a terrible purity. I did not, God knows, wish to injure Gavin or to destroy him—only that he should not be allowed to forget the vision I thought he had all but lost. But it is not the way of that world to bend the will, which is at all times free to turn away; only at the Last Judgement must every soul face the God within. In that world there may be no difference in value between the divine mercy and the divine anger; but who is pure enough to dare to invoke that world's vengeance? It may be that oblivion of the soul calls, before the tribune of the gods, for the awakening lightning; the only aspect the divine mercy can assume in the face of our extreme resistance; for that oblivion is a spiritual state more deadly than any suffering which may serve to awaken us from it. Yet those who cry, as I did, for justice, cannot afterwards beg for mercy; I invoked the most terrible epiphany of all; and perhaps my prayer was answered.

CHAPTER TWO

The Lion's Mouth

THAT golden string which had once (or so I imagined) united me with Gavin had become a severed cord from whose living substance my life bled away continually, so that I lost all power to lift up my heart; and this for several years during which I did not see him. Of these years one memory will serve for all: the hired car standing outside what had been my own house to take the groom to his wedding. For what seemed unrelated reasons, I had passed the end of Paultons Square at that time of all times. 'The marriage-hearse' was the phrase that came to my mind. Of course, I may only have imagined that the car had come for Gavin; but that he married on that day, that I did not imagine.

He had sent me an invitation to the large reception to be held a few days later; and I even wondered whether, so that his friends and mine should know that he was marrying with my good will, and himself feel no shadow of trouble on my account I ought to compel myself to go. It was John Hayward who brought me to my senses, pointing out that a man on the eve of his wedding would be thinking of his bride, not of me at all; that his guests and hers would be from a world in which my very existence would be unknown; that my presence would be neither here nor there. 'No one, after all, ever imagined Gavin would marry *you*,' John concluded. Illogically it was John whom I did not forgive; I took his salutary advice but did not see him again for two years.

Only in this cold January of 1976 can I bring myself to face a memory I had not recorded. Before I had left Paultons Square I had been warned; but had put away the warning. Gavin had said to me, one day, that he had been thinking of marrying; I did not take this very seriously at the time, and indeed nothing came of it then. But he had spoken very gently to me, saying, 'I would like you to accept my wife, as you are the two people who know me best.' I had not responded to that request directly, but had said, also so quietly, more to myself than to him, that he may no more have noted my words than I his—on both sides it seemed as though we were each speaking to ourselves, not to one another, 'Then I will go away.' I could not believe it; and yet that is what I did; I withdrew myself from Gavin's life, little by little, always hoping to be recalled; and I was not recalled.

Yet I had waited. Someday, someday I would surely hear from him, or meet him. And one day his letter came, and my heart gave a leap of joy to

327

see the familiar hand-writing Then I read it; he was going to marry a friend of many years; she had been married to a friend of Gavin's but was now free; a woman of his own world, of course. The letter asked me, again, to accept and love for his sake, his wife.

Gavin's letter reached me when I was staying with Willa Muir in the house at Swaffham Prior where she and Edwin had lived for a few happy years until Edwin's death in 1959. I had given up my Research Fellowship at Girton, grateful as I had been for Muriel Bradbrook's kindness in inviting me back to my old College, there to continue in some financial security my work on Blake.

I am sure my natural friends must have thought it a pity that I could not have settled in Academe, that happy, civilized world, where work so valuable may be done, in a freedom unimaginable elsewhere. I enjoyed teaching the young, too, although this never presented itself to me as my task in life. Why could I not have done so? I enjoyed many friendships, too, in Cambridge. C. S. Lewis arrived in Cambridge in the same year as myself, to take up his Regius Professorship; installed in those same rooms in Magdalene where so many years before William Empson had been my host; now it was C. S. Lewis—not sitting on the windowbox, but standing with, on one side Owen Barfield and on the other A. C. Harwood, the Anthroposophist; like three Eldils from one of his own science fictions. Tom Henn, too, who read Yeats to us in what an Irishman in Sligo called 'his great cathedral voice that comes from the heart;' there was Muriel Bradbrook herself; and many peripheral figures who adorned that world. It was partly through myself, and also through John Holloway and David Daiches, that Edwin and Willa themselves came to settle at Swaffham Prior; Edwin was honoured by the University with a Doctor's degree; and he came often to visit Muriel Bradbrook and myself at Girton. It all seemed so perfect.

When my friend Rafael Nadal (Lorca's closest friend, and a member of that group of Spanish Intellectuals whose master had been Unamuno; Bunuel and Salvador Dali had been of his circle) came to visit me, 'What a *beautiful* room, he had exclaimed with that Spanish enthusiasm of his; then added, 'you *must* get away from here!' A spiritual friend. He was right, of course. If the record of my life shows any pattern is it not a series of returns to the wild places? I am wild and of the wilds, the inspirers meet me there; only there am I not, in some measure, an exile, playing (however enjoyably) a part.

My scholarship was always incidental to the needs of the poet for knowledge of a certain kind. Like Thomas Taylor, I read the books of wisdom for the sake of that wisdom, seeing scholarship always as a means to an end, never as an end in itself. But it is I suppose before all else the needs

of the poet that have driven me away from those 'straight roads' made by
education. My war-job at Bush House seemed more like a fantastic dream
than a reality; the British Council still more so. My attempts to
Christianise myself have all failed; and now Academe. I felt, in some
indescribable way, in a false position; just as I had felt with the Church.
My friends were poets and painters, all wild like myself; not Bohemia—I
seldom set foot in any 'pub', and then only as the guest of Louis MacNeice
or some other—and I do not enjoy that dropping of barriers of the world
where 'poets' (usually very minor ones, for any serious artist must live a
life in some sense disciplined) move in a kind of promiscuous
gregariousness. My personal life was never at any time, after I had left
Charles, emotionally involved within 'the literary world', with which my
relations were so to say professional. But every true poet is wild in a
different way. David Jones, in his magical room in Harrow; 'He still lives
in a dug-out,' I remember someone saying of him with much perception.
Winifred Nicholson belonged to Cumberland and its luminous grey skies.
Edwin and Willa floated like clouds among us. 'Edwin will never go into
anything unless he can see *an out*,' Willa once said. Dylan Thomas, it is
true, was the typical poet of the pubs, although even he did not write his
poems in that Dionysiac world, but in his native Wales. His friend Vernon
Watkins was quietly wild on his headland on the Gower Peninsula; he too
had fled from Cambridge many years before.

Eliot, indeed, from his office in Russell Square wore the impeccable
mask of the distinguished publisher and man of letters he was; but was
there not some truth in Tambi's words, 'But he is really a wild man, like
me.'? The poet must protect his wildness as best he may, with whatever
camouflage he can create; a principle inherited from the shy animal world
from a millennial past. And for a poet whose theme was the city, the city,
also, must be his protective disguise.

Not living poets only, or principally, but the dead also are, in that sense,
our own people in a way that for the critic is not so. The critic's work
begins where the work of the poet ends—with 'the words on the page';
and the processes of commentary are far other than those of formulating
some mood or vision or realization, one of those instantaneous intellections that come with a leap of the heart or a flash of imagination. When
the words are on the page the poet's work is done; in the hope that the
words may evoke in the reader the same flash, or mood, or intellection;
and on the whole the simpler the reader the more likely this is to take
place; and the best of critics—Coleridge is of course the best of critics—
can help the reader towards this. Some years ago, to make more room on
my bookshelves I threw out (not literally, of course: I sold them) all works
of criticism not written by poets. Scholarship is another matter, and

works of scholarship I did not throw out. I remember 'Jack' Lewis asking me once if I had ever found myself helped in my appreciation of any work of literature by any work of criticism; and when I said no, never, he said that neither had he. So perhaps I was not wrong in being unable to breathe the cold dry air of a Cambridge still in so many ways dominated by the kind of thought—and indeed by the same people—as I had encountered in my student days.

Cambridge soil may be fertile enough, but my own native Grass of Parnassus will not grow in those English gardens. Or was there in me some lack of adaptability, of some quite simple human trait that would have enabled me there to take root; as I think Muriel Bradbrook would have liked me to do? At all events, she gave me the chance.

So in Girton I could not, the second time more than the first, take root. Some homing instinct had taken me back to Paultons Square as the only place left where I might still pick up the threads of the broken pattern of my life, and I had already taken the lease of the house (no longer No. 9) that is still mine; though it has never seemed, in quite the same way, home. But I had let the house for the months I was to spend in America to give my Andrew Mellon lectures on Blake at the National Gallery in Washington; and now, at the beginning of a new Academic year, I was staying as Willa's guest until the time for departure. How happy Priory Cottage had been, while Edwin lived; how often had I, alone or with Muriel, taken the 'bus that dropped us by those two churches at Swaffham Prior, where the pigeons and the jackdaws, much to Edwin and Willa's delight and amusement, disputed the two towers. Now Willa was alone. I had seen her, at Edwin's funeral, stricken with grief, and looking ready to throw herself into the grave with her beloved Edwin. But she had begun to live again, to build up a world with her cat Popsy, and the various visiting cats, like 'Johnnie the Vicar' with his 'face like a chrysanthemum', as Willa said. She fed all who came through the cat-door in the kitchen. Willa had the gift of creating round herself a 'little' world alongside the main world, of cats, jackdaws, cleaning-women and tradesmen's boys, a fine firm bright texture of all the little daily things. But the centre of it all was Popsy and the rhythm of her saucers, exits, entrances, privileges, and daily rounds of house and garden. Living, then, with Willa, I understood very well how she had sustained Edwin. She and he had cared little for necessities, but much for small luxuries. Willa made 'drop-scones' fresh and hot; drank only the best tea (blended by herself in varying proportions from a family of tea-caddies) properly made with boiling water in a heated teapot; kept a bottle of Drambuie, from which she gave us tiny drams in the Bohemian glasses she and Edwin had brought with them from Czechoslovakia; could eat only the freshest and cleanest of food, though the dust lay thick under the bookcases. She was, as I often told her, like the Princess who could not sleep because of a pea hidden under nine mattresses; if I made the tea, she could tell to a tealeaf if my blending had been ill done. She had, besides, a gift which should be, but seldom is, accounted one of woman's greatest beauties—the softness of her touch. She could always, so she said, 'gentle' Edwin with the caress of her hand, with its fine tapering fingers. My mother's hands, too, had that soft, thrilling gentleness. One of my three granddaughters inherits it, though I do not.

'I'm soft-centred,' she used to say; some, who had hoped to talk with Edwin, were daunted by her aggressive conversational manner; but was she not, perhaps, just the protector of his silences that Edwin needed? A dragon to strangers, but to him, gentleness itself? 'Edwin had all the best of me,' she used to say; for him she had been—and knew she had been—a person she could never be for any other, because only Edwin, whom she loved, could evoke that side of her. And in their wandering homeless life, she said, 'my home was Edwin's bosom'.

I was with Willa, then, on the morning when that letter came; and when I had read it, her gentle hand comforted me. Later I was with Helen, and she, too, was infinitely compassionate and gentle. But it was Willa (who in any case on principle always took the woman's side) who comforted me then. I remember mechanically taking the 'bus into Cambridge, as I had planned to do, to work, I suppose, at the University library. I remember walking round the market, looking for I knew not what, and buying for myself a little necklace of mother-of-pearl beads; Sandaig shore, Sandaig shells. I remember that I could not swallow—could scarcely swallow for several days. However our grief may be self-caused, self-inflicted, and deserved, how we suffer! What a capacity for suffering a human being has! And I suffered to the extreme limit of my capacity. Yet fortitude had long been with me so habitual that I carried on with my life. I could not break down if I tried, so habitual with me has it become, in the course of a life in which I have carried my own burdens, to go on, from day to day. Perhaps, like my father, I am very strong physically; but also it is hard to break down when there is no one there to pick us up again. I remember Willa saying (and we had been speaking of Gavin), 'What a wonderful thing it is that men and women mean so much to one another!' And indeed it is so; immeasurably much, whether in a relationship, like her own with Edwin, cemented by mutual love; or no less in a doomed relationship like my own with Gavin. For even though I can now see how at every step I acted blindly and selfishly, God knows he was everything to me.

For the last day or two before embarking on the *Queen Mary* on my passage to New York I was staying with Rupert and Helen Gleadow, in their flat in Cheyne Row, just round the corner from Paultons Square; and on `the day after Gavin's marriage I sailed. Among the first-class passengers (thank God I was in the cabin class) was that very friend Gavin had brought to Sandaig on the fatal day of the rowan-tree.

I went to face the world as a scholar, a moment of success come at last, in a state of all but unbearable suffering. How I got through those months, which demanded of me a best I could not, under these circumstances, give, God only knows. By an irony of fate Washington's élite set themselves to welcome and entertain me. My lectures, fortunately, had already been written the previous summer before Gavin's letter-card, telling me of his engagement, had destroyed in me, with the long-nursed hope of ultimate reconciliation, the power to work.

In the night following the day that letter had reached me, as the mortally ill or wounded sometimes experience a partial separation from the suffering bodies they see lying on some bed below as if they themselves were other, I had been able, passing through and beyond my delirium of anguish, to see Gavin and his chosen bride in the full light of a love which had now been put to the test of a total renunciation (by that paradox by which the beloved asks most of the lover when he asks nothing at all). It had seemed, from that clear solitude above the snow-line of suffering, that I could love for his sake the woman he loved (that was what his brief conventional note had asked of me), that I could be glad he would have children. Perhaps I then allowed myself to fancy, he would bring his wife to visit me, would say to her, 'This is Kathleen, of whom I have told you'; perhaps they would invite me to cross again the threshold of the house that had been mine, to see that first-born for whose sake I would be glad to have lost what I valued most. I had, to Gavin, committed myself absolutely; but this was the one sacrifice I had never expected to be asked to make. Death would have been less painful, and infinitely less humiliating; yet, knowing how Gavin had loved our animal-child, how could I not wish for him a human son? It was as if, during that night, I saw all our lives as from some place beyond these brief life-times as stars sent out from the same source, each in its inmost nature immortal, beautiful, only and for ever to be loved: how then could I hate another woman whose nature was in essence the same as my own, who, loving Gavin, would be giving him the same love of which all are only channels, instruments? As in the order of angels message and messenger are one, so, in that altitude of freedom, I perceived that the ten thousand thousand agents of the one mind come and go within the universal sympathy in which no life or love is separate from the one life in all. In that insight, that freedom from myself, I beheld in that term and source of all existences a profound joy, wherein for a while I seemed almost to participate, as I lay, literally beside myself, outside myself in this almost unendurable confrontation with a reality by which my individual existence seemed in process of destruction.

I wrote, of course, to Gavin; very briefly. In the outer world (as John Hayward in the clear light of that world had pointed out to me) it made little difference what I wrote, or whether I wrote at all. But I had known too long of that second world, invisible to sense, in which thoughts have the reality of things, and acts. It was not enough to write; I must send out to Gavin no deadly thoughts, must lay no curse upon him, or his bride.

One night, in a dream, Gavin's bride came, and kissed me. But upon that exaltation, barely attained and scarcely held, followed mere grief. I lived, through that winter, only in the night, dragging myself through each day to the threshold, there to take up the invisible work which awaited me in an interior country which had no longer any frontier with the outer and common world. I longed for each empty day to end, so that I could resume my task, follow as best I could the bleeding severed thread of my life which led me now, like Blake's 'soul exploring the recesses of the grave' to discover 'the secrets of a land unknown'. I wanted only to be alone, taking up my grief each night, like the woman in the fairy-tale who must spin and weave the nettles that grow on graves into redemptive garments. I strove to learn my sorrow, to understand, to possess myself of it not as pain but as knowledge. Suffering, I was still inhabiting my love; but more than an inability to relinquish drove me on; that was the way the clue led. Into the heart of grief itself I sought to penetrate, as if there I should discover some secret that would resolve all. It was not courage, either (the hope to be free by facing the thing feared); this was my quest, the task love itself had laid upon me, and therefore sacred.

'*Il faut que vous mettez la tête dans la gueule du lion,*' Alexis Léger said to me, I remember: the advice of the great St. John Perse, author of *Exile*; for whom all the ways of the world lead into the future, open to the conquest of imagination. In the garden of Dumbarton Oaks, on a bench among the violets, it was. I had met him several years before on my first visit to the United States; then as an obscure 'visiting poet', now in a more honourable guise. But he had been kind—more than kind to me on that first visit. I had been the guest of William Empson's brother Charles and his wife Monica, my old neighbour in Martindale years; and I had been taken to call on the poet by Robert Richman, who organized such meetings for poets reading their works at his Institute of Contemporary Arts; which he had founded in admiration of, and with the help of, our dear mutual friend Herbert Read. M. Léger then invited me to lunch, and I was spellbound by his conversation—monologue rather—as vivid and as enthralling as that of Othello and no less full of 'Anthropophagi, and men whose heads do grow beneath their shoulders'—or the like 'marvels' of the world. Some as simple as the fungi whose soil is the glue of posters in the heart of cities; others as rare as some citrous fruit that grows only on one tree, in the Imperial garden of the Chinese Emperor (M. Léger had known China before the Revolution), of which one cutting was given to I have forgotten whom, and grew now on Bird Island off New Orleans. He was a man more akin to Gavin than any other poet I have known, caring more for the solitary places and the sea, for the marvels of nature, the earth and its teeming inexhaustible fecundity, than for the 'literary world' which he studiously avoided; or the Academic world, in which he refused absolutely to set foot. 'Do you not', I had said to the poet of *Anabase*, 'miss the wildernesses of the earth here in Washington?' And he had pointed to the vultures circling above the city; the wild places are everywhere, he had said, and there are, besides, tracts of earth in the United States as virgin as any on the surface of the moon. It was W. H. Hudson who had told him about the fungi who have made their habitat the glue of posters; Hudson, whom he had met through Conrad, who had in his youth been his friend and admired master. He had wondered that the great writer should have given him his friendship, an obscure young Frenchman of whom no one had heard. Conrad had said—I hope I reproduce the sense, though not the words (he always spoke French though he understood English better than he liked to have it known)— that chance had brought him, and the obligation towards whatever chance brings is absolute. 'You had in common your love of the sea,' I said; for he had been telling me of the harbours of the world known to him as well as to Odysseus—he even knew the Hebrides, Gavin's waters—but he said No, Conrad hated the sea; the sea, for him, was the antagonist, the enemy.

One must never go back, he said; he had himself sailed round the island of Guadeloupe, his native isle, paradise of his boyhood; but he had known that he must not go on shore. One must go on, never looking back; and his wonderful eyes seemed always to see into distances opening before him. Not eyes wonderful to be looked into, but eyes that wonderfully looked out, and far away, beholding '*les merveilles*' that the earth everywhere generates.

I had of course no intention of inviting the advances of the poet I consider as the greatest, after the death of Eliot and of Yeats. I belonged to Gavin; Gavin, who on that first visit to the States had driven me to the airport, and who had given me, when we parted, a little cowrie shell from the Sandaig shore. Why do I find it so hard to confess, even now, twenty years later, that I gave that cowrie shell to Alexis Léger? It seemed, then, the only thing I had worthy of him. Yet Gavin's parting gift should not have been given away; again, as I come to write this story, I find that I was the betrayer, not he. The smallest of shells; but symbol of so much.

On my next visit to Washington, M. Léger called on me at once; and we always met, thereafter, and were fellow guests both at the house of Francis and Margaret Biddle (the poetess Margaret Chapin) and of Mildred Woods Bliss. Now, among the violets in those beautiful gardens of Dumbarton Oaks I poured out to him my grief. He had admonished me, on a previous occasion, to live like a poet; for to be a poet, he reminded me, is a way of life; not to him would I have had to explain why I could not live in Cambridge. We are not poets, he reminded me, merely when we are writing verse; our imagination must at all times be attuned to the imagination of the world as it flows on, ceaselessly, into the future. It comforted me a little that, scorned by Gavin ('nobody ever thought he would marry *you*') I found that St. John Perse was so real a friend; and he told me to put my head in the lion's mouth.

A few days later, carrying out from one of Washington's dazzling assemblies our champagne onto the terrace, I seemed, with the lights of the city outspread below like a tray of jewels, in the unknown night of the world's spaces, in the company of the poet for whom the earth is itself like a region of the imagination, to stand poised on the brink of Plato's 'moving image of eternity'; we ourselves, and the assembly behind us, uplifted on the bright crest of the world's ever-advancing wave. To those who can relinquish the past—and how much had Alexis Léger relinquished—was not this vision of the future the reward? The former Minister of France's foreign affairs had relinquished more than a private past, a private sorrow; though doubtless these also. Yet I could not let go. Like Lot's wife, I was bound to the past.

Nor did I, after all, go into the arena to meet the lion face to face; and through cowardice, was only mauled by it. Gay Taylor assured me that, astrologically, she thought it more than unlikely that Gavin's marriage would last; and I am bound to admit that I waited for it to end. She had proved right, God knows, in foreseeing sorrow as the outcome of our meeting. But could I not, perhaps, outwait the stars? I was, besides, the prey of an invincible incredulity. When I heard from Canetti that Gavin's brief marriage was in fact over, I said, as I remember, 'God is not merciful but He is just.' Canetti, who could not bring himself to admit any good in the Demiurge nevertheless replied, with a certain solemnity, 'I would not say that; but there is a Law.' Only then was I able to take up my life again. I could have listened to many stories current at the time of the explosive break-up of that marriage, but I refused to do so. I remember one, however—from Canetti. Gavin's wife had said to him 'But you are treating me just as you treated Kathleen!' No doubt she had thought, as I had thought, that she, unlike all others who had failed, could meet his needs. I found comfort, even companionship, in that reported phrase.

And what if Gavin's marriage had been under a blessing, if that child for whose sake I could not have withheld the consent of my love, had become a reality? Would I then have been glad, at last? God knows; 'there is a Law', and the outcome was what it was. For the marriage to have been under a blessing, for that son to have been born, everything would have had to be different, not just some one or other element in the situation. And in that case I might have been, at last, glad with him, and for him. I do not know; for I was not put to that test. But I think I would have loved Gavin's child, had I been given the smallest opportunity to do so.

Neither was my incredulity, perhaps, mere egoism; in it there may have been insight too, the knowledge that no one can with impunity snatch from life anything and everything; we must know what is ours.

What I could not face, then and for long after, was the realization that the One Mind that brought us together, had also parted us. I swung, instead, between the extremes of my despair: the useless protest that since Gavin and I had been to one another Heaven-sent, it could only be by a miscarriage of divine justice that we were parted; and the retrospective denial of what had been. I reached a point when I seemed dispossessed even of my own past; for in his departure Gavin had taken with him my very identity, inseparable from our shared world and all its texture of memories; not recent and shared memories only, but the regions of my childhood, made over to him like a domain to its rightful heir after long absence returned. If ever by chance I was asked if I knew Gavin, I answered no, feeling this point-blank denial to be the mere truth. I might almost have given the same answer if I had been asked 'do you know Kathleen Raine', for all the country of imagination the poet had inhabited I had lost in losing Gavin; even 9 Paultons Square had become a house memory dared not enter. All that was left me was Ilford, in whose shameful heritage Gavin had no part; but also my learning. William Blake and the Neoplatonists were still, in the separation of our regions of imagination, incontestably my own, lending their dignity to my destitution. Many women whose loss has been as great have had less with which to spin their nettle-yarn.

When a bird can no longer fly on that invisible beam which guides it to its own place, because that place is gone, it must circle, unable to alight, inner and outer reality no longer congruous. I travelled far afield, to America, to Greece, to Italy, as if moving in outer space, on and on with no centre to draw me back. Since this is a record of inner experience I shall not describe these journeys which so mercifully distracted me, by day, from the far other journeyings of my nights. I began to write this record because I could not relinquish the life I could no longer live. Driven from the living reality I had to rebuild my world, memory by memory, or I had nothing; that is the truth of it, so far as I know it—I must live still in my love's house or I could not live at all. So much beauty how could I see lost? For my life—not because mine but because a life—seemed to me to have been something of infinite value, infinite meaning. Everything was there, if I could only discover what. Yet at the same time I needed to be rid of it, to free myself of myself. In giving birth is the motive to rid the body of an intolerable burden or to give life? Motives and intentions have no place in the hidden will that determines the processes of life. Useless to ask the spinners and weavers and builders of shells and nests and webs and combs why they must do what they do—why sea-molluscs must add lamina after lamina to the rim of some iridescent geometric shell they themselves are without sense to perceive. The law which decrees those shells neither begins nor ends with these blind labourers, inseparable from the single whole of nature. Like them we may have to labour at tasks of consciousness, whose shining structures are visible to spirits of an order as remote from us as we from the toilers between the tides.

Once, some months after his marriage, I met Gavin by chance outside the chemist's shop on the corner of Beaufort Street, by the traffic-lights. Meeting so, for the duration of a heart-beat, I was back in life. He kissed me, for all the world as if we had been the people we formerly were; it seemed natural to meet, to exchange those daily small things friends communicate because a relationship is continuous: except for one thing, that the moment was a fragment from a world which no longer existed. Like the sensation of an amputated limb, that irresolvable discord of joy and pain bore no relation to present reality.

For in the end of my relationship with Gavin was a finality I recognized as being altogether different in kind from anything I had ever known; I did not hope for anything more of life, not from hopelessness but because I neither desired nor needed anything more; I knew that my fate was, in the most profound sense, completed, that more would be superfluous; I can only put it so. If anyone had attempted to console me by saying that I might perhaps love again, or find some other thing, I would not have disbelieved them from despair but from a kind of plenitude; life, could give me no more, for there was nothing more I could ever need or want. There was work to be done, but the work of the daimon; death I still must face, but death is not, perhaps, to me serious as an issue—my greatest fear is that it should come before my work is finished. I was, in any case, almost an old woman: what had I to lose but a few years? To relinquish the future is nothing when the thing loved is in the past.

Nothing remained but to write. I wrote the first draft of my story in Helen Sutherland's house, soon after my return from Washington; carried

my volume to Italy, where as the guest of Hubert and Lelia Howard, I
worked in the earthly paradise of Ninfa; continued work on the island of
Euboea, looking from Philip Sherrard's white house to Parnassus and
Helicon across the sound where the Argonauts sailed, and where now
Gavin's brother's yacht floated at its moorings below; a spar from the
wreck of my world. I carried it to Canna, where the Cuillin, whose jagged
leaping summit had, from Sandaig, lain to the west, lay now in the wake
of the ship's path, to the east, a mirage bright in the declining sun. 'Those
infinite mountains of light' which had once been the Wannies, and once
again the hills of Skye.

> Last night I dreamed a weary dream
> Beyond the Isle of Skye.

There are times and places when the outer world seems perfectly to
image the inner, to reflect back to us, by 'correspondence', meanings,
metaphysical intuitions. Perhaps it does so always, no less than when it,
gives back to us chaos for chaos, opacity for opacity, than when all is clear
as in Boehme's 'vegetable glass' of wonders. Because love had made all
there sacramental, or because of the clarity of that glass, I still found, in
the Western Highlands, forms that answered my imagination. There is a
natural symbol of peculiar beauty which meets us wherever the sun rises
or sets over water: that track of light which travels from the sun to the
place where we stand. For each there is a path always silently at our feet,
summoning us to walk over the water. In Greece I used to swim out along
that track until the great ball of blood the setting sun there resembles
dropped behind Mount Parnassus. In the Hebrides it is said that the newly
dead leave the land and travel towards the west; do they then walk that
track of liquid gold which seems at times to turn the water of the sea to
light? Nowhere on earth does the summoning path shine with such
splendour; but west of the Hebrides lies the edge of the world. Looking in
imagination along the ever-present ever-summoning way, I could not yet
follow it; the centre that drew me was still the rowan-tree of Sandaig, on
the landward side, *terra firma*. I was not ready to take the way of no
return, to go with that great fire of light on its night-journey.

If I here say little of the friends who received me, in my exile, into their
houses, it is because the interchange of ideas, the sharing of impressions
and knowledge, the laughter, the conversations, all these pleasant things
belong to an impersonal order on the far side of the personal fate of which
this book is the record.

All these sanctuaries of my friends' houses have in common one thing:

all are dedicated, almost, it might be said, consecrated, as monastic houses are ('at least in principle', as Marco Pallis would say) to something besides personal ends. Margaret Campbell told me, when first I was her guest at Canna House, of the prayer she had made that all who came to the isle should receive its blessing. She and John Lorne Campbell are converts to the Catholic faith, 'the auld religion', strongest of many bonds with the people of the Isles living and dead. Hubert and Lelia Howard, latest and perhaps last custodians of the diminished but still great estates of the dukes of Sermoneta (Lelia's inheritance) regard that feudal task as a sacred trust; something no longer imaginable in a profane world which seeks to possess absolutely, and not, as in the older civilization, 'under God'. The planting of orchards and crops and trees, the restoration of the castle of Sermoneta as a summer-school for young musicians (selling pieces of land to restore equivalent pieces of the ancient roof, or to build bathrooms and students' cubicles into the great keeps like honey-comb into an ancient tree) are works undertaken within the framework of the Christian *civitas dei*. There was truth (the historian's tag notwithstanding) in the concept of a Christian Roman empire to whose holiness the works of her artificers bear witness. Is not civilization, as such, the empire of the human imagination, of that in man which is precisely not determined by economic pressures and the instincts of the *bête humaine?* Who, in the city well-named eternal, since so much of eternity is reflected in its works of three successive civilizations, can fail to be aware of this? Art is the city of the soul. Hubert and Lelia Howard, like those painted donors whose grave intelligent faces look up at some golden vision of virgin and angels, still served that holy city as their ancestors had done in unbroken succession since Aeneas founded his colony.

I was given, on my last visit to Ninfa, the room which had belonged to Marguerite Caetani, the last duchess, patron of poets, whose magazines *Commerce* and *Botteghe Oscure* made literary history. Alexis Léger had written for *Commerce*. How could I, writing at her table, forget that what I write must abide the judgement of civilization, of that unbroken tradition carried into my own present by T. S. Eliot (her cousin) and her friends Alexis Léger and Paul Valéry? Now that I had gained admission to that company, I saw with shame how I had neglected the work of the poet through personal unhappiness (and personal happiness also, though less often) forgetting that these are, in the light of eternity, only the furnaces in which natural experience is transmuted into those unageing forms.

Two especially, among Rome's treasures of the imagination, put me to shame. The first was that dungeon of San Pietro ad Vinculam where the barbarian chieftains conquered in battle were kept alive until such time as some general should arrive in Rome to hold his Triumph; they were decapitated at the end of the show. The long list of their names is there; and with them those of the Apostles Peter and Paul; obscure figures in such company. It was St. Paul whose spirit spoke to me, that slight, indomitable Jew, writing (a stone's throw from the not dissimilar prison of the Christians' fellow-victims, the lions) to his friends to pray, not for his release, but 'that God would open unto us a door of utterance, to speak the mystery of Christ'.

In the city which itself embodies all the dreams and visions of the Christian cult, that dungeon, unadorned as a coal-hole, most deeply moved me just because it preceded all embodiment. One could not get nearer than this to the source of Christendom. St. Paul could not have known that his Christ would rule in the city of the Emperors, nor that his own letters would be read throughout a civilization which did not then exist, and which came into existence solely through the triumph of imagination over power, and over the *bête humaine*. He, unlike those tragic and romantic chieftains, was free in his bonds (you can see the stone to which they were tied) and in his death beyond the reach of the executioners, who have no power over the kingdom not of this world. I then began to understand why freedom is to be found only in the lion's mouth; not only because every lesser kind must assuredly be lost, since this world in its very nature imperils all, takes all in the end; but because only untrammelled by hopes and fears can we contemplate existence as it appears to the one mind within whose unity our wholes are parts; fear blinds us to the glory of many 'portions of eternity too great for the eye of man'. The martyrs, courting that death, had aspired to total freedom; not to death as such, not a death-wish. No civilization was ever founded on a death-wish.

Hubert Howard took me, one afternoon in a downpour of rain, to visit the Keats museum. The room where Keats died is a little larger than the dungeon of the barbarian kings and Christian apostles, and much more beautiful, with its painted rafters and view of the Spanish steps; a fitting room for the poet to die in who had perceived the truth of beauty. We were shown the treasures by the custodian and his wife; and I must have said to Hubert something about Keats and Shelley (who in the great company of Rome seemed diminished to the stature of friends and members of one's own family) being over-shadowed by those greater legislators of the world who (in their lifetimes more unacknowledged than any poet) had created Christendom. Hubert, deeply Catholic though he is in faith and by family tradition, replied, 'but they too gave all they had'. It seemed to me then that all the enduring works and living memories of the Eternal City are sacrifices which the gods to whom they were made have accepted because of their purity.

I returned from Italy by way of Corsica, exchanging the austere sweet grandeur of the Palazzo Caetani for Homer's land of the Laestrygonians, those cannibals who attacked Odysseus and his mariners (coasting from Polyphemus' cave below the Cyclopian city of Norma, on the hill behind Ninfa and its fountains) with showers of sling-stones. I went there to visit Frederica Rose who (herself a Laestrygonian by affinity, a General's daughter whose early passion was reckless hunting) had found in Corsica, where she had lived for many years, the counterpart of her own nature. (She was the first to light upon those carved menhirs of Filitosa, seen one way archaic warriors armed with swords, seen the other, uncompromisingly phallic.) Here I felt myself more remote from all familiar land-marks than in any place I have ever been. Greece I seemed to have known always, as if in some former life I had been native there. Of the Italy of art, all civilized Europeans are in some degree citizens; but until I set foot on the harbour of Bastia (Balzac, that admirer of Napoleon, I found, had been there before me, however) Corsica had had no existence for me at all, real or imaginary. As if rising into existence for the first time, therefore, I watched the unfolding panorama of those savage snow-jagged alps, those deep romantic chasms hung with chestnut-forests, those Laestrygonian bastions of Calvi, the citadel of Sartène perched like the Tibetan Potala on its rock. The luxuriant olive-trees, the *maquis* whose lentisk and arbutus (on the dry mountains of Greece barely waist-high) forms a dense and fragrant woodland of evergreen filled with blackbird-song, rose before me unsullied by any hopes or fears of mine, memories or anticipations. From Bastia to Calvi we travelled in a little *michelin* train on a railway-track which suggested, in the smallness of its scale in relation to that vertiginous and rugged scenery, a 00-gauge model railway, for ever taking hairpin-bends round precipices, plunging into tunnels hewn through the clean rock, often with goats or cattle running along the track in front of us. The autumn moon which travelled with us seemed to be plunging down into gorges, or suddenly reappearing high overhead, now in front, now behind; unfolding, as in a dream, the savage and enchanted interior landscape of Kubla Khan. Our fellow-travellers, women with bulging baskets, men with guns, were speaking the Corsican language, defence of their race against the encroachments of successive civilizations whose remains (Graeco-Roman, Genoese, French Imperial) seem so strangely alien, as if shipwrecked on the rocks and submerged reefs of an indomitable barbarism. I listened to that tongue, never spoken by civilized man or woman, wondering what unguessed meanings and modes of feeling and being, incommunicable except in that speech, were preserved, by those archaic words, in the consciousness of the living; attitudes and thoughts of the Laestrygonians and the builders of megaliths.

At one point there had been a landslide on the line, and we all had to get out, carrying our baggage through the freshly fallen rock and earth, to where the other *michelin*, from the Calvi side, was waiting to take us on. The episode, slight in itself, reappeared later in a dream, from which I wrote a poem; but the dream's symbolic content must have come less from the impact of Corsican scenery (to me that island was and remains a place of impenetrable strangeness) than from my conversations with Frederica. In that relentless isle she had worked out her salvation, returning, after years in the wilderness, to the Church (of England, at that, true to her native Gloucestershire). I had known her first as a Marxist, an elegant and gallant traitor to her own traditions; and now, after adventures which in risk and action rivalled Conrad, in romantic dedication to love *jusqu' au bout* some film of Greta Garbo (or was it Marlene Dietrich who on such well-bred naked feet walked her knife-edge of burning desert after some irretrievable *légionnaire?*). She had found, at the end of it all, that to which all loves, even the most deluded, lead in the end: one can but say, God. ('Call it X,' I tried saying to Ivor Richards once, hesitating to use a word, like its only Scriptural equation, too often abused. 'No, no, you have to say God, there is no synonym'—and the author of Basic English, if anyone, should know.) 'At least she knew where she wanted to get to,' Frederica said, as she closed the book of saints in which we had looked up the story of how St. Mary of Egypt had worked her passage to Jerusalem as a prostitute. She believed in the miraculous, having made a vow to pray in every church in Corsica for the salvation of some incorrigible lover, and she had, in a sudden illumination, realized that the grace she had asked for him, was offered likewise to herself: a thing that seldom occurs to women in love, set only upon drawing up the beloved out of the depths.

Hubert Howard, on whose ancestral tree hang popes and Catholic martyrs like golden apples among the emperors and earls, had not once said to me 'go back to the Church'; it was Frederica, who had been, in her own words, 'scraped across the stony bed of the universe', who said go back, accept the divine forgiveness offered to all.

In part I clung to my remorse because that last painful strand still bound my life to Gavin; in part because I feared to entrust myself, yet again, to hope, for fear of being once more dashed down. Yet I knew she was right, it was time to relinquish personal hopes and fears. That confrontation must have been decisive; for when I dreamed of stepping out of a train that had come to a halt among high wild mountains, I knew the dream was a symbol of freedom; a state which, as I began slowly to enter upon it, seemed of a quality scarcely discernible, like air. No longer to be impelled or compelled by desire or fear was, in that dream, like getting out of the train at Penrith with my children in October 1940, and smelling, in the darkness, the forgotten scent of hills and sheep.

Those who enter a religious order, who leave, as it is said, the world, take a new name; and this represents a truth; for the former human personality is (at least in principle, and in many instances in reality) left behind. Life, from this time on, is no longer lived in terms of the human ego, its desires and hopes and fears; another principle takes over, and the new man or woman has become an instrument of another principle. St. Paul's 'not I, but Christ liveth in me' is not an exclamation of emotion, but an exact expression of that new mode of life; which can only begin when the renunciation of the personal existence is absolute. I had now reached this threshold, reached an understanding, at least, of what was now demanded of me; understood, too, not without anguish, that no renunciation less than absolute is a renunciation at all, but a mere bargaining for the thing most desired at the price of everything else. My life had hitherto been a series of such gambler's losses; but now if I could not place myself beyond these hopes and despairs, I could not go on. I knew enough of the literature of the Perennial Philosophy to know at what parting of the ways I stood; and, confronted with a choice I had hoped never to have to make, knew that others had made it, that the way of absolute renunciation of hopes and fears and desires had a thousand times been found to be the way of freedom; the terrible words 'he that loseth his life, the same shall find it' met me. But still I could not turn away from the past, which seemed to contain all the treasure of my life, to enter the emptiness of—not an unknown future, for of the future I neither asked nor expected anything—but of a new mode of being altogether, a futureless condition which is nevertheless freedom itself, as such; that poverty, or emptiness, of whose great joy many have told, but all saying that the price to be paid is the relinquishment of the hopes and fears of which natural life is an incessant flow. I sheltered myself in the last tatters of my egoism, remorse. And if, besides, I argued with myself, catastrophe had followed my most sincere attempt to perfect even one relationship, had I not better keep away from the gods altogether, as dangerous destroyers? I refused to draw the obvious conclusion, that since what had happened was what had to happen, given all the circumstances, it therefore was, (as all reality can only be) the expression of the divine will, terrible to me and to Gavin only insofar as the judgement passed upon us was not what either would have wished. But at every moment, that Judgement is passed in the inexorable terms of reality itself; there are no mistakes.

Those patterns of lives Plato's Er saw spread out for the souls to choose were varied, better and worse, good and bad; and so it is in Indian and Tibetan accounts of incarnation and reincarnation; but all say that good and bad alike must be discarded by the souls who seek for freedom; for all

those patterns are but variations on a single theme, the suffering conse-
quent upon all that has in time its beginning, middle and end, birth and
death, rise and decline. What are the typically fated people, Oedipus and
Macbeth, Deirdre, or Balzac's Rafael de Valentin, but the doers and
sufferers of calamity? Saints, sages, musicians like Mozart, seem to enter
the world already free, knowing more than experience can ever teach
those who struggle through its toils. Blake knew that knowledge belongs
to the state of innocence, and his annals of experience are all the devious
wanderings of ignorance in 'Satan's labyrinth'. I can now myself say that I
have learned nothing from experience, from my mistakes, from trial and
error, or from the mere passage of time: only through rifts in these clouds,
as if from another order of knowledge altogether. Tragedies, after all,
however nobly enacted and grandly endured, are, as seen by wisdom, the
storms of illusion, the webs woven in ignorance and passion by those who
'do but slenderly know themselves'. In tragedy we can finally admire only
the grandeur of humanity's never-abandoned struggle to attain the
moment of transcendence; without which there can be no catharsis, no
liberation. Having myself at last perhaps emerged, stunned and exhausted
and too late, only what lies on the far side of that moment seems now to
matter. The term of all the devious roads lives are is another condition of
being altogether, known only to those who have experienced it; who are
perhaps more numerous than profane literature might lead one to
suppose. The people in the cave may pity as 'disillusioned' those others
who no longer care for the shadow-prizes nor compete for them. But the
loss of illusion, for Plato as for the followers of the Buddhist or any other
way of enlightenment, is known to be the threshold of that state of being
which is its own joy.

CHAPTER THREE

The Light of Common Day

IF ANY reader has read thus far perhaps such a one will ask how I could
have lived my life with my head in the clouds, so unaware of the world
around me. Yet if I have written my story upon the assumption that mental
things are real and constantly act as the causes of events, operating through

thought no less than through physical action, it can hardly be said that the belief makes life easier; on the contrary, for the sins of the heart are agents. So indeed is the heart's love and goodness, but my attempts at these can scarcely be called successful. However, if my attempts to live 'up to' my view of reality have failed, I have not, either, spared myself its inevitable judgement.

If I have written, then, of an inner world and its events it is not because I have had no occasion to notice the outer world, as this appears to a society indoctrinated with the notion that the material level is all. That level has its virtues too—feeding the hungry, tending the sick, and the many other social virtues of our society. Platonic love would be meaningless in materialist terms. It may be said that my own adventure into such a relationship will hardly commend it. But if I cannot defend my failure I can at least defend my values because I believe these inevitably follow from the real nature of things. If the mental world is a world of causes; if man is not only an animal, but also a soul and a spirit, then the issues I so terribly encountered cannot be evaded.

By the logic of circumstances, no doubt, one of those far-off figures of the Cambridge of my student years whose falsehoods had so bedevilled me, reappeared for a moment. I remembered her face as one I had seen; perhaps at the Heretics, those Sunday evening meetings which it had been 'advanced' to attend in that world now so remote both in time and in more important respects; or perhaps her face only resembled other faces bearing the imprint of the same ideology. How easily, in those days, had I been put out of countenance when one of those bright clever 'emancipated' faces had happened to focus on me (such people always look you straight in the face, seeing no reason to respect the privacy or mystery of another being) with 'I'm afraid I don't understand what you mean by the word "beauty"'—or whatever it might be. They didn't of course; but what was implied was that there was no such thing. It was always some qualitative word that such people met with some unanswerable negation based upon the premiss that only the quantifiable is 'real'. As a schoolgirl I had lacked both the knowledge and the courage to defend Keats's 'beauty is truth, truth beauty' against the reduction of man, nature and works of art to material terms (human will to animal instinct, animal instinct to chemistry, and so on down). I had not taken the measure of their ignorance; had not realized that I was confronting people who had not (for example) the sense of the holy, or of intellectual beauty, and who were not therefore in a position to compare these qualities with their own quantitative standards. How certain people come to represent materialist ideologies can, for the present argument, be disregarded; for whatever reason many people do so; 'for we wrestle not against flesh and blood' but against ideologies and power-structures in high places, in the 'mass media', the Universities, and among the well-meaning when these are governed by false values.

Confronted with a mind which had so remarkably retained the stamp and style of the twenties, I knew with shame that I was in the presence of a mental deformity I had myself once been in haste to assume, and which I had allowed to plunge me into the loveless inhuman courses of my early years. As, for example, by way of conversation on psychiatry, I said that as I did not believe the Freudian doctrine to be true I was mistrustful of psychoanalysis; and she replied that she was far from being a 'strict' Freudian herself: 'An elderly spinster, for instance, for whom it is *too late* is much better left with her sublimations.' To such a statement there is no answer given the premiss: that that for which it may be 'too late' (the sexual act) is self-evidently a greater good than 'sublimations', which include in effect religion and all the arts, besides such lesser pleasures as gardening, keeping a cat or a dog, indeed practically all human activities not directly or indirectly concerned with the survival and reproduction of the physical body.

Yet she spoke without any trace of irony and in perfect good humour; without the saving bitterness of the 'double-take' such an utterance might have implied. The tone was, rather, conciliatory; meeting me half way, as if here at least two women who shared a Cambridge background could meet in agreement. Her remark was made, besides, with the assurance with which only received opinion is repeated; there was no question in 1965, as there might have been in 1925, of an 'advanced', daring or controversial statement. In behaviourist circles the remark would have passed as no more strange than a platitude upon the weather; and yet the question begged nothing less than Job's and Oedipus' and Blake's question, 'What is man?'

Perhaps Freud, a civilized man, was being paradoxical when he wrote of all the arts as mis-directed sexual libido; not so much mis-directed, he probably said, as re-directed. But the fact remains that Jung, who knew him well (and honoured him, as all must, as the first to chart the landfall of that great unexplored mental continent, 'the unconscious') parted with him on precisely that issue. There are, besides, plenty of people who so understand him and see nothing unacceptable in a theory whose strict and literal application must lead to a reversion of man to the human animal. It is not for me to point the moral of Poe's story of the lunatic asylum whose inmates locked up the sane men and conducted the establishment on their own lines. The 'cure', these days, is so often worse than the disease; and to remove from a human soul its conflicts and its suffering may be more kill than cure.

This person and I had on another occasion a conversation still more astonishing. She spoke of a medical colleague who 'specialized' in homosexuality. 'Is he successful?' I asked. 'Oh, yes—but of course it is easier to graft a vagina on a man than a penis on a woman' (or it may have been the other way round). Again there was nothing to be said; I wonder what the author of the *Phaedrus* would have thought; though the joke might have appealed to Aristophanes, whose spherical proto-lovers were certainly anatomical oddities. Yet given the behaviourist premiss that love is the rubbing together of little fleshy appendages the rest follows. What other felicity, what other view of love, homosexual or otherwise, have those to offer who deny the soul? I thought with affection of that great Catholic sinner the Baron de Charlus who in Charlie Morel beheld (rightly or wrongly or both) the Archangel Michael .... *'Quand le monde moderne avilit,'* Péguy wrote, *'mettons que c'est alors qu'il travaille de sa partie.'*

It seemed to me that the Utopias of atheism may well be the hells of the spirit; and the sexual orgasm itself, emptied of the spiritual dimension which makes of marriage a Christian sacrament, and the act of sex in both Buddhist and Hindu iconography a symbol of the eternal generation of the world by God, one of the torments of those hells.

A more famous and austere atheist is said to have said that sex should be as simple a matter as drinking a glass of water. Against Lenin's colourless odourless and tasteless draught I set that cup of water given 'for my sake'; and those six water-pots at the wedding-feast whose transmutation was the first evidence of the presence in Galilee of the divine principle. The gods are forever turning water into wine, drawing milk and honey from springs and fountains, offering another kind of bread than that made from stones; only they can. Materialism reverses the process.

Winifred Nicholson tells an anecdote of her great-grand-mother, who was also Bertrand Russell's grandmother (that same Lady Stanley whose portrait looks down, still critical, upon the generations of Girton students) remarking, after a visit from her grandson, 'I don't know why it is that all my grandchildren are so *stupid.*' I don't know why she thought the great logician 'stupid' at that time; but the 'stupidity' of logical positivism lies, if anywhere, in its premisses. Logicians never admit that their premisses are open to question; perhaps do not know it. If it is true that the crassness of English philosophy (Yeats observed that the English have the poorest philosophic literature in the world) has lain always in the quality of its premisses Lady Stanley may in this respect have been right about her grandson's 'stupidity'. Yet I no longer believe that these apparently impervious rationalists who demand so aggressively that we others should 'explain what you mean by....' (God, love, beauty, the good, the soul, the Logos,) are always victims of what the Church calls 'invincible ignorance', that stupidity against which the gods themselves are said to struggle in vain. To judge others by myself I would guess that in many more it is the will that has at some time denied and rejected spiritual knowledge. In the choice of premises the will is free: logic cannot dictate the ground from which its conclusions proceed; and I wonder whether the loveless beautyless state is not the cause rather than the effect of such systems? If, disregarding those superstructures so dazzling to ignorance, we regard their foundations, these will be seen for what they are. Blake never answered Urizen's arguments, but merely drew his portrait.

Premisses, I suppose the positivists would argue, are necessarily simple sense-experiences of physical objects, 'positive', like the kitchen table Virginia Woolf took as her primary philosophical solid. But is even the kitchen table only what it seems to so limited an experience of reality as a quantitative philosophy allows? Is not that perhaps just the point? Science is forever boasting of knowing and discovering 'more' about the universe; but the only 'more' with which it is concerned is quantitative; why, then, should we look to science to tell us 'more' about the nature of the things it measures and describes? Going to the moon, or splitting the atom is only (Blake again) 'the same dull round', more of the same thing. But what if there were a qualitative 'more', of which we remain for the most part unaware?

Whatever 'nature-mysticism' may be it is not 'the pathetic fallacy', but a perception as 'positive' as barking one's shin on Virginia Woolf's kitchen table, or stubbing one's toe on Dr. Johnson's stone. It is possible to perceive more, or less, of what is there, in a sense immeasurable in terms of quantity. It is not the logic of the materialists which precludes this knowledge, but a kind of consciousness; and to their 'I don't understand what you mean by...' one can but quote Blake, 'Reason, or the ratio of what we have already known, is not the same as it shall be when we know more.' It is just in these primary experiences that the difference lies; the mystic and the positivist do not see different things; neither do they see the same things and draw different conclusions; they see the same things, but differently.

For certain kinds of knowledge (my mother's vision of the moor as 'alive', or my own hyacinth) once is enough. Those who have had the experience recognize instantly what is meant by others who speak of it; those who have not can never argue it away by logic, or dissect it by science. The terrible thing is that spiritual realities should have ceased to be premisses. I would despair were it not for the irreversible nature of knowledge; we may come to know but we cannot un-know.

Emerging from my ten years' work on Blake, from my years with Gavin engaged in what was, though the part I had played may have been played amiss, a spiritual drama, I realized that I was engaged in a great battle now being fought in the world: my own story took its place within a much wider context. The battlefield was upon me; but where, now, were the strongholds against the ever-rising tide?

I took my father (he had always loved the theatre) to the first production of Osborne's *Look Back in Anger*. He was incredulous and indignant. Why could not that young fellow, who had had the advantage (in my father's boyhood given to few) of a university education, have set himself to work for the good of society? Teaching, for example—then his ill-nature would have evaporated (as ill-nature always does) as an unacknowledged state of being (rightly) ashamed of himself gave place to the satisfaction of work well done? My father, his years of work behind him, had no sympathy for the self-pity of Jimmy Porter. My father's life had been a life of work well done; the modern 'left' with its endless demand for 'rights', with its ever-diminishing sense of duty, puzzled and distressed him. My father's kind had not wished to disrupt, and to air their grievances, but to reform, to extend the Good and the Best to more people, in theory to everybody; for my father would never have admitted that Shakespeare and Wordsworth and Euclid, and above all Jesus Christ, could be less than universal in their humanity. 'We needs must love the highest when we see it' was one of those too glibly repeated maxims in which he felt that much wisdom was summarized. My father's generation of Christian socialists had been Blake's 'golden builders' of the New Jerusalem, the city 'coming down from heaven'. He could see no other socialism than that of the kingdom of Christ on earth. But if my father refused to admit that the new subversive socialism, and even communism itself, is inseparable from its root in atheist materialism, I, living a generation later, could not fail to see that this was so. In that philosophy all the legion manifestations of the nihil have their common ground. There has been much talk of the 'two cultures' as if this were a simple opposition of 'arts' against 'sciences' or a political matter; but the issue, under every guise, is between atheist humanism and the *sophia perennis*. For my father Christianity was the religion of the poor, of the slaves and the dispossessed who were those 'early Christians' whose catacombs were not unlike the coal-mines of his own County Durham Methodist people. A godless proletariat was, for him, the most bitter disillusionment; but history is unanswerable.

Not so much the phenomena in themselves ('Conduct and work grow coarse, and coarse the soul') struck fear into me, but what lay behind. Some instinct told me to re-read *The Possessed*; which when I first read it had seemed to me (under Western eyes) an almost incredible account of the triumph of nihilism over social order and human dignity; but then Russia was a 'backward' country where things were possible which could not happen in our more civilized society. Now it seemed like a commentary upon England in the 1960s: 'Do you know that we are tremendously powerful already? Our party does not consist only of those who commit murder and arson, fire off pistols in the traditional fashion, or bite colonels. They are only a hindrance.... Listen, I've reckoned them all up: a teacher who laughs with children at their God and at their cradle is on our side. The lawyer who defends an educated murderer because he is more cultured than his victims and could not help murdering them to get money is one of us. The school-boys who murder a peasant for the sake of sensation are ours. The juries who acquit every criminal are ours. The prosecutor who trembles at a trial for fear he should not seem advanced enough is ours. Among officials and literary men we have lots, lots, and they don't know it themselves.... When I left Russia, Littré's dictum that crime is insanity was all the rage; I come back and I find that crime is no longer insanity, but simply common sense, almost a duty; anyway, a gallant protest.'

I felt myself impelled to rally to some standard; but where discover a sanctuary and custodian of the spiritual values threatened in a world whose purpose to destroy was becoming increasingly undisguised, but in the Church? I began to attend Mass on Sunday mornings, as the strongest political protest I was able to make; in sheer contempt of the slip-shod lie-about newspaper-reading English atheist Sunday morning I went at 8 a.m; there is something cleansing in the mere discipline of early-rising; the arriving at a certain place at a certain time sets a form upon the day. Near the back of the Church of the Holy Redeemer I would sit where I could look at the photograph of the face of the Holy Shroud which hangs in a small side-chapel. Far other faces were illustrated on the pages of those Sunday newspapers which lay still unopened on the doorsteps of Paultons Square along with the milk bottles (since even atheist man does not live by bread alone—better perhaps if he did) as I returned from Mass. I do not read the Sunday newspapers; but those who do so might, so I felt, judge world affairs more truly in the light of that daily-enacted symbolic restoration. I began to feel that I ought to return to the Church. All very well for me, who had read Proclus and the Upanishads; but if I, over the years, had become learned in the literature of spiritual knowledge, for the unlearned only the Christian religion makes accessible that knowledge, and a way of life consistent with it.

I was, besides, ashamed of my lack of simplicity. In Cambridge one evening Frances Cornford had so put me to shame; I had been cavilling at this or that in the Christian religion, and she said, I remember, in her thrilling tragic voice, 'I only know that there I find water and I go to drink.' But though I had often forced myself through church doors I never had found water there. Or perhaps I am one of those who cannot be made to drink.

Again, it was the politics of this world, rather than any inner impulse of assent, that drove me to conclude, once more, that in Western Europe Christianity alone stands (for all but the learned few) for the values of eternity. Kafka saw that 'Mankind can only become a grey, formless, and therefore nameless mass through a fall from the Law which gives it form. But in that case there is no above and below any more; life is levelled out to mere existence; there is no struggle, no drama, only the consumption of matter, decay'; words now no longer a prophecy but the description of a grey formlessness everywhere present where current ideologies prevail.

Of all the teachers of my generation I am perhaps most indebted to Jung. At all events, I continue to be aware of the debt, when others are forgotten; for Jung points the way to a living access to the originals of which the myths and symbols of religion are formulations. If I have come to understand the power and depth of the Christian mythology, it is, I must confess, by way of study and experience, and not because these icons have ever moved me. It is true that the more I have come to know, both of life and of metaphysics, the greater my reverence for these symbols of the cult has become; but the cult has in no way moved me, the symbols have not lived for me, as the symbols of poetry have lived, or those mysteries unveiled, sometimes, in dreams. Jung is surely right in divining that at this time what was once encountered 'outside' must be encountered within the *psyche*, an interior world no longer, as perhaps once it was, inclined to project itself upon cult-images. I have read nearly all Jung's published works, some with greater interest, some with less, all with imaginative delight at the rediscovery of the lost kingdom of the gods. Yet I could never quite call him master; in his *Answer to Job* 'God', by a sleight-of-hand, is made to appear as something less than Job, something man is 'enduring' within himself. Martin Buber (it was Louis MacNeice who first told me to read *I and Thou*, and David Gascoyne re-read that seminal book repeatedly) never compromised the vision of the divine transcendence which is the glory of the ancient Hebrew poem; nor Kafka either.

I had myself made a study of certain traditional myths in the course of my Blake work (Cupid and Psyche, the Two Goddesses, Narcissus, and other themes relating to the descent and return of souls) and I discovered in the course of my work a number of Jungian re-interpretations to be (assuming the meaning of the myths to be those understood by the cultures which created and made use of them) in the simple academic sense, incorrect; but also less far-reaching, less subtle, less poetically and philosophically amenable, than the interpretations of Porphyry and Plotinus, Proclus and Sallust, and that central mainstream of imaginative learning which flows in unbroken continuity from Orpheus to Ovid, carrying a perpetual renaissance from the Florentine school into all poetic traditions, continuous throughout English poetry down to Yeats's Ireland. I had discovered that knowledge of myths is a kind of learning not to be had in a day; and having in this field myself become passably literate, could see in even Jungian psychologists a tendency to rush in with the inadequate interpretations of an insufficient learning. For the psychologists are in truth newcomers in the great field of symbolic thought and discourse. They are inclined to forget—or, rather, have not yet discovered —that mythology is a language inseparable from the metaphysics of the Perennial Philosophy, whose expression it is.

René Guénon's bitter diatribes and intellectual pride suited my mood, and his masterly discourse on the metaphysical aspect of traditional symbols commanded my respect. Coomaraswamy's books on the aesthetics of the *philosophia perennis* I already knew. On Philip Sherrard's introduction I went to see Marco Pallis, the *éminence grise* of that school in England, himself a Buddhist, who had studied in the monasteries of Tibet, and a friend and correspondent of Frithjof Schuon, and others of the school of Tradition. Where, I asked Marco, could we turn?

Any one of the 'revealed' traditions, he said, might be followed; all were valid 'ways'; the essential thing was to adhere wholly to one, and to avoid eclecticism, since each is in itself a whole whose parts are not separable from that totality. One may, according to circumstances (which include personal sympathies and dyspathies) follow any one of these Ways. Very occasionally highly gifted souls may be able to dispense with these traditional forms; but none can deny their adequacy. One must, besides, participate in a living tradition; the Pythagorean and neo-Platonic learning is a dead language, for the Mysteries of the ancient world are no longer practised. So there I was back again at the point from which I had hoped to escape; I said I supposed, then, that he advised me to return to the Catholic church. 'I did not say anything of the kind,' Marco would say, with his super-subtle Greek smile, 'I merely stated the arguments.' He, like myself, did not 'like' Christianity, and found himself, even though born in the Greek Orthodox world, out of sympathy with it—'but that is not to deny its validity', he would hasten to add. He himself having lived in India and travelled in Tibet, had a pretext, so to say, for choosing Buddhism. I wished I could think of any pretext for following Vedanta; but I knew that to do so would, in my own case, be mere exoticism.

I don't know what I had expected or hoped for; what unimagined, unimaginable enlightenment. And do not, Marco said, suppose that the Eastern religions are less in decadence than is Christianity; so near the end of the *kali yuga* all means fail. 'But so long as I am myself alive,' he added, 'Buddhism will continue to exist.' Surely there are Christians who still keep the Church open as a spiritual channel? How could I doubt this? And yet, and yet.

I am doubtless in closer sympathy with Marco's school than with any other; had I not, in discovering the secret of Blake's 'originality' found it to lie precisely in his fidelity to these origins and originals? But even with these initiates of wisdom I could not wholly identify myself.

Not one of the principal exponents of that school was in fact living within the tradition to which they themselves were native. Coomaraswamy, praising Hinduism, was educated in England and lived his adult life in America. Of all their writings, those of Schuon most illuminate Christianity, but their author is a Moslem convert. Several members of the group are, as was Guénon himself, Moslems; Marco, born into a Greek Orthodox family, a Buddhist. Were they not all, under the disguise of strict adherence to tradition, in fact refugees, or rebels, and by the very assumption of Islam, or Mahayana Buddhism, as the case might be, changing the nature of the tradition assumed? Even while denouncing the confusion of the different traditions, were they not all carried on an interfusing tide? How could Marco's Buddhism not be coloured by Greek Orthodox Christianity? Or Philip Sherrard's Greek Orthodoxy by his Bloomsbury background and his training as a Cambridge historian? Was not Guénon's Islam that of an embittered French intellectual? Eclecticism, whether or not desirable, is in practice unavoidable, its implicit syncretism may even be the best contribution of this school. If I were to try once again to make a Catholic of myself, only what I had learned from Indian and Platonic sources could make that return tolerable.

My second doubt was whether these defenders of the ancient springs would recognize the 'wind that blows where it listeth. We hear the sound thereof, and it is gone.' The parable of the new wine in old bottles might, I felt, be applied to the school of Guénon. Forms will always be new. These people, I sensed, did not live by the imagination; was there, even, a certain hatred, or envy of the creative spirit in the monotonously negative judgements passed (for example) upon Jung and Teilhard de Chardin who, whatever their limitations, are seminal imaginative thinkers? God knows I myself was sick of the cant of progress and evolution, most often heard in those quarters where spiritual, intellectual and moral retrogression is most evident; and inherently probable as I felt the opposite view to be (the decline towards an Armageddon) a view supported not least by the very evidence of 'progress' the evolutionists point to with most confidence and pride, yet I could not relinquish my poet's faith in the prophetic spirit, which has never failed.

Nor am I convinced that the neo-Platonic tradition is no longer viable. Marco might say that the Eleusinian Mysteries were, like the Mass, kept alive not by the imagination but by the informing gods; but in Plato's Garden of the Muses (call it Jung's world of the archetypes, or Yeats's and Edwin Muir's *anima mundi*), poets may still find the living immortal presences, whether like Keats or Hölderlin they name the gods by their old names, or like Blake re-clothe them in the dress of the present. Are poets initiated not in an apostolic but in a poetic succession, still held in the chain of magnetized rings of which Plato spoke? Perhaps the springs and fountains are now only a thin trickle; but can I not say of my tradition, as Marco of the Buddhism of a Tibet which in 1965 no longer exists, so long as I live the poetic transmission shall not die?

If the One Consciousness is now seeking some other form than a 'Church' (and Jung too saw with dismay, in that mind, such a change of mode,) it is not that the reality to be communicated is other than it was and forever is; the new mode seems rather a change in our manner of receiving than in what is to be received. 'A church in the hearts of men,' Gay Taylor was told in a dream. It is as if the informing presences have abandoned their old habitations, the cult-images, and once more

> . . . the chill marble seems to sweat
> While each peculiar power forgoes his wonted seat.

Only now it is the Christian Saints who are departing from their shrines. We must, it seems, now meet the gods on other ground; in the psyche, as Jung affirmed. 'Reality' cannot be defined, but only experienced; and if for other ages reality took up its abode in cult images and liturgy, for ours it is not so; if we meet the gods it is within. Having there (in dream or vision) beheld them, we may see plainly enough that the cult-images are their true portraits; but there must be others like myself who have recognized the truth of these aids and props of faith only retrospectively, having come to the reality otherwise; they do not evoke for us, as for earlier Christian centuries, the realities they embody. However we may assent to the truth of these old depictions, it is no longer through them we receive that which they depict; they are no longer icons, but pictures; imperceptibly the walls where they hang have ceased to be the walls of churches and have become the walls of museums.

That reality, as such, is not bound by any of those forms which may at one time or another embody it is self-evident to any Hindu or Buddhist;

which makes it for me easier to talk with my Indian or Buddhist friends than to even the most intelligent Christian. In India it is taken for granted that people in different degrees of spiritual development necessarily need, or necessarily outgrow, supports of certain kinds. May it not be that it is not some particular form of liturgy, or school of religious art, which time is at this moment sweeping away, but the whole concept of the cult, as such, the whole use of spiritual supports of this kind?

Lisa Hill, until her retirement Professor of Russian in Cambridge, described to me how with her own eyes (and, what is more, in America) she had seen a weeping icon of the Virgin, whose tears, as minute as seed-pearls, proportionate to her paper face, ran down ceaselessly, so that the bottom of the cheap print was sodden like blotting-paper. It is all the same whether the weeping figure be of paper or of dream; that which weeps may use any vehicle; for there is a weeper! We are surprised, incredulous, even shocked, when the vehicle of the tears is of paint or paper; but if in a dream the Virgin weeps, we do not doubt the reality of the sorrower. If once the sacramental seemed to inhere in the icons and symbolic enactments of the cult, the power to trans-substantiate to reside in its priests, this is no longer the truth of experience. For me the Church has not been the trans-substantiator; and the sacramental, the trans-substantiate, we can meet only where itself meets us.

I do not know how, unless by that quality itself, we may recognize the holy, the numinous; and in certain dreams and visions (and also when the curtain of nature has been lifted) I have known that presence. Those 'images of wonder' brought forth, in dreams, like the sacred objects carried by the priest celebrating the Orthodox liturgy from behind the icon-painted screen (the Book, the Cup, the bread and the wine) itself an emblem of the gate or barrier between two worlds now open, now closed and all that comes and goes between, have seemed mysteries for a moment shown, given from the One Mind. No one, as Edwin Muir says, knows the whole Fable; only parts of it. Perhaps the soul is, in its very nature, 'naturally Christian'; but who can set limits to the inexhaustible in-dwelling Imagination? Of those few I have been shown in dreams most are themselves central symbols of the Christian mysteries: the Tree, holy well, the sign of the Cross, and that sword of light once held in my dreaming hand. May not the withdrawal of the numinosity formerly projected upon the symbolic enactments of the cult to the source itself, within the ever-living imagination within each of us, be a sign not of irreligion but of spiritual maturity? If I spoke only for myself I would hesitate to say this; but the experience is widespread, not among those who do not believe, but among those who do.

Living in this leaf-fall of a civilization (or is it of a world?) I have witnessed with sorrow and with fear the showering down of dead leaves which were once—even within my own memory—informed with life. Not only from churches but from the civil order (insofar as this is an expression of spiritual and intangible values) the life has been progressively withdrawn. In the generation before my own, T. S. Eliot remained within the tradition he would have wished to see continue; he, and David Jones, were perhaps the last poets of that tradition. Yeats saw the darkness approaching, the tide rising; but his hope lay not in any turning or stemming of the tide, but in that which lies beyond civilizations, the mystery of the gyres, the Indian Brahman whose outbreathings create worlds and whose inbreathings withdraw them from existence. But Yeats too was still among the artificers of Byzantium, the Graeco-Christian civilization, preserved in Ireland beyond its time elsewhere. It is my generation which has seen the end.

I would not have tried so hard to adhere to the Church from personal motives—indeed I have never looked to religion for spiritual support, rather the reverse: if my adherence would help to save the Church, mainstay of civilization, then I would willingly adhere. But if I am to be true to what I imaginatively perceive (for what such intuitions are worth) I must say that it is of no use to try to keep the leaves from falling, green though they once were, and lament as we must their fading. The nihilists would agree; but they desire the death of the tree, the dismantling of civilization, nor do they believe in those divine originals Christendom has embodied and reflected. Yet it is not those leaves which cling longest against the wind of change that are obedient to the tree's life, but the seed cast adrift, the end as it is the beginning of the life-cycle. The great tree is at this time showering down its leaves in a process of death which cannot be arrested, and whose record is everywhere to be read in the nihilism of the arts, of social life, in a thousand images of disintegration, in the reversion of civilized society, it may be, to a state of barbarism.

Those who are indissolubly wedded to the external forms, whether of a religion or of a culture, must at this time despair; unable to withdraw from these what for centuries has been projected into them, they lose, when these fail, portions of their souls; but those who are able to rediscover within themselves all that has been progressively withdrawn from our dismantled world, need not fear the withdrawal of the informing presence from the beautiful forms itself created.

The process of death cannot be arrested, civilizations cannot be saved; but there are the seeds, the living among the dead, who do not participate in the collective disintegration, but guard their secret of immortality, the essence of what has been and may be again. Who can say into what soil these seeds may be sown, or into what region of the universe the harvest of the world is gathered?

(And re-reading this manuscript in 1976, I dreamed, last night, the words, repeated again and again, 'Set the axe to the root of the tree'.)

CHAPTER FOUR

A Judgement

HARDEST of all to write; for here, if at all, I must confess that mortal truth which throughout a lifetime I have sought to evade; or declare that immortal truth which I have looked for. The one as hard as the other; and how related? I do not know. Here I reach only the boundaries of my own ignorance. Every being is finite, can contain only so much of either knowledge; and yet what each is capable of experiencing, of attaining, must suffice. Has my own life sufficed? That, it now seems to me, is the only question which in the end remains. For happiness and suffering alike become, once past, something else altogether.

But since it has been above all poetic truth I have followed, tried to discover always that good, that best Socrates never ceased to speak of, poetic justice it must have been (the only kind I have ever acknowledged) that brought me at last to stand my judgement in Greece itself.

I had written thus far when, in 1966, there came a letter from Philip Sherrard, to whom I had shown my work in progress:

'I've been thinking about the last part of your book, and it seems to me that what you have to do is not to say anything at all about the Church or about Traditional doctrine or anything of this kind—you've said all that in your Blake book, and anyhow it's not what is wanted. What is wanted is something absolutely simple and what is the heart of your life and what has been distilled from the experience and the suffering, and this put down in words that are free from jargon, even of the most exalted kind. And I'm sure that what this thing is—what you have found and what you can communicate from within as perhaps few other people can—is connected with, almost born from . . . your relationship with Gavin, and that is the extraordinary insight this has given you into that fantastic mystery which we call love. Love human and love divine—love divino-human—human love moving into eternity, eternity moving into human life through love: isn't that your theme?'—and a page or two on:

'... when one thinks of the absolute travesty of love and sex in our age, its vilification and emptiness, its lack of beauty—could there be anything better to do than to try to clean this filthy slate—not from the outside but from the inside?... But this living of the central mystery and miracle, that is what I would ask to learn and be initiated into.'

So I decided to go to Greece, there to finish my work in the Sherrards' house, in a bare room with bed, chair and table where I have often worked. I brought the record of my life to place before Philip's judgement; the judgement of a lover of poetry, an Orthodox Christian, more well-read than I am myself in all the literature of the world's wisdom; he would read my record in the light of that perennial truth by which all must finally be judged; which has long been, for Philip as for myself, the only measure; and—I see it now very well—a friend on whose partiality I could rely not to judge me too hardly.

In that room I found in a book some words from Conrad's *The Arrow of Gold*; which seem a better comment than any I might make upon Philip's letter: 'In every, even terrestrial, mystery there is as it were a sacred core. A sustained commentary on love is not fit for every eye. A universal experience is exactly the sort of thing which is most difficult to appraise justly in a particular instance.'

But that perennial wisdom had appointed for me another judge; I had invoked the Judge of whose coming no one knows the day or the hour; and the one consciousness that pierces up and down through every plane of being brought it about that in the appointed hour the judge should appear who was to pronounce that sentence against which we cannot plead.

So perfect is the pattern of destiny that, at the time when it was necessary we should meet, Gavin and I were once more brought together. Nearly seven years had passed; our houses in London had been mere yards apart, in physical distance; I had visited mutual friends in Scotland; yet never once had circumstances brought us together. Since the exchange of letters at the time of his marriage there had been no communication between us; only that one meeting in the street, when we had scarcely paused, he on his way, I on mine. And as our first meeting had come unsought, so now again.

I say unsought; but was this really so? Had I not, all these years, been waiting for Gavin, though only inwardly, not overtly? I had made it a rule, which had become second nature, never to look across Paultons Square towards No. 9; some sense of honour forbade me to do so, as it forbade me to try to learn anything beyond the bare minimum about Gavin or his activities. If he wished me to know, he would tell me; if he wished to seek me out, he would do so. It was through no doing of mine that from the house of Philip Sherrard (who is, after all, one of my oldest and most

A Judgement

valued friends) I could look down on the pantile roof of Gavin's brother's house. Sometimes that brother invited me to drink ouzo with him on a terrace looking over the sea to Mount Parnassus between a palm and a cypress whose shapes stood, like the rowan and the waterfall pool at Sandaig, in Gavin's consciousness also. Just as, when I visited Gavin's friends (and through him now my friends) John Lorne Campbell, of Canna, and his wife Margaret Fay Shaw, I returned, above all, to Gavin's horizon, waiting always to catch a glimpse, from the *Loch Arkaig* or the *Western Isles*, of a speck in the distance that was the Sandaig lighthouse.

The day after my own arrival, Gavin came on a visit to his brother; for Gavin, not Philip, was my appointed judge. And the divine justice was to be more terrible than anything I had ever dreamed, because altogether different from anything I had foreseen.

Heaven knows I did not seek him out; would have avoided him, had he so wished; but this was not so; perhaps he too wanted to make peace. He came and stood on the shore where I was bathing and waited for me. He looked as if he too had suffered; as if a dark shadow enveloped him. We talked, all that noon, down under the olives outside the little *taverna* by the mother-of-pearl sea; for many hours. He told me, in outline, the story of his life in those intervening years.

What folly made me suggest that he should read the manuscript of my autobiography, which I had with me? I had not, after all, written it in order to publish it—during the lifetime of my parents I could not in any case have done so—but under the compelling necessity to understand, and by understanding, make somehow bearable, my life. I was not attempting to justify myself, indeed, but to discover the truth. And yet how ugly the self-portrait I had drawn, I had not realized. It is one thing to write such a record; quite another to read it. I was probably the last person capable of doing that. Why did I feel I must show it to Gavin? Perhaps I still wanted him, in Helen's word, to 'see'; but was unable to understand, even now, *what* he would see. I thought of him still, I suppose, as part of myself; so accustomed was I to talking to him in my thought as if he were there, as if he were the daimon whose image I suppose some Jungian would say I had projected on him, that I did not think how painful such a reading might be to him. Helen Sutherland had read my manuscript, and Philip; but they saw everything, including myself, from quite another standpoint.

So he read the book; as far as the curse and the Tree, no farther. After he had done so we met again; and while the moon travelled from her rising behind pine-clad Kandile to throw down for us her unheeded path of light across the water as she moved from Helicon to Parnassus, from Parnassus towards Pelion, the full bitterness of the truth I had not seen was laid bare; Gavin's truth.

359

Cecil Collins had read the auguries in my tea-leaves before I left England; 'You are now asked', he said, 'to make a complete sacrifice.' Sacrifice, I then thought, what more have I to lose? It seemed unlikely that my death could be meant, for in this there would be nothing which could be called sacrificial. But he was right; I still had certain memories which I treasured; and I was asked, now, to sacrifice not only the present, but the past as well; to abandon all the places recollection might still have visited; of my days of happiness at Sandaig, nothing was to be left me now, or for the future. I have to live the rest of my life with the retrospective know-ledge that in those times and places in which I had been happy because I had thought myself invisibly companioned, I had been alone. Fortunately for my power to survive the intervening years I did not know then what I learned that night; nor do I think I could have believed it, my imagination would not have encompassed it, so near those days whose deep beauty was an experience lived and not a memory only. For Gavin was entirely to disown and to deny any participation in a relationship I had thought mutual; 'outrageous' was the word he used. Canetti had been quite right when he had so solemnly assured me, 'Gavin does not love you, Kathleen.' Not in any sense of the word love; not at any time. Canetti had, it is true, done his utmost to undermine my own love for Gavin: 'You do realize, Kathleen,' he had once said, 'that Gavin *dyes his hair?*' Useless, of course; I only retorted with Yeats's lines about

> . . . looking for the face I had
> Before the world was made

Our standards, Canetti's and mine, were, first and last incommensurable.

And yet I had seemed to have my reasons; why had Gavin, then, lent me his house, not once but many times, speaking of it always, as I did also, as of a place we shared? Why, once when we were speaking of death, had Gavin when I had asked him what, if he were dying, he would do, said 'send for you'; why asked his brother to rent me an old and beautiful tower on his estate on whose spiral stone stair the doves laid their eggs undisturbed? These and like memories had long been like fixed stars in my firmament; but now the stars fell from heaven.

'What a long time ago all that seems' he said; to him an episode almost forgotten, to me the forever-written story of my book of life. Yet have not I myself written of my marriage with Charles as something long past, because I had chosen to forget, as Gavin had forgotten me? Is anything ever cancelled from that dread Book of Judgement, and may we not, at death, have to read those pages, made present again before our eyes, which we have thought to blot out by putting them from our minds?

Gavin too, though my judge, must himself be judged; though not by me.

He had not loved me; Tambi, who had consigned Gavin to my care (and had I not, at the time, wondered what could be wrong about a situation which brought Gavin to my door through Tambi's introduction?) had at the same time forced me upon Gavin; who had, for his part, never heard of me. 'That woman is very lonely,' he had said, and nagged Gavin to invite me out, and so forth; and he had done so, perhaps because he was under some obligation to Tambi, who was useful to him at the time. Gavin laughed—we both did—when this double plot came to light; so like Tambi; and a good idea, so far as it went. All sorts of things fitted into place—a painter friend of Tambi's who some years before had inexplicably sent me boxes of *soleil d'or* narcissi from the Scilly Isles. Had Tambi long had in mind that I needed a lover? But how dangerous a thing it is to practise such deceptions. Hardy's Farmer Maybold might have lived quietly enough as Bathsheba's neighbour, but for that valentine, which he took to be an overture. When we think our love is welcome, we lay aside our defences. It is not in my nature to make a first advance, even in friendship. That had been my one defence; a defence also, perhaps, for others too, against my too extreme emotions.

And Canetti; had he too deceived me? True he had warned me; but that Gavin had a mistress, even at the time when, first visiting Sandaig, I had thought my place in his life the counterpart of his in mine—that Canetti had not told me. My instinct to fly when I had seen that pair of gloves in Gavin's studio had been right. I asked him, later, whether he had known of this; if, indeed, it was true—for Gavin might only have been trying, after all, to hurt me as much as he could. Yes, Canetti said; he had known, but had carefully—how carefully!—kept it from me; because, he said, I could not have endured to know the truth. Truth again! Canetti's truth this time; the truth of the compassionate man who does not trust God; who builds for us little saving edifices, vital illusions. What folly, what presumption! For they collapse in the end, long before the end. *Magna est veritas et praevalebit*; but only the truth of God. Into what net of lies I had allowed myself to be woven! Gavin told me, that night, of another parallel: to him Canetti had said, 'Kathleen for you is the abyss;' as to me he had said, 'Gavin for you is the abyss.' Canetti denies having said this, and I am willing to believe him, but not to lose the symmetry of the pattern; for if he did not say it, he should have said it, for it proved true. But as to Gavin being for me 'the abyss', I have learned from William Blake to commit myself to the void.

But Gavin himself—what had his motives been? God knows; perhaps he had really set out to be kind to me; perhaps even pitied me? and when I received with tears what for love was too little but for friendship very much, what could he have done? *'Il faut aimer pour savoir qu'on n'est pas aimé. Quand on n'aime plus, on est toujours assez aimé.'* Perhaps he liked me well enough while I, like poor Proust, suffered all the while from not being loved; liked me well enough until he could stand no more of my love, and broke out in irritation; or withdrew himself inwardly as I would have done myself had I ever allowed any one in love with me to get even a foot inside the door of my life. Gavin, it seems, had been kinder, infinitely kinder, than I would have been, in his situation.

Of course Canetti spared me nothing, afterwards; told me all he had then withheld, confirmed what Gavin himself had told me; and so did Sonia Orwell, and so did others. What concerns us we always come to know, in the end; and this is right. What an atrocious deception to keep any human being in a state of ignorance or illusion in matters of vital concern to us! And yet, I could not, then, have believed what even as Gavin spoke the words, there at Katounia, seemed like a dream.

It may seem a strange irony that Philip should, of all things, have written that it is only on the theme of love that he would ask to learn from me. 'If one is in love one can invent many reasons why one's love is unlike anybody else's, both in quality and kind, and this I think you have done somewhat naïvely. You should not forget that your readers will judge you by this account of your life.' That was Gavin's comment, which may stand, for what it is worth, beside Conrad's 'sacred core', which, of course, belongs to every true experience of love, not, certainly, to mine only. I am concerned with values, not with my own case-history. I do not suppose my love to be 'unlike anybody else's', except in detail; but I had hoped, in exploring my own experience, to discover, perhaps, universal things. All poetry makes the same assumption of universality in particulars.

If that vision of perfection Plato and Dante and Shelley saw (beholding in imperfect humanity the image and inprint of eternal beauty) then, yes, I know a little about love. But if by love the spirit that suffereth long and is kind, I know almost nothing. 'Tell me one single person who has been close to you in your life,' Gavin said, 'whom you have not destroyed— your parents, your children, your husband, myself whom you say you loved. What was your love for me but an infatuation? You are a destroyer, Kathleen.' I could not defend myself; for it is so. But all was not best at the close, nor was there peace nor consolation from the event.

Yet I had felt Gavin, often enough, to be my destroyer. I think his judgement was just, and my own mere self-deception; I thought because I suffered that it was he who was making me suffer; whereas it was nobody but myself. Suffering is of all things the most deceptive; for when we are suffering we are unaware of the pain we may ourselves be causing; often by the very fact of the state of suffering we are in.

A Judgement

Beyond the inner circle of those in my life—and Gavin was right about the suffering I had caused my parents and my children—I have, I suppose, done as much good as harm, harm as good; neither more nor less than most human beings; all of which counts for nothing at all before the judgement of the God within. I have, in this record, told my truth, not concealing faults of which I was aware. I had written, even before my fateful encounter with Gavin, that ignorance ignores precisely that of which it is ignorant.

The poets are always blamed, more or less, for the same thing: they are ruthless, or that which drives and possesses them is. Yet that is not how it seems to those who, perceiving immortal beauty, can do no other than follow it and strive to give it expression. 'Looked at from the shadow-side, ideals are not beacons on mountain-peaks, but task-masters and gaolers...foisted upon mankind by a clever ruse.' Jung said that. Blake had said much the same, in much better prose, about 'the delights of Genius, which to Angels look like torments and insanity....' I had all these years thought I was holding up before Gavin (in the poetry of the relationship as I saw it no less than in my published work) the reflected images of holy things. I had thought that by holding before him this beauty I could do him every good; and perhaps after all he did glimpse something in that glass.

I had been at first wounded at heart by what seemed a wilful denial of a shared vision; and if afterwards my bewilderment intensified to an anguish in which I invoked the divine avengers it was because I saw all those heavenly and holy treasures profaned as if they had no value, no existence. If to Gavin what to me seemed most real, seemed reality itself, was as if non-existent, was not he the loser?

Laurens van der Post has somewhere told a Bushman fairy-tale of a heavenly milk-maid married by a mortal. She made one condition—that until she gave him leave he should not open a basket she had brought with her from the sky. Of course he did so; and laughed at her because he found it empty. 'Empty?' she asked; then told him that it had in fact been filled with heavenly treasures; but because he did not see them, she was compelled to leave him and return whence she had come. So long ago the world had known the secret of every woman's love. And if he has good sight to say that I did not meet his need, I can say the same: had he given me that intangible support I as a poet needed so greatly (Tambi was right there) had he not begun, little by little, to undervalue and misconceive me, I might have done better, and all those years of desolation which were to follow been, instead, fruitful. I believe our relationship should have been what I dreamed it was—a lifelong Platonic love. But—so it was, and the cause of failure lay in ourselves.

Parting, the moon casting our shadows on the spent dust; exhausted by hours of torment given and received, we kissed, at last, as long ago we would have kissed at parting, and Gavin said, 'write *something* kind about me.' And even then I did not realize that I had not, in fact, written anything kind about Gavin; only my own dreams and fantasies.

Comparing the harvest of our lives over those seven years, I could show only a few poems; he, *Ring of Bright Water* and all his later books. And if I had brought on those nearest to me nothing but unhappiness, he, of all those he had taken under his protection, had not lost one; all had been set on their ways by his compassionate understanding and active help. I reminded him how, long ago, he had quoted, as his own deepest belief, Traherne's 'Never was anything in this world loved too much but many things have been loved in a false way: and all in too short a measure.' Now I saw it as possible that the little friendship Gavin had felt for me had been more generous than my much 'love'; for I had not answered his needs, but wound about him the trammels of my emotions. I did not know I was making emotional demands at all; nor is love a 'demand' when it is returned—who calls the love of children 'demanding'? Children take for granted that they will be loved, and what is most terrible is that they should ever not be. Why is it so seemingly impossible for grown men and women to love one another with the same simplicity? It seemed to me, as we sat under the vine and the olive, unable, like two children, to make up our quarrel, that probably we would both have done so, if we could; that both of us knew, at the bottom of our hearts, that we still were, and always would be, as much part of one another's lives as we had always been; but neither of us could say this, things had gone too far, we were too old, too tired really to care enough; like two old animals who go their lonely ways. Or rather, two different things were simultaneously true—all that Gavin had said, all that I had believed; and none of it. Children understand this perfectly; and that too seems to be a capacity lost with age. In fact I said something of the kind to Gavin as we parted: that I had not taken all this so very seriously; and he replied, with what seemed relief, 'I didn't really think you had.' I think it possible that all Gavin's sexual adventures and misadventures, all my wrongs and heroics, are only superficial, are nothing but children's make-believe in comparison with what really was and is and always will be between us. But I may be mistaken.

January the fourteenth, 1976. In my three-roomed cottage on the Border, bought with my mother's legacy, and near the places she loved and the places I loved; near Gavin's Solway, where the skeins of geese fly over, in spring and autumn, and the childhood home that he had loved, I conclude my story. The sky is grey and the north-east wind is howling and rumbling, the wild free wind I loved as a child at Bavington; not many miles away. A long way from Cambridge; a sanctuary, though not a paradise.

Am I any nearer to the truth now than on the day Gavin and I so fatefully, indeed so fatally, met? God knows; nor does it matter any more, for Gavin is dead, and what help now can my thoughts be to him? Or are our thoughts, above all, important to the dead? Or have I not, all the time, tried to disguise from myself the real situation, saying that I experienced this or understood that—the plain facts—facts, not dreams—that I lost Mij; and that I laid on Gavin a curse that may have caused his death. He was younger than I; he should have been living now, and how much he would have found still to do, among his wild creatures.

I began to write my story all those years ago because, in my own suffering—for the suffering was real enough though perhaps all self-caused, and in no way an extenuating circumstance—I had to try to understand. Why had I to try to understand? What impells us? We do not make ourselves, we are what causes unknown, rooted in the past, in the universe itself, in the physical earth and in whatever spiritual worlds there may be, have made us. A growing-point, each of us, of the one life, of the 'one consciousness'. What the final purpose is none living knows; only the imperative. I did not write this record in order to publish it, to justify or condemn myself before men and women; nor yet to withhold it. I wrote it because I must and if it can serve any useful purpose to others struggling, as I have struggled, to live a life, why should fear of ridicule or censure hold me back? I am aware that the person who emerges from these pages is as terrible as that demon-face of the Lady Rokujo in the Noh play of *Aoi*. And yet, all my life, how hard I have tried—tried to understand, to discover the good and to live by it, to bear witness, to accomplish something. Not for myself, in particular; but because of that innate imperative. I wish I could say 'for the greater glory of God'; that is what I would have wished to be able to say. Only the word, God, should perhaps be avoided; it has meant too many things to mean anything. But at the end of this story I see how ridiculous such a claim would be. I have been blind and evil; but perhaps the devils also struggle as best they can to do what they must.

Well, Gavin wrote and published his story: *Raven Seek thy Brother*. Of how I had laid on him a curse to which he thereafter attributed all the tragic disasters that befell him. My poor father wanted to sue Gavin and his publishers for libel, little knowing how much truth lay in his story. Longmans, so I was told (it may only be rumour but it could well be true) were a little nervous about libel, but Gavin assured them that they need have no fear. And he was right, of course: right for two reasons—the first, that knowing me he knew that I would never bring a libel suit ever, under any circumstances, against any one, least of all himself; and, more important, that I would not deny the truth of what he had written; even though, for good measure, he had thrown in an added clause to my curse, extending it to his circle of friends and any of these who might visit Sandaig. But even in that invention there may have been a basic truth, that I was perhaps jealous or disapproving of some of these. It might have been so. Nor indeed can I blame Gavin for writing such a book, since he had after all, seen mine.

'Gavin is lucky to be able to blame everything on you,' his brother said to me. There is some truth in that; for he was, after all, very well able to make mistakes on his own account. He made the mistake of marrying; he made the mistake of leaving Sandaig and his otters Edal and Teko in the care of young, and if only for that reason, irresponsible people. He involved himself in various Evelyn Waugh-like adventures in North Africa; many things which he cannot, by any stretch of credibility, lay to my charge. When first I met Gavin he was involved already in one of his periodic crises; and truth to say he was ever at his best when, having got himself into some desperate situation, he set to work not only to extricate himself from it, but to turn it to account... This was his temperament; for Gavin, the very idea of security and peace and quiet was unimaginable. That was after all why I—and why through his books so many others—loved him.

But the fire which destroyed the house at Sandaig, and Edal? Was that the result of my terrible invocation, 'Let Gavin suffer here as I am suffering now'? If it is so, then indeed I am guilty. Casting my mind back I remember how once, going down the hill to Sandaig, long before we had so fatally quarrelled, I had thought the house was on fire, and had said so to Mary Macleod, who was with me, and could confirm it if she would. I dare say she holds me responsible for all. Was it some trick of light, or a precognition? Or both? I was greatly alarmed at the time, I remember, being myself then in charge of the house. When I read in the press of the burning of the house at Sandaig it never crossed my mind that I was the cause or that Gavin could have thought me so. I sent him a telegram of sympathy—for had not that house, to me also, been the place most dear on earth? I knew what it must mean to him. And he wrote me in reply and we did then in some measure begin to make up our quarrel. It was not until *Raven Seek thy Brother* was published that I realized that Gavin really did attribute the burning of the house to my curse. And even then— for I was both hurt and angry that after all my only place in any book of Gavin's was not as a friend who had loved and helped him once but as the woman who had laid a curse on him. But if that was how Gavin saw me, it was, if only in that respect, the truth. I never wished him ill; and in those

A *Judgement*

long years of separation there was in my own heart only the ragged pain
of the longing to be reconciled. Perhaps he felt that longing dragging at
him and interpreted that as ill-will; for, certainly, the sense of another
person's unwanted thoughts flowing towards one constantly, could well
be felt so. For good or ill we were, after all, attuned. To me Gavin was like
a part of myself; he may well have felt something of the kind, however
much he might have wished it not to be so.

Yet it had all seemed so different at the time; as if one were to draw
a picture blindfold, and then, the bandage removed, see some terrible
shape . . . .

Raven Seek thy Brother concludes with an open question: after the fire
which destroyed his house and his otter, was the curse spent? In that open
question Gavin was to lay his own death to my charge. For nothing,
thereafter, went well with him. He bought the little lighthouse isle between Kyle of Loch Alsh and Kylakin, on Skye; but that little rocky islet,
with its views of wild cold grandeur to the north, with its eider-colony, its
secure enclosure for Teko, was not for Gavin what Sandaig had been. I
visited him there twice; the first time soon after *Raven Seek thy Brother*
had been published. It is characteristic of our relationship that there were
no recriminations whatsoever on either side. I have said that there was
much of our childhood in what we were to one another; and when we
behaved like children, who forget the dreadful things they have just done
to one another as if nothing had happened, all was well. As adults,
nothing went well between us.

Gavin tried to make me stay on but I did not; he asked me to come back
soon; but when I did so we again quarrelled bitterly. Justly proud of the
success of the film of his *Ring of Bright Water* he spoke of this, and played
me a record of a piece of 'pop' music written to the words: my words, from
a poem I had written at Sandaig in happy days. I had waited for some word
about the film which might have recognized that I had ever played any part
in that story, other than as the cause of Mij's death. But he said no word,
not even that he hoped I had not minded too much a film in which my own
part was, after all, re-enacted. Or so my friends told me, for my own pain
was too great for me to have ventured to see the film. It was only after
Gavin's death that I at last forced myself to read *Ring of Bright Water*;
though I had carried the book half round the world with me, unread. And
after listening to that record—it was very pleasant, I remember—it was not
the music as such that hurt me—I had said in bitterness of heart not,
indeed, what really made my heart bitter, which was that he had not
spoken that word I had waited for, of—not gratitude, but recognition,
companionship, even compassion—at all events something that made of
me not a stranger—something about the use he had made of my poem

367

which made him think—or pretend he thought—that I was trying in some way to 'cash in' on his fame. Now that of course is, even allowing that Gavin truly saw the shadow-side of me that my friends were not aware of—the devouring female spider of emotional possessiveness—unthinkable. I have never in my life done anything for money, and from Gavin that was the last form of restitution I wanted—but I was too proud to say, what I hoped he might have understood, that his *Ring of Bright Water*, that was to become a film, and then a legend, because it was written in his heart's blood, was written in my heart's blood also.

And yet, why could I not see that to Gavin Mij's death must have cancelled any former debt of love between us? Yet I could not bring myself to face this, or to realize that in assigning to me only the part of the woman who had laid on him a curse, I was assigned my due. Why did I continue to hark back to a paradise I had myself destroyed?

So real that paradise had been that I still could not believe that the end of the story had been the end; and I still went on hoping that I could still have the place in his life that I had thought was mine, the participation, the shared experience from which *Ring of Bright Water* had been written. Perhaps a murderer feels so—hoping still for the love of the wife or lover he has killed (why do I say 'he' when it is 'she'—myself—I mean?); and goes on acting as if it had not happened, not from the desire of deceiving others but because unable to believe what has been done in an instant has undone the reality of a lifetime. So Gavin supposed that I—who had, so long ago, lent him, or fancied I lent him, the support of my poor little reputation in 'the literary world'—was trying in some way to exploit his fame! Among the many bitter things we said to one another, I remember I exclaimed— unforgivably—'*My* work will be remembered when yours is forgotten.' That was the eye of the tornado; for he always did value my poetry; my books were all, even then, laid on his table. 'That,' he said, 'may very well be true.'

I do not think it is. I believe his *Ring of Bright Water* will live on. I believe also that some poems of mine will live on. I also believe that if I had suffered less in and through my disastrous relationship with Gavin, I would have achieved more. But that is doubtless my fault, not his.

I was, on that occasion, beside myself with misery; it was like a nightmare in which we are unable to move or act.

We seemed fatally at cross-purposes, as if we were playing our parts from two different plays. As indeed in some ways we were. And yet, in our poetry how close our roots. Those things we both loved—the hills and the wild places of our childhood, and the earthly paradise we had shared, and destroyed. These things were, for both of us, not only, I believe, our common ground but our deepest reality.

A Judgement

What I had hoped, on that worst of all days, was some word of recognition that I had played in his life and his work some part other than that he assigned to me in *Raven Seek thy Brother*; which to me seemed, against all the evidence, unbelievable. I had wanted him, as Helen understood—as I think any woman would have understood—to *see*; or perhaps simply to understand how much I was suffering and to stop hurting me: it was as simple as that. But many a murderer has perhaps felt just as I did.

I even wondered—or rather some of my friends did—if in *Raven Seek thy Brother* Gavin had not exploited the theme of the curse laid on him because it made a good story. But I do not think, now, that this was altogether so. He had, in the early days, an almost superstitious faith in my power to help him; and I too had believed with my whole being that I could do so. And that one-pointedness of thought is, after all, the secret of the power of all magic. At least I had tried to do so, and he had drawn strength from the faith I had had in him and in my own power. So what more natural than that the dark face of that power should have turned me into a witch in his eyes? And in reality? Of all criminals it is with murderers that I feel most akin, in the terrible realization of how easily a crime of passion can be committed; perhaps I did after all commit just that crime. There are many murders besides those committed with arsenic or pistol.

Gavin was already ill, on that last visit, though he did not then know how seriously, for the doctors who had examined him had said there was nothing serious amiss. He suffered from headaches, especially on one side of his head. And one last time I tried to bring him magic help; though not my own magic.

Long ago when Mijbil had been a cub, and was living, still, in Gavin's London studio, some injury to his back had seemed to threaten his life; his hind quarters seemed to be paralysed; and the expert at the Zoo had given little hope and no help. Gavin was in despair; and I bethought me, as a last resort (for at worst it could do no harm) of a certain Brigadier Firebrace, whom I had met with my friends Rupert and Helen Gleadow, who were always much interested in occult matters. This Brigadier had spoken, that evening, of the healing sometimes effected by so-called 'radionics'. This distant treatment presumed non-physical 'radiations' which could be brought to play on some distant patient, if on the 'box' there was a specimen (blood, or spittle or hair or the like) by whose means the healing ray could be 'attuned'. So in our desperation I had taken a small piece of Mij's fur and sent it to Brigadier Firebrace. Mij, on the 'box', made a perfect recovery. Coincidence? I wonder. Gavin had friends, too, whose experience had been similar. There could be, with animals, at least no question of 'suggestion'; and Gavin's friends had well-authenticated evidence of race-horses having been cured in this way. Gavin at the time did not think it was coincidence and neither did I.

When I had left Sandaig for the last time, it had been Edal whose life was despaired of; she was suffering from toothache, and Gavin had taken her to Inverness, to the most skilful vet to be found; who had been quite unable to do anything for her, so strongly rooted are an otter's teeth; and again he was in despair. He scarcely heeded me when I begged, again, for a piece of fur; but finally I was given what I asked for; and sent the fur to the 'box'; but, this time, with my own most passionate prayer for her recovery. Only let Edal recover, I had prayed, and I will never hope to see Gavin again. Edal, against all Gavin's expectation, recovered. Again coincidence perhaps. That time he certainly never gave the matter another thought. This time I begged Gavin to give me a drop of his own blood for the same purpose. Again, it could do no harm, and might help. Is it not foolish to refuse to try everything, even if we do not understand the laws that operate on levels other than the physical? If there are no such laws the worst that can happen is nothing at all. But this time it was of no use.

We made up our last furious quarrel, before I departed. And Gavin asked me to look, on my way to Inverness, into a certain tree-trunk to see if there were young jack-daws in it. There were. I telephoned him that evening from the house of the friend (Gavin's friend) where he had arranged that I should stay; and I heard his beautiful voice, then, for the last time.

Soon after that visit Gavin wrote to me that he had been re-examined and that he was suffering from inoperable, incurable cancer. There was absolutely no hope; he might live for a year, perhaps, and intended, before that time, to come to London. 'I am writing to ask you to accompany me in spirit,' he said. And, God forgive me, in the grief of his dying, I could yet find comfort in those words that surely were, in some sense, more real than all the superficial storms there had been between us, words of love.

I never saw Gavin again; death came mercifully soon. I was in Dublin when I received the telegram. But I knew before I heard. Over my head, on the evening of the day he died, a V-shaped flight of curlew had flown low, reminding me of Gavin's beloved grey-lag geese. I have a photograph given me by him years ago of such a flight, taken as they flew over the Solway. Long ago, in the first weeks of our meeting, we had read together Yeats's *Wild Swans at Coole*; and for those birds that, like his own Solway grey-lags

> . . . lover by lover
> They paddle in the cold,
> Companionable streams

A Judgement

I had seen tears gather in Gavin's blue eyes. In the first poems I ever wrote for him there had been the image of migrant birds, homing to this earth. And as that formation of curlew flew low over me, I had thought, 'Gavin!'. That was a message he would have known I would understand.

> Among what rushes will they build,
> By what lake's edge or pool
> Delight men's eyes when I awake some day
> To find they have flown away?

So I took an aeroplane from Dublin to Glasgow, and travelled on and on, towards Mallaig, and to Canna House, where Margaret and John Campbell took me in and comforted me as best they could. Gavin had been their friend too; to him I owed their friendship. Even too much so—they were ever inclined to believe too well of me, too ill of him.

His ashes were to be buried at Sandaig where the house had stood. Bruce Watt, of the *Western Isles*, who had long ago been one of Gavin's crew on the *Sea Leopard* in the days of Soay and the shark-fishing, took me to Sandaig; we landed there, as so often, in the past, with Mij. I was glad to have Bruce standing beside me; for when the party arrived with Gavin's ashes and I spoke to Mary Macleod, once my friend, as I had thought, she was cold and distant; believing doubtless that I was the witch who had caused his death. And that, too, was a realization that came to me slowly: that to Gavin's friends I could only seem so. And perhaps they are right. I laid in his grave a bunch of rowan-berries from the Tree.

He left me his Order of the Garter tie-pin, which he always wore, and that had been his grandfather's. He left very few personal bequests; not even to his brother; perhaps because death came sooner than he foresaw. So that I do take comfort from his having, after all, at the end, thought of me as a friend; with love? affection? compassion? Or simply as, for better and for worse, 'the woman in his life'?

Three years ago this month I was on Canna for the New Year, and set out on a stormy morning to cross to Mallaig on the *Western Isles*. I was the only passenger, and Bruce called me into his cabin. Presently the weather calmed, and he gave me the wheel; I guided the boat from Rhum to Eigg, and, leaving Eigg, he said, 'Just hold her towards Sgriol;' and so I steered the *Western Isles* holding her prow towards the mountain above Sandaig, where one mid-summer eve Mary and I had seen the fairy-gold of the globe-flowers. Bruce talked of his cruises to St. Kilda; of Hugh Miller's *Old Red Sandstone*, and the geological formation of the isles. He did not mention 'the Major'; Western Highland courtesy is perfect. And neither did I, because it would have been too painful to speak his name. But

371

Bruce's arm, very gently and lightly, was laid round my waist. I understood very well what he wished to communicate but could not say.

LaVergne, TN USA
03 December 2009
165869LV00003B/30/P

9 781597 313322